THE NEW PALGRAVE

MONEY

EDITED BY

JOHN EATWELL · MURRAY MILGATE · PETER NEWMAN

W·W·NORTON

NEW YORK · LONDON

Contents

Contents

Acknowledgements

The following contributors (articles shown in parentheses) acknowledge support from public bodies or permission to reprint copyright material:

Don Patinkin (Neutrality of Money), Central Research Fund of the Hebrew University of Jerusalem.

General Preface

The books in this series are the offspring of *The New Palgrave*: *A Dictionary of Economics*. Published in late 1987, the *Dictionary* has rapidly become a standard reference work in economics. However, its four heavy tomes containing over four million words on the whole range of economic thought is not a form convenient to every potential user. For many students and teachers it is simply too bulky, too comprehensive and too expensive for everyday use.

By developing the present series of compact volumes of reprints from the original work, we hope that some of the intellectual wealth of *The New Palgrave* will become accessible to much wider groups of readers. Each of the volumes is devoted to a particular branch of economics, such as econometrics or general equilibrium or money, with a scope corresponding roughly to a university course on that subject. Apart from correction of misprints, etc. the content of each of its reprinted articles is exactly the same as that of the original. In addition, a few brand new entries have been commissioned especially for the series, either to fill an apparent gap or more commonly to include topics that have risen to prominence since the dictionary was originally commissioned.

As *The New Palgrave* is the sole parent of the present series, it may be helpful to explain that it is the modern successor to the excellent *Dictionary of Political Economy* edited by R.H. Inglis Palgrave and published in three volumes in 1894, 1896 and 1899. A second and slightly modified version, edited by Henry Higgs, appeared during the mid-1920s. These two editions each contained almost 4,000 entries, but many of those were simply brief definitions and many of the others were devoted to peripheral topics such as foreign coinage, maritime commerce, and Scottish law. To make room for the spectacular growth in economics over the last 60 years while keeping still to a manageable length, *The New Palgrave* concentrated instead on economic theory, its originators, and its closely cognate disciplines. Its nearly 2,000 entries (commissioned from over 900 scholars) are all self-contained essays, sometimes brief but never mere definitions.

Apart from its biographical entries, *The New Palgrave* is concerned chiefly with theory rather than fact, doctrine rather than data; and it is not at all clear how theory and doctrine, as distinct from facts and figures, *should* be treated in an encyclopaedia. One way is to treat everything from a particular point of view. Broadly speaking, that was the way of Diderot's classic *Encyclopédie raisonée* (1751–1772), as it was also of Léon Say's *Nouveau dictionnaire d'économie politique* (1891–2). Sometimes, as in articles by Quesnay and Turgot in the *Encyclopédie*, this approach has yielded entries of surpassing brilliance. Too often, however, both the range of subjects covered and the quality of the coverage itself are seriously reduced by such a self-limiting perspective. Thus the entry called '*Méthode*' in the first edition of Say's *Dictionnaire* asserted that the use of mathematics in economics 'will only ever be in the hands of a few', and the dictionary backed up that claim by choosing not to have any entry on Cournot.

Another approach is to have each entry take care to reflect within itself varying points of view. This may help the student temporarily, as when preparing for an examination. But in a subject like economics, the Olympian detachment which this approach requires often places a heavy burden on the author, asking for a scrupulous account of doctrines he or she believes to be at best wrong-headed. Even when an especially able author does produce a judicious survey article, it is surely too much to ask that it also convey just as much enthusiasm for those theories thought misguided as for those found congenial. Lacking an enthusiastic exposition, however, the disfavoured theories may then be studied less closely than they deserve.

The New Palgrave did not ask its authors to treat economic theory from any particular point of view, except in one respect to be discussed below. Nor did it call for surveys. Instead, each author was asked to make clear his or her own views of the subject under discussion, and for the rest to be as fair and accurate as possible, without striving to be 'judicious'. A balanced perspective on each topic was always the aim, the ideal. But it was to be sought not *internally*, within each article, but *externally*, between articles, with the reader rather than the writer handed the task of achieving a personal balance between differing views.

For a controversial topic, a set of several more or less synonymous headwords, matched by a broad diversity of contributors, was designed to produce enough variety of opinion to help form the reader's own synthesis; indeed, such diversity will be found in most of the individual volumes in this series.

This approach was not without its problems. Thus, the prevalence of uncertainty in the process of commissioning entries sometimes produced a less diverse outcome than we had planned. 'I can call spirits from the vasty deep,' said Owen Glendower. 'Why, so can I,' replied Hotspur, 'or so can any man;/ But will they come when you do call for them?' In our experience, not quite as often as we would have liked.

The one point of view we did urge upon every one of *Palgrave*'s authors was to write from an historical perspective. For each subject its contributor was asked to discuss not only present problems but also past growth and future prospects. This request was made in the belief that knowledge of the historical development of any theory enriches our present understanding of it, and so helps to construct better theories for the future. The authors' response to the request was generally so positive that, as the reader of any of these volumes will discover, the resulting contributions amply justified that belief.

Peter Newman
Murray Milgate
John Eatwell

Preface

'Money is not such a vital subject as is often supposed'...'A monetary system is like some internal organ; it should not be allowed to take up very much of our thoughts when it goes right, but it needs a deal of attention when it goes wrong.'   D.H. Robertson, *Money* (1922)

The little work from which these quotations are taken was probably the most enduring – as it is the most endearing – of all the *Cambridge Economic Handbooks*, a famous series edited by J.M. Keynes between the two World Wars. Robertson's sharp mind and nimble prose made his exposition so clear to countless undergraduates that a revised edition of his book was still in print thirty years later, even after the grave monetary upsets of depression and world war. Yet the two quotations above, the beginning and end respectively of the very first section of the first chapter of the first edition, are in literal contradiction. If the monetary system needs 'a deal of attention' when it goes wrong, then that must be because its proper working is indeed vital to the whole body economic.

This contradiction between quotations neatly exaggerates the discord between two intuitive feelings about money which are held simultaneously by most economists most of the time. The first is that, at least in the long run, 'money does not matter' to the *real* economy, i.e. to the determination of relative prices, output and employment. This idea is well captured in Robertson's further remark that one must 'try from the start to pierce the monetary veil in which most business transactions are shrouded'; interestingly enough, this seems to be the first use in English of the now hackneyed metaphor of money as a 'veil'.

The second intuition is that 'money does matter', at least in the short run, i.e. that inappropriate management of the money supply (a concept not easily defined) can result in serious damage to the economy and society, not only via the distribution of income and wealth (which is bad enough) but also through real effects on prices and output. Just as pathology illuminates physiology, so these adverse consequences are exhibited in stark and grievous fashion by such disasters as the Hungarian hyperinflations after the two World Wars, where for example in July 1946, prices rose at the *monthly* rate of 4.2×10^{16} per cent. In a sense, the history of monetary theory could be written in terms of the tension between these two warring intuitions.

A striking feature of monetary economics is its intertwining of practical debate and theoretical development. The earliest systematic formulations of the quantity theory of money, for example, were consequences of pressing practical concerns, beginning a pattern that has continued ever since. Debate has followed debate over the centuries, each giving rise to new theoretical understanding; to name just a few – the Bullionist Controversy; the Banking School–Currency School–Free Banking School debates; the controversy over bimetallism; the perennial arguments over when to go off or on the gold standard, and at what parity; the contemporary many-sided disputes between Keynesians (neo-, post-, and old original), monetarists, and 'new classical macroeconomists'.

Accounts of these debates, and more, will be found in the pages which follow.

The Editors

Quantity Theory of Money

MILTON FRIEDMAN

Lowness of interest is generally ascribed to plenty of money. But...augment-ation [in the quantity of money] has no other effect than to heighten the price of labour and commodities...In the progress toward these changes, the augmentation may have some influence, by exciting industry, but after the prices are settled...it has no manner of influence.

[T]hough the high price of commodities be a necessary consequence of the increase of gold and silver, yet it follows not immediately upon that increase; but some time is required before the money circulates through the whole state.... In my opinion, it is only in this interval of intermediate situation, between the acquisition of money and rise of prices, that the increasing quantity of gold and silver is favourable to industry.... [W]e may conclude that it is of no manner of consequence, with regard to the domestic happiness of a state, whether money be in greater or less quantity. The good policy of the magistrate consists only in keeping it, if possible, still increasing...

(David Hume, 1752).

In this survey, we shall first present a formal statement of the quantity theory, then consider the Keynesian challenge to the quantity theory, recent develop-ments, and some empirical evidence. We shall conclude with a discussion of policy implications, giving special attention to the likely implications of the worldwide fiat money standard that has prevailed since 1971.

1. THE FORMAL THEORY

(a) NOMINAL VERSUS REAL QUANTITY OF MONEY. Implicit in the quotation from Hume, and central to all later versions of the quantity theory, is a distinction between the *nominal* quantity of money and the *real* quantity of money. The nominal quantity of money is the quantity expressed in whatever units are used to designate money – talents, shekels, pounds, francs, lira, drachmas, dollars, and so on. The real quantity of money is the quantity expressed

1

in terms of the volume of goods and services the money will purchase.

There is no unique way to express either the nominal or the real quantity of money. With respect to the nominal quantity of money, the issue is what assets to include – whether only currency and coins, or also claims on financial institutions; and, if such claims are included, which ones should be, only deposits transferable by cheque, or also other categories of claims which in practice are close substitutes for deposits transferable by cheque. More recently, economists have been experimenting with the theoretically attractive idea of defining money not as the simple sum of various categories of claims but as a weighted aggregate of such claims, the weights being determined by one or another concept of the 'moneyness' of the various claims.

Despite continual controversy over the definition of 'money', and the lack of unanimity about relevant theoretical criteria, in practice, monetary economists have generally displayed wide agreement about the most useful counterpart, or set of counterparts, to the concept of 'money' at particular times and places (Friedman and Schwartz, 1970, pp. 89–197; Barnett, Offenbacher and Spindt, 1984; Spindt, 1985).

The real quantity of money obviously depends on the particular definition chosen for the nominal quantity. In addition, for each such definition, it can vary according to the set of goods and services in terms of which it is expressed. One way to calculate the real quantity of money is by dividing the nominal quantity of money by a price index. The real quantity is then expressed in terms of the standard basket whose components are used as weights in computing the price index – generally, the basket purchased by some representative group in a base year.

A different way to express the real quantity of money is in terms of the time duration of the flow of goods and services the money could purchase. For a household, for example, the real quantity of money can be expressed in terms of the number of weeks of the household's average level of consumption its money balances could finance or, alternatively, in terms of the number of weeks of its average income to which its money balances are equal. For a business enterprise, the real quantity of money it holds can be expressed in terms of the number of weeks of its average purchases, or of its average sales, or of its average expenditures on final productive services (net value added) to which its money balances are equal. For the community as a whole, the real quantity of money can be expressed in terms of the number of weeks of aggregate transactions of the community, or aggregate net output of the community, to which its money balances are equal.

The reciprocal of any of this latter class of measures of the real quantity of money is a velocity of circulation for the corresponding unit or group of units. For example, the ratio of the annual transactions of the community to its stock of money is the 'transactions velocity of circulation of money', since it gives the number of times the stock of money would have to 'turn over' in a year to accomplish all transactions. Similarly, the ratio of annual income to the stock of money is termed 'income velocity'. In every case, the real quantity of money is calculated at the set of prices prevailing at the date to which the calculation refers. These prices are the bridge between the nominal and the real quantity of money.

The quantity theory of money takes for granted, first, that the real quantity rather than the nominal quantity of money is what ultimately matters to holders of money and, second, that in any given circumstances people wish to hold a fairly definite real quantity of money. Starting from a situation in which the nominal quantity that people hold at a particular moment of time happens to correspond at current prices to the real quantity that they wish to hold, suppose that the quantity of money unexpectedly increases so that individuals have larger cash balances than they wish to hold. They will then seek to dispose of what they regard as their excess money balances by paying out a larger sum for the purchase of securities, goods, and services, for the repayment of debts, and as gifts, than they are receiving from the corresponding sources. However, they cannot as a group succeed. One man's spending is another man's receipts. One man can reduce his nominal money balances only by persuading someone else to increase his. The community as a whole cannot in general spend more than it receives; it is playing a game of musical chairs.

The attempt to dispose of excess balances will nonetheless have important effects. If prices and incomes are free to change, the attempt to spend more will raise total spending and receipts, expressed in nominal units, which will lead to a bidding up of prices and perhaps also to an increase in output. If prices are fixed by a custom or by government edict, the attempt to spend more will either be matched by an increased in goods and services or produce 'shortages' and 'queues'. These in turn will raise the effective price and are likely sooner or later to force changes in customary or official prices.

The initial excess of nominal balances will therefore tend to be eliminated, even though there is no change in the nominal quantity of money, by either a reduction in the real quantity available to hold through price rises or an increase in the real quantity desired through output increases. And conversely for an initial deficiency of nominal balances.

Changes in prices and nominal income can be producted either by changes in the real balances that people wish to hold or by changes in the nominal balances available for them to hold. Indeed, it is a tautology, summarized in the famous quantity equations, that all changes in nominal income can be attributed to one or the other – just as change in the price of any good can always be attributed to a change in either demand or supply. The quantity theory is not, however, this tautology. On an analytical level, it has long been an analysis of the factors determining the quantity of money that the community wishes to hold; on an empirical level, it has increasingly become the generalization that changes in desired real balances (in the demand for money) tend to proceed slowly and gradually or to be the result of events set in train by prior changes in supply, whereas, in contrast, substantial changes in the supply of nominal balances can and frequently do occur independently of any changes in demand. The conclusion is that substantial changes in prices or nominal income are almost always the result of changes in the nominal supply of money.

3

(b) QUANTITY EQUATIONS. Attempts to formulate mathematically the relations just presented verbally date back several centuries (Humphrey, 1984). They consist of creating identities equating a flow of money payments to a flow of exchanges of goods or services. The resulting quantity equations have proved a useful analytical device and have taken different forms as quantity theorists have stressed different variables.

The transactions form of the quantity equation. The most famous version of the quantity equation is doubtless the transactions version formulated by Simon Newcomb (1885) and popularized by Irving Fisher (1911):

$$MV = PT, \tag{1}$$

or

$$MV + M'V' = PT. \tag{2}$$

In this version the elementary event is a transaction – an exchange in which one economic actor transfers goods or services or securities to another actor and receives a transfer of money in return. The right-hand side of the equations corresponds to the transfer of goods, services, or securities; the left-hand side, to the matching transfer of money.

Each transfer of goods, services or securities is regarded as the product of a price and quantity; wage per week times number of weeks, price of a good times number of units of the good, dividend per share times number of shares, price per share times number of shares, and so on. The right-hand side of equations (1) and (2) is the aggregate of such payments during some interval, with P a suitably chosen *average* of the prices and T a suitably chosen *aggregate* of the quantities during that interval, so that PT is the total nominal value of the payments during the interval in question. The units of P are dollars (or other monetary unit) per unit of quantity; the units of T are number of unit quantities per period of time. We can convert the equation from an expression applying to an *interval* of time to one applying to a *point* in time by the usual limiting process of letting the interval for which we aggregate payments approach zero, and expressing T not as an aggregate but as a rate of flow. The magnitude T then has the dimension of quantity per unit time; the product of P and T, of dollars (or other monetary unit) per unit time.

T is clearly a rather special index of quantities: it includes service flows (man-hours, dwelling-years, kilowatt-hours) and also physical capital items yielding such flows (houses, electric-generating plants) and securities representing both physical capital items and such intangible capital items as 'goodwill'. Since each capital item or security is treated as if it disappeared from economic circulation once it is transferred, any such item that is transferred more than once in the period in question is implicitly weighted by the number of times it enters into transactions (its 'velocity of circulation', in strict analogy with the 'velocity of circulation' of money). Similarly, P is a rather special price index.

The monetary transfer analysed on the left-hand side of equations (1) and (2) is treated very differently. The money that changes hands is treated as retaining its identity, and all money, whether used in transactions during the time interval in question or not, is explicitly accounted for. Money is treated as a stock, not as a flow or a mixture of a flow and a stock. For a single transaction, the breakdown into M and V is trivial: the cash that is transferred is turned over once, or $V = 1$. For all transactions during an interval of time, we can, in principle, classify the existing stock of monetary units according as each monetary unit entered into 0, 1, 2, ... transactions – that is, according as the monetary unit 'turned over' 0, 1, 2, ... times. The weighted average of these numbers of turnover, weighted by the number of dollars that turned over that number of times, is the conceptual equivalent of V. The dimensions of M are dollars (or other monetary unit); of V, number of turnovers per unit time; so, of the product, dollars per unit time.

Equation (2) differs from equation (1) by dividing payments into two categories: those effected by the transfer of hand-to-hand currency (including coin) and those effected by the transfer of deposits. In equation (2) M stands for the volume of currency and V for the velocity of currency, M' for the volume of deposits, and V' for the velocity of deposits.

One reason for the emphasis on this particular division was the persistent dispute about whether the term *money* should include only currency or deposits as well. Another reason was the direct availability of date on $M'V'$ from bank records of clearings or of debits to deposit accounts. These date make it possible to calculate V' in a way that is not possible for V.

Equations (1) and (2), like the other quantity equations we shall discuss, are intended to be identities – a special application of double-entry bookkeeping, with each transaction simultaneously recorded on both sides of the equation. However, as with the national income identities with which we are all familiar, when the two sides, or the separate elements on the two sides, are estimated from independent sources of data, many differences between them emerge. This statistical defect has been less obvious for the quantity equations than for the national income identities – with their standard entry 'statistical discrepancy' – because of the difficulty of calculating V directly. As a result, V in equation (1) and V and V' in equation (2) have generally been calculated as the numbers having the property that they render the equations correct. These calculated numbers therefore embody the whole of the counterpart to the 'statistical discrepancy'.

Just as the left-hand side of equation (1) can be divided into several components, as in equation (2), so also can the right-hand side. The emphasis on transactions reflected in this version of the quantity equation suggests dividing total transactions into categories of payments for which payment periods or practices differ: for example, into capital transactions, purchases of final goods and services, purchases of intermediate goods, and payments for the use of resources, perhaps separated into wage and salary payments and other payments. The observed value of V might well depend on the distribution of total payments among categories. Alternatively, if the quantity equation is interpreted not as an identity but as a functional relation expressing desired velocity as a function of other variables, the distribution of payments may well be an important set of variables.

The income form of the quantity equation. Despite the large amount of empirical work done on the transactions equations, notably by Irving Fisher (1911, pp. 280–318; 1919, pp. 407–9) and Carl Snyder (1934, pp. 278–91), the ambiguities of the concepts of 'transactions' and the 'general price level' – particularly those arising from the mixture of current and capital transactions – have never been satisfactorily resolved. More recently, national or social accounting has stressed income transactions rather than gross transactions and has explicitly if not wholly satisfactorily dealt with the conceptual and statistical problems involved in distinguishing between changes in prices and changes in quantities. As a result, since at least the work of James Angell (1936), monetary economists have tended to express the quantity equation in terms of income transactions rather than gross transactions. Let Y = nominal income, P = the price index implicit in estimating national income at constant prices, N = the number of persons in the population, y = per capita national income in constant prices, and $y' = Ny$ = national income at constant prices, so that

$$Y = PNy = Py'. \tag{3}$$

Let M represent, as before, the stock of money; but define V as the average number of times per unit time that the money stock is used in making *income* transactions (that is, payment for final productive services or, alternatively, for final goods and services) rather than all transactions. We can then write the quantity equation in income form as

$$MV = PNy = Py' \tag{4}$$

or, if we desire to distinguish currency from deposit transactions, as

$$MV + M'V' = PNy. \tag{5}$$

Although the symbols P, V, and V' are used both in equations (4) and (5) and in equations (1) and (2), they stand for different concepts in each pair of equations. (In practice, gross national product often replaces national income in calculating velocity even though the logic underlying the equation calls for national income. The reason is the widespread belief that estimates of GNP are subject to less statistical error than estimates of national income).

In the transactions version of the quantity equation, each intermediate transaction – that is, purchase by one enterprise from another – is included at the total value of the transaction, so that the value of wheat, for example, is included once when it is sold by the farmer to the mill, a second time when the mill sells flour to the baker, a third time when the baker sells bread to the grocer, a fourth time when the grocer sells bread to the consumer. In the income version, only the net value added by each of these transactions is included. To put it differently, in the transactions version, the elementary event is an isolated exchange of a physical item for money – an actual, clearly observable event. In the income version, the elementary event is a hypothetical event that can be inferred but is not directly observable. It is a complete series of transactions involving the exchange of productive services for final goods, via a sequence of money payments, with all the intermediate transactions in the income circuit netted out. The total value of all transactions is therefore a multiple of the value of income transactions only.

For a given flow of productive services or, alternatively, of final products (two of the multiple faces of income), the volume of transactions will be affected by vertical integration or disintegration of enterprises, which reduces or increases the number of transactions involved in a single income circuit, and by technological changes that lengthen or shorten the process of transforming productive services into final products. The volume of income will not be thus affected.

Similarly, the transactions version includes the purchase of an existing asset – a house or a piece of land or a share of equity stock – precisely on a par with an intermediate or final transaction. The income version excludes such transactions completely.

Are these differences an advantage or disadvantage of the income version? That clearly depends on what it is that determines the amount of money people want to hold. Do changes of the kind considered in the preceding paragraphs, changes that alter the ratio of intermediate and capital transactions to income, also alter in the same direction and by the same proportion the amount of money people want to hold? Or do they tend to leave this amount unaltered? Or do they have a more complex effect?

The transactions and income versions of the quantity theory involve very different conceptions of the role of money. For the transactions version, the most important thing about money is that it is transferred. For the income version, the most important thing is that it is held. This difference is even more obvious from the Cambridge cash-balance version of the quantity equation (Pigou, 1917). Indeed, the income version can perhaps best be regarded as a way station between the Fisher and the Cambridge version.

Cambridge cash-balance approach. The essential feature of a money economy is that an individual who has something to exchange need not seek out the double coincidence – someone who both wants what he has and offers in exchange what he wants. He need only find someone who wants what he has, sell it to him for general purchasing power, and then find someone who has what he wants and buy it with general purchasing power.

For the act of purchase to be separated from the act of sale, there must be something that everybody will accept in exchange as 'general purchasing power' – this aspect of money is emphasized in the transactions approach. But also there must be something that can serve as a temporary abode of purchasing power in the interim between sale and purchase. This aspect of money is emphasized in the cash-balance approach.

How much money will people or enterprises want to hold on the average as a temporary abode of purchasing power? As a first approximation, it has generally been supposed that the amount bears some relation to income, on the assumption that income affects the volume of potential purchases for which the individual or enterprise wishes to hold cash balances. We can therefore write

$$M = kPNy = kPy' \qquad (6)$$

where M, N, P, y, and y' are defined as in equation (4) and k is the ratio of money stock to income – either the observed ratio so calculated as to make equation (6) an identity or the 'desired' ratio so that M is the 'desired amount of money, which need not be equal to the actual amount. In either case, k is numerically equal to the reciprocal of the V in equation (4), the V being interpreted in one case as measured velocity and in the other as desired velocity.

Although equation (6) is simply a mathematical transformation of equation (4), it brings out sharply the difference between the aspect of money stressed by the transactions approached and that stressed by the cash-balance approach. This difference makes different definitions of money seem natural and leads to placing emphasis on different variables and analytical techniques.

The transactions approach makes it natural to define money in terms of whatever serves as the medium of exchange in discharging obligations. The cash-balance approach makes it seem entirely appropriate to include in addition such temporary abodes of purchasing power as demand and time deposits not transferable by check, although it clearly does not require their inclusion (Friedman and Schwartz, 1970, ch. 3).

Similarly, the transactions approach leads to emphasis on the mechanical aspect of the payments process: payments practices, financial and economic arrangements for effecting transactions, the speed of communication and transportation, and so on (Baumol, 1952; Tobin, 1956; Miller and Orr, 1966, 1968). The cash-balance approach, on the other hand, leads to emphasis on variables affecting the usefulness of money as an asset: the costs and returns from holding money instead of other assets, the uncertainty of the future, and so on (Friedman, 1956; Tobin, 1958).

Of course, neither approach enforces the exclusion of the variables stressed by the other. Portfolio considerations enter into the costs of effecting transactions and hence affect the most efficient payment arrangements; mechanical considerations enter into the returns from holding cash and hence affect the usefulness of cash in a portfolio.

Finally, with regard to analytical techniques, the cash-balance approach fits in much more readily with the general Marshallian demand-supply apparatus than does the transactions approach. Equation (6) can be regarded as a demand function for money, with P, N, and y on the right-hand side being three of the variables on which the quantity of money demanded depends and k symbolizing all the other variables, so that k is to be regarded not as a numerical constant but as itself a function of still other variables. For completion, the analysis requires another equation showing the supply of money as a function of these and other variables. The price level or the level of nominal income is then the resultant of the interaction of the demand and supply functions.

Levels versus rates of change. The several versions of the quantity equations have all been stated in terms of the levels of the variables involved. For the analysis of monetary change it is often more useful to express them in terms of rates of change. For example, take the logarithm of both sides of equation (4) and differentiate with respect to time. The result is

$$\frac{1}{M}\frac{dM}{dt} + \frac{1}{V}\frac{dV}{dt} = \frac{1}{P}\frac{dP}{dt} + \frac{1}{y'}\frac{dy'}{dt} \tag{7}$$

or, in simpler notation,

$$g_M + g_V = g_P + g_{y'} = g_{Y'}, \tag{8}$$

where g stands for the percentage rate of change (continuously compounded) of the variable denoted by its subscript. The same equation is implied by equation (6), with g_V replaced by $-g_k$.

The rate of change equations serve two very different purposes. First, they make explicit an important difference between a once-for-all change in the level of the quantity of money and a change in the rate of change of the quantity of money. The former is equivalent simply to a change of units – to substituting cents for dollars or pence for pounds – and hence, as is implicit in equations (4) and (6), would not be presumed to have any effect on real quantities, on neither V (nor k) nor y', but simply an offsetting effect on the price level, P. A change in the rate of change of money is a very different thing. It will tend, according to equations (7) and (8), to be accompanied by a change in the rate of inflation (g_P) which, as pointed out in section d below, affects the cost of holding money, and hence the desired real quantity of money. Such a change will therefore affect real quantities, V and g_V, y' and $g_{y'}$, as well as nominal and real interest rates.

The second purpose served by the rate of change equations is to make explicit the role of time, and thereby to facilitate the study of the effect of monetary change on the temporal pattern of response of the several variables involved. In recent decades, economists have devoted increasing attention to the short-term pattern of economic change, which has enhanced the importance of the rate of change versions of the quantity equations.

(c) THE SUPPLY OF MONEY. The quantity theory in its cash-balance versions suggests organizing an analysis of monetary phenomena in terms of (1) the conditions determining supply (this section); (2) the conditions determining demand (section (d) below); and (3) the reconciliation of demand with supply (section (e) below).

The factors determining the nominal supply of money available to be held depend critically on the monetary system. For systems like those that have prevailed in most major countries during the past two centuries, they can usefully be analysed under three main headings termed the proximate determinants of the quantity of money: (1) the amount of high-powered money – specie plus notes or deposit liabilities issued by the monetary authorities and used either as currency or as reserves by banks; (2) the ratio of bank deposits to bank holdings of high-powered money; and (3) the ratio of the public's deposits to its currency holdings (Friedman and Schwartz, 1963b, pp. 776–98; Cagan, 1965; Burger, 1971; Black, 1975).

It is an identity that

$$M = H \cdot \frac{\frac{D}{R}\left(1 + \frac{D}{C}\right)}{\frac{D}{R} + \frac{D}{C}}, \tag{9}$$

where H = high-powered money; D = deposits; R = bank reserves; C = currency in the hands of the public so that (D/R) is the deposit-reserve ratio; and (D/C) is the deposit-currency ratio. The fraction on the right-hand side of (9), i.e., the ratio of M to H, is termed the money multiplier, often a convenient summary of the effect of the two deposit ratios. The determinants are called proximate because their values are in turn determined by much more basic variables. Moreover, the same labels can refer to very different contents.

High-powered money is the clearest example. Until some time in the 18th or 19th century, the exact date varying from country to country, it consisted only of specie or its equivalent: gold, or silver, or cowrie shells, or any of a wide variety of commodities. Thereafter, until 1971, with some significant if temporary exceptions, it consisted of a mixture of specie and of government notes or deposit liabilities. The government notes and liabilities generally were themselves promises to pay specified amounts of specie on demand, though this promise weakened after World War I, when many countries promised to pay either specie or foreign currency. During the Bretton Woods period after World War II, only the USA was obligated to pay gold, and only to foreign monetary agencies, not to individuals or other non-governmental entities; other countries obligated themselves to pay dollars.

Since 1971, the situation has been radically different. In every major country, high-powered money consists solely of fiat money – pieces of paper issued by the government and inscribed with the legend 'one dollar' or 'one pound' and the message 'legal tender for all debts public and private'; or book entries, labelled deposits, consisting of promises to pay such pieces of paper. Such a worldwide fiat (or irredeemable paper) standard has no precedent in history. The 'gold' that central banks still record as an asset on their books is simply the grin of a Cheshire cat that has disappeared.

Under an international commodity standard, the total quantity of high-powered money in any one country – so long as it remains on the standard – is determined by the balance of payments. The division of high-powered money between physical specie and the fiduciary component of government-issued promises to pay is determined both by the policies of the various monetary authorities and the physical conditions of supply of specie. The latter provide a physical anchor for the quantity of money and hence ultimately for the price level.

Under the current international fiat standard, the quantity of high-powered money is determined solely by the monetary authorities, consisting in most countries of a central bank plus the fiscal authorities. What happens to the quantity of high-powered money depends on their objectives, on the institutional and political arrangements under which they operate, and the operating procedures they adopt. These are likely to vary considerably from country to country. Some countries (e.g., Hong Kong, Panama) have chosen to link their currencies rigidly to some other currency by pegging the exchange rate. For them, the amount of high-powered money is determined in the same way as under an international commodity standard – by the balance of payments.

The current system is so new that is must be regarded as in a state of transition. Some substitute is almost sure to emerge to replace the supply of specie as a long-term anchor for the price level, but it is not yet clear what that substitute will be (see section 5 below).

The deposit-reserve ratio is determined by the banking system subject to any requirements that are imposed by law or the monetary authorities. In addition to any such requirements, it depends on such factors as the risk of calls for conversion of bank deposits to high-powered money; the cost of acquiring additional high-powered money in case of need; and the returns from loans and investments, that is, the structure of interest rates.

The deposit-currency ratio is determined by the public. It depends on the relative usefulness to holders of money of deposits and currency and the relative cost of holding the one or the other. The relative cost in turn depends on the rates of interest received on deposits, which may be subject to controls imposed by law or the monetary authorities.

These factors determine the *nominal*, but not the *real*, quantity of money. The real quantity of money is determined by the interaction between the *nominal* quantity supplied and the *real* quantity demanded. In the process, changes in demand for real balances have feedback effects on the variables determining the nominal quantity supplied, and changes in nominal supply have feedback effects on the variables determining the real quantity demanded. Quantity theorists have generally concluded that these feedback effects are relatively minor, so that the *nominal* supply can generally be regarded as determined by a set of variables distinct from those that affect the *real* quantity demanded. In this sense, the nominal quantity can be regarded as determined primarily by supply, the real quantity, primarily by demand.

Instead of expressing the nominal supply in terms of the identity (9), it can also be expressed as a function of the variables that are regarded as affecting H, D/R, and D/C, such as the rate of inflation, interest rates, nominal income, the extent of uncertainty, perhaps also the variables that are regarded as determining the decisions of the monetary authorities. Such a supply function is frequently written as

$$M^S = h(R, Y, \ldots), \tag{10}$$

where R is an interest rate or set of interest rates, Y is nominal income, and the dots stand for other variables that are regarded as relevant.

(d) THE DEMAND FOR MONEY. The cash-balance version of the quantity theory, by stressing the role of money as an asset, suggests treating the demand for money as part of capital or wealth theory, concerned with the composition of the balance sheet or portfolio of assets.

From this point of view, it is important to distinguish between ultimate wealth holders, to whom money is one form in which they choose to hold their wealth, and enterprises, to whom money is a producer's good like machinery or inventories (Friedman, 1956; Laidler, 1985; Friedman and Schwartz, 1982).

Demand by ultimate wealth holders. For ultimate wealth holders the demand for money, in real terms, may be expected to be a function primarily of the following variables:

1. *Total wealth.* This is the analogue of the budget constraint in the usual theory of consumer choice. It is the total that must be divided among various forms of assets. In practice, estimates of total wealth are seldom available. Instead, income may serve as an index of wealth. However, it should be recognized that income as measured by statisticians may be a defective index of wealth because it is subject to erratic year-to-year fluctuations, and a longer-term concept, like the concept of permanent income developed in connection with the theory of consumption, may be more useful (Friedman, 1957, 1959).

The emphasis on income as a surrogate for wealth, rather than as a measure of the 'work' to be done by money, is perhaps the basic conceptual difference between the more recent analyses of the demand for money and the earlier versions of the quantity theory.

2. *The division of wealth between human and non-human forms.* The major asset of most wealth holders is personal earning capacity. However, the conversion of human into non-human wealth or the reverse is subject to narrow limits because of institutional constraints. It can be done by using current earnings to purchase non-human wealth or by using non-human wealth to finance the acquisition of skills, but not by purchase or sale of human wealth and to only a limited extent by borrowing on the collateral of earning power. Hence, the fraction of total wealth that is in the form of non-human wealth may be an additional important variable.

3. *The expected rates of return on money and other assets.* These rates of return are the counterparts to the prices of a commodity and its substitutes and complements in the usual theory of consumer demand. The nominal rate of return on money may be zero, as it generally is on currency, or negative, as it sometimes is on demand deposits subject to net service charges, or positive, as it sometimes is on demand deposits on which interest is paid and generally is on time deposits. The nominal rate of return on other assets consists of two parts: first, any currently paid yield, such as interest on bonds, dividends on equities, or cost, such as storage costs on physical assets, and, second, a change in the nominal price of the asset. The second part is especially important under conditions of inflation or deflation.

4. *Other variables determining the utility attached to the services rendered by money relative to those rendered by other assets – in Keynesian terminology, determining the value attached to liquidity proper.* One such variable may be one already considered – namely, real wealth or income, since the services rendered by money may, in principle, be regarded by wealth holders as a 'necessity', like bread, the consumption of which increases less than in proportion to any increase in income, or as a 'luxury', like recreation, the consumption of which increases more than in proportion.

Another variable that is important empirically is the degree of economic stability expected to prevail, since instability enhances the value wealth-holders attach to liquidity. This variable has proved difficult to express quantitatively although qualitative information often indicates the direction of change. For example, the outbreak of war clearly produces expectations of greater instability. That is one reason why a notable increase in real balances – that is, a notable decline in velocity – often accompanies the outbreak of war. Such a decline in velocity produced an initial *decline* in sensitive prices at the outset of both World War I and World War II – not the rise that later inflation would have justified.

The rate of inflation enters under item 3 as a factor affecting the cost of holding various assets, particularly currency. The variability of inflation enters here, as a major factor affecting the usefulness of money balances. Empirically, variability of inflation tends to increase with the level of inflation, reinforcing the negative effect of higher inflation on the quantity of money demanded.

Still another relevant variable may be the volume of trading in existing capital goods by ultimate wealth holders. The higher the turnover of capital assets, the larger the fraction of total assets people may find it useful to hold as cash. This variable corresponds to the class of transactions omitted in going from the transactions version of the quantity equation to the income version.

We can express this analysis in terms of the following demand function for money for an individual wealth holder:

$$M^D = P \cdot f(y, w; R_M^*, R_B^*, R_E^*; u), \qquad (11)$$

where M, P, and y have the same meaning as in equation (6) except that they relate to a single wealth-holder (for whom $y = y'$); w is the fraction of wealth in non-human form (or, alternatively, the fraction of income derived from property); an asterisk denotes an expected value, so R_M^* is the expected nominal rate of return on money; R_B^* is the expected nominal rate of return on fixed-value securities, including expected changes in their prices; R_E^* is the expected nominal rate of return on physical assets, including expected changes in their prices; and u is a portmanteau symbol standing for other variables affecting the utility attached to the services of money. Though the expected rate of inflation is not explicit in equation (11), it is implicit because it affects the expected nominal returns on the various classes of assets, and is sometimes used as a proxy for R_E^*. For some purposes it may be important to classify assets still more finely – for example, to distinguish currency from deposits, long-term from short-term fixed-value securities, risky from relatively safe equities, and one kind of physical assets from another.

Furthermore, the several rates of return are not independent. Arbitrage tends to eliminate differences among them that do not correspond to differences in perceived risk or other nonpecuniary characteristics of the assets, such as liquidity. In particular, as Irving Fisher pointed out in 1896, arbitrage between real and nominal assets introduces an allowance for anticipated inflation into the nominal interest rate (Fisher, 1896; Friedman, 1956).

The usual problems of aggregation arise in passing from equation (11) to a corresponding equation for the economy as a whole – in particular, from the possibility that the amount of money demanded may depend on the distribution among individuals of such variables as y and w and not merely on their aggregate or average value. If we neglect these distributional effects, equation (11) can be regarded as applying to the community as a whole, with M and y referring to per capita money holdings and per capita real income, respectively, and w to the fraction of aggregate wealth in non-human form.

Although the mathematical equation may be the same, its significance is very different for the individual wealth-holder and the community as a whole. For the individual, all the variables in the equation other than his own income and disposition of his portfolio are outside his control. He takes them, as well as the structure of monetary institutions, as given, and adjusts his nominal balances accordingly. For the community as a whole, the situation is very different. In general, the nominal quantity of money available to be held is fixed and what adjusts are the variables on the right-hand side of the equation, including an implicit underlying variable, the structure of monetary institutions, which, in the longer run, at least, adjusts itself to the tastes and preferences of the holders of money. A dramatic example is provided by the restructuring of the financial system in the US in the 1970s and 1980s.

In practice, the major problems that arise in applying equation (11) are the precise definitions of y and w, the estimation of *expected* rates of return as contrasted with actual rates of return, and the quantitative specification of the variables designed by u.

Demand for business enterprises. Business enterprises are not subject to a constraint comparable to that imposed by the total wealth of the ultimate wealth-holder. They can determine the total amount of capital embodied in productive assets, including money, to maximize returns, since they can acquire additional capital through the capital market.

A similar variable defining the 'scale' of the enterprise may, however, be relevant as an index of the productive value of different quantities of money to the enterprise. Lack of data has meant that much less empirical work has been done on the business demand for money than on an aggregate demand curve encompassing both ultimate wealth-holders and business enterprises. As a result, there are as yet only faint indications about the best variable to use: whether total transactions, net value added, net income, total capital in nonmoney form, or net worth.

The division of wealth between human and non-human form has no special relevance to business enterprises, since they are likely to buy the services of both forms on the market.

Rates of return on money and on alternative assets are, of course, highly relevant to business enterprises. These rates determine the net cost of holding money balances. However, the particular rates that are relevant may differ from those that are relevant for ultimate wealth-holders. For example, the rates banks charge on loans are of minor importance for wealth-holders yet may be extremely important for businesses, since bank loans may be a way in which they can acquire the capital embodied in money balances.

The counterpart for business enterprises of the variable u in equation (11) is the set of variables other than scale affecting the productivity of money balances. At least one subset of such variables – namely, expectations about economic stability and the variability of inflation – is likely to be common to business enterprises and ultimate wealth-holders.

With these interpretations of the variables, equation (11), with w excluded, can be regarded as symbolizing the business demand for money and, as it stands, symbolizing aggregate demand for money, although with even more serious qualifications about the ambiguities introduced by aggregation.

Buffer stock effects. In serving its basic function as a temporary abode of purchasing power, cash balances necessarily fluctuate, absorbing temporary discrepancies between the purchases and sales they mediate.

Though always recognized, this 'buffer stock' role of money has seldom been explicitly modelled. Recently, more explicit attention has been paid to the buffer stock notion in an attempt to explain anomalies that have arisen in econometric estimates of the short-run demand for money (Judd and Scadding, 1982; Laidler, 1984; Knoester, 1984).

(e) THE RECONCILIATION OF DEMAND WITH SUPPLY. Multiply equation (11) by N to convert it from a per capita to an aggregate demand function, and equate it to equation (10), omitting for simplicity the asterisks designating expected values, and letting R stand for a vector of interest rates:

$$M^S = h(R, Y, \dots) = P \cdot N \cdot f(y, w, R, g_P, u). \qquad (12)$$

The result is quantity equation (6) in an expanded form. In principle, a change in any of the underlying variables that produces a change in M^S and disturbs a pre-existing equilibrium can produce offsetting changes in any of the other variables. In practice, as already noted earlier, the initial impact is likely to be on y and R, the ultimate impact predominantly on P.

A frequent criticism of the quantity theory is that its proponents do not specify the transmission mechanism between a change in M^S and the offsetting changes in other variables, that they rely on a black box connecting the input – the nominal quantity of money – and the output – effects on prices and quantities.

15

This criticism is not justified insofar as it implies that the transmission mechanism for the quantity equation is fundamentally different from that for a demand-supply analysis of a particular product – shoes, or copper, or haircuts. In both cases the demand function for the community as a whole is the sum of demand functions for individual consumer or producer units, and the separate demand functions are determined by the tastes and opportunities of the units. In both cases, the supply function depends on production possibilities, institutional arrangements for organizing production, and the conditions of supply of resources. In both cases a shift in supply or in demand introduces a discrepancy between the amounts demanded and supplied *at the pre-existing price.* In both cases any discrepancy can be eliminated only by either a price change or some alternative rationing mechanism, explicit or implicit.

Two features of the demand-supply adjustment for money have concealed this parallelism. One is that demand-supply analysis for particular products typically deals with flows – number of pairs of shoes or number of haircuts per year – whereas the quantity equations deal with the stock of money at a point in time. In this respect the correct analogy is with the demand for, say, land, which, like money, derives its value from the flow of services it renders but has a purchase price and not merely a rental value. The second is the widespread tendency to confuse 'money' and 'credit', which has produced misunderstanding about the relevant price variable. The 'price' of money is the quantity of goods and services that must be given up to acquire a unit of money – the inverse of the price level. This is the price that is analogous to the price of land or of copper or of haircuts. The 'price' of money is not the interest rate, which is the 'price' of credit. The interest rate connects stocks with flows – the rental value of land with the price of land, the value of the service flow from a unit of money with the price of money. Of course, the interest rate may affect the quantity of money demanded – just as it may affect the quantity of land demanded – but so may a host of other variables.

The interest rate has received special attention in monetary analysis because, without quite realizing it, fractional reserve banks have created part of the stock of money in the course of serving as an intermediary between borrowers and lenders. Hence changes in the quantity of money have frequently occurred through the credit markets, in the process producing important transitory effects on interest rates.

On a more sophisticated level, the criticism about the transmission mechanism applies equally to money and to other goods and services. In all cases it is desirable to go beyond equality of demand and supply as defining a stationary equilibrium position and examine the variables that affect the quantities demanded and supplied and the dynamic temporal process whereby actual or potential discrepancies are eliminated. Examination of the variables affecting demand and supply has been carried farther for money than for most other goods or services. But for both, there is as yet no satisfactory and widely accepted description, in precise quantifiable terms, of the dynamic temporal process of adjustment. Much research has been devoted to this question in recent decades;

yet it remains a challenging subject for research. (For surveys of some of the literature, see Laidler, 1985; Judd and Scadding, 1982.)

(f) FIRST-ROUND EFFECTS. Another frequent criticism of the quantity equations is that they neglect any effect on the outcome of the source of change in the quantity of money. In Tobin's words, the question is whether 'the genesis of new money makes a difference', in particular, whether 'an increase in the quantity of money has the same effect whether it is issued to purchase goods or to purchase bonds' (1974, p. 87).

Or, as John Stuart Mill put a very similar view in 1844, 'The issues of a *Government* paper, even when not permanent, will raise prices; because Governments usually issue their paper in purchases for consumption. If issued to pay off a portion of the national debt, we believe they would have no effect' (1844, p. 589).

Tobin and Mill are right that the way the quantity of money is increased affects the outcome in some measure or other. If one group of individuals receives the money on the first round, they will likely use it for different purposes than another group of individuals. If the newly printed money is spent on the first round for goods and services, it adds directly at that point to the demand for such goods and services, whereas if it is spent on purchasing debt, or simply held temporarily as a buffer stock, it has no immediate effect on the demand for goods and services. Such effects come later as the initial recipients of the 'new' money dispose of it. However, as the 'new' money spreads through the economy, any first-round effects tend to be dissipated. The 'new' money is merged with the old and is distributed in much the same way.

One way to characterize the Keynesian approach (see below) is that it gives almost exclusive importance to the first-round effect by putting primary emphasis on flows of spending rather than on stocks of assets. Similarly, one way to characterize the quantity-theory approach is to say that it gives almost no importance to first-round effects.

The empirical question is how important the first-round effects are compared with the ultimate effects. Theory cannot answer that question. The answer depends on how different are the reactions of the recipients of cash via alternative routes, on how rapidly a larger money stock is distributed through the economy, on how long it stays at each point in the economy, on how much the demand for money depends on the structure of government liabilities, and so on. Casual empiricism yields no decisive answer. Maybe the first-round effect is so strong that it dominates later effects; maybe it is highly transitory.

Despite repeated assertions by various authors that the first-round effect is significant, none, so far as I know, has presented any systematic empirical evidence to support that assertion. The apparently similar response of spending to changes in the quantity of money at widely separated dates in different countries and under diverse monetary systems establishes something of a presumption that the first-round effect is not highly significant. This presumption is also supported by

17

several empirical studies designed to test the importance of the first-round effect (Cagan, 1972).

(g) THE INTERNATIONAL TRANSMISSION MECHANISM. From its very earliest days, the quantity theory was intimately connected with the analysis of the adjustment mechanism in international trade. A commodity standard, in which money is specie or its equivalent, was taken as the norm. Under such a standard, the supply of money in any one country is determined by the links between that country and other countries that use the same commodity as money. Under such a standard, the same theory explains links among money, prices, and nominal income in various parts of a single country – money, prices, and nominal income in Illinois and money, prices, and nominal income in the rest of the United States – and the corresponding links among various countries. The differences between interregional adjustment and international adjustment are empirical: greater mobility of people, goods, and capital among regions than among countries, and hence more rapid adjustment.

According to the specie-flow mechanism developed by Hume and elaborated by Henry Thornton, David Ricardo and their successors, 'too' high a money stock in country A tends to makes prices in A high relative to prices in the rest of the world, encouraging imports and discouraging exports. The resulting deficit in the balance of trade is financed by shipment of specie, which reduces the quantity of money in country A and increases it in the rest of the world. These changes in the quantity of money tend to lower prices in country A and raise them in the rest of the world, correcting the original disequilibrium. The process continues until price levels in all countries are at a level at which balances of payments are in equilibrium (which may be consistent with a continuing movement of specie, for example, from gold- or silver-producing countries to non-gold- or silver-producing countries, or between countries growing at different secular rates).

Another strand of the classical analysis has recently been revived under the title 'the monetary theory of the balance of payments'. The specie-flow mechanism implicitly assumes that prices adjust only in response to changes in the quantity of money produced by specie flows. However, if markets are efficient and transportation costs are neglected, there can be only a single price expressed in a common currency for goods traded internationally. Speculation tends to assure this result. Internally, competition between traded and nontraded goods tends to keep their relative price in line with relative costs. If these adjustments are rapid, 'the law of one price' holds among countries. If the money stock is not distributed among countries in such a way as to be consistent with the equilibrium prices, excess demands and supplies of money will lead to specie flows. Domestic nominal demand in a country with 'too' high a quantity of money will exceed the value of domestic output and the excess will be met by imports, producing a balance of payments deficit financed by the export of specie; and conversely in a country with too 'low' a quantity of money. Specie flows are still the adjusting mechanism, but they are produced by differences between demand for output in nominal terms and the supply of output at world prices rather than by discrepancies in prices. Putative rather than actual price differences are the spur to adjustment. This description is highly oversimplified, primarily because it omits the important role assigned to short- and long-term capital flows by all theorists – those who stress the specie-flow mechanism and even more those who stress the single-price mechanism (Frenkel, 1976; Frenkel and Johnson, 1976).

In practice, few countries have had pure commodity standards. Most have had a mixture of commodity and fiduciary standards. Changes in the fiduciary component of the stock of money can replace specie flows as a means of adjusting the quantity of money.

The situation is still different for countries that do not share a unified currency, that is, a currency in which only the name assigned to a unit of currency differs among countries. Changes in the rates of exchange between national currencies then serve to keep prices in various countries in the appropriate relation when expressed in a common currency. Exchange rate adjustments replace specie flows or changes in the quantity of domestically created money. And exchange rate changes too may be produced by actual or putative price differences or by short- or long-term capital flows. Moreover, especially during the Bretton Woods period (1945–71), but more recently as well, governments have often tried to avoid changes in exchange rates by seeking adjustment through subsidies to exports, obstacles to imports, and direct controls over foreign exchange trans-actions. These measures involved either implicit or explicit multiple rate systems and were accompanied by government borrowing to finance balance-of-payments deficits, or governmental lending to offset surpluses. They sometimes led to severe financial crises and major exchange rate adjustments – one reason the Bretton Woods system finally broke down in 1971. Since then, exchange rates have supposedly been free to float and to be determined in private markets. In practice, however, governments still intervene in an attempt to affect the exchange rates of their currencies, either directly by buying or selling their currency on the market, or indirectly, by adopting monetary or fiscal or trade policies designed to alter the market exchange rate. However, most governments no longer announce fixed parities for their currencies.

2. KEYNESIAN CHALLENGE TO THE QUANTITY THEORY. The depression of the 1930s produced a wave of scepticism about the relevance and validity of the quantity theory of money. The central banks of the world – the Federal Reserve in the forefront – proclaimed that, despite the teachings of the quantity theory, 'easy money' was proving to be ineffective in stemming the depression. They pointed to the low level of short-term interest rates as evidence of how 'easy' monetary policy was. Their claims seemed credible not only because of the confusion between 'lowness of interest' and 'plenty of money' pointed out by Hume but also because of the absence of readily available evidence on what was happening to the quantity of money. Most observers at the time did not know, as we do now, that the Federal Reserve permitted the quantity of money in the United States to decline by one-third between 1929 and 1933, and hence that the accompanying contraction in economic activity and deflation of prices was

entirely consistent with the quantity theory. Monetary policy was incredibly 'tight' not 'easy'.

The scepticism about the quantity theory was further heightened by the publication of John Maynard Keynes's *The General Theory of Employment, Interest and Money* (Keynes, 1936) which offered an alternative interpretation of economic fluctuations in general and the depression in particular. Keynes emphasized spending on investment and the stability of the consumption function rather than the stock of money and the stability of the demand function for money. He relegated the forces embodies in the quantity theory to a minor role, and treated fiscal rather than monetary policy as the chief instrument for influencing the course of events. Received wisdom both inside and outside the economics profession became 'money does not matter'.

Keynes did not deny the validity of the quantity equation, in any of its forms – after all, he had been a major contributor to the quantity theory (Keynes, 1923). What he did was something very different. He argued that the demand for money, which he termed the liquidity-preference function, had a special form such that *under conditions of underemployment* the *V* in equation (4) and the *k* in equation (6) would be highly unstable and would passively adapt to whatever changes independently occurred in money income or the stock of money. Under such conditions, these equations, though entirely valid, were largely useless for policy or prediction. Moreover, he regarded such conditions as prevailing much, if not most of the time.

That possibility rested on two other key propositions. First, that, contrary to the teachings of classical and neoclassical economists, the *long-run equilibrium* position of an economy need not be characterized by 'full employment' of resources even if all prices are flexible. In his view, unemployment could be a deep-seated characteristic of an economy rather than simply a reflection of price and wage rigidity or transitory disturbances. This proposition has played an important role in promoting the acceptance of Keynesianism, especially by non-economists, even though, by now, it is widely accepted that, as a *theoretical* matter, the proposition is false. Keynes's error consisted in neglecting the role of wealth in the consumption function. There is no fundamental 'flaw in the price system' that makes persistent structural unemployment a possible or probable natural outcome of a fully operative market system (Haberler, 1941, pp. 242, 389, 403, 491–503; Pigou 1947; Tobin, 1947; Patinkin, 1948; Johnson, 1961). The concept of 'underemployment equilibrium' has been replaced by the concept of a 'natural rate of unemployment' (see section 3 below).

Keynes's final key proposition was that, as an *empirical* matter, prices, especially wages, can be regarded as rigid – an institutional datum – for *short-run economic fluctuations*; in which case, the distinction between real and nominal magnitudes that is at the heart of the quantity theory is irrelevant for such fluctuations. This proposition, unlike the other two, did not conflict with the teachings of the quantity theory. Classical and neoclassical economists had long recognized that price and wage rigidity existed and contributed to unemployment during cyclical contractions, and to labour scarcity during cyclical booms. But to them, wage rigidity was a defect of the market; to Keynes, it was a rational response to the possibility of underemployment equilibrium (Keynes, 1936, pp. 269–71).

In his analysis of the demand for money (i.e., the form of equation (6) or (11), Keynes treated the stock of money as if it were divided into two parts, one part, M_1, 'held to satisfy the transactions- and precautionary-motives', the other, M_2, 'held to satisfy the speculative-motive' (Keynes, 1936, p. 199). He regarded M_1 as a roughly constant fraction of income. He regarded the demand for M_2 as arising from '*uncertainty* as to the future course of the rate of interest' (Keynes, 1936, p. 168) and the amount demanded as depending on the relation between current rates of interest and the rates of interest expected to prevail in the future. Keynes, of course, recognized the existence of a whole complex of interest rates. However, for simplicity, he spoke in terms of 'the rate of interest', usually meaning by that the rate on long-term securities that were fixed in nominal value and that involved minimal risks of default – for example, government bonds. In a 'given state of expectations', the higher the current rate of interest, the lower would be the (real) amount of money that people would want to hold for speculative motives for two reasons: first, the greater would be the cost in terms of current earnings sacrificed by holding money instead of securities, and, second, the more likely it would be that interest rates would fall, and hence bond prices rise, and so the greater would be the cost in terms of capital gains sacrificed by holding money instead of securities.

To formalize Keynes's analysis in terms of the symbols we have used so far, we can write his demand (liquidity-preference) function as

$$M/P = M_1/P + M_2/P = k_1 y' + f(R - R^*, R^*) \tag{13}$$

where R is the current rate of interest, R^* is the rate of interest expected to prevail, and k_1, the analogue to the inverse of the income velocity of circulation of money, is treated as determined by payment practices and hence as a constant at least in the short run. Later writers in this tradition have argued that k_1 too should be regarded as a function of interest rates (Baumol, 1952; Tobin, 1956).

Although expectations are given great prominence in developing the liquidity function expressing the demand for M_2, Keynes and his followers generally did not explicitly introduce an expected interest rate into that function as is done in equation (13). For the most part, in practice, they treated the amount of M_2 demanded as a function simply of the current interest rate, the emphasis on expectations serving only as a reason for attributing instability to the liquidity function. Moreover, for the most part, they omitted P (and replaced y' by Y) because of their assumption that prices were rigid.

Except for somewhat different language, the analysis up to this point differs from that of earlier quantity theorists, such as Fisher, only by its subtle analysis of the role of expectations about future interest rates, its greater emphasis on current interest rates, and its narrower restriction of the variables explicitly considered as affecting the amount of money demanded.

Keynes's special twist concerned the empirical form of the liquidity-preference function at the low interest rates that he believed would prevail under conditions of underemployment equilibrium. Let the interest rate fall sufficiently low, he argued, and money and bonds would become perfect substitutes for one another; liquidity preference, as he put it, would become absolute. The liquidity-preference function, expressing the quantity of M_2 demanded as a function of the rate of interest, would become horizontal at some low but finite rate of interest. Under such circumstances, an increase in the quantity of money by whatever means would lead holders of money to seek to convert their additional cash balances into bonds, which would tend to lower the rate of interest on bonds. Even the slightest lowering would lead speculators with firm expectations to absorb the additional money balances by selling any bonds demanded by the initial holders of the additional money. The result would simply be that the community as a whole would hold the increased quantity of money without any change in the interest rate; k would be higher and V lower. Conversely, a decrease in the quantity of money would lead holders of bonds to seek to restore their money balances by selling bonds, but this would tend to raise the rate of interest, and even the slightest rise would induce the speculators to absorb the bonds offered.

Or, again, suppose nominal income increases or decreases for whatever reason. That will require an increase or decrease in M_1, which can come out of or be transferred to M_2 without any further effects. The conclusion is that, *under circumstances of absolute liquidity preference*, income can change without a change in M and M can change without a change in income. The holders of money are in metastable equilibrium, like a tumber on its side on a flat surface; they will be satisfied with whatever the quantity of money happens to be.

Keynes regarded absolute liquidity preference as a strictly 'limiting case' of which, though it 'might become practically important in future', he knew 'of no example...hitherto' (1936, p. 207). However, he treated velocity as if in practice its behaviour frequently approximated that which would prevail in this limiting case.

Keynes's disciples went much farther than Keynes himself. They were readier than he was to accept absolute liquidity preference as the actual state of affairs. More important, many argued that when liquidity preference was not absolute, changes in the quantity of money would affect only the interest rate on bonds and that changes in this interest rate in turn would have little further effect. They argued that both consumption expenditures and investment expenditures were nearly completely insensitive to changes in interest rates, so that a change in M would merely be offset by an opposite and compensatory change in V (or a change in the same direction in k), leaving P and y almost completely unaffected. In essence their argument consists in asserting that only paper securities are substitutes for money balances – that real assets never are (see Hansen, 1957, p. 50; Tobin, 1961).

The apparent success during the 1950s and 1960s of governments committed to a Keynesian full-employment policy in achieving rapid economic growth, a high degree of economic stability, and relatively stable prices and interest rates, for a time strongly reinforced belief in the initial Keynesian views about the unimportance of variations in the nominal quantity of money.

The 1970s administered a decisive blow to these views and fostered a revival of belief in the quantity theory. Rapid monetary growth was accompanied not only by accelerated inflation but also by rising, not falling, average levels of unemployment (Friedman, 1977), and by rising, not declining, interest rates. As Robert Lucas put it in 1981,

> Keynesian orthodoxy ... appears to be giving seriously wrong answers to the most basic questions of macroeconomic policy. Proponents of a class of models which promised $3\frac{1}{2}$ to $4\frac{1}{2}$ percent unemployment to a society willing to tolerate annual inflation rates of 4 to 5 percent have some explaining to do after a decade [i.e., the 1970s] such as we have just come through. A forecast error of this magnitude and central importance to policy has consequences (pp. 559–60).

This experience undermined the belief that the price level could be regarded as rigid – or at any rate as determined by forces unrelated to the quantity of money; that the nominal quantity of money undemanded could be regarded as a function primarily of the nominal interest rate, and that absolute liquidity preference was the normal state of affairs. No teacher of elementary economics since the late 1970s can, as so many did in the 1940s, 1950s, and 1960s, draw on the blackboard a downward sloping liquidity-preference diagram with the nominal quantity of money on the horizontal axis and a nominal interest rate on the vertical axis and confidently proclaim that the only important effect of an increase in the nominal quantity of money would be to lower the rate of interest. The distinction between the nominal interest rate and the real interest rate introduced by Irving Fisher in 1896 has entered – or re-entered – received wisdom (Fisher, 1896).

Despite its subsidence, the Keynesian attack on the quantity theory has left its mark. It has reinforced the tendency, already present in the Cambridge approach, to stress the role of money as an asset and hence to regard the analysis of the demand for money as part of capital or wealth theory, concerned with the composition of the balance sheet or portfolio of assets. The Keynesian stress on autonomous spending and hence on fiscal policy remains important in its own right but also has led to greater emphasis on the effect of government fiscal policies on the demand for money. Keynes's stress on expectations has contributed to the rapid growth in the analysis of the role and formation of expectations in a variety of economic contexts. Conversely, the revival of the quantity theory has led Keynesian economists to treat changes in the quantity of money as an essential element in the analysis of short-term change.

Finally, the controversy between Keynesians and quantity theorists has led both groups to distinguish more sharply between long-run and short-run effects of monetary changes; between 'static' or 'long-run equilibrium' theory and the dynamics of economic change.

As Franco Modigliani put it in his 1976 presidential address to the American Economic Association, there are currently 'no serious analytical disagreements between leading monetarists [i.e., quantity theorists] and leading nonmonetarists [i.e., Keynesians]' (1977, p. 1).

However, there still remain important differences on an empirical level. These all centre on the dynamics of short-run change – the process whereby a change in the quantity of money affects aggregate spending and the role of fiscal variables in the process.

The Keynesians regard a change in the quantity of money as affecting in the first instance 'the' interest rate, interpreted as a market rate on a fairly narrow class of financial liabilities. They regard spending as affected only 'indirectly' as the changed interest rate alters the profitability and amount of investment spending, through the multiplier, affects total spending. Hence the emphasis they give in their analysis to the interest elasticities of the demand for money and of investment spending.

The quantity theorists, on the other hand, stress a much broader and more 'direct' impact of spending, saying, as in section 1a above, that individuals will seek 'to dispose of what they regard as their excess money balances by paying out a larger sum for the purchase of securities, goods, and services, for the repayment of debts, and as gifts than they are receiving from the corresponding sources'.

The two approaches can be readily reconciled on a formal level. Quantity theorists can describe the transmission mechanism as operating 'through' the balance sheet and 'through' changes in interest rates. The attempt by holders of money to restore or attain a desired balance sheet after an unexpected increase in the quantity of money tends initially to raise the prices of assets and reduce interest rates, which encourages spending to produce new assets and also spending on current services rather than on purchasing existing assets. This is how an initial effect on balance sheets gets translated into an effect on income and spending. The resulting increase in spending tends to raise prices of goods and services which, in turn, by lowering the real value of the quantity of money and of nominal assets, tends to eliminate the initial decline in interest rates, even overshooting in the process.

The difference between the quantity theorists and the Keynesians is less in the nature of the process than in the range of assets considered. The Keynesians tend to concentrate on a narrow range of marketable assets and recorded interest rates. The quantity theorists insist that a far wider range of assets and interest rates must be taken into account – such assets as durable and semi-durable consumer goods, structures, and other real property. As a result, the quantity theorists regard the market rates stressed by the Keynesians as only a small part of the total spectrum of rates that are relevant.

This difference in the assumed transmission mechanism is largely a by-product of the different assumptions about price. The rejection of absolute liquidity preference forced Keynes's followers to let the interest rate be flexible. This chink in the key assumption that prices are an institutional datum was minimized by interpreting the 'interest rate' narrowly, and market institutions made it easy to do so. After all, it is most unusual to quote the 'interest rate' implicit in the sales and rental prices of houses and automobiles, let alone furniture, household appliances, clothes, and so on. Hence the prices of these items continued to be regarded as an institutional datum, which forced the transmission process to go through an extremely narrow channel. On the side of the quantity theorists there was no such inhibition. Since they regard prices as flexible, though not 'perfectly' flexible, it was natural for them to interpret the transmission mechanism in terms of relative price adjustments over a broad area rather than in terms of narrowly defined interest rates.

Less important differences are the tendency for Keynesians to stress the short-run as opposed to the long-run impact of changes to a far greater extent than the quantity theorists; and, a related difference, to give greater scope to the first-round effect of changes in the quantity of money.

3. THE PHILLIPS CURVE AND THE NATURAL RATE HYPOTHESIS. A major postwar development that contributed greatly to the revival of the quantity theory grew out of criticism by quantity theorists of the 'Phillips curve' – an allegedly stable inverse relation between unemployment and the rate of change of nominal wages such that a high level of unemployment was accompanied by declining wages, a low level by rising wages. Though not formally linked to the Keynesian theoretical system, the Phillips curve was widely welcomed by Keynesians as helping to fill a gap in the system created by the assumption of rigid wages. In addition, it appeared to offer an attractive trade-off possibility for economic policy: a permanent reduction in the level of unemployment at the cost of a moderate sustained increase in the rate of inflation. The Keynesian assumption that prices and wages could be regarded as institutionally determined made it easy for them to accept a relation between a nominal magnitude (the rate of change of wages) and a real magnitude (unemployment).

By contrast, the quantity theory distinction between real and nominal magnitudes implies that the Phillips curve is theoretically flawed. The quantity of labour demanded is a function of real not nominal wages; and so is the quantity supplied. Under any given set of circumstances, there is an equilibrium level of unemployment corresponding to an equilibrium structure of *real* wage rates. A higher level of unemployment will put downward pressure on real wage rates. The level of unemployment consistent with the equilibrium structure of real wage rates has been termed the 'natural rate of unemployment' and defined as

> the level that would be ground out by the Walrasian system of general equilibrium equations, provided there is imbedded in them the actual structural characteristics of the labour and commodity markets, including market imperfections, stochastic variability in demands and supplies, the cost of gathering information about job vacancies and labour availabilities, the cost of mobility, and so on (Friedman, 1968, p. 8).

The nominal wage rate that corresponds to any given real wage rate depends on the level of prices. Whether that nominal wage rate is rising or falling depends on whether prices are rising or falling. If wages and prices change at the same rate, the real wage rate remains the same. Hence, in the long run, there need be no relation between the rate of change of *nominal* wages and the rate of change of *real* wages, and hence between the rate of change of nominal wages and the level of unemployment. In the long run, therefore, the Phillips curve will tend to be vertical at the natural rate of unemployment – a proposition that came to be termed the Natural Rate Hypothesis.

Over short periods, an *unanticipated* increase in inflation reduces real wages as viewed by employers, inducing them to offer higher nominal wages, which workers erroneously view as higher real wages. This discrepancy simultaneously encourages employers to offer more employment and workers to accept more employment, thereby reducing unemployment, which produces the inverse relation encapsulated in the Phillips curve. However, if the higher rate of inflation continues, the anticipations of workers and employers will converge and the decline in unemployment will be reversed. A negatively sloping Phillips curve is therefore a short-run phenomenon. Moreover, it will not be stable over time, since what matters is not the nominal rates of change of wages and prices but the difference between the actual and the *anticipated* rates of change. The emergence of stagflation in the 1970s quickly confirmed this analysis, leading to the widespread replacement of the original Phillips curve by an expectations-adjusted Phillips curve (Friedman, 1977).

Acceptance of the natural rate hypothesis has had far-reaching effects not only on received wisdom among economists but also on economic policy. It became widely recognized that expansionary monetary and fiscal policies at best gave only a temporary stimulus to output and employment and if long continued would be reflected primarily in inflation.

4. THE THEORY OF RATIONAL EXPECTATIONS. A subsequent theoretical development was the belated flowering of a seed planted in 1961 by John F. Muth, in a long-neglected article on 'Rational expectations and the theory of price movements' (Muth, 1961). The theory of rational expectations offers no special insight into stationary-state or long-run equilibrium analysis. Its contribution is to dynamics – short-run change, and hence potentially to stabilization policy.

It has long been recognized by writers of all persuasions that, as Abraham Lincoln put it over a century ago, 'you can't fool all of the people all of the time'. The tendency for the public to learn from experience and to adjust to it underlies David Hume's view that monetary expansion 'is favourable to industry' only in its initial stages, but that if it continues, it will come to be anticipated and will affect prices and nominal interest rates but not real magnitudes. It also underlies the companion view associated with the natural rate hypothesis that a 'full employment' policy in which monetary, or for that matter fiscal, measures are used to counteract any increase in unemployment will almost inevitably lead not simply to uneven inflation but to uneven inflation around a rising trend – a conclusion often illustrated by analogizing inflation to a drug of which the addict must take larger and larger doses to get the same kick.

Nonetheless, the importance of anticipations and how they are formed in determining the dynamic response to changes in money and other magnitudes remained largely implicit until Lucas and Sargent applied the Muth rational expectations idea explicitly to the reliability of econometric models of the economy and to stabilization policies (Fisher, 1980; Lucas, 1976; Lucas and Sargent, 1981).

The theory of rational expectations asserts that economic agents should be treated as if their anticipations fully incorporate both currently available information about the state of the world and a correct theory of the interrelationships among the variables. Anticipations formed in this way will on the average tend to be correct (a statement whose simplicity conceals fundamental problems of interpretation, Friedman and Schwartz, 1982, pp. 556–7).

The rational expectations hypothesis has far-reaching implications for the validity of econometric models. Suppose a statistician were able to construct a model that predicted highly accurately for a past period all relevant variables; also, that a monetary rule could be devised that if used during the past period with that model could have achieved a particular objective – say keeping unemployment between 4 and 5 percent. Suppose now that that policy rule were adopted for the future. It would be nearly certain that the model for which the rule was developed would no longer work. The economic equivalent of the Heisenberg indeterminacy principle would take over. The model was for an economy without that monetary rule. Put the rule into effect and it will alter rational expectations and hence behaviour. Even without putting the rule into effect, the model would very likely continue to work only so long as its existence could be kept secret because if market participants learned about it they would use it in forming their rational expectations and thereby falsify it to a greater or lesser extent. Little wonder that every major econometric model is always being sent back to the drawing board as experience confounds it, or that their producers have reacted so strongly to the theory of rational expectations.

The implication of one variant of the theory that has received the most attention and generated the most controversy is the so-called neutrality hypothesis about stabilization policy – in particular, about discretionary monetary policy directed at promoting economic stability. Correct rational expectations of economic agents will include correct anticipation of any systematic monetary policy; hence such policy will be allowed for by economic agents in determining their behaviour. Given further the natural rate hypothesis, it follows that any systematic monetary policy will affect the behaviour only of nominal magnitudes and not of such real magnitudes as output and employment. The authorities can affect the course of events only by 'fooling' the participants, that is, by acting in an unpredictable, *ad hoc* way. But, in general, such strictly ad hoc intervention will destabilize the economy, not stabilize it, serving simply to introduce another series of random shocks into the economy to which participants must adapt and which reduce their ability to form precise and accurate expectations.

This is a highly oversimplified account of the rational expectations hypothesis and its implications. All otherwise valid models of the economy will not be falsified by being known. All real effects of systematic and announced governmental policies will not be rendered nugatory. Serious problems have arisen in formulating the hypothesis in a logically satisfactory way, and in giving it empirical content, especially in incorporating multi-valued rather than single-valued expectations and allowing for non-independence of events over time. Research in this area is exploding; rapid progress and many changes in received opinion can confidently be anticipated before the rational expectations revolution is fully domesticated.

5. EMPIRICAL EVIDENCE. There is perhaps no empirical regularity among economic phenomena that is based on so much evidence for so wide a range of circumstances as the connection between substantial changes in the quantity of money and in the level of prices. There are few if any instances in which a substantial change in the quantity of money per unit of output has occurred without a substantial change in the level of prices in the same direction. Conversely, there are few if any instances in which a substantial change in the level of prices has occurred without a substantial change in the quantity of money per unit of output in the same direction. And instances in which prices and the quantity of money have moved together are recorded for many centuries of history, for countries in every part of the globe, and for a wide diversity of monetary arrangements.

The statistical connection itself, however, tells nothing about direction of influence, and this is the question about which there has been the most controversy. A rise or fall in prices, occurring for whatever reason, could produce a corresponding rise or fall in the quantity of money, so that the monetary changes are a passive consequence. Alternatively, changes in the quantity of money could produce changes in prices in the same direction, so that control of the quantity of money implies control of the prices. The second interpretation – that substantial changes in the quantity of money are both a necessary and a sufficient condition for substantial changes in the general level of prices – is strongly supported by the variety of monetary arrangements for which a connection between monetary and price movements has been observed. But of course this interpretation does not include a reflex influence of changes in prices on the quantity of money. The reflex influence is often important, almost always complex, and, depending on the monetary arrangements, may be in either direction.

Evidence from specie standards. Until modern times, money was mostly metallic – copper, brass, silver, gold. The most notable changes in its nominal quantity were produced by sweating and clipping, by governmental edicts changing the nominal values attached to specified physical quantities of the metal or by discoveries of new sources of specie. Economic history is replete with examples of the first two and their coincidence with corresponding changes in nominal prices (Cipolla, 1956; Feavearyear, 1931). The specie discoveries in the New World in the 16th century are the most important example of the third. The association between the resulting increase in the quantity of money and the price revolution of the 16th and 17th centuries has been well documented (Hamilton, 1934).

Despite the much greater development of deposit money and paper money, the gold discoveries in Australia and the United States in the 1840s were followed by substantial price rises in the 1850s (Cairnes, 1873; Jevons, 1863). When growth of the gold stock slowed, and especially when country after country shifted from silver to gold (Germany in 1871–3, the Latin Monetary Union in 1873, the Netherlands in 1875–6) or returned to gold (the United States in 1879), world prices in terms of gold fell slowly but fairly steadily for about three decades. New gold discoveries in the 1880s and 1890s, powerfully reinforced by improved methods of mining and refining, particularly commercially feasible methods of using the cyanide process to extract gold from low-grade ore, led to much more rapid growth of the world gold stock. Further, no additional important countries shifted to gold. As a result, world prices in terms of gold rose by 25 to 50 percent from the mid-1890s to 1914 (Bordo and Schwartz, 1984).

Evidence from great inflations. Periods of great monetary disturbances provide the most dramatic evidence on the role of the quantity of money. The most striking such periods are the hyperinflations after World War I in Germany, Austria, and Russia, and after World War II in Hungary and Greece, and the rapid price rises, if not hyperinflations, in many South American and some other countries both before and after World War II. These 20th-century episodes have been studied more systematically than earlier ones. The studies demonstrate almost conclusively the critical role of changes in the quantity of money (Cagan, 1965; Meiselman, 1970; Sargent, 1982).

Substantial inflations following a period of relatively stable prices have often had their start in wartime, though recently they have become common under other circumstances. What is important is that something, generally the financing of extraordinary governmental expenditures, produces a more rapid growth of the quantity of money. Prices start to rise, but at a slower pace than the quantity of money, so that for a time the real quantity of money increases. The reason is twofold: first, it takes time for people to readjust their money balances; second, initially there is a general expectation that the rise in prices is temporary and will be followed by a decline. Such expectations make money a desirable form in which to hold assets, and therefore lead to an increase in desired money balances in real terms.

As prices continue to rise, expectations are revised. Holders of money come to expect prices to continue to rise, and reduce desired balances. They also take more active measures to eliminate the discrepancy between actual and desired balances. The result is that prices start to rise faster than the stock of money, and real balances start to decline (that is, velocity starts to rise). How far this process continues depends on the rate of rise in the quantity of money. If it remains fairly stable, real balances settle down at a level that is lower than the initial level but roughly constant – a constant expected rate of inflation implies a roughly constant level of desired real balances; in this case, prices ultimately rise at the same rate as the quantity of money. If the rate of money growth declines, inflation will follow suit, which will in turn lead to an increase in actual and desired real balances as people readjust their expectations; and conversely. Once the process is in full swing, changes in real balances follow with a lag changes in the rate of change of the stock of money. The lag reflects the fact that people apparently base their expectations of future rates of price change partly on an average of experience over the preceding several years, the period of averaging being shorter the more rapid the inflation.

In the extreme cases, those that have degenerated into hyperinflation and a complete breakdown of the medium of exchange, rates of price change have been so high and real balances have been driven down so low as to lead to the widespread introduction of substitute moneys, usually foreign currencies. At that point completely new monetary systems have had to be introduced.

A similar phenomenon has occurred when inflation has been effectively suppressed by price controls, so that there is a substantial gap between the prices that would prevail in the absence of controls and the legally permitted prices. This gap prevents money from functioning as an effective medium of exchange and also leads to the introduction of substitute moneys, sometimes rather bizarre ones like the cigarettes and cognac used in post-World War II Germany.

Other evidence. The past two decades have witnessed a literal flood of literature dealing with monetary phenomena. Expressed in broad terms, the literature has been of two overlapping types – qualitative and econometric – and has dealt with two overlapping sets of issues – static or long-term effects of monetary change and dynamic or cyclical effects.

Some broad findings are:

(1) For both long and short periods there is a consistent though not precise relation between the rate of growth of the quantity of money and the rate of growth of nominal income. If the quantity of money grows rapidly, so will nominal income, and conversely. This relation is much closer for long than for short periods.

Two recent econometric studies have tested the long-run effects using comparisons among countries for the post-World War II period. Lothian concludes his study for 20 countries for the period 1956–80:

> In this paper I have examined three sets of hypotheses associated with the quantity theory of money: the classical neutrality proposition [i.e., changes in the nominal quantity of money do not affect real magnitudes in the long run], the monetary approach to exchange rates [i.e., changes in exchange rates between countries reflect primarily changes in money per unit of output in the several countries], and the Fisher equation [i.e., differences in sustained rates of inflation produce corresponding differences in nominal interest rates]. The data are completely consistent with the first two and moderately supportive of the last (1985, p. 835).

Duck concludes his study for 33 countries and the period 1962 to 1982 – which uses overlapping data but substantially different methods:

> Its [the study's] findings suggest that (i) the real demand for money is reasonably well explained by a small number of variables, principaly real income and interest rates; (ii) nominal income is closely related to the quantity

of money, but is also related to the behaviour of other variables, principally interest rates; (iii) most changes in nominal income or its determinants are absorbed by price increases; (iv) even over a 20-year period some nominal income growth is to a significant degree absorbed by real output growth; (v) the evidence that expectations are rational is weak (1985, p. 33).

(2) These findings for the long run reflect a long-run real demand function for money involving, as Duck notes, a small number of variables, that is highly stable and very similar for different countries. The elasticity of this function with respect to real income is close to unity, occasionally lower, generally higher, especially for countries that are growing rapidly and in which the scope of the money economy is expanding. The elasticity with respect to interest rates is, as expected, negative but relatively low in absolute value. The real quantity demanded is not affected by the price level (i.e., there is no 'monetary illusion') (Friedman and Schwartz, 1982; Laidler, 1985).

(3) Over short periods, the relation between growth in money and in nominal income is often concealed from the naked eye partly because the relation is less close for short than long periods but mostly because it takes time for changes in monetary growth to affect income, and how long it takes is itself variable. Today's income growth is not closely related to today's monetary growth; it depends on what has been happening to money in the past. What happens to money today affects what is going to happen to income in the future.

(4) For most major Western countries, a change in the rate of monetary growth produces a change in the rate of growth of nominal income about six to nine months later. This is an average that does not hold in every individual case. Sometimes the delay is longer, sometimes shorter. In particular, it tends to be shorter under conditions of higher and highly variable rates of monetary growth and of inflation.

(5) In cyclical episodes the response of nominal income, allowing for the time delay, is greater in amplitude than the change in monetary growth, so that velocity tends to rise during the expansion phase of a business cycle and to fall during the contraction phase. This reaction appears to be partly a response to the pro-cyclical pattern of interest rates; partly to the linkage of desired cash balances to permanent rather than measured income.

(6) The changed rate of growth of nominal income typically shows up first in output and hardly at all in prices. If the rate of monetary growth increases or decreases, the rate of growth of nominal income and also of physical output tends to increase or decrease about six to nine months later, but the rate of price rise is affected very little.

(7) The effect on prices, like that on income and output, is distributed over time, but comes some 12 to 18 months later, so that the total delay between a change in monetary growth and a change in the rate of inflation averages something like two years. That is why it is a long row to hoe to stop an inflation that has been allowed to start. It cannot be stopped overnight.

(8) Even after allowance for the delayed effect of monetary growth, the relation

is far from perfect. There's many a slip over short periods 'twixt the monetary change and the income change.

(9) In the short run, which may be as long as three to ten years, monetary changes affect primarily output. Over decades, on the other hand, as already noted, the rate of monetary growth affects primarily prices. What happens to output depends on real factors: the enterprise, ingenuity and industry of the people; the extent of thrift; the structure of industry and government; the relations among nations, and so on. (*In re* points 3 to 9, Friedman and Schwartz, 1963a, 1963b; Friedman, 1961, 1977, 1984; Judd and Scadding, 1982).

(10) One major finding has to do with severe depressions. There is strong evidence that a monetary crisis, involving a substantial decline in the quantity of money, is a necessary and sufficient condition for a major depression. Fluctuations in monetary growth are also systematically related to minor ups and downs in the economy, but do not play as dominant a role compared to other forces. As Friedman and Schwartz put it,

> Changes in the money stock are...a consequence as well as an independent source of change in money income and prices, though, once they occur, they produce in their turn still further effects on income and prices. Mutual interaction, but with money rather clearly the senior partner in longer-run movements and in major cyclical movements, and more nearly an equal partner with money income and prices in shorter-run and milder movements – this is the generalization suggested by our evidence (1963b, p. 695; Friedman and Schwartz, 1963a; Cagan, 1965, pp. 296–8).

(11) A major unsettled issue is the short-run division of a change in nominal income between output and price. The division has varied widely over space and time and there exists no satisfactory theory that isolates the factors responsible for the variability (Gordon, 1980, 1981, 1982; Friedman and Schwartz, 1982, pp. 59–62).

(12) It follows from these propositions that *inflation is always and everywhere a monetary phenomenon* in the sense that it is and can be produced only by a more rapid increase in the quantity of money than in output. Many phenomena can produce temporary fluctuations in the rate of inflation, but they can have lasting effects only insofar as they affect the rate of monetary growth. However, there are many different possible reasons for monetary growth, including gold discoveries, financing of government spending, and financing of private spending. Hence, these propositions are only the beginning of an answer to the causes and cures for inflation. The deeper question is why excessive monetary growth occurs.

(13) Government spending may or may not be inflationary. It clearly will be inflationary if it is financed by creating money, that is, by printing currency or creating bank deposits. If it is financed by taxes or by borrowing from the public, the main efect is that the government spends the funds instead of the taxpayer or instead of the lender or instead of the person who would otherwise have borrowed the funds. Fiscal policy is extremely important in determining what fraction of total income is spent by government and who bears the burden of

that expenditure. It is also extremely important in determining monetary policy and, via that route, inflation. Essentially all major inflations, especially hyper-inflations, have resulted from resort by governments to the printing press to finance their expenditures under conditions of great stress such as defeat in war or internal revolution, circumstances that have limited the ability of governments to acquire resources through explicit taxation.

(14) A change in monetary growth affects interest rates in one direction at first but in the opposite direction later on. More rapid monetary growth at first tends to lower interest rates. But later on, the resulting acceleration in spending and still later in inflation produces a rise in the demand for loans which tends to raise interest rates. In addition, higher inflation widens the difference between real and nominal interest rates. As both lenders and borrowers come to anticipate inflation, lenders demand, and borrowers are willing to offer, higher nominal rates to offset the anticipated inflation. That is why interest rates are highest in countries that have had the most rapid growth in the quantity of money and also in prices – countries like Brazil, Chile, Israel, South Korea. In the opposite direction, a slower rate of monetary growth at first raises interest rates but later on, as it decelerates spending and inflation, lowers interest rates. That is why interest rates are lowest in countries that *have had* the slowest rate of growth in the quantity of money – countries like Switzerland, Germany, and Japan.

(15) In the major Western countries, the link to gold and the resultant long-term predictability of the price level meant that until some time after World War II, interest rates behaved as if prices were expected to be stable and both inflation and deflation were unanticipated; the so-called Fisher effect was almost completely absent. Nominal returns on nominal assets were relatively stable; real returns unstable, absorbing almost fully inflation and deflation.

(16) Beginning in the 1960s, and especially after the end of Bretton Woods in 1971, interest rates started to parallel rates of inflation. Nominal returns on nominal assets became more variable; real returns on nominal assets, less variable (Friedman and Schwartz, 1982, pp. 10–11).

6. POLICY IMPLICATIONS. On a very general level the implications of the quantity theory for economic policy are straightforward and clear. On a more precise and detailed level they are not.

Acceptance of the quantity theory means that the quantity of money is a key variable in policies directed at controlling the level of prices or of nominal income. Inflation can be prevented if and only if the quantity of money per unit of output can be kept from increasing appreciably. Deflation can be prevented if and only if the quantity of money per unit of output can be kept from decreasing appreciably. This implication is by no means trivial. Monetary authorities have more frequently than not taken conditions in the credit market – rates of interest, availability of loans, and so on – as criteria of policy and have paid little or no attention to the quantity of money per se. The emphasis on credit as opposed to the quantity of money accounts both for the great contraction in the United States from 1929 to 1933, when the Federal Reserve System allowed the stock of money to decline by one-third, and for many of the post-World War II inflations.

The quantity theory has no such clear implication, even on this general level, about policies concerned with the growth of real income. Both inflation and deflation have proved consistent with growth, stagnation, or decline.

Passing from these general and vague statements to specific prescriptions for policy is difficult. It is tempting to conclude from the close average relation between changes in the quantity of money and changes in money income that control over the quantity of money can be used as a precision instrument for offsetting other forces making for instability in money income. Unfortunately the loose relation between money and income over short periods, the long and variable lag between changes in the quantity of money and other variables, and the often conflicting objectives of policy-makers precludes precise offsetting control.

An international specie standard leaves only limited scope for an independent monetary policy. Over any substantial period, the quantity of money is determined by the balance of payments. Capital movements plus time delays in the transmission of monetary and other impulses leave some leeway, which may be more or less extensive, depending on the importance of foreign transactions for a country and the sluggishness of response. As a result, monetary policy under an effective international specie standard has consisted primarily of banking policy, directed towards avoiding or relieving banking and liquidity crises (Bagehot, 1873).

Until 1971, departures from an international specie standard, at least by major countries, took place infrequently and only at times of crisis. Surveying such episodes, Fisher concluded in 1911 that 'irredeemable paper money has almost invariably proved a curse to the country employing it' (1911, p. 131), a generalization that has applied equally to most of the period since, certainly up to 1971, and that explains why such episodes were generally transitory.

The declining importance of the international specie standard and its final termination in 1971 have changed the situation drastically. 'Irredeemable paper money' is no longer an expedient grasped at in times of crisis; it is the normal state of affairs in countries at peace, facing no domestic crises, political or economic, and with governments fully capable of obtaining massive resources through explicit taxes. This is an unprecedented situation. We are in unexplored terrain.

As Keynes pointed out in 1923, monetary authorities cannot serve two masters: as he put it, 'we cannot keep *both* our own price level *and* our exchanges stable. And we are compelled to choose' (p. 126). Experience since has converted his dilemma into a trilemma. In principle, monetary authorities can achieve any two of the following three objectives: control of exchange rates, control of the price level, freedom from exchange controls. In practice, it has in fact proved impossible to achieve the first two by accepting exchange controls. Such controls have proved extremely costly and ultimately ineffective. The Bretton Woods system was ultimately wrecked on this trilemma. The attempts by many countries to pursue an independent monetary policy came into conflict with the attempt to maintain pegged exchange rates, leading to the imposition of exchange controls, repeated monetary crises, accompanied by large, discontinuous changes in exchange rates, and ultimately to the abandonment of the system in 1971.

Since then, most countries have had no formal commitment about exchange rates, which have been free to fluctuate and have fluctuated widely. Nonetheless, Keynes's dilemma is still alive and well. Monetary authorities have tried to influence the exchange rates of their currency and, at the same time, achieve internal objectives. The result has been what has been described as a system of managed floating.

One recent strand of policy discussions has consisted of attempts to devise a substitute for the Bretton Woods arrangements that would somehow combine the virtues of exchange rate stability with internal monetary stability. For example, one proposal, by McKinnon (1984), is for the USA, Germany, and Japan to fix exchange rates among their currencies, and set a joint target for the rate of increase of the total quantity of money (or high-powered money) issued by the three countries together. So far, no such proposal has gained wide support among either economists or a wider public.

A different strand of policy discussions has been concerned with the instruments, targets, and objectives of monetary authorities. One element of the quantity theory approach that has had considerable influence is emphasis on the quantity of money as the appropriate intermediate target for monetary policy. Most major countries now (1985) follow the practice of announcing in advance their targets for monetary growth. That is so for the USA, Great Britain, Germany, Japan, Switzerland, and many others. The record of achievement of the announced targets varies greatly – from excellent to terrible. Recently, a considerable number of economists have favoured the use of a nominal income (usually nominal gross national product) as the intermediate target. The common feature is the quantity theory emphasis on nominal magnitudes.

A more abstract strand of policy discussions has been concerned with the optimum quantity of money: what rate or pattern of monetary growth would in principle promote most effectively the long-run efficiency of the economic system – meaning by that a Pareto welfare optimum. This issue turns out to be closely related to a number of others, in particular the optimum behaviour of the price level; the optimum rate of interest; the optimum stock of capital, and the optimum structure of capital (Friedman, 1969, pp. 1–50).

One widely accepted answer is based on the observation that no real resource cost need be incurred in increasing the real quantity of money since that can be done by reducing the price level. The implication is that the optimum quantity of money is that at which the marginal benefit from increasing the real quantity is also zero. Various arrangements are possible that will achieve such an objective, of which perhaps the simplest, if money pays no interest, is a pattern of monetary growth involving a decline in the price level at a rate equal to the real interest rate (Mussa, 1977; Ihori, 1985).

This answer, despite its great theoretical interest, has had little practical

35

consequence. Short-run considerations have understandably been given precedence to such a highly abstract long-run proposition.

Finally, there has been a literal explosion of discussion of the basic structure of the monetary system. One component derives from the belief that Fisher's generalization about irredeemable paper money will continue to hold for the present world fiat money system and that we are headed for a world monetary collapse ending in hyperinflation unless a specie (gold) standard is promptly restored. In the United States, this monetary belief was powerful enough to lead Congress to establish a Commission on the Role of Gold. In its final report, 'the Commission concludes that, under present circumstances, restoring a gold standard does not appear to be a fruitful method for dealing with the continuing problem of inflation.... We favor no change in the flexible exchange rate system' (Commission, 1982, vol. 1, pp. 17, 20). The testimony before the Commission revealed that agreement on a 'gold standard' concealed wide differences in the precise meaning of the phrase, varying from a system in which money consisted of full-bodied gold or warehouse receipts for gold to one in which the monetary authorities were instructed to regard the price of gold as one factor affecting their policy.

A very different component of the discussion has to do with possible alternatives to gold as a long-term anchor to the price level. This includes proposals for subjecting monetary authorities to more specific legislative or constitutional guidelines, varying from guidelines (price stability, rate of growth of nominal income, real interest rate, etc.) to guidelines specifying a specific rate of growth in money or high-powered money. Perhaps the most widely discussed proposal along this line is the proposal for imposing on the authorities the obligation to achieve a constant rate of growth in a specified monetary aggregate (Friedman, 1960, pp. 92–5; Commission, 1982, vol. 1, p. 17). Other proposals include freezing the stock of base money and eliminating discretionary monetary policy, and denationalizing money entirely, leaving it to the private market and a free banking system (Friedman, 1984; Friedman and Schwartz, 1986; Hayek, 1976; White, 1984a).

Finally, a still more radical series of proposals is that the unit of account be separated from the medium of exchange function, in the belief that financial innovation will establish an efficient payment system dispensing entirely with the use of cash. The specific proposals are highly sophisticated and complex, and have been sharply criticized. So far, their value has been primarily as a stimulus to a deeper analysis of the meaning and role of money. (For the proposals, see Black, 1970; Fama, 1980; Hall, 1982a, 1982b; Greenfield and Yeager, 1983; for the criticisms, see White, 1984b; McCallum, 1985).

One thing is certain: the quantity theory of money will continue to generate agreement, controversy, repudiation, and scientific analysis, and will continue to play a role in government policy during the next century as it has for the past three.

BIBLIOGRAPHY

Angell, J.W. 1936. *The Behaviour of Money.* New York: McGraw-Hill.
Bagehot, W. 1873. *Lombard Street.* London: Henry S. King; reprint of the 1915 edn, New York: Arno Press, 1969.

Barnett, W.A., Offenbacher, E.K. and Spindt, P.A. 1984. The new Divisia monetary aggregates. *Journal of Political Economy* 92(6), December, 1049–85.

Baumol, W.J. 1952. The transactions demand for cash: an inventory theoretic approach. *Quarterly Journal of Economics* 66, November, 545–56.

Black, F. 1970. Banking and interest rates in a world without money: the effects of uncontrolled banking, *Journal of Bank Research* 1(3), Autumn, 2–20.

Black, H. 1975. The relative importance of determinants of the money supply: the British case. *Journal of Monetary Economics* 1(2), April, 25–64.

Bordo, M.D. and Schwartz, A.J. (eds) 1984. *A Retrospective on the Classical Gold Standard, 1821–1931.* Chicago: University of Chicago Press for the National Bureau of Economic Research.

Burger, A.E. 1971. *The Money Supply Process.* Belmont: Wadsworth.

Cagan, P. 1965. *Determinants and Effects of Changes in the Stock of Money, 1875–1960.* New York: Columbia University Press for the National Bureau of Economic Research.

Cagan, P. 1972. *The Channels of Monetary Effects on Interest Rates.* New York: National Bureau of Economic Research.

Cairnes, J.E. 1873. Essays on the gold question. In J.E. Cairnes, *Essays in Political Economy,* London: Macmillan.

Cipolla, C.M. 1956. *Money, Prices, and Civilization in the Mediterranean World, Fifth to Seventeenth Century.* Princeton: Princeton University Press.

Commission on the Role of Gold in the Domestic and International Monetary Systems. 1982. *Report to the Congress,* March. Washington, D.C.: The Commission.

Duck, N.W. 1985. Money, output and prices: an empirical study using long-term cross country data. Working Paper, University of Bristol, September.

Fama, E.F. 1980. Banking in the theory of finance. *Journal of Monetary Economics* 6(1), January, 39–57.

Feavearyear, A.E. 1931. *The Pound Sterling: a History of English Money.* 2nd edn, Oxford: Clarendon Press, 1963.

Fischer, S. (ed.) 1980. *Rational Expectations and Economic Policy.* Chicago: University of Chicago Press for the National Bureau of Economic Research.

Fisher, I. 1896. *Appreciation and Interest.* New York: American Economic Association.

Fisher, I. 1911. *The Purchasing Power of Money.* 2nd revised edn, 1926; reprinted New York: Kelley, 1963.

Fisher, I. 1919. Money, prices, credit and banking. *American Economic Review* 9, June, 407–9.

Frenkel, J.A. 1976. Adjustment mechanisms and the monetary approach to the balance of payments. In *Recent Issues in International Monetary Economics,* ed. E. Claassen and P. Salin, Amsterdam: North-Holland.

Frenkel, J.A. and Johnson, H.G. 1976. The monetary approach to the balance of payments: essential concepts and historical origins. In *The Monetary Approach to the Balance of Payments,* ed. J.A. Frenkel and H.G. Johnson, Toronto: University of Toronto Press.

Friedman, M. 1956. The quantity theory of money – a restatement. In *Studies in the Quantity Theory of Money,* ed. M. Friedman, Chicago: University of Chicago Press.

Friedman, M. 1957. *A Theory of the Consumption Function.* Princeton: Princeton University Press for the National Bureau of Economic Research.

Friedman, M. 1959. The demand for money: some theoretical and empirical results. *Journal of Political Economy* 67, August, 327–51. Reprinted as Occasional Paper No. 68, New York: National Bureau of Economic Research, and in Friedman (1969).

Friedman, M. 1960. *A Program for Monetary Stability.* New York: Fordham University Press.

Friedman, M. 1961. The lag in effect of monetary policy. *Journal of Political Economy* 69, October, 447–66. Reprinted in Friedman (1969).

Friedman, M. 1968. The role of monetary policy. *American Economic Review* 58(1), March, 1–17. Reprinted in Friedman (1969).

Friedman, M. 1969. *The Optimum Quantity of Money and Other Essays.* Chicago: Aldine.

Friedman, M. 1977. Inflation and unemployment (Nobel lecture). *Journal of Political Economy* 85(3), June, 451–72.

Friedman, M. 1984. Monetary policy for the 1980s. In *To Promote Prosperity: U.S. domestic policy in the mid-1980s,* ed. J.H. Moore, Stanford: Hoover Institution Press.

Friedman, M. and Schwartz, A.J. 1963a. Money and business cycles. *Review of Economics and Statistics* 45(1), Supplement, February, 32–64. Reprinted in Friedman (1969).

Friedman, M. and Schwartz, A.J. 1963b. *A Monetary History of the United States, 1867–1960.* Princeton: Princeton University Press for the National Bureau of Economic Research.

Friedman, M. and Schwartz, A.J. 1970. *Monetary Statistics of the United States.* New York: Columbia University Press for the National Bureau of Economic Research.

Friedman, M. and Schwartz, A.J. 1982. *Monetary Trends in the United States and the United Kingdom: Their Relation to Income, Prices, and Interest Rates, 1867–1975.* Chicago: University of Chicago Press for the National Bureau of Economic Research.

Friedman, M. and Schwartz, A.J. 1986. Has government any role in money? *Journal of Monetary Economics* 17(1), January 37–62.

Gordon, R.J. 1980. A consistent characterization of a near-century of price behavior. *American Economic Review* 70(2), May, 243–49.

Gordon, R.J. 1981. Output fluctuations and gradual price adjustment. *Journal of Economic Literature* 19(2), June, 493–530.

Gordon, R.J. 1982. Price inertia and policy ineffectiveness in the United States, 1890–1980. *Journal of Political Economy* 90(6), December, 1087–117.

Greenfield, R.L. and Yeager, L.B. 1983. A laissez-faire approach to monetary stability. *Journal of Money, Credit, and Banking* 15(3), August, 302–15.

Haberler, G. 1941. *Prosperity and Depression.* 3rd edn, Geneva: League of Nations; 3rd edn, Lake Success, New York: United Nations, 1946.

Hall, R.E. 1982a. Explorations in the gold standard and related policies for stabilizing the dollar. In *Inflation: Causes and Effects,* ed. R.E. Hall, Chicago: University of Chicago Press.

Hall, R.E. 1982b. 'Monetary trends in the United States and the United Kingdom': a review from the perspective of new developments in monetary economics. *Journal of Economic Literature* 20(4), December, 1552–6.

Hamilton, E.J. 1934. *American Treasure and the Price Revolution in Spain, 1501–1650.* Harvard Economic Studies, Vol. 43, New York: Octagon, 1965.

Hansen, A. 1957. *The American Economy.* New York: McGraw-Hill.

Hayek, F.A. 1976. *Denationalization of Money.* 2nd extended edn, London: Institute of Economic Affairs, 1978.

Hume, D. 1752. Of interest; of money. In *Essays, Moral, Political and Literary,* Vol. 1 of *Essays and Treatises,* a new edn, Edinburgh: Bell and Bradfute, Cadell and Davies, 1804.

Humphrey, T.M. 1984. Algebraic quantity equations before Fisher and Pigou. *Economic Review,* Federal Reserve Bank of Richmond 70(5), September-October, 13–22.

Ihori, T. 1985. On the welfare cost of permanent inflation. *Journal of Money, Credit, and Banking* 17(2), May, 220–31.

Jevons, W.S. 1863. A serious fall in the value of gold. In *Investigations in Currency and Finance,* 2nd edn, London: Macmillan, 1909; New York: A.M. Kelley, 1964.

Johnson, H.G. 1961. *The General Theory* after twenty-five years. *American Economic Association, Papers and Proceedings* 51, May, 1–17.

Judd, J.P. and Scadding, J.L. 1982. The search for a stable money demand function. *Journal of Economic Literature* 20(3), September, 993–1023.

Keynes, J.M. 1923. *A Tract on Monetary Reform*. Reprinted London: Macmillan for the Royal Economic Society, 1971; New York: St. Martin's Press.

Keynes, J.M. 1936. *The General Theory of Employment, Interest, and Money*. Reprinted London: Macmillan for the Royal Economic Society, 1973; New York: Harcourt, Brace.

Knoester, A. 1984. Pigou and buffer effects in monetary economics. Discussion Paper 8406 G/M, Institute for Economic Research, Erasmus University, Rotterdam.

Laidler, D. 1984. The 'buffer stock' notion in monetary economics. *Economic Journal* 94, Supplement, 17–34.

Laidler, D. 1985. *The Demand for Money: theories, evidence, and problems*. 3rd edn, New York: Harper & Row.

Lothian, J.R. 1985. Equilibrium relationships between money and other economic variables. *American Economic Review* 75(4), September, 828–35.

Lucas, R.E., Jr. 1976. Econometric policy evaluation: a critique. *Journal of Monetary Economics* supplementary series 1, 19–46.

Lucas, R.E., Jr. 1981. Tobin and monetarism: a review article. *Journal of Economic Literature* 19(2), June, 558–67.

Lucas, R.E., Jr. and Sargent, T.J. (eds.) 1981. *Rational Expectations and Economic Practice*. 2 vols, Minneapolis: University of Minnesota Press.

McCallum, B. 1985. Bank deregulation, accounting systems of exchange and the unit of account: a critical review. *Carnegie-Rochester Conference Series on Public Policy* 23, Autumn.

McKinnon, R. 1984. *An International Standard for Monetary Stabilization*. Cambridge, Mass: MIT Press.

Meiselman, D. (ed.) 1970. *Varieties of Monetary Experience*. Chicago: University of Chicago Press.

Mill, J.S. 1844. Review of books by Thomas Tooke and R. Torrens. *Westminster Review*, June.

Miller, M.H. and Orr, D. 1966. A model of the demand for money by firms. *Quarterly Journal of Economics* 80(3), August, 413–35.

Miller, M.H. and Orr, D. 1968. The demand for money by firms: extensions of analytical results. *Journal of Finance* 23(5), December, 735–59.

Modigliani, F. 1977. The monetarist controversy, or should we forsake stabilization policies? *American Economic Review* 67(2), March, 1–19.

Mussa, M. 1977. The welfare cost of inflation and the role of money as a unit of account. *Journal of Money, Credit, and Banking* 9(2), May, 276–86.

Muth, J.F. 1961. Rational expectations and the theory of price movements. *Econometrica* 29, July, 315–35. Reprinted in Lucas and Sargent (1981).

Newcomb, S. 1885. *Principles of Political Economy*. New York: Harper & Brothers.

Patinkin, D. 1948. Price flexibility and full employment. *American Economic Review* 38, September, 543–64. Revised and reprinted in F.A. Lutz and L.W. Mints (American Economic Association), *Readings in Monetary Theory*, Homewood, Ill.: Irwin, 1951.

Phelps, E.S. 1967. Phillips curves, expectations of inflation, and optimal unemployment over time. *Economica* 34(135), August 254–81.

Pigou, A.C. 1917. The value of money. *Quarterly Journal of Economics* 32, November, 38–65. Reprinted in F.A. Lutz and L.W. Mints (American Economic Association), *Readings in Monetary Theory*, Homewood, Ill.: Irwin, 1951.

Pigou, A.C. 1947. Economic progress in a stable environment. *Economica* 14(55), August, 180–88.

Sargent, T.J. 1982. The ends of four big inflations. In *Inflation: Causes and Effects*, ed. R.E. Hall, Chicago: University of Chicago Press.

Snyder, C. 1934. On the statistical relation of trade, credit, and prices. *Revue de l'Institut International de Statistique* 2, October, 278–91.

Spindt, P.A. 1985. Money is what money does: monetary aggregation and the equation of exchange. *Journal of Political Economy* 93(1), February, 1975–2204.

Tobin, J. 1947. Money wage rates and employment. In *The New Economics*, ed. S. Harris, New York: Knopf.

Tobin, J. 1956. The interest-elasticity of transactions demand for cash. *Review of Economics and Statistics* 38, August, 241–47.

Tobin, J. 1958. Liquidity preference as behavior toward risk. *Review of Economic Studies* 25, February, 65–86.

Tobin, J. 1961. Money, capital and other stores of value. *American Economic Review, Papers and Proceedings* 51, May, 26–37.

Tobin, J. 1974. Friedman's theoretical framework. In *Milton Friedman's Monetary Framework: a Debate with His Critics*, ed. R.J. Gordon, Chicago: University of Chicago Press.

White, L.H. 1984a. *Free Banking in Britain: Theory, Experience and Debate, 1800–1845*. New York: Cambridge University Press.

White, L.H. 1984b. Competitive payments systems and the unit of account. *American Economic Review* 74(4), September, 699–712.

Banking School, Currency School, Free Banking School

ANNA J. SCHWARTZ

Historians of economic thought conventionally represent British monetary debates from the 1820s on as centred on the question of whether policy should be governed by rules (espoused by adherents of the Currency School), or whether authorities should be allowed discretion (espoused by adherents of the Banking School). In fact many other questions were in dispute, including those raised by neglected or misidentified participants in the debates – adherents of the Free Banking School.

Among the questions in dispute were the following: (1) Should the banking system follow the Currency School's principle that note issues should vary one-to-one with the Bank of England's gold holdings? (2) Were the doctrines of the Banking School – real bills, needs of trade and the law of reflux – valid? (3) Was a monopoly of note issue desirable or, as the Free Banking School contended, destabilizing? (4) Was overissue a problem and, if so, who was responsible? (5) How should money be defined? (6) Why do trade cycles occur? (7) Should there be a central bank? No, was the Free Banking School answer to the final question; yes, was the answer of the other two schools, with disparate views, as indicated, on the question of rules *vs*. authorities. What was not in dispute was the viability of the gold standard system with gold convertibility of Bank of England notes.

On what grounds did the schools oppose each other? Each of the first three questions identifies the central doctrines that the adherents of one of the schools shared; on the remaining questions, individual views within each school varied. Before establishing the positions of each school in the monetary debates, we introduce the institutional background and the principal participants.

INSTITUTIONAL BACKGROUND. The Bank of England, incorporated in 1694 as a private institution with special privileges, stood at the head of the British banking system at the time of the debates. Until 1826 the Bank's charter was interpreted to mean the prohibition of other joint stock banks in England. As a result banking establishments were either one-man firms or partnerships with not more than six members. Two types of banks predominated in England: the wealthy London private banks which had voluntarily surrendered their note-issuing privilege, and the country banks which depended almost exclusively on the business of note issues. Numerous failures among the country banks demonstrated that the effect of the Bank's charter was to foster the formation of banking units of uneconomical size.

Banking in Ireland was patterned on English lines. The Bank of Ireland, chartered in 1783 with the exclusive privilege of joint stock banking in Ireland, surrendered its monopoly in 1821 in places farther than fifty miles from Dublin. Joint-stock banking in the whole of Ireland was legalized in 1845.

The Bank of Scotland was founded in 1695 with privileges similar to those of the Bank of England, except that it was formed to promote trade, not to support the credit of the government. It lost its monopoly in 1716, and no further monopolistic banking legislation was enacted in Scotland. With free entry possible, many local private and joint stock banks, most of the latter well capitalized, where established, and a nationwide system of branch banking developed. Unlike the English system, overissue was not a problem in the Scottish system. The banks accepted each other's notes and evolved a system of note exchange. Shareholders of Scottish joint stock banks (except for three chartered banks) assumed unlimited liability. At the time of the debates banking in Scotland was at a far more advanced stage than in England.

PRINCIPALS IN THE DEBATES. The leading spokesmen for the Currency School side in the debates were McCulloch, Loyd (later Lord Overstone), Longfield, George Warde Norman, and Torrens. Norman, a director of the Bank of England for most of the years 1821–72, and of the Sun Insurance Company, 1830–64, was active in the timber trade with Norway. The principal Banking School representatives were Tooke, Fullarton, and John Stuart Mill, while James Wilson held views that straddled Banking and Free Banking School doctrines. The most prominent members of the Free Banking School were Parnell (later Baron Congleton), James William Gilbart, and Poulett Scrope. Gilbart, a banker, was general manager of the London and Westminster Bank, the first of the joint stock banks authorized by the Bank Charter Act of 1833.

CURRENCY SCHOOL PRINCIPLE. The objective of the Currency School was to achieve a price level that would be the same whether the money supply were fully metallic or a mixed currency including both paper notes and metallic currency. According to Loyd, gold inflows or outflows under a fully metallic currency had the immediate effect of increasing or decreasing the currency in circulation, whereas a mixed currency could operate properly only if inflows or outflows of gold were exactly matched by an increase or decrease of the paper component. He and others of the Currency School regarded a rise in the price level and a fall in the bullion reserve under a mixed currency as symptoms of excessive note issues. They advocated statutory regulation to ensure that paper money was neither excessive nor deficient because otherwise fluctuations in the currency would exacerbate cyclical tendencies in the economy. They saw no need, however, to regulate banking activities other than note issue.

The Banking School challenged these propositions. Fullarton denied that overissue was possible in the absence of demand, that variations in the note issue could cause changes in the domestic price level, or that such changes could cause a fall in the bullion reserve ([1844] 1969, pp. 57, 128–9). Under a fully metallic as well as under a mixed currency bank, deposits, bills of exchange, and all forms of credit might influence prices. Moreover, inflows and outflows of gold under a fully metallic currency might change bullion reserves but not prices. If convertibility were maintained, overissue was not feasible and no statutory control of note issues was required. An adverse balance of payments was a temporary phenomenon that was self-correcting when, for example, a good harvest followed a bad one. According to the Free Banking School, the possibility of overissue and inflation applied only to Bank of England notes but could not occur in a competitive banking system.

BANKING SCHOOL PRINCIPLES. The Banking School adopted three principles that for them reflected the way banks actually operated as opposed to the Currency School principle which they dismissed as an artificial construct of certain writers (White, 1984, pp. 119–28).

The first Banking School principle was the doctrine that liabilities of deposits and notes would never be excessive if banks restricted their earning assets to real bills. One charge levelled by modern economists against the doctrine is that it leaves the quantity of money and the price level indeterminate, since it links the money supply to the nominal magnitude of bills offered for discount. Some members of the school may be exculpated from this charge if they regarded England as a small open economy, its domestic money stock a dependent variable determined by external influences. However, because it ignored the role of the discount rate in determining the volume of bills generated in trade, the doctrine was vulnerable. In addition, the Banking School confused the flow demand for loanable funds, represented by the volume of bills, with the stock demand for circulating notes, although the two magnitudes are non-commensurable.

Free Banking School members who also adopted the real bills doctrine erroneously attributed overissue by the Bank of England to its purchase of assets other than real bills, when overissue was possible with a portfolio limited to real bills, acquired at an interest rate that led to a stock of circulating medium inconsistent with the prevailing price level (Gilbart, 1841, pp. 103–5; 119–20). The Currency School regarded the real bills doctrine as misguided since it could promote a cumulative rise in the note issue and hence in prices.

A second Banking School principle was the 'need of trade' doctrine, to the effect that the note circulation should be demand-determined – curtailed when business declined and expanded when business prospered, whether for seasonal or cyclical reasons. An implicit assumption of the doctrine was that banks could either vary their reserve ratios to accommodate lower or higher note liabilities, or else offset changes in note liabilities by opposite changes in deposit liabilities. For non-seasonal increases in demand for notes, the doctrine implied that expanding banks could obtain increased reserves from an interregional surplus of the trade balance. The Currency School regarded an increase in the needs of trade demand to hold notes accompanying increases in output and prices as unsound because it would ultimately produce an external drain. The Free Banking School countered that such an objection by the Currency School was paradoxical since the virtue of a metallic currency according to the latter was that it accommodated the commercial wants of the country, and therefore for a mixed currency to respond to the needs of trade could not be a vice. The modern objection to the needs of trade doctrine as procyclical is an echo of the Currency School view.

The third Banking School principle was the law of the reflux according to which overissue was possible only for limited periods because notes would immediately return to the issuer for repayment of loans. This was a modification of the real bills doctrine that Tooke and Fullarton advanced, since adherence to the doctrine supposedly made overissue impossible. They made no distinction between the speed of the reflux for the Bank of England and for competitive banks of issue – a distinction at the heart of the Free Banking position. For the latter, reflux of excess notes was speedy only if the notes were deposited in rival banks. These would then return the notes to the issuing banks and accordingly bring an end to relative overissue by individual banks. The Bank of England, on the contrary, could overissue for long periods because it had no rivals. Fullarton, however, made the unwarranted assumption that notes would be returned to the Bank to repay previous loans at a faster rate than the Bank was discounting new loans, hence correcting the overissue. Moreover, he believed that if the Bank overissued by open market purchases, the decline in interest rates would quickly activate capital outflows, reducing the Bank's bullion and forcing it to retreat. Tooke was sounder in arguing for the law of reflux on the ground that excess issues would not be held if they did not match the preferences of holders for notes rather than deposits.

The Banking School had no legislative programme for reform of the monetary system. Good bank management, in the view of the school, could not be legislated.

FREE BANKING SCHOOL PRINCIPLE. As the name suggests, the principle the Free Banking School advocated was free trade in the issue of currency convertible into specie. Members of the school favoured a system like the Scottish banking system, where banks competed in all banking services, including the issue of notes, and no central bank held a monopoly of note issue. They argued that in such a system banks did not issue without limit but indeed provided a stable quantity of money. Although the costs of printing and issuing were minimal, to keep notes in circulation required restraint in their issue. The profit-maximizing course for competitive banks was to maintain public confidence in their issues by maintaining convertibility into specie on demand, which required limiting their quantity.

Loyd's response to the argument for free trade in currency was that unlike ordinary trades, what was sought was not the greatest quantity at the cheapest price but a regulated quantity of currency. The Free Banking School denied that free banking would debase the currency, and contended that the separation of banking from note issue, the Banking School proposal, was impractical. Scrope (1833a. pp. 32–3) asked why the Currency School objected to an unregulated issue of notes but not to that of deposits, questioning Loyd's assumption that an issuing bank's function was to produce money, when in fact its function was to substitute its bank notes for less well-known private bills of exchange that were the bank's assets. Scrope and other Free Banking adherents (Parnell, 1827, p. 143) neglected the distinction between a banknote immediately convertible into gold and a commercial bill whose present value varied with time to maturity and the discount rate. Contrary to Loyd, they reasoned that free trade and competition were applicable to currency creation because the business of banks was to produce the scarce good of reputation.

Loyd's second disagreement with the argument for free trade in banking was that miscalculations by the issuers were borne not by them but by the public. Moreover, individuals had no choice but to accept notes they received in ordinary transactions, and trade in general suffered as a result of overissue. The Free Banking School answer to this externalities argument turned on the ability of holders to refuse notes of issuers without reputation. Protection against loss could also be provided if joint stock banks were allowed to operate in place of country banks limited to six or fewer partners. In addition, if banks were required to deposit security of government bonds or other assets, noteholders would be further protected (Scrope, 1832, p. 455; 1833b, p. 424; Parnell, 1827, pp. 140–44). Free Banking School members who argued in this vein failed to recognize that they were thereby acknowledging a role for government intervention in currency matters.

In the 1820s the Free Banking School championed joint stock banking both in the country bank industry and in direct competition in note issue with the Bank of England in London. Although the six-partner rule for banks of issue at least 65 miles from London was repealed in 1826 after a spate of bank failures, the Bank retained its monopoly of note circulation in the London area. In addition, the Bank was permitted to establish branches anywhere in England. The Parliamentary inquiry in 1832 on renewal of the Bank's charter was directed to the question of prolonging the monopoly. The Act of 1833 eased entry for joint stock banks within the 65-mile limit but denied them the right of issue and made the Bank's notes legal tender for redemption of country bank notes, in effect securing the Bank's monopoly. The doom of the Free Banking cause was finally pronounced by the Bank Charter Act of 1844. It restricted note issues of existing private and joint stock banks in England and Wales to their average circulation during a period in 1843. Note issue by banks established after the act was prohibited.

WAS OVERISSUE A PROBLEM? Participants in the debates understood overissue to mean a stock of notes, whether introduced by a single issuer or banks in aggregate, in excess of the quantity holders voluntarily chose to keep as assets, given the level of prices determined by the world gold standard. Was overissue of a convertible currency possible? According to the Free Banking School, interbank note clearing by competitive banks operated to eliminate excess issued by a single bank. The check to excess issues by the banking system as a whole was an external drain through the price-specie flow mechanism. In this respect the school acknowledged that the result of overissue by a competitive banking system as a whole was the same as for a monopoly issuer. However, they held that overissue was a phenomenon that the monopoly of the Bank of England encouraged but a competitive system would discourage.

The Currency School, on the other hand, regarded both the Bank of England and the Scottish and country banks as equally prone to overissue and did not grant that a check to overissue by a single bank or banks in the aggregate was possible through the interbank note clearing mechanism. For them, regulation of a monopoly issuer promised a stable money supply that was not attainable with a plural banking system.

The Free Banking School's explanation of the Bank of England's ability to overissue rested on the absence of rivals for the Bank's London circulation, so no interbank note clearing took place; the absence of competition in London from interest-bearing demand deposits; and the fact that London private banks held the Bank's notes as reserves. Hence the demand for its notes was elastic. The Free Banking and Currency Schools agreed that there was a substantial delay before an external drain checked overissue, so the Bank's actions inescapably inflicted damage on the economy. Scrope (1830, pp. 57–60), who attributed the Bank's willingness to overexpand its note issues to its monopoly position, advocated abrogating that legal status.

The Banking School dismissed the question of overissue as irrelevant, for noteholders could easily exchange unwanted notes by depositing them. What they failed to examine was the possibility that a broader monetary aggregate could be in excess supply resulting in an external drain.

HOW SHOULD MONEY BE DEFINED? Currency School members favoured defining money as the sum of metallic money, government paper money, and bank notes (Norman, 1833, pp. 23, 50; McCulloch, 1850, pp. 146–7). The Free Banking School, like the Currency School, focused on bank notes as the common medium of exchange, ignoring demand deposits that were not usually subject to transfer by check outside London. The Banking School definition of money is sometimes represented as broader than that of the other schools, but in fact was narrower – money was restricted to metallic and government paper money. Bank notes and deposits were excluded, since they were regarded as means of raising the velocity of bank vault cash but not as adding to the quantity of money (Tooke [1848], 1928, pp. 171–83; Fullarton [1844], 1969, pp. 29–36; Mill [1848], 1909, p. 523). In the short run, the school held that all forms of credit might influence prices, but only money as defined could do so in the long run, because the domestic price level could deviate only temporarily from the world level of prices determined by the gold standard.

WHY DO TRADE CYCLES OCCUR? The positions of the three schools on the impulses initiating trade cycles were not dogma for their members. In general the Currency and Banking Schools held that nonmonetary causes produced trade cycles, whereas the Free Banking School pointed to monetary causes, but individual members did not invariably hew to these analytical lines. McCulloch (1937, p.63), Loyd (1857, p. 317), and Longfield (1840, pp. 222–3) essentially attributed cycles to waves of optimism and pessimism to which the banks then responded by expanding and contracting their issues. Banks accordingly never initiated the sequence of expansion and contraction. Hence the Currency School principle of regulating the currency to stabilize prices and business did not imply that cycles would thereby be eliminated. Cycles would, however, no longer be amplified by monetary expansion and contraction, if country banks were denied the right to issue and the Bank of England's circulation were governed by the 'currency principle'. Torrens (1840, pp. 31, 42–3), unlike other Currency School members, attributed trade cycles to actions of the Bank of England. That was also the position of the Free Banking School, although in an early work Parnell (1827, pp. 48–51) of that school held that cycles were caused by nonmonetary factors. For the Banking School, however, monetary factors accounted for both the origin and spread of trade cycles. Tooke (1840, pp. 245, 277), for example, believed that overoptimism would prompt an expansion of trade credit for which the banks were in no way responsible. Collapse of optimism would then lead to shrinkage of trade credit. For Fullarton ([1844] 1969, p. 101) nonmonetary causes produced price fluctuations to which changes in note circulation were a passive response. Proponents of the nonmonetary theory of the onset of trade cycles provided no explanation of the waves of optimism and pessimism themselves. For the Free Banking School the waves were precipitated by the Bank of England's expansion and ultimate contraction of its liabilities. Initially, the Bank's actions depressed interest rates and ultimately forced them up, as loanable funds increased in supply and then decreased. The Bank's monopoly position enabled it to create such monetary disturbances, whereas competitive country banks had no such power.

SHOULD THERE BE A CENTRAL BANK? The Currency and Banking Schools were in agreement that a central bank with the sole right of issue was essential for the health of the economy. McCulloch (1831, p. 49) regarded a system of competitive note issuing institutions as one of inherent instability. Tooke (1840, pp. 202–7) favoured a monopoly issuer as promoting less risk of overissue and greater safety because it would hold sufficient reserves. The two schools differed on the need for a rule to regulate note issues, the Currency School pledged to a rulebound authority, the Banking School to an unbound authority. The Free Banking School disapproved of both a rule and a central bank authority, instead favouring a competitive note-issuing system that it held to be self-regulating. For that school proof that centralized power was inferior to a competitive system was revealed by cyclical fluctuations that had been caused by errors of the Bank of England.

A CONTINUING DEBATE. The Bank Charter Act of 1844 ended the right of note issue for new banks in England and Wales. Scottish banks, however, were treated differently from Irish banks by the Act of 1845 and from English provincial banks by the Act of 1844. Like the latter, authorized circulation for the Scottish banks was determined by the average of a base period, but they could exceed the authorized circulation provided they held 100 per cent specie reserves against the excess – a provision also imposed on the Bank of England.

The Free Banking School thus lost its case for an end of the note issue monopoly of the Bank of England. The death of Parnell in 1842, a leading Parliamentary spokesman, had hurt the cause. Others of the school were mainly country and joint stock bankers. The Acts conferred benefits on them by restricting entry into the note-issuing industry and by freezing market shares (White, 1984, pp. 78–9). Their voices were note raised in opposition. Only Wilson was critical of the privileges the Bank of England was accorded ([1847] 1849, pp. 34–66).

The Banking School objected not only to the Act but claimed vindication for its point of view by the necessity to suspend it in 1847, 1857 and 1866. The Currency School responded that the suspensions were of no great significance (Loyd, 1848, pp. 393–4). The recommendations of the Currency School prevailed to set a maximum for country bank note issues and the eventual transfer of their circulation to the Bank of England.

The monetary debates that were initiated in the 1820s were not conclusive. No point of view carried the day. Long after the original participants had passed from the scene, the doctrines of the schools found supporters. Even the Free Banking School position in opposition to monopoly issue of hand-to-hand currency that seemed to be buried has recently been revived by new adherents (White, 1984, pp. 137–50). The debate on all the questions in dispute in the 19th century continues to be live.

BIBLIOGRAPHY

Fullarton, J. 1844. *On the Regulation of Currencies.* London: John Murray. Reprinted, New York: Augustus M. Kelley, 1969.

Gilbart, J.W. 1841. Testimony before the Select Committee of the House of Commons on Banks of Issue. British Sessional Papers, vol. 5 (410).

Gregory, T.E. 1928. Introduction to *Tooke and Newmarch's A History of Prices.* London: P.S. King.

[Longfield, S.M.] 1840. Banking and currency. *Dublin University Magazine.*

Loyd, S.J. 1848. Testimony before the Secret Committee of the House of Commons on Commercial Distress. British Sessional papers, 1847–8, vol. 8, part 1 (584).

Loyd, S.J. 1857. *Tracts and Other Publications on Metallic and Paper Money.* London.

[McCulloch, J.R.] 1831. *Historical Sketch of the Bank of England.* London: Longman.

[McCulloch, J.R.] 1837. The Bank of England and the country banks. *Edinburgh Review,* April.

[McCulloch, J.R.] 1850. *Essays on Interest, Exchange, Coins, Paper Money, and Banks.* London.

Mill, J.S. 1848. *Principles of Political Economy*, Ed. W.J. Ashley, London: Longmans & Co., 1909.

Norman, G.W. 1833. *Remarks upon Some Prevalent Errors, with Respect to Currency and Banking.* London: Hunter.

Parnell, H.B. 1827. *Observations on Paper Money, Banking and Overtrading.* London: James Ridgway.

Scrope, G.P. 1830. *On Credit-Currency, and its Superiority to Coin, in Support of a Petition for the Establishment of a Cheap, Safe, and Sufficient Circulating Medium.* London: John Murray.

[Scrope, G.P.] 1832. The rights of industry and the banking system. *Quarterly Review*, July, 407–55.

Scrope, G.P. 1833a. *An Examination of the Bank Charter Question.* London: John Murray.

Scrope, G.P. 1833b. *Principles of Political Economy.* London: Longman.

Tooke, T. 1840. *A History of Prices and of the State of the Circulation in 1838 and 1839.* London: Longman. Reprinted, London: P.S. King, 1928.

Tooke, T. 1848. *History of Prices and of the State of the Circulation, from 1839 to 1847 inclusive.* London: Longmans. Reprinted, London: P.S. King, 1928.

Torrens, R. 1840. *A Letter to Thomas Tooke, Esq. in Reply to His Objections against the Separation of the Business of the Bank into a Department of Issue and a Department of Discount: With a Plan of Bank Reform.* London: Longman.

White, L.H. 1984. *Free Banking in Britain: Theory, Experience, and Debate, 1800–1845.* Cambridge and New York: Cambridge University Press.

Wilson, J. 1847. *Capital, Currency, and Banking: being a collection of a series of articles published in the Economist in 1845 ... and in 1847.* London: The office of the Economist. 2nd edn, London: D.M. Aird, 1859.

Bank Rate

A.B. CRAMP

This was the label applied to the rate at which the Bank of England would discount first-class bills of exchange in the London market: by extension, it has come to mean the rate at which any central bank makes short-term loans available to domestic commercial banks. The UK Bank Rate's practical significance dates from the Bank Charter Act of 1833, Section 7 of which exempted bills of a currency up to three months from the provisions of usury laws which had previously imposed a 5 per cent interest ceiling. This relaxation had been recommended in 1802 by Henry Thornton as a means of containing demand for discounts, which passed along a chain from country banks to London banks to the nascent last-resort central bank, and threatened to become excessive when market forces would have pushed rates above the ceiling. The urgency of such containment was increased as a result of (a) these 'internal' gold drains being reinforced by 'external' analogues related to the expansion of international trade and capital movements; (b) the imposition by the 1844 Bank Charter Act of a limit to the fiduciary issue, of Bank of England notes backed by holdings of securities, designed to ensure the maintenance of convertibility of notes into gold. The 1847 liquidity crisis forced the Government to promise a retrospective act of indemnity should this limit be breached, freeing the Bank to act as lender of last resort to whatever extent the exigencies of the crisis might require – but on condition that a Bank Rate of not less than 8 per cent be imposed.

Henceforward, and until the final abandonment of the gold standard in 1931, Bank Rate changes were the major technique by which the Bank of England protected its reserve. The technique was powerul at least until the First World War, after which its effectiveness was compromised by political and economic disorder, and by the rise of New York as an international financial centre alternative to London. Understanding of the causes of the pre-1914 power of Bank Rate increases (reductions tended to represent rather passive reactions to relaxation of pressures) is facilitated by distinguishing responses in the spheres of, respectively, the London money market; external trade and payments; and internal economic activity.

Within the London money market, matters hinged – in the manner adumbrated by Thornton – on bankers' response to the rise in Bank Rate to a 'penalty' level, above the market rate(s) at which the bankers had themselves acquired bills. Bank Rate thus operated, in Walter Bagehot's phrase, as a 'fine on unreasonable timidity' in regard to the liquidation of banks' assets with a view to strengthening reserve ratios, against the possibility of a run on banks by nervous depositors. Originally, it is to be noted, the initiative lay with the commercial banks rather than with the developing central bank; the shortage of cash (= deposits at the Bank of England) resulted from increased demand by the former, rather than from reduction of supply engineered by the latter; autonomous pressures were already raising (short-term) interest rates, and Bank Rate changes were an important – probably overriding – influence on the extent of the rise by virtue of the Bank of England's position as key supplier of an essential margin of funds. There was thus no real problem in 'making Bank Rate effective', that is to say ensuring that it exerted appropriate influence on market rates. Nor was there any call for assistance from the weapon, not in any case developed until after World War I, of open-market sales of securities at central bank initiative. These points warn modern theorists against the temptation to read back into the 19th century later-developed notions suggesting that the rise in *price* (short-term interest rates) either reflected, accompanied or caused a reduction in *quantity* (bank credit flows, or bank deposit totals). The relationship between Bank Rate changes and 'the quantity of money' was, as Keynes argued (see below) much more diffuse and complex than modern monetarist styles of theory can easily envisage; its character can hardly begin to emerge until repercussions outside the money market have been considered.

Of these repercussions, those relating to external flows, rather than to internal adaptations, were the main focus of attention in Bank Rate's classical period, and we first consider the external side. Ricardian thought, in the early part of the period, encouraged attention to the trade balance; but in practice, as the 19th century wore on, the action was increasingly seen to occur in the sphere of international payments and capital movements. This was mainly a reflection of structural changes which produced a consistently strong UK trade balance, massive long-term overseas lending, and a growing mass of internationally mobile bills of exchange (principally the 'bill on London'). It was also, by the turn of the century, a reflection of (probably fortuitously) helpful policy by the Bank of France, the focal point of London's only rival as a financial centre. The Bank of France kept more substantial gold reserves than the Bank of England; and it was willing to allow those reserves to vary in order to exert stabilizing influence on continental interest rates. As a result, a rise in London's Bank Rate tended to increase the differential between UK and foreign short-term rates, and to tilt the balance of short-term flows in London's favour. An increase in Bank Rate, opined the Cunliffe Committee in 1918, would 'draw gold from the moon'; in practice, the metal did not travel quite so far.

A highly significant implication of this (at the time, ill-understood) conjuncture, was that the Bank of England discovered a power to protect its reserve without significant damage to UK overseas trade. The validity of this judgement is witnessed by the decline in the volume of complaints from traders about the burden of high short-term interest rates. Such complaints were quite substantial in the early decades of intermittently high and rising Bank Rate levels. The present author has established (1962), however, that the grievances were much more closely related to the *availability* of short-term credit than to its *cost*. A rise in Bank Rate (from even quite low levels) was seen, with good reason, as heralding a potential liquidity shortage that might be transformed quickly into a liquidity crisis: alert bankers and traders at once began to exercise caution in undertaking new commitments. This is undoubtedly the historical origin of what would otherwise be a rather puzzling strand in the Bank Rate tradition, namely the idea that a rise in Bank Rate operated as an 'Index', a storm signal enjoining caution. This strand persisted in financiers' folk-memories long after its realistic basis had declined, and resurfaced in the 1950s in a new form: sterling crises could be countered by a 'package deal' of measures, of which a Bank Rate rise constituted an essential element, as an *index* of the UK authorities' determination to inflict whatever pain might be necessary to rectify external imbalance.

In just what this pain might consist had been a matter of debate, intermittently vigorous, among academic economists – whose primary attention, in the 20th century, came to focus on the internal economy, and the effects thereon of what the 1918 Cunliffe Committee saw as a Bank Rate-induced (? accompanied) general rise of interest rates and restriction of credit. The emphasis on credit restriction was by then probably exaggerated, and traceable to the folk-memories just noted. The emphasis on generally rising interest rates undoubtedly exaggerated Bank Rate's *direct* influence on the structure of interest rates. It is true that, by 1900, commercial bank borrowing and lending rates were widely (not universally) linked to Bank Rate – an administrative link reflecting a market reality for, as indicated above and as Bagehot had argued, an institution (the Bank of England) that regularly supplied the market with the necessary residual margin of cash almost automatically exercised what we should call 'price leadership', its own price for short-term accommodation dominating other influences. Keynes was thus justified, in his *Treatise on Money* (1930), in treating Bank Rate as representative of the general level of *short* rates, on the assumption that Bank Rate changes were normally 'effective' in influencing market rates. The further link to *long* rates, however, was more problematic, and a source of disagreement between Keynes and R.G. Hawtrey (1938).

Hawtrey tended to downplay the link, on the argument that the direct influence on long rates of a rise in short rates depended on the period for which the rise was expected to last – which period, because of Bank Rate's external power described above, was typically brief. His view was doubtless influenced by his tenacious, and fairly isolated, adherence to the theory that Bank Rate's external power was mediated primarily by its influence on the cost of holding inventories. His theory was that individual merchants would have a strong inducement to respond to a Bank Rate increase by reducing purchases from manufacturers, designed to effect a temporary reduction of inventory levels during the limited period for which the higher Bank Rate was expected to last. But collectively these mercantile responses so reduced demand that manufacturers restricted their purchases of raw materials from merchants, and the 'vicious circle of deflation' was joined. Hawtrey claimed support for his theory from oral testimony, notably before House of Commons committees of inquiry into liquidity crises. But later investigation (Cramp, 1962) demonstrated that John Torr, Chairman of the Liverpool Chamber of Commerce during the 1857 crisis, was typical in arguing that what mattered to traders was 'not so much the rate of interest as the impossibility of getting the medium of exchange', that is, not so much the cost of credit as its availability, which gradually became more reliable as the techniques of commercial and central banking improved.

It was Keynes's view, in the *Treatise* and in the Report of the Macmillan Committee which he dominated, that exercised the more substantial and enduring influence on academic opinion. Unlike Hawtrey, he tended to emphasize the link through to long-term interest rates, perhaps implicitly assuming – by this juncture – the support of appropriate open-market operations, security sales by the central bank. He was by this stage urging that such sales should include bonds as well as bills, facilitating direct influence on long rates. Such advocacy was not uncongenial to a central bank now ever-anxious to 'fund the floating debt', reflecting fears of repetition of the experience of feeling constrained by government borrowing needs during the inflationary boom of 1920–21.

Keynes was thus enabled to presume that a rise in Bank Rate would be accompanied by supporting measures appropriate to the exertion of a strong *indirect* influence on the structure of interest rates. In this way, he justified retrospectively the Cunliffe Committee's rejection of Alfred Marshall's dismissal of the effect of Bank Rate changes as 'a ripple on the surface', and also inaugurated the era of academic preoccupation with the link between 'the rate of interest' (essentially, the long-term rate) and the level of expenditures on fixed investment. He contended (*Treatise*, I, pp. 154–5) that 'a rise in Bank rate tends, in so far as it modifies the effective rates of interest, to depress price levels'.

The theoretical model deployed to explain this proposition is significant for the history of monetary theory as well as that of Bank Rate. Keynes appealed to Wicksell's celebrated (1898) concepts, to argue that a Bank Rate increase represented a rise in the market of interest, relative to the natural rate which would equate desired levels of investment and saving. The link to prices, however, would come principally, not through the monetary route of reduced bank-lending flows and bank-deposit stocks, but through the impact of higher market interest rates on the decision to invest. A higher rate of discount would be applied to the stream of future yields anticipated from an act of investment. Such acts would be postponed, the more readily when the higher Bank Rate was regarded as a temporary divergence from the normal level, the more ineluctably on account of the likely difficulty in such market conditions of floating new issues on the capital market. Aggregate demand and prices would thus tend to be depressed, by processes which would result in reduced demand for money balances. The money market tightness would be superficially eased from the domestic side, as it would also be relieved from the foreign side – quickly on account of reduced lending to overseas borrowers, more slowly and fundamentally as the domestic deflation improved the trade balance.

The *General Theory*, of course, was soon to initiate a prolonged phase of even greater scepticism about the strength of the linkage between money and prices. It appeared at a time when cheap money was also causing de-emphasis on the role of changes in Bank Rate. From 1932 to 1951, Bank Rate was held, apart from a hiccough when war began in 1939, at the level of 2 per cent. Academic discussion continued of the relationship between the level of interest rates and decisions to invest, but it was largely severed from consideration of money-market techniques and policies. When inflationary fears began to surface late in the cheap money era, as Professor R.S. Sayers (1979) notes, D.H. Robertson 'addressed the world not on the question "What has happened to Bank Rate?" but "What has happened to the Rate of Interest?"'

The desire to restrain inflationary tendencies prompted the beginning in 1951 of a period of experimentation with the revival of monetary policy techniques, a trend which within a decade or so was to receive very substantial impetus from the anti-Keynesian monetarist counter-revolution originating principally in Chicago. In the earlier phases of this postwar period, Bank Rate changes were reintroduced to the authorities' armoury of measures, but somewhat tardily and half-heartedly, being subordinated to the then still quite fashionable preference for direct controls, e.g. on the volume of bank advances. As noted above, there was some disposition to regard a Bank Rate increase as an essential element in a restrictive 'package deal', but no-one seemed quite sure why, except that folk-memories even yet favoured it (*those* were the days, when even gold on the moon was magnetized!), and market enthusiasts instinctively welcomed a price element in a package consisting primarily of quantity controls. In the later, monetarist-influenced, phases of the postwar period, quantity controls were precisely what influential opinion desired, but because that opinion favoured achieving them by market rather than by administrative measures, interest-rate changes were acknowledged to have a significant, though subsidiary, role.

Thus was Keynes's sequence, which as we have seen began from Bank Rate, reversed. Bank Rate was renamed, under the 'Competition and Credit Control' regime operated in the UK in the 1970s. It became 'Minimum Lending Rate' (MLR). It was ostensibly linked to the Treasury Bill rate emerging from the weekly tender, and consequently moved much more frequently than of yore, although every so often the authorities uncoupled the link, when they desired an old-fashioned 'index effect' – on external fund flows – from a rise in short-term rates clearly engineered by themselves.

Under the new (and nameless) UK monetary control regime of the 1980s, the ghost of Bank Rate became yet more evanescent. The continuous posting of MLR was formally suspended, though the authorities reserved the right 'in some circumstances to announce in advance the minimum rate which, for a short period ahead, it would apply in lending to the market'. This right has on occasion been actified. Bank Rate lives, just. Treatises on money no longer contain, as did Keynes's, a chapter on its *modus operandi*. But as in so many directions in economics, it would be a bold observer who projected the existing trend indefinitely, and predicted Bank Rate's final demise. There are continuities in economics, albeit disguised by irregular cycles in opinion and practice; trends persist, even in a new high-technological age.

BIBLIOGRAPHY

Bank of England. 1971. Competition and credit control. *Quarterly Bulletin,* June.

Cramp, A.B. 1962. *Opinion on Bank Rate 1822–60.* London: G. Bell.

Cunliffe (Lord), et al. 1918. *Committee on Currency and Foreign Exchanges, First Interim Report.* London: HMSO.

Hawtrey, R.G. 1938. *A Century of Bank Rate.* London: Longman.

Keynes, J.M. 1930. *A Treatise on Money.* London: Macmillan; New York: St. Martin's Press, 1971.

Keynes, J.M. 1936. *General Theory of Employment, Interest and Money.* London: Macmillan; New York: Harcourt, Brace.

Sayers, R.S. 1981. *Bank Rate in Keynes's Century.* London: The British Academy.

Wicksell, K. 1898. *Interest and Prices.* Trans. R.F. Kahn, London: Macmillan for the Royal Economic Society, 1936; New York: A.M. Kelley, 1965.

Bonds

DONALD D. HESTER

A bond is a contract in which an issuer undertakes to make payments to an owner or beneficiary when certain events or dates specified in the contract occur. The term has medieval origins in a system where an individual was bound over to another or to land. Subsequently, goods were put in a bonded warehouse until certain conditions (e.g. payments of taxes or tariffs) were satisfied; individuals were released from jail when a bail bond guaranteeing their appearance in court was supplied; and individuals were allowed to perform certain tasks when a surety or performance bond guaranteeing satisfaction was provided. Governments and individuals have borrowed from others since earliest recorded history, as Sumerian documents attest. Perhaps public bonds first appeared in modern form with the establishment of the Monte in Florence in 1345. Monte shares were interest bearing, negotiable, and funded by the Commune.

In contemporary economic discourse, a bond is commonly understood to be a debt instrument in which a borrower, typically a government or corporation, receives an advance of funds and contracts to make future payments of interest and principal according to an explicit schedule. The remainder of this entry focuses exclusively on these debt instruments. Terms of bonds are designed to protect the rights of borrowers and creditors; they are heterogeneous and their interpretations and enforceability vary across legal jurisdictions.

The distinction between bonds and other evidences of debt such as loans or notes is inherently arbitrary and imprecise. Bonds tend to have rather long specified maturities when issued, or none at all in the case of consols. However, issuers may reserve the right to call them after they have been outstanding for a specified time interval. While bonds ordinarily convey no equity stake in an enterprise, some corporate bonds include a clause that allows bondholders to convert bonds to shares of the issuer's common stock at a specified conversion value. Formulas for determining the values of such options are discussed by Black and Scholes (1973).

Bonds tend to be negotiable and can usually be traded on an established second market. Once bonds are issued, bondholders are strategically

56

vulnerable to actions of a firm's management, equity holders, and short-term lenders as has been argued by Bulow and Shoven (1978), especially if an issuer's financial condition deteriorates. Default occurs if a bond issuer fails to make scheduled payments of interest or principal or violates other covenants of a contract. A bondholder's rights in a default situation are circumscribed by terms of the contract and by judicial authority.

The yield on a bond is the flow of interest income to its holders. Apart from defaults, bonds traditionally pay interest in fixed amounts on specified dates that are indicated by coupons on the bond. Coupon bearing bonds may allow investors to choose portfolios that nearly match interest and amortization streams with their own nominal future requirements for funds. A portfolio is said to be perfectly *immunized* against interest rate fluctuations if such matching is achieved. Bonds that have no coupons are called discount bonds; they provide no interim cash flow and are retired at maturity with a payment equal to their face or par value, which is higher than the issue price. Default free bonds thus afford nominal *income certainty* to investors as was explained by Robinson (1951), but do not guarantee that an investor's spending goals can be achieved when inflation is unpredictable.

The nominal return from holding a bond is the sum of its interest payments and the change in its price over an arbitrary holding period. For example, if there are no transactions costs and taxes, the return from holding a multiyear bond for two years is:

$$\text{return} = y_1 + y_2 - P_p + P_s \tag{1}$$

where P_p and P_s are respectively the purchase and selling price and y_1 and y_2 are annual interest payments. If interest payments are assumed to be paid at year end, the nominal annual rate of return, r, from this two-year investment is obtained by solving the polynomial:

$$P_p = y_1/(1+r) + y_2 + P_s)/(1+r)^2 \tag{2}$$

If the bond is actually bought at P_p and sold at P_s, a bond trader is said to *realize* a capital gain (loss) if P_p is less (more) than P_s.

A condition for equilibrium in a bond market is that expected rates of return from holding similar bonds are similar. If this condition were not satisfied, bond traders could improve portfolio earnings by selling the bond with the lower rate of return and buying the bond with the higher rate of return so long as the difference exceeds transactions costs. When transactions costs are zero, bonds are perfectly *reversible*. When expected rates of return rise, prices on outstanding bonds fall and rates of return *experienced* by existing bondholders fall; capital losses are experienced by holders of all but maturing bonds. Bond traders attempt to buy bonds immediately before market rates of return fall so that they may realize capital gains by buying at a low price and selling at a high price. Similarly, speculative traders of bonds seek to sell bonds immediately before market rates of return rise. A distinctive feature of bonds is that their future prices are unpredictable; rates of return and prices move inversely.

Bonds are issued by governments and corporations to finance deficits and acquire assets. While neither issuer can afford to ignore imminent movements in interest rates, their time schedules of outlays are somewhat inflexible. Deficits must be financed and it is shortsighted to delay purchasing high rate of return assets to take advantage of interest rate movements. Firms needing funds may choose to finance a long-term asset with short-term borrowings from banks, with a long-term bond whose interest rate varies or *floats* over time in a fixed relation to short-term rates, or with a long-term fixed coupon bond. Bank borrowing to finance long-term assets exposes firms to the risk that banks may unilaterally alter loan terms or refuse to renew maturing loans. Firms avoid non-renewal risk by borrowing with bonds. A firm's choice between issuing conventional fixed rate bonds or floating rate bonds to finance an asset depends in part on the correlation between returns from the asset being acquired and short-term interest rates for reasons that are developed by Cox, Ingersoll and Ross (1982). Other things being equal, a floating rate bond exposes a firm to less risk when short-term rates and the rate of return on the acquired asset are positively correlated.

Government deficits are financed by issuing fiat or *outside* money, short-term treasury bills and notes, and bonds. Central banks control the ratio of outside money to interest-bearing government debt when conducting monetary policy. Central bank sales (purchases) of bonds decrease (increase) bond prices and increase (decrease) bond interest rates in the market place. Other things being equal, an increase in bond interest rates increases the cost of financing new capital equipment and causes marginal investment projects to become unprofitable. Control of bond and other market interest rates by central banks is one handle through which monetary policy affects the level of macroeconomic activity. It has also been argued by Tobin (1963) that the composition of outstanding interest-bearing government debt can importantly influence the level of macro-economic activity. If bonds are closer substitutes for physical capital in investors' portfolios than are treasury bills, a debt management policy of selling bonds and buying an equivalent amount of bills discourages private sector capital formation.

Since about 1970 bond markets have experienced a number of major institutional changes and innovations that promise to have enduring and uncertain consequences. The establishment of futures markets for bonds has modified the role of bonds in investor portfolios. Hedging and speculative positions are more inexpensively achieved in a futures market than they are by assuming long and/or short positions in a bond market. A market has also been established in *stripped* bonds where all a bond's coupons are separated from the body of a bond, and both parts are traded as separate entities. The body of the bond becomes a discount bond.

A large off-shore Eurobond market has developed where governments and corporations issue bonds denominated in currencies that may differ from the domestic currency unit of the issuer. This large and expanding market qualifies the effects of a monetary policy action in a country and complicates credit evaluation of potential bond issuers. In the United States and elsewhere, quasi-official agencies of governments have been issuing large amounts of bonds or collateralized securities that differ inconsequentially from government bonds; the effects of this development are similar to those of the expanding Euro-bond market.

Finally, automation in bond markets has reduced costs of trading bonds and made them more convenient to hold. Most government bonds in the United States are no longer issued in certificate form; they are only computer entries. They are readily transferable in a computer and can be lent or sold at low cost whenever a borrower requires cash. By making bonds more reversible, automation has reduced the distinction between bonds and outside money, a distinction that is crucial for the success of central bank open market operations.

BIBLIOGRAPHY

Black, F. and Scholes, M.S. 1973. The pricing of options and corporate liabilities. *Journal of Political Economy* 81(3), May/June, 637–54.

Bulow, J.I. and Shoven, J.B. 1978. The bankruptcy decision. *Bell Journal of Economics* 9(2), Autumn, 437–56.

Cox, J.C., Ingersoll, J.E., Jr. and Ross, S.A. 1981. The relation between forward prices and future prices. *Journal of Financial Economics* 9(4), December, 321–46.

Robinson, J. 1951. The rate of interest. *Econometrica* 19, April, 92–111.

Tobin, J. 1963. An essay on the principles of debt management. In *Fiscal and Debt Management Policies*, prepared for the Commission on Money and Credit, Englewood Cliffs, NJ: Prentice-Hall.

The Bullionist Controversy

DAVID LAIDLER

'Bullionist Controversy' is the label conventionally attached to the series of debates about monetary theory and policy which took place in Britain over the years 1797-1821, when the specie convertibility of Bank of England notes was suspended. The protagonists in this controversy are usually classified into two camps – 'bullionist' supporters of specie convertibility who were critics of the Bank of England, and 'anti-bullionist' adherents of an opposing viewpoint. Such labels are useful as organizing devices, but it is dangerous to apply them rigidly. The bullionist controversy was a series of debates about a variety of issues, and those debates involved a shifting cast of participants, whose views sometimes changed as controversy continued.

Although contemporary policy problems provided most of the immediate impetus for debate, the bullionist controversy was not a series of arguments about the application of well-known economic principles to a particular set of circumstances. On the contrary, much of the debate was about fundamental questions of economic theory; and though the literature of the controversy consists largely of pamphlets, reviews, letters to newspapers, parliamentary speeches and reports, it contains contributions of crucial and lasting importance to monetary theory.

I. The Bank of England, a privately owned joint stock company, was founded in 1694 with the aim of creating a market for, and an institution to manage, the government debt arising from William III's participation in the wars against the France of Louis XIV. By the end of the 18th century its monopoly of note issue in the London area, and its status as the only note-issuing joint stock bank in England, had given it a pivotal position in the British monetary system. It had in fact evolved into the central bank at least of England, though not of the United Kingdom; for Ireland at this time had its own largely independent monetary system, with commercial banks operating on a reserve base provided by the Bank of Ireland in Dublin, which held its reserves in specie rather than in claims upon

60

London. Scottish Banks too belonged to a distinct system, albeit one which held its reserves in London. Though reforms of the coinage beginning in 1696 and culminating in that supervised by Sir Isaac Newton in 1717 had been intended to create a bimetallic system, their undervaluation of silver had instead placed Britain on a *de facto* gold standard that was firmly entrenched by the last decade of the century.

By the 1790s the 'circulating medium', to use a contemporary phase, consisted of gold coin, Bank of England and Country (i.e., non-London) Bank notes, while bills of exchange and bank deposits were widely used means of payment in wholesale transactions. Country Banks mainly held reserves on deposit with private London banks, which did not emit notes, and which in turn held reserves in the form of Bank of England liabilities. Britain's specie reserves were mainly held by the Bank of England in the form of bullion. The degree of concentration here was not as absolute as it would become later in the 19th century, but, to put it in modern parlance, Bank of England liabilities were high-powered money, and any difficulties in the banking system at large quickly put pressure on the Bank's specie reserves.

The outbreak of hostilities between Britain and Revolutionary France in 1793 precipitated just such pressure. A drain of reserves from the banking system into domestic private sector portfolios, to which the Bank of England responded by contracting its note issue, created a liquidity crisis. The crisis was alleviated by a government issue of exchequer bills, and this very fact speaks eloquently of the lack of appreciation, on the part of the Bank and Government alike, of the role and responsibilities of a Central Bank in the monetary and financial system which characterized the state of knowledge at the beginning of the bullionist controversy. Not the least of that controversy's enduring contributions was to advance understanding of these matters.

As France recovered from the political chaos associated with the Terror, and the monetary chaos created by the Assignats, the war began to go badly for Britain and her allies. By the beginning of 1797 France was clearly in the ascendant. Indeed, the completion of Bonaparte's Italian campaign at the end of that year would see only Britain remaining in the field against her. During 1795–6 the Bank of England had again attempted to counter a continuing drain of specie from its reserves by a contraction of its liabilities, and had probably thereby accentuated its difficulties. This certainly was the opinion of commentators such as Walter Boyd (1800), while Henry Thornton's (1802) analysis of the general importance of a Central Bank's standing ready to lend freely in the face of a domestic run on its reserves in order to restore and maintain confidence may be read, in part, as a criticism of the Bank of England's behaviour during this episode.

Be that as it may, by February of 1797, pressure on the Bank was again strong, and rumours of an impending French invasion – a small force of French troops did land in Wales but was quickly captured – provoked a run on the banking system. This run began in Newcastle and quickly spread. To the Government and the Bank of England it seemed to put that institution in jeopardy, and an

Order in Council of 26 February, confirmed in May by an Act of Parliament, suspended the specie convertibility of Bank of England notes. This 'temporary' suspension, initially supposed to end in June 1797, was to last until 1821. The management of an inconvertible currency – or rather partially convertible, for gold and some subsidiary silver coin continued to circulate, and during the suspension period the Bank did from time to time declare some of its small denomination notes convertible – would have been difficult enough in peacetime; but down to 1815 the Bank of England's task was frequently complicated by the need to make large transfers abroad to subsidise allies and support British forces fighting on the Continent, not to mention the disruptive effects of the Napoleonic 'Continental System' on British trade.

The body of economic analysis which a modern economist would deploy in dealing with these matters was not available in Regency Britain. The Cantillon (1734)–Hume (1752) version of the quantity theory of money, and its associated analysis of the price-specie flow mechanism was well enough known; but that dealt with a commodity money system, not with one dominated by banks, in which a large proportion of the 'circulating medium' consisted of bank notes and deposits (or cheques drawn upon them), not to mention various commercial bills. The *Wealth of Nations* (Smith, 1776) contained extensive discussions of banking, but those discussions, as Checkland (1975) has argued, were largely based on Scottish oral tradition; they therefore dealt with the competitive operations of commercial banks against the background of specie convertibility and had next to nothing to say about central banking.

Much available knowledge about the operation of inconvertible paper systems was of a practical nature. It drew on the French experience with John Law's scheme, and later the Assignats, on many North American experiments before, during and after the American War of Independence, and, to a lesser extent, the 18th-century experience of Russia and Sweden with paper money. Though the Swedish experience had generated controversy which in many respects anticipated the British bullionist debate, as Eagly (1968) has shown, there seems to be no evidence that the Swedish literature was known in Britain, even to those who, like Henry Thornton, were aware of the events that had generated it.

In short, by the 1790s, institutional developments in the British monetary system had run far ahead of systematic knowledge of what we would now call the theory of money and banking. The difficulties of the suspension period focused attention on this fact, and the analysis developed during the course of the bullionist controversy had to solve fundamental problems in monetary theory as well as cope with contemporary policy issues. It is because it dealt with the first of these tasks with such success that the controversy is of enduring importance to monetary economists, and not just to historians of economic thought and economic historians.

II. The 18th-century experiences with inconvertible paper referred to above were, with few exceptions, unhappy, and it is scarcely surprising that, at the very outset, opponents of restriction in Britain warned of dire inflationary consequences.

However, it was not until 1800 that rising prices, a decline in the value of Bank of England paper in terms of bullion, and an associated depreciation of the sterling exchange rate on Hamburg gave warning that all was not well. (We need not concern ourselves here with the complications caused by the fact that Hamburg was on a silver and not a gold standard.) These events generated a flurry of pamphlets, and it is generally agreed that Walter Boyd's (1800) *Letter to...William Pitt* was the most noteworthy of these. It stated a simple version of what was to become known as the bullionist position, namely that the suspension of convertibility had permitted the Bank of England unduly to expand its note issue and that overexpansion had in turn brought about the above-mentioned interrelated consequence.

The fact that agricultural prices had risen considerably more than the value of bullion made it possible for defenders of the Bank of England, such as Sir Francis Baring, to argue that the problem lay elsewhere than in the banking system *per se*. The Bank's defenders also raised at this early stage of the debate what was to become an important bone of contention in later monetary debates, namely the possibility that the Country Banks, by varying their note issue, could and indeed did exert an influence on the behaviour of the price level independently of the Bank of England. The preliminary 'skirmish' of 1800–1802 as Fetter (1965) called it was indecisive, but it produced Henry Thornton's *Paper Credit...*(1802), an extraordinary treatise which systematically expounds the intellectual basis of what Viner (1937) termed the 'moderate bullionist' position in subsequent discussions.

Von Hayek suggests in his introduction to *Paper Credit* that Thornton may have been working on it as early as 1796, but in its published form, this book was a defence, albeit a constructively critical defence, of the Bank of England's policy during the early years of restriction. It was published during a lull in the debate, and its *direct* influence on the course of the bullionist controversy was therefore minor. During the 19th century the work dropped from sight, and its true stature was not thereafter widely appreciated until the appearance of von Hayek's (1939) edition. Indirectly, however, *Paper Credit* was of the first order of importance. Its author was an influential member both of the Committee of the House of Commons that investigated Irish currency issues in 1804 – see Fetter (1955) on this episode – and of the so-called Bullion Committee itself, whose 1810 report marked the high point of the controversy. Moreover, the chairman of the latter committee, Francis Horner, who, with help from Thornton and William Huskisson, was the principal author of its Report, had devoted a long and favourable review article to *Paper Credit...* in the first issue of the *Edinburgh Review*.

III. The immediate cause of the renewed controversy that led to the setting up by Parliament of the *Select Committee on The High Price of Gold Bullion* in February 1810 was a re-emergence of inflationary pressures in early 1809, whose most noticeable symptoms to observers not equipped with even the concept of a price index, let alone a serviceable example of such a device, where a declining exchange rate for sterling and marked rise in the price of specie in terms of Bank of England notes. Both of these symptoms were more marked than they had been in 1800–1802, but the positions taken up in the controversy that preceded the committee's formation and accompanied its deliberations were very much those established in the preliminary skirmish of those years.

What Viner (1937) terms the 'extreme bullionist' position had been stated by John Wheatley as early as 1803, and was subsequently maintained by him. David Ricardo, whose contributions to the *Morning Chronicle* in 1809 represent his first published work in economics also argued this position, though a little more flexibly than Wheatley, notably in his (1810–11) essay on *The High Price of Gold Bullion*. Simply put, the extreme bullionist position was that the decline in the exchanges, and the increase in the price of bullion, were solely due to an excessive issue of Bank of England notes, an excessive issue which could not have taken place under convertibility. Against such views, the anti-bullionist defenders of the Bank argued that the decline in the exchanges was due to pressures exerted by extraordinary wartime foreign remittances and had nothing to do with the Bank's domestic policy. Moreover, they argued, because the Bank confined itself to making loans on the security of high quality commercial bills, drawn to finance goods in the course of production and distribution, it was impossible that its note issue could be excessive and could cause prices to rise. The first of these arguments deals with what we would now call the 'transfer problem' and the second is a statement of the infamous *Real Bills Doctrine*.

At the outset of the bullionist controversy there existed little in the way of coherent analysis of the transfer problem under conditions of convertibility, let alone of inconvertibility. Adam Smith (1776) had stated that foreign remittances would in fact be effected by a transfer of goods rather than specie abroad, but had not explained how, while during the bullionist controversy the directors of the Bank of England consistently argued that any transfer must initially involve an outflow of specie equal in amount to the transfer itself. This position was not far removed from the naïve mercantilist analysis which Hume had so effectively attacked in 1752, and was, as Fetter (1965) has noted, quite inconsistent with the actual behaviour of the Bank's specie reserves during the French wars.

A key contributor to the analysis of the transfer problem was Thornton, and the influence of ideas first expounded in *Paper Credit* is quite evident in the Committee's *Bullion Report* of 1810 (Cannan, 1919). He had shown in *Paper Credit* how a transfer of goods would be brought about under a convertible currency as a result of monetary contraction in the country making the transfer and expansion in the recipient country, and had stressed income effects as well as price level changes as critical links in the mechanism. Though he did not distinguish clearly between a convertible and an inconvertible currency, he also argued that, under post-1797 arrangements (which because of the continued circulation of gold coin did not amount to a clear-cut inconvertible system), the mechanisms in question would lead to a temporary exchange rate depreciation, even if domestic policy was such as to promote what we would now term domestic price level stability. The limits to the possible depreciation here would be set by the costs of evading legal prohibitions on the melting and export of coin.

In 1802 this analysis had formed part of Thornton's defence of Bank of England policy against bullionist critics, and it was further refined in the course of the deliberations of the Parliamentary Committee of 1803 which investigated the depreciation of the Irish pound, and on which Thornton served. At least two authors, John Hill and J.C. Herries (both anti-bullionists) were later to supplement it with the observation that a temporary depreciation created scope for short-term capital movements to help in making a transfer effective.

By 1810–11, the view that transfers could temporarily depress the exchanges under conditions of inconvertibility, and a growing scarcity of gold coin had moved the system much closer to such conditions than it had been a decade earlier, set the analysis of moderate bullionists, including Thomas R. Malthus, and of course the Bullion Committee itself, apart from that of Ricardo and Wheatley, who denied that even a temporary exchange rate depreciation could take place in the absence of a simultaneous excessive issue of domestic paper. Either this latter argument involves an implicit definition of 'excessive' and is circular; or, as Viner has suggested, it is erroneous and provides an unfortunate example of the 'Ricardian vice' of giving answers relevant to the long run equilibrium outcome of particular situations to questions having to do with the intermediate stages whereby long run equilibrium is achieved.

Disagreement among the bullionists was about temporary effects, however. Moderate bullionists were in complete agreement with their more extreme colleagues that an apparently permanent exchange depreciation could not be put down to the effects of once and for all transfers. Their view, as expressed in the 1810 *Report*, was that sterling's initial depreciation had probably been the consequence of foreign remittances, and of the effects of the Continental System on trade, but that its subsequent failure to recover was caused by an overissue of paper money by the Bank of England. They thus rejected the Bank of England's claim that it was powerless to affect the purchasing power of paper money so long as it confined its issues to those called forth by the supply for discount of good quality bills of exchange.

The analysis of the Real Bills Doctrine set out in the *Bullion Report* is in all its essentials the same as that to be found in *Paper Credit*, and is marked by a careful discussion of the mechanisms whereby the policies espoused by the Bank could lead to overissue. In this respect it is superior to that of Ricardo, who in his essay of 1810–11, without going into any details about the processes whereby the economy might move from one long run equilibrium to another, concentrated on giving an exceptionally clear statement of the nature of the long run equilibrium relationship that rules between the quantity of paper money, the exchange rate and the price of specie (which, as Hollander (1979) persuasively argues, is to be understood in this context as standing as a proxy for what we would now term the general price level).

The Real Bills Doctrine is attributable to Adam Smith (1776) but in his work it appears mainly as a rule of behaviour for the individual commercial bank operating in a competitive system against a background of specie convertibility. To discount only good short-term bills is not perhaps bad practice for such an institution if it wishes to secure its long-term viability. To claim such a principle to be a sufficient guarantee of price level stability if adopted by a Central Bank managing something akin to an inconvertible paper currency is another thing altogether, but that is what the directors of the Bank of England did, giving to the Bullion Committee what Bagehot (1874) was later to term 'answers almost classical by their nonsense' when questioned on this matter. Adherence to the Real Bills Fallacy was by no means confined to the Bank of England. It had many defenders and even so able an economist as Robert Torrens espoused the doctrine during the bullionist controversy, though in later debates he was to be one of its most vigorous opponents. Moreover, despite its definitive refutation by Thornton and the Bullion Committee, this doctrine was to reassert itself with great regularity throughout the 19th century, and into the 20th, as Mints (1945) in particular has so carefully documented.

The critical flaw in the Real Bills Doctrine arises from its implicitly treating the nominal quantity of bills of exchange offered for discount as being determined, independently of the policies of the banking system, by the real volume of goods under production in the economy, rather than by the perceived profitability of engaging in production and trade. The latter, as Thornton, the Bullion Committee and all subsequent critics of the doctrine have pointed out, depends upon the relationship between the rate of interest at which the banking system stands ready to lend, and the rate of return that borrowers expect to earn. To put it in the language of Knut Wicksell (1898), whose analysis of these matters closely follows Thornton – even though he appears to have been unaware of *Paper Credit* – everything depends on the relationship between the 'money rate of interest' and the 'natural rate of interest'.

As the Bullion Committee argued, with the rate of interest at which banks would lend set below the anticipated rate of profit, the potential supply of bills for discount would be without limit. Under specie convertibility, a banking system that had fixed its lending rate too low would find the associated expansion of money causing a drain of reserves and the central bank would be forced to raise its lending rate. Without the crucial check of convertibility, prices and the money supply would begin to rise, as would the nominal value of new bills of exchange offered for discount in a self-justifying inflationary spiral. The Real Bills Doctrine, a relatively harmless precept under specie convertibility, thus becomes, under inconvertibility, a recipe for unlimited inflation and exchange depreciation. This conclusion is of enduring importance and is perhaps the most significant result that emerged from the bullionist controversy.

The Real Bills Doctrine was particularly dangerous in the circumstances of 1810. The then current usury laws set an upper limit of 5 per cent to the rate of interest at which loans could be made, and the ability of the public to convert paper money into gold coin, and then melt the latter for export, an illegal but seemingly widely practised check on overissue in the earlier days of the suspension, had become less effective by 1810 as gold coin had become scarce. Moreover, what we would now term inflationary expectations had begun to become established in the business community. Though the point was not raised explicitly in the *Bullion Report*, in a parliamentary speech of 1811 on the *Report*, Thornton showed himself well aware of the implications of this for the relationship between nominal and real interest rates and the inflationary process, thus anticipating the insights of Irving Fisher (1896) by 85 years.

In placing the blame for the persistence of sterling's depreciation on the Bank of England, the Bullion Committee also took the position that the Country Banks' note issue had not exerted a major independent influence on prices. Their *Report* contained nothing approaching a formal analysis of what we would nowadays term the 'bank credit multiplier'; such analysis did not appear until the early 1820s, when it was first developed by Thomas Joplin and James Pennington, and indeed it was not widely understood until well into the 20th century. The Committee nevertheless took the position that the Country Banks' note issue, not to mention the other privately emitted components of the circulating medium, tended to expand and contract in rough harmony with Bank of England liabilities. This is a point of some interest, since in the debates of the 1830s and 1840s, the Currency School, who in their opposition to the Real Bills Doctrine were the intellectual heirs to the bullionists, took a diametrically opposite view of the significance of the Country Bank note issue and were eventually successful in having it suppressed.

In matters of monetary theory and the diagnosis of contemporary problems it is hard to fault the Bullion Committee even today. No other discussion of economic policy issues prepared by working politicians has had so sound an intellectual basis and has stood the test of time so well. It is more difficult to praise the *Report*'s key policy proposal, however. So worried were its authors about sterling's depreciation, and about the capacity of the Bank of England to conduct policy competently, that in the midst of major war, and at a time when sterling had significantly depreciated, they recommended a return to specie convertibility at the prewar parity within two years. The *Bullion Report* was laid before the House of Commons in May 1811 where debate on its substance was organized around a series of resolutions and counter-resolutions. Though the Commons rejected the whole *Report* it is not without interest that the specific proposal to resume convertibility within two years failed by a significantly larger majority than did any other. It should be noted though, that in rejecting the Bullion Committee's recommendations, the House of Commons simultaneously supported resumption once peace was re-established.

IV. Subsequent experience was to prove the Bullion Committee's fears of future Bank of England profligacy unfounded. Whatever the Bank's directors may have said about their operating procedures, they clearly relied on more than a real bills rule, and, as commentators from Bagehot on have noted, their policy was, if judged by results, reasonably responsible, particularly after 1810, which saw the peak of wartime inflationary pressures. Thus debate about monetary issues had died down by 1812, but that year saw the crucial defeat of Napoleon's army in Russia. The decline in his fortunes thereafter, leading to his final surrender in 1815, set the stage for the next phase of the bullionist controversy. This dealt mainly with the problems of implementing resumption, though the first decisive peacetime monetary measure, taken by Parliament in 1816, was to remove the legal ambiguity which had persisted since 1717 about the status of silver in Britain's monetary system by formally placing the country on a gold standard, albeit one in which convertibility was still suspended.

The end of a war that had lasted for more than two decades was inevitably an occasion for considerable economic dislocation. Agriculture and metalworking industries in particular suffered badly from the re-establishment of peacetime patterns of production and trade. A simultaneous general fall of prices in terms of gold, upon which was superimposed a contraction of Bank of England liabilities and therefore an approach of sterling to its prewar parity, was associated with widespread distress. In such circumstances, it is hardly surprising that there was much political opposition to early resumption. By and large, this opposition was not grounded in any coherent economic analysis, except in Birmingham. In this city, the centre of the metalworking industries, opposition to resumption was articulated by Thomas and Matthias Attwood and their associates, and the Birmingham School showed a keen appreciation of the effects of monetary contraction and deflation upon employment, and an understanding than an appropriately managed monetary system based on inconvertible paper might, in principle, be a viable method of avoiding such problems.

At their best the Birmingham School anticipated Keynesian insights of the 1930s, but their analysis often degenerated into crude inflationism, particularly in their later writings. In any event, they were always a small minority among those whom we would nowadays recognize as economists. The vast majority of these always supported the principle of resumption at the 1797 parity. The value of Bank of England paper in terms of gold was either regarded as a good measure of its purchasing power over goods in general, or stability in the good value of money was looked upon as 'natural' and desirable in its own right; and there was widespread agreement that wartime inflation had been unjust to creditors. The problems of those who had incurred debts during the war, after paper had depreciated, provided some of the impetus to popular opposition to resumption immediately after the war, particularly in agricultural areas, but it is nevertheless fair to argue that a curious moral one-sidedness about the redistributive effects of inflation emerged among the majority of economists during this stage of the bullionist controversy. This one-sidedness, which perhaps had its roots in Hume's view of credit markets in which the typical borrower is an improvident consumer and the typical lender a frugal producer, has played an important role in debates about inflation ever since.

If there was, then, wide agreement about the ultimate desirability of resuming convertibility at the 1797 parity, its advocacy was nevertheless tempered with caution after 1812. In contrast to the *Bullion Report*'s unconcern about such matters, later discussion did pay attention to the potentially disruptive effects on output and employment of the deflation needed to implement it. Two problems were recognized: first, deflation was needed to restore sterling to its old parity with gold; and, second, there was the possibility that the increased demand for gold implied by a resumption of convertibility might itself create more deflation by driving up the relative price of specie. The end of the war was, as we have already noted, the occasion for significant price level falls, both in terms of gold, but even more in terms of Bank of England paper, whose quantity in circulation contracted considerably. The latter contraction was not, according to Fetter (1965), the result of any conscious policy decision on the part of the Bank of England, but it did have the effect of weakening any practical case against resumption by reducing the amount of further deflation needed to implement it.

Ricardo dominated the later stages of the bullionist controversy, as Thornton had dominated its earlier stages, and he is often regarded as having been unconcerned about deflation. Such unconcern would be consistent with the Ricardian vice off underplaying the importance of the short run in economic life, but, as Hollander (1979) has shown, this view of his position is not sustainable. Ricardo's 1816 *Proposals for An Economical and Secure Currency* were motivated by a desire to mitigate further deflation as well as by a desire to put the British monetary system upon an intellectually sound basis. He argued that, with resumption, Britain adopt a paper currency rather than one with a high proportion of gold coin, and that the Bank of England should hold against it a reserve of gold ingots in terms of which notes could be redeemed. One practical advantage of this scheme was that by economizing on gold, it would put little upward pressure on its value when it was implemented, and Ricardo pointed out this advantage. He mainly justified his proposal in more general terms, though, stressing the desirability *per se* of economizing on scarce precious metals when paper would serve equally well as currency, an argument which harked back to Adam Smith's defence of paper money in the *Wealth of Nations*.

Ricardo's ingot plan was adopted in 1819 by Parliament, of which he was by then a member, as a basis for resumption; but second thoughts about it soon set it, for quite practical reasons. Counterfeiting of bank notes had been virtually unknown before 1797, but the increased circulation of low denomination Bank of England notes thereafter had offered considerable temptation to forgers. The years 1797–1817 saw over 300 capital convictions for the offence. These convictions and, as Fetter (1965) records, the fact that clemency seems to have been granted or refused on the recommendation of the Bank, brought much opprobrium upon that institution from a public among which opposition to the widespread use of capital punishment was becoming intense. A paper currency backed by gold ingots might have been economical and secure, but it did not remove the temptation to forgery. Hence Ricardo's ingot plan was dropped, and when resumption was finally implemented in 1821, gold coins replaced small denomination notes in circulation. Ricardo's ingot plan was not forgotten, however; it was to be the starting point of Alfred Marshall's symmetallic proposals of (1887), and something very like it was implemented in Britain in 1925 when the country once again resumed gold convertibility in the wake of a wartime suspension. The similarities here were no accident. The literature of the bullionist controversy, not least Ricardo's contributions to it, was much read and cited throughout the 19th century and into the 20th, not least by participants in the monetary debates of the 1920s.

V. The resumption of 1821 was not the unmitigated disaster that the 1925 return to gold was to be, not least because the amount of deflation needed after 1819 to make the 1797 parity effective was rather minor. Nevertheless, resumption did not put an end either to monetary problems or to debate. Even the rather small amount of deflation needed after 1819 was hard for the economy to digest, and a fitful recovery thereafter ended, in 1825, in the first of a series of financial crises that were to recur at roughly decennial intervals for the next half century. Thus, if 1821 marked the end of the bullionist controversy, it also marked the beginning of a new period of debate about the monetary system, and in particular about the conduct of monetary policy and the design of monetary institutions under a gold standard. This debate would, in due course, culminate in a second famous controversy, that between the Currency School and the Banking School.

There is considerably continuity between these later debates and the bullionist controversy, and this simple fact attests to the important contributions which were made during its course. In only a quarter century, 18th-century analysis of commodity money mechanisms had been adapted to the circumstances of a modern banking system, and the monetary economics of the open economy under fixed and flexible exchange rates had taken on a form that is recognizable even today. Moreover, the foundations of the theory of central banking under commodity and paper standards were also developed. It is hard to think of any other episode in the history of monetary economics when so much was accomplished in so short a period.

BIBLIOGRAPHY

Bagehot, W. 1874. *Lombard Street, A Description of the Money Market*. Ed. Frank C. Genovese, Granston, Illinois: Richard Irwin, 1962.

Boyd, W. 1800. *Letter to the Right Honourable William Pitt on the Influence of the Stoppage of Issue in Specie at the Bank of England; on the Prices of Provisions, and other Commodities*. London.

Cannan, E. (ed.) 1919. *The Paper Pound of 1797–1821: The Bullion Report*. London: P.S.King & Son. Second (1921) edition, reprinted by Augustus M. Kelley, New York, 1969.

Cantillon, R. 1734. *Essai sur la nature du commerce en général*. Trans. and edited by Henry Higgs, London: re-issued for the Royal Economic Society by Frank Cass & Co., 1959.

Checkland, S. 1975. Adam Smith and the bankers. In *Essays on Adam Smith*, ed. A.S. Skinner and T. Wilson, Oxford: The Clarendon Press.

Eagly, R.V. 1968. The Swedish and English Bullionist Controversies. In *Events Ideology and Economic Theory*, ed. R.V. Eagly, Detroit, Mich.: Wayne State University Press.

Fetter, F.W. 1955. *The Irish Pound 1797–1826*. London: Allen & Unwin.

Fetter, F.W. 1965. *Development of British Monetary Orthodoxy 1797–1875*. Cambridge, Mass.: Harvard University Press.

Fisher, I. 1896. Appreciation and interest. *AEA Publications* 3(11), August, 331–442.

Hollander, S. 1979. *The Economics of David Ricardo*. Toronto: University of Toronto Press.

Hume, D. 1752. Of Money, Of the Balance of Trade and Of Interest. In *Political Discourses*, Edinburgh: Fleming. Subsequently incorporated in the 1758 edition of *Essays, Moral Political and Literary*. London. Reprinted London: Oxford University Press, 1962.

Marshall, A. 1887. Remedies for fluctuations of general prices. *Contemporary Review*, March; reprinted as ch. 8 of *Memorials of Alfred Marshall*, ed. A.C. Pigou, London: Macmillan, 1925; New York: A.M. Kelley, 1966.

Mints, L. 1945. *A History of Banking Theory*. Chicago: University of Chicago Press.

Ricardo, D. 1809. Contributions to the *Morning Chronicle*. Reprinted in *Works and Correspondence of David Ricardo*, ed. P. Sraffa, Vol. III, Cambridge: Cambridge University Press, 1951; New York: Cambridge University Press, 1973.

Ricardo, D. 1810–11. *The High Price of Gold Bullion, A Proof of the Depreciation of Bank Notes*. Reprinted in *Works...*, ed. P. Sraffa, Vol. III, Cambridge: Cambridge University Press, 1951; New York: Cambridge University Press, 1973.

Ricardo, D. 1816. *Proposals for an Economical and Secure Currency*, Reprinted in *Works...*, ed. P. Sraffa, Vol. IV, Cambridge: Cambridge University Press, 1951; New York: Cambridge University Press, 1973.

Smith, A. 1776. *An Inquiry into the Nature and Causes of the Wealth of Nations*. London. Reprinted in two vols, ed. R.H. Campbell, A.S. Skinner and W.B. Todd, Oxford: Clarendon Press, 1976.

Thornton, H. 1802. *An Enquiry into the Nature and Effects of the Paper Credit of Great Britain*. London. Edited with an Introduction by F.A. von Hayek, London: George Allen & Unwin, 1939; reprinted, New York: Augustus Kelley, 1962.

Viner, J. 1937. *Studies in the Theory of International Trade*. New York: Harper Bros.

Wheatley, J. 1803. *Remarks on Currency and Commerce*. London.

Wicksell, K. 1898. *Interest and Prices*. Trans. R.F. Kahn, London: Macmillan for the Royal Economic Society, 1936; New York: A.M. Kelley, 1965.

Capital, Credit and Money Markets

BENJAMIN M. FRIEDMAN

The markets for money, credit and capital represent a fundamental dimension of economic activity, in that the many and varied functions of the modern economy's financial markets both reflect and help shape the course of the economic system at large. Financial markets facilitate such central economic actions as producing and trading, earning and spending, saving and investing, accumulating and retiring, transferring and bequeathing. Development of the financial system is a recognized hallmark of economic development in the broadest sense.

Neither the important role played by the financial side of economic activity nor economists' awareness of it is a recent phenomenon. Economic analysis of the roles of money, credit and capital constitutes a tradition as old as the discipline itself. Nevertheless, in comparison with other equally central objects of economic analysis this tradition is as remarkable for its continuing diversity as for the richness of the insights it has generated. A century after Marshall and Wicksell and Bagehot, a half-century after Keynes and Robertson and Hicks, and a quarter-century after the initial path-breaking work of Tobin and Modigliani and Milton Friedman, there is still no firm consensus on many of the more compelling questions in the field: What are the most important determinants of an economy's overall level of capital intensity? How does risk affect the allocation of that capital? Do leverage and intermediation of debt matter for aggregate economic outcomes? Does money matter – and, if so, what is it?

The absence of universally accepted answers to these and other fundamental questions does not signify a failure to develop conceptual understanding of how the markets for money, credit and capital function, or of the basic elements of these markets' interactions with non-financial economic activity. The persistent diversity of thought on these unresolved questions has instead reflected the inability of empirical analysis, hindered by the continual and at times rapid evolution of actual financial systems, to provide persuasive evidence on issues characterized both by a multiplicity of plausibly relevant determining factors and by the inherent unobservability of some of the most important among them – for example, ex ante perceptions of risks as well as rewards.

THE MARKET FOR CAPITAL. The essential reason for having a capital market in any economy stems from the nature of the productive process. In all economies anyone has ever observed, and the more so in the more developed among them, production of goods and services to satisfy human wants relies on capital as well as labour. If capital is to exist to use in production, someone must own it; and in economies in which this ownership function lies with individuals or other private entities, the primary initial role of the capital market is to establish the terms on which capital is held. In market-oriented economies the terms on which capital is (or may be) held provide incentives affecting the further accumulation of new capital, so that over time the capital market plays an additional, logically consequent role in determining the economy's existing amount of capital and hence its potential ability to produce goods and services.

In conceptualizing how the market mechanism sets the terms on which an economy's capital is held, economists have traditionally paired the role of capital as an input to the production process with the role of capital as a vehicle for conveying wealth – that is, ultimate command over goods and services – forward in time. The capital marekt is therefore the economic meeting place between the theory of production, often in the derivative form of the theory of investment, and the theory of consumption and saving. Different assumptions forming the underlying theory on either side in general lead to differing characterizations of how the capital market establishes the terms on which capital is held, and consequently differing characterizations of how the market affects the economy's accumulation of capital over time and hence its capital intensity at any point in time. Among the critical features of production theory and consumption-saving theory that have featured prominently in this analysis of their intersection are the substitutability of capital for other production inputs, the source and nature of technological progress, and the interest elasticity of saving. In most modern treatments, these specifics in turn depend on more basic assumptions like the respective specifications of the production function constraining producers and the intertemporal utility function maximized by wealth-holders.

Notwithstanding the central importance of this basic economic role of the capital market, as well as the insight and ingenuity with which economists over many years have elaborated their understanding of it, what gives the modern study of capital markets much of its particular richness is the focus on one particular factor that could, in principle, be entirely absent from this economic setting, but that is ever present in reality: uncertainty.

The essential feature of capital from this perspective is its durability. Because capital is durable – that is, its use in production does not instantly consume or destroy it – it provides those who hold it with not just the ability but the necessity to convey purchasing power forward in time in a specific form. Precisely because of this durability, capital necessarily exposes those who hold it to whatever uncertainties characterize both the production process and the demand for wealth-holding in the future.

Not just reward but risk too, therefore, are inherent features of capital that must accrue to some holders, somewhere in the economy, if the economy is to enjoy the advantages of production based in part on durable capital inputs. The introduction of risk has profound implications for consumption-saving behaviour. In addition, when the absence of perfect rental markets leads producers who use capital to be also among the holders of capital, the introduction of risk in this way affects production-investment behaviour too. Hence via at least one side of the capital market nexus, and via both sides under plausibly realistic assumptions, the risk consequent upon the durability of capital alters the determination of the terms on which capital is held, and thereby alters the determination of the economy's capital accumulation. Increasingly in recent years, the study of capital markets by economists has focused on the market pricing of this risk. The context in which this risk pricing of function matters, however, remains the consequences, for wealth-holding and for investment and production, of the terms on which capital is held.

The implications of the risk inherent in durable capital depend, of course, on many aspects of the capital market environment. Two prominent features of existing capital markets in particular have importantly shaped the explosive development of the capital markets risk-pricing literature during the past quarter-century. First, durable capital is not the only available form of wealth holding. Other assets may be risky too, but at least some assets exist which do not expose holders to the risks, involving unknown outcomes far in the future, that are consequent on the durability of typical capital assets. Second, even capital assets are not all identical. Heterogenous capital assets expose their holders to risks that not only are not identical but also, are not in general independent.

Following Markowitz (1952) and Tobin (1958), the investigation of the allocation of wealth-holding between a single risk-free asset and a single risky asset readily establishes the terms on which (risky) capital is held, in the form of the excess of its expected return over the known return on the alternative (presumed risk-free) asset. In the simplest case of a single-period-at-a-time decision horizon, for example, the maximization of utility exhibiting constant relative risk aversion in the sense of Pratt (1964) and Arrow (1965), subject to the assumption that the uncertain return to capital is normally distributed, leads to the result that an investor's demand for capital, expressed in proportion to the investor's total wealth, depends linearly on the expected excess return:

$$\frac{1}{W} \cdot A_K^D = \frac{1}{\rho \cdot \sigma_K^2} \cdot [E(r_K) - \bar{r}] \tag{1}$$

where W is the investor's total wealth, A_K^D is the quantity demanded of the risky asset, ρ is the coefficient of relative risk aversion, $E(r_K)$ and σ_K^2 are respectively the mean and variance of the ex ante distribution describing assessments of the uncertain asset return, and $\bar{r}$ is the known return on the alternative asset. (This simple result is both convenient and standard, but it can be only an approximation because normally distributed asset returns are strictly incompatible with utility functions exhibiting constant relative risk aversion.) If it is possible to represent the economy's aggregate asset demands in a form corresponding to (1) for individual investors, then the requirement that the existing amount of each asset must equal to the amount demanded leads to the result that the expected excess return on capital depends linearly on the composition of the existing wealth:

$$E(r_K) = \bar{r} + \rho \sigma_K^2 \cdot \frac{A_K}{W} \tag{2}$$

where A_K is the actual existing quantity of the risky asset. If the market equilibration process works via changes in the price of the risky asset, rather than its stated per-unit return, then both A_K and W are jointly determined with $E(r_K)$ and the resulting relationship is analogous though no longer linear:

$$E(r_K) = \bar{r} + \rho \sigma_K^2 \cdot \frac{P[E(r_K)] \cdot \bar{A}_K}{A_F + P[E(r_K)] \cdot \bar{A}_K} \tag{3}$$

where A_F is the existing quantity of the risk-free asset (taken to have unit price), $\bar{A}_K$ is the quantity of the risky asset in physical units, and P is the price of the risky asset with $[dP/dE(r_K)] < 0$. (If capital is infinitely lived, $P = 1/E(r_K)$.) The addition of this element of the theory of risk pricing thus allows the capital market, in the context of a general economic equilibrium, to establish the terms on which durable capital is held – and hence the incentive to capital accumulation – when other, non-durable assets are also present.

The second major aspect of actual capital assets motivating the development of the economic analysis of capital markets is heterogeneity. Capital assets differ from one another not only because of actual physical differences but also because, with imperfect rental markets, the application of identical capital items to different uses in production has some permanence, so that ownership of a particular capital asset typically implies ongoing participation in a specific production activity. In general, each kind of capital asset, categorized not only by physical characteristics but also by production application, exposes those who hold it to a unique set of uncertainties. Moreover, in general the different risks associated in this way with different capital assets are not independent.

The elaboration of the single-risky-asset model in (1)–(3) due to Sharpe (1964) and Lintner (1965) readily represents the determination of relative returns in the capital market, in this context of heterogeneous capital assets with interdependent risks, and hence enables the outcomes determined in the capital market to affect not just the aggregate quantity but also the allocation of the company's capital accumulation. The multi-variate analogues of (1) and (2) are simply

$$\frac{1}{W} \cdot \mathbf{A}_K^D = \frac{1}{\rho} \Omega^{-1} [E(\mathbf{r}_K) - \bar{r} \cdot \mathbf{1}] \tag{4}$$

$$E(\mathbf{r}_K) = \bar{r} \cdot \mathbf{1} + \rho \Omega \cdot \frac{1}{W} \cdot \mathbf{A}_K \tag{5}$$

where $\mathbf{A}_K^D$, $\mathbf{A}_K$ and $\mathbf{r}_K$ are vectors with individual elements respectively corresponding to A_K^D, A_K and r_K, Ω is the variance-covariance structure associated with expectations $E(\mathbf{r}_K)$, and $\mathbf{1}$ is a vector of units. In (4) the demand for each specific capital asset depends linearly on the expected excess return over the risk-free rate not only of that asset but of all other capital assets as well, with the substitutability between any two assets – that is, the response of the demand for one asset to the expected return on another – determined by the investor's risk aversion as well as by the interdependence among the respective returns on all of the risky assets. In (5) the equilibrium expected excess return on each capital asset at any time therefore depends (linearly) on the existing quantities of all assets expressed as shares of the economy's total wealth. Under conventional models of investment behaviour, the accumulation of each specific kind of capital over time depends in turn on the entire set of equilibrium returns determined in this way.

Moreover, this role of the capital market in guiding the allocation of capital does not depend in any fundamental way on the presence of an alternative asset with risk-free return. If all assets bear uncertain returns, either because capital assets are the only existing assets, or because even the returns on other assets are uncertain (because of uncertain price inflation, for example), the analogue of (4) is

$$\frac{1}{W} \cdot \mathbf{A}_K^D = \frac{1}{\rho}[\Omega^{-1} - (\mathbf{l}'\Omega^{-1}\mathbf{l})^{-1}\Omega^{-1}\mathbf{l}\mathbf{l}'\Omega^{-1}] \cdot E(\mathbf{r}_K) + (\mathbf{l}'\Omega^{-1}\mathbf{l})^{-1}\Omega^{-1}\mathbf{l}. \tag{6}$$

The second term in (6) represents the composition of the minimum-variance portfolio, which in the absence of a risk-free asset is a unique combination of risky assets, expressed as a vector of asset shares adding to unity. The first term in (6) expresses the investor's willingness to hold a portfolio different from this minimum-variance combination. The transformation of Ω contained in the first term maps what is in general a variance-covariance matrix of full rank into a matrix of rank reduced by one, as is implied by the balance sheet constraint emphasized by Brainard and Tobin (1968). Because the resulting matrix is of less than full rank, however, no exact analog of (5) then exists.

Combining the description of asset demands in (6) with the requirement of market clearing therefore determines the relative expected returns among all assets – in other words, determines the absolute expected returns on all assets but one, given the expected return on that one – but cannot determine absolute expected returns without at least some reference point fixed outside the risk pricing mechanism. This result is in fact analogous to the implication of (5) (or (3)), in that (5) determines the expected return on each risky asset only in relation to the fixed benchmark of the known return on the alternative risk-free asset. In either case the analysis of risk pricing alone is insufficient to determine absolute returns without something else, presumably grounded in the fundamental interrelation between the respective roles of capital in production and in wealth-holding, to anchor the overall return structure.

Actual capital markets perform these functions of pricing risk and thereby guiding the accumulation and allocation of new capital, in essentially all advanced economies with well developed financial systems. In most such economies, the most immediately visible focus of the risk pricing mechanism is the trading on stock exchanges of existing claims to capital in the form of equity ownership shares in ongoing business enterprises. Equity shares are composite capital assets not only in the sense that each business firm typically owns a variety of different kinds of physical capital but also because the value of most firms consists in part of intangible capital in the form of existing knowledge, organization and reputation. In the context of what are often very large costs of establishing new enterprises, together with highly imperfect secondary markets for physical capital assets, even in principle the prices of equity securities need not correspond in any direct way to the liquidation value of a firm's separate items of plant and equipment. Given transactions costs and imperfect secondary markets, the existing enterprise itself is just as much an aspect of an advanced economy's long-lived production technology as is the sheer physical durability of capital.

Markets in which existing equity shares are traded also present the opportunity for the initial sale to investors of new equity shares issued by business enterprises in order to augment their available financial resources. In addition to guiding capital accumulation and allocation by establishing the relevant risk pricing, therefore, capital markets also play a direct role in facilitating capital accumulation by offering firms the opportunity to raise new equity funds directly. Even so, given firms' ability to increase their equity base by retaining their earnings rather than distributing them fully to shareholders – and also given the availability of debt financing (see the discussion of credit markets immediately below) – the extent to which firms actually rely on new issues of equity varies widely from one economy to another. In the United States, for example, well established firms typically do not issue new equity shares in significant volume, and the market for new issues is primarily a resource for new enterprises of a more speculative character. (The aggregate net addition to equity in the US market each year is typically negative, in that equity retirements and repurchases exceed gross new issues.) In most other economies, too, new issues of equity shares provide only small amounts of net funds for business.

Even when new equity additions via new shares issues are small, however, the risk pricing function of the capital market still guides an economy's capital accumulation and allocation process. Internal additions to equity from retained earnings are by far the major source of equity funds for the typical business in most economies, and – at least in theory – the retention of distribution of earnings by firms reflects in part considerations of expected return and associated risk as priced in the capital markets. Firms in lines of business in which new investment is less profitable (after allowance for risk) than the economy's norm not only cannot issue new equity shares on attractive terms but also must either distribute their earnings or face undervaluation of their outstanding shares by market investors. Conversely, firms with unusually profitable prospects at the margin of new investment can favourably issue new shares or can retain their earnings to fund their expansion.

Finally, two further features of actual modern capital markets bear explicit notice. Each, appropriately considered, is consistent with the notion of capital markets serving the basic function of pricing risk, and thereby guiding an economy's capital accumulation and allocation.

First, highly developed capital markets are characterized by enormous volumes of trading. In principle, the risk-pricing mechanism could function with little trading of existing securities, and under the right conditions it could function with none at all. If investors all agreed on the appropriate set of price relationships, there would be neither the incentive nor the need to effect actual transactions. The agreed-upon set of prices might fluctuate widely or narrowly, depending upon changes in assessments of risk and return, but as long as the assessments were universally shared there would be little if any trading.

The huge trading volumes typical of actual modern capital markets therefore suggest that, in fact, investors do not share identical risk and return assessments. Annual trading volume on the New York Stock Exchange, for example, is normally near one-half the total value of listed existing shares. Although the continually changing circumstances of both individual and institutional investors no doubt play some role, it is difficult to explain this phenomenon except in the context of substantial heterogeneity in the response of investors' risk and return assessments to the flow of new information.

The possibility that investors' opinions differ is only a minor complication for the theory of risk pricing as sketched above. Lintner (1969) showed that competitive capital markets with heterogeneous investors determine outcomes for the pricing of risky assets that just reflect an appropriately constructed aggregation over all individual investors' differing assessments (as well as their differing preferences), weighted by their respective wealth positions. The question remains, however, why investors' assessments differ. One line of analysis, initiated by Grossman (1976), has emphasized systematic differences in assessments due to underlying differences in information available to different investors. By contrast, Shiller (1984) suggested the importance of unsystematic differences not readily explainable within the conventional analytic framework based on rational maximization. The question remains unsettled but important nonetheless.

The second additional feature of actual modern capital markets that bears explicit attention is the proliferation of increasingly complex securities, including options, warrants, futures, and so forth. Given heterogeneity among investors, this development fits naturally in the context of the capital markets' basic economic role of establishing the terms on which the risks inherent in a capital-intensive production technology are to be borne. When investors differ among themselves in age, or wealth, or preferences, or risk and return assessments, in general the most efficient allocation of those risks does not consist of all investors' holding portfolios embodying identical risks and prospective returns. Instead, different investors will hold differing portfolios, and a further role of an economy's capital markets is to allocate the bearing of specific risks across different investors.

Heterogeneity among different kinds of physical assets would itself facilitate such specialization, and heterogeneity among the business enterprises whose equity shares constitute the asset units in actual capital markets typically does so to an even greater extent. Still, even this resulting degree of feasible specialization in risk bearing apparently falls well short of what would be fully consistent with the existing extent of investor heterogeneity.

Complex securities enable the capital markets to achieve a more efficient allocation of risk across heterogeneous investors by more finely dividing the risk inherent in economy's production technology. Options, for example, permit an investor not merely to hold a (positive or negative) position in the equity of a specific firm but to hold positions corresponding only to designated parts of the distribution describing the possible outcomes for that firm's performance as reflected in the price of its equity shares. While the existing array of complex securities presumably does not approach the set of contingent claims necessary to span the space of possible outcomes in the sense of Arrow (1964) and Debreu (1959), developments along these lines in recent years have presumably rendered risk bearing more efficient. Moreover, following Merton (1973a) and Black and Scholes (1973), the analysis of the market pricing of risk has extended to explicitly contingent claims the central features of market equilibrium. The analysis is richer, therefore, and the outcome more efficient, but the end result of the economic process remains the pricing of the risk associated at any time with the existing stock of capital, with consequent effects on the total accumulation and allocation of capital over time.

THE MARKET FOR CREDIT. The presence of heterogeneity among different participants in a market economy also provides an economic rationale for credit markets. The primary initial role of the credit market is to facilitate borrowing and lending – that is, the transfer of purchasing power by the issuing and acquiring (and trading) of money-denominated debts. In establishing the terms on which such transfers take place, the credit market plays a role in guiding the allocation of the economy's resources that is parallel to that played by the capital market.

If all market participants were identical, such a market could establish terms on which the representative agents would be willing to borrow or lend, but no actual borrowing or lending would take place. Under those circumstances the credit market would be of little economic importance. By contrast, actual economies consist of an almost infinite variety of differently positioned participants. Individuals differ from business enterprises, and private-sector entities differ from governments. Even just among individuals, there are old and young, rich and poor, highly and weakly risk-averse, favourably and unfavourably taxed, home-owners and renters, and so on in ever more dimensions and ever greater detail. As a result, the credit market does not just establish a putative price for strictly hypothetical trades. It facilitates transfers that in turn make possible resource allocations which could not otherwise come about.

At the most basic level, economists since Fisher (1930) have emphasized the role of borrowing and lending in achieving a separation between production and consumption decisions. Here the function of the credit market is to enable individuals to shift purchasing power forward or backward in time, so as to free the timing pattern of consumption streams from the corresponding timing pattern of earnings from production (while still preserving, of course, the relevant constraint connecting the appropriately discounted totals). The overall result of this intertemporal separation is, in general, to achieve more efficient resource allocations in the sense both of greater production from given available inputs as well as higher utility from given available consumption. Without such a separation it would be impossible to construe the intertemporal theory of consumption and saving as in any way distinct from the theory of production and investment. Even the limited heterogeneity between firms and households is sufficient to give rise to borrowing and lending along these lines.

Nevertheless, the question of why money-dominated debts should serve this intertemporal transfer function – rather than having all obligations take the form of direct ownership claims to capital, for example – opens up a whole series of further important issues. Following the analysis of capital markets immediately above, the most readily apparent answer is that debt obligations isolate the specific risks associated with the purchasing power of the unit of denomination (in other words, inflation risk) and risks associated with the borrower's ability to meet the stated obligation (default risk), and that this conventional compartmentalization is evidently convenient for a variety of reasons. Inflation risk and default risk are in general not independent, however. In addition, it is just as easy to imagine alternative conventions that might be just as convenient, like the predominant use of debts denominated in purchasing-power units.

Given the conventional monetary denomination of debt obligations, the function of the credit market in most modern economies is to redistribute immediate claims to purchasing power, in exchange for future claims, along three major dimensions of heterogeneity: between individuals and firms, between the private sector and the government, and between domestic and foreign entities. In addition, redistributions among individuals (and, to a lesser extent, among firms) are often a further important credit market function.

Business firms typically apply to investment not only their equity additions from retained earnings and any new share issues but also funds raised by borrowing. Modigliani and Miller (1958) set forth conditions under which the firm's reliance on debt versus equity financing would be a matter of indifference, in that it would not affect the firm's total value, but conditions prevailing in actual economies and their capital and credit markets do not meet these conditions closely. Business reliance on debt financing is typically large, and it varies systematically across countries and across industries within a given country. Prominent aspects of the divergence of actual economies from the Modigliani-Miller irrelevance conditions which the ensuing voluminous literature has emphasized, include tax structures, risks and costs of bankruptcy by the firm, differential borrowing rates for firms and individuals (due to, for example, risks and costs of bankruptcy by individuals), monitoring costs required to minimize risks, and restrictive features of debt contracts intended to reduce risks due to moral-hazard effects of imperfectly compatible incentive structures.

The resulting substantial reliance on debt financing by business means that credit markets, like capital markets, play a major economic role in guiding an economy's accumulation and allocation of capital over time. When any or all of the factors cited above lead business enterprises to finance a new investment with some combination of additional equity (from retained earnings or new share issues) and additional debt, the appropriate calculation of investment incentives involves the cost to the firm in both the capital market and the credit market. In circumstances in which the financing margin corresponding to marginal new investment is a debt margin – as is often the case in the United States, for example, where firms' reliance on external funds is typically synonymous with issuance of debt – the relevant cost at the margin is the cost in the credit market.

Use of the credit market to finance government spending is among the oldest and most prevalent forms of financial transactions, and it has, understandably, generated an entire literature unto itself. In practical terms, government reliance on the credit markets in most modern economies is important not only in that governments often issue debt to finance large portions of their total spending but also because government borrowing often absorbs a large amount of the total funds advanced in the market by lenders. As is the case for private borrowers, government debt issues separate in time the ability to spend from the need to raise revenue. In addition, however, because under some circumstances governments need not repay debt obligations at all (they may refinance them forward indefinitely), and also because of uncertainty over the identity of the responsible taxpayers even in the case of future repayment, government debt is in part net wealth to the aggregate of private holders in a way that private debts are not.

The distinguishing feature of government debt in many economies is its essential freedom from default risk. In addition, in most economies the market for government debt is among the most efficiently functioning of all financial markets. Hence the existence of government debt enables the credit market to establish a base, with risk factors limited to inflation and real discounting values, from which it can then price privately issued debts subject to risks associated with default as well. The practice of giving government guarantees to the payment of interest and principal on selected private debts, which has greatly proliferated in recent years, has further increased the variety of forms of default-free debt securities. Yet another important implication of the default-free nature of government debt is that, to the extent that government borrowing takes the place of borrowing that individuals could do on their own account only at higher cost or not at all, government debt is in part net wealth to the private sector even if it is necessarily repaid and even if the identity of the responsible taxpayers is fully known.

International borrowing and lending has also greatly increased in recent years, as technological advances in communications have brought the world's financial markets closer together in the relevant physical sense, while individual countries' governments have progressivelly relaxed legal and regulatory barriers that impede international capital flows. From the perspective of any one country, the possibility of international borrowing and lending serves a separation function analogous to the fundamental Fisherian separation of production and consumption decisions in a closed economy. An economy that can borrow or lend abroad need not balance its imports and exports at each moment of time. Moreover, once an economy builds up a positive net international creditor position, it can indefinitely finance an excess of imports over exports from the associated interest income. (Conversely, once an economy builds up a net international debtor position, it must indefinitely export in excess of its imports so as to finance the debt service.) From the perspective of the world economy as a whole, international borrowing and lending is even more closely analogous to the closed economy model, in that it facilitates a more efficient allocation of resources across national boundaries.

Apart from these categorical heterogeneities, credit markets also reallocate immediate purchasing power among individuals and among business firms. The need for individuals in differing circumstances to make a complementary arrangement for divergences among their respective income and spending streams is basic to any life-cycle or overlapping-generations model of consumer behaviour. On the borrowing side, practical market limitations on individuals' issuance of equity-type claims contingent on their future earnings means that the only effective way for most individuals to shift command over purchasing power from the future to the present is through ordinary money-denominated debts. In fact, in most economies individuals' ability to borrow against no security other than future earnings is severely limited in any form, so that most borrowing by individuals occurs in conjunction with the purchase of homes, automobiles or other specific durable goods. On the lending side, individuals choosing to carry purchasing power into the future can hold wealth in any of its available forms, and in fact most individuals hold by far the greater part of their wealth in forms other than credit market instruments. Hence the great bulk of the borrowing done by individuals respresents funds advanced by financial intermediary institutions rather than directly by other individuals.

Direct borrowing and lending among business firms is also a significant part of credit market activity especially in highly developed financial systems. On the borrowing side, firms' reliance on debt finance is readily understandable for reasons sketched above, irrespective of whether the funds raised come from individuals, from financial intermediaries or from other businesses. On the lending side, debt held by business firms usually takes the form of very short-term liquid instruments intended to provide maximum flexibility in the future disposition of the purchasng power thus deferred.

In sum, the credit markets play the fundamental role of enabling an economy populated by heterogeneous agents to achieve superior resource allocations by redistributing immediate purchasing power in exchange for money-denominated claims on the future. Because of the intensive use of debt to finance both business and residential investment, in establishing the terms on which such transfers take place also play a consequent role in guiding the economy's capital accumulation and capital allocation over time that is analogous to – and, in some economies, as important as – the parallel incentives provided by the capital markets. In addition, in part because those elements of total spending that are typically debt-financed bulk large in aggregate demand, in many economies fluctuations of overall economic activity are as closely related to the movement of total credit as to the movements of any other financial aggregates (like any measure of money, for example).

Finally, as in the case for capital markets, several other features of actual credit markets that in principle need not be so, but in fact are so, have exerted a strong influence on the way in which economists have studied these markets over many years. One of the most important in this regard is the fact, noted above, that individuals directly hold relatively few credit market instruments. Instead, the great bulk of the borrowing and lending in any even moderately advanced economy takes place through specialized financial intermediaries, including commercial banks, non-bank thrift institutions, insurance companies, pension funds, mutual funds, and so on.

Standard rationales underlying financial intermediation include the minimization of information and transactions costs, and the diversification of risks, in a world in which assets are imperfectly divisible and both asset returns and wealth-holders' cash-flow positions are imperfectly correlated. In principle, rationales apply to capital markets as well as credit markets, and in many countries institutions like mutual funds and pension funds do play an important role in holding equity shares. In practice, however, in many countries the bulk of the existing equity securities is still held directly by individuals rather than through financial intermediaries, while the opposite is true for debt instruments. As a result, the study of financial intermediation in general, and of specific kinds of intermediary institutions in particular, has been a major focus of the economic analysis of credit markets.

Another feature of actual credit markets that has likewise attracted a voluminous economic literature has been the simultaneous existence of a great variety of different debt instruments, especially including debts that differ according to their respective stated maturities. Although in principle only a single form of debt instrument, with a unique maturity, would enable the credit market to serve much of its economic functions, in fact almost all known credit markets are characterized by the simultaneous existence of many debt instruments with differing terms to maturity. The need for the market to price these debts – that is, to establish a term structure of interest rates – not only raises issues of risk analogous to those discussed above in relation to capital markets but also makes explicit the need for a more general intertemporal framework of analysis.

At least since Hicks (1939), economists have been aware at some level that short-term and long-term debts are both risky assets, each from a particular time perspective. Apart from risks associated with default and inflation, short-term debt provides a certain return to holders over a short-time horizon, so that short-term government debt could plausibly constitute the risk-free asset in a no-inflation version of the standard capital asset pricing model represented by (1) and (2) above. Over a longer horizon, however, short-term debt preserves capital value only by exposing both borrowers and lenders to an income risk if interest rates fluctuate. Conversely, long-term debt maintains income streams only by exposing borrowers and lenders to the risk of fluctuating capital value over any time horizon shorter than the stated term to maturity. At an *a priori* level, there is no way to establish which form of risk is more important, and hence no way to establish even the sign of the expected return premium that risk-averse borrowers and lenders would establish in pricing short-term and long-term debts relative to one another.

Following both Hicks and Keynes (1936), most economists have assumed as an empirical matter that typically prevailing preferences are such that lenders require, and borrowers are willing to pay, a positive expected return premium for the capital risk inherent in long-term debt. Hence the subsequent development of the term structure literature has taken a form at least in principle compatible with the single-period capital asset pricing model. More recently, however, following Stiglitz's (1970) explicit demonstration of the connection between the risk pricing of receipt streams and preferences with respect to consumption streams, the economic literature of asset pricing has tended to return to the position that there is no general answer to the question of whether short-term or long-term debts are more risky. Instead, the preferred form of analysis has increasingly become an explicitly intertemporal model, like Merton's (1973b) intertemporal capital asset pricing model or, more recently, Ross's (1976) arbitrage pricing model as generalized by Cox et al. (1985).

MONEY MARKETS. The economic role played by the money market is more difficult to establish than that of the markets for capital and credit, in part because 'money' is not straightforward to define. The standard practice among non-economists, which often creates unexpected confusion for economists, is to refer to 'money' indistinguishably from short-term forms of credit, so that 'the money market' is just that segment of the credit market devoted to issuing and trading short-term debts, and 'money rates' are correspondingly the stated nominal interest rates on money market instruments thus defined. By contrast, economists have traditionally viewed money as distinct from credit, and have given money a central place in macroeconomic analysis which typically appeals to some form of aggregation argument to assume away the existence of credit altogether.

Two lines of thinking, neither necessarily easy to convert into an operational definition of 'money', have traditionally dominated economists' thinking on the subject. One has emphasized the role of money as a form of wealth (in traditional language, a store of value). The problem then is to define which forms of wealth constitute money and which do not. The emphasis in drawing such distinctions has typically rested on the safety and liquidity of the asset, in the sense of its relative freedom from default risk and its ease of conversion, at a predetermined rate of exchange, into whatever is the economy's means of payment. Although the general idea behind such thinking is clear enough, in actually existing economies it has proved impossible to draw the requisite line between money and non-money assets without imposing arbitrary distinctions. Typically, the more highly developed an economy's financial system, the greater is the need for such arbitrary judgements.

The alternative line of traditional thinking has been to emphasize the role of money in effecting transactions, and hence to define as money just those assets that are acceptable as means of payment. One problem here is that both legalities and common business practice sometimes make ambiguous what constitutes an acceptable means of payment. Indeed, in highly developed financial systems an increasing volume of transactions is effected without requiring the actual holding of any specific asset identifiable as money. Moreover, this approach leads to further difficulties, even apart from definitional problems. If money is used as one side of every transaction in the respective markets for all goods and services and all other assets, then the meaning of 'the money market' is unclear except in the sense that there exists a demand for money equal to the net supply of all other tradeables, and, correspondingly, a supply of money equal to the net demand for all other tradeables.

Under either the store-of-value approach or the means-of-payment approach, the central role conventionally attached to the money market in modern macroeconomic analysis primarily reflects the standard institutional structure within which monetary policy consists in the first instance of actions by the central bank that, either directly or through the financial intermediary system, affect the supply of money however it is defined. Market equilibrium then requires a corresponding change in the demand for money – that is, in the demand for highly liquid assets or for the means of payment, depending on the definitional approach assumed. In either case, the required shift in the public's aggregate portfolio demands presumably requires, in turn, a shift in the structure of expected asset returns, with consequent implications for non-financial economic activity under any of a variety of familiar theories of consumption, investment and production behaviour.

The specifics of this process, however, depend crucially on the definition of 'money'. Under the approach that identifies money with assets meeting sufficient criteria of safety and liquidity, the demand for money is merely a by-product of the theory of risk-averse portfolio selection under uncertainty. Under this approach, what is more difficult is to specify the process connecting the supply of money, so defined, to the central bank's actions. To the extent that the supply of assets defined as money consists largely of the liabilities of depository intermediaries, and to the extent that the relevant institutional arrangements require intermediaries to hold reserves against their liabilities, the connection between money supply and central bank actions that provide or withdraw intermediary reserves is apparent enough. When there is no reserve requirement, however – because either specific kinds of intermediary institutions or specific kinds of intermediary liabilities face no reserve requirement – the connection between monetary policy actions and money supply is more problematic.

The situation under the approach that identifies money with the means of payment is roughly the opposite. Because more economies' means of payment consist largely of the direct liabilities of the central bank and the reservable liabilities of specific intermediaries, connecting the supply of money to central bank reserve actions is relatively straightforward. What is more difficult under this approach is establishing the link to the demand for money thus defined, and hence ultimately the effect on non-financial economic activity. When assets other than the means of payment also provide safety and liquidity, the standard theory of portfolio selection no longer suffices to determine the demand for the means of payment itself. Economic analysis of this problem has largely developed along the inventory-theoretic lines laid out initially by Baumol (1952) and Tobin (1956) and by Miller and Orr (1966). Especially in modern circumstances that readily permit transactions on a credit basis, however, the relevance of such 'cash in advance' models is unclear.

Regardless of the specific conceptual approach taken to define money, it is clear that the deposit liabilities of financial intermediaries bulk large in individuals' direct wealth holding in most actual economies, so that economists' study of money markets has heavily focused on the role of intermediaries and intermediation. The reasons for the prominent position of intermediary liabilities in individuals' direct wealth-holdings are not difficult to understand. The deposits of banks and similar intermediaries typically provide the most convenient means of settling most transactions, and the asset transformation provided by financial intermediations makes it attractive for most individuals to participate in the market for many kinds of assets via intermediaries rather than directly.

As a result, 'the money market' in most actual economies consists largely of financial intermediaries on one side and both individuals and business firms on the other. Here, as elsewhere in modern economies, the profusion of differentiated financial products is vast. Money market assets in this sense consist of checkable and non-checkable deposits, demand deposits and deposits for stated terms ranging from a few days to many months, deposits with fixed (nominal) returns and variable returns, and so on. Moreover, in the eyes of most market participants, short-term credit market claims that are close portfolio substitutes for inter-mediary deposits (commercial paper) are money market instruments too.

BIBLIOGRAPHY
Arrow, K.J. 1964. The role of securities in the optimal allocation of risk-bearing. *Review of Economic Studies* 31, April, 91–6.
Arrow, K.J. 1965. *Aspects of the Theory of Risk-Bearing.* Helsinki: The Yrjo Jahnsson Foundation.
Baumol, W.J. 1952. The transactions demand for cash: an inventory theoretic approach. *Quarterly Journal of Economics* 66, November, 545–56.
Black, F. and Scholes, M. 1973. The pricing of options and corporate liabilities. *Journal of Political Economy* 81(3), May–June, 637–54.
Brainard, W.C. and Tobin, J. 1968. Pitfalls in financial model-building. *American Economic Review, Papers and Proceedings* 58, May, 99–122.
Cox, J.C., Ingersoll, J.E., Jr. and Ross S.A. 1985. A theory of the term structure of interest rates. *Econometrica* 53(2), March, 385–407.

Debreu, G. 1959. *Theory of Value: An Axiomatic Analysis of Economic Equilibrium.* New Haven: Yale University Press.

Fisher, I. 1930. *The Theory of Interest.* New York: The Macmillan Company.

Grossman, S.J. 1976. On the efficiency of competitive stock markets when traders have diverse information. *Journal of Finance* 31(2), May, 573–85.

Hicks, J.R. 1939. *Value and Capital.* Oxford: Oxford University Press; 2nd edn, New York: Oxford University Press, 1946.

Keynes, J.M. 1936. *The General Theory of Employment, Interest and Money.* London: Macmillan; New York: Harcourt, Brace & World.

Lintner, J. 1965. The valuation of risk assets and the selection of risky investments in stock portfolios and capital budgets. *Review of Economics and Statistics* 47, February, 13–37.

Lintner, J. 1969. The aggregation of investors' diverse judgements and preferences in purely competitive securities markets. *Journal of Financial and Quantitative Analysis* 4(4), December, 347–400.

Markowitz, H. 1952. Portfolio selection. *Journal of Finance* 7, March, 77–91.

Merton, R.C. 1973a. Theory of rational option pricing. *Bell Journal of Economics and Management Science* 4(1), Spring, 141–83.

Merton, R.C. 1973b. An intertemporal capital asset pricing model. *Econometrica* 41(5), September, 867–87.

Miller, M.H. and Orr, D. 1966. A model of the demand for money by firms. *Quarterly Journal of Economics* 80, August, 413–35.

Modigliani, F. and Miller, M.H. 1958. The cost of capital, corporation finance, and the theory of investment. *American Economic Review* 48, June, 261–97.

Pratt, J.W. 1964. Risk aversion in the small and in the large. *Econometrica* 32, January–April, 122–36.

Ross, S.A. 1976. The arbitrage theory of capital asset pricing. *Journal of Economic Theory* 13(3), December, 341–60.

Sharpe, W.F. 1964. Capital asset prices: a theory of market equilibrium under conditions of risk. *Journal of Finance* 19, September, 425–42.

Shiller, R.J. 1984. Stock prices and social dynamics. *Brookings Papers on Economic Activity* No. 2, 457–510.

Stiglitz, J.E. 1970. A consumption-oriented theory of the demand for financial assets and the term structure of interest rates. *Review of Economic Studies* 37(3), July, 321–51.

Tobin, J. 1956. The interest-elasticity of transactions demand for cash. *Review of Economics and Statistics* 38, August, 241–7.

Tobin, J. 1958. Liquidity preference as behaviour toward risk. *Review of Economic Studies* 25, February, 65–86.

Central Banking

CHARLES GOODHART

When the first government-sponsored banks were founded in Europe, for example the Swedish Riksbank (1668) and the Bank of England (1694), there was no intention that these should undertake the functions of a modern central bank, that is, discretionary monetary management and the regulation and support, for example through the 'lender of last resort' function, of the banking system. Instead, the initial impetus was much more basic, generally relating to the financial advantages a government felt that it could obtain from the support of such a bank, whether a State bank, as in the case of the Prussian State Bank, or a private bank, like the Bank of England. This naturally involved some favouritism, often supported by legislation, by the government for this particular bank in return for its financial assistance. The favoured bank was often granted a monopoly advantage, for example over the note issue in certain areas, or as the sole chartered joint stock bank in the country; and this may have had the effect in some countries, such as England and France, of weakening the early development of other commercial banks, so that, at the outset, the foundation of a government-sponsored bank was a mixed blessing for the development of banking in such countries.

Other government-sponsored central banks, for example the Austrian National Bank founded in 1816 at the end of the Napoleonic wars, were established to restore the value of the national currency, notably after its value had been wrecked by government over-issue in the course of war finance. Others were founded partly in order to unify what had become in some cases (e.g. in Germany, Switzerland and Italy) a somewhat chaotic system of note issue; to centralize, manage and protect the metallic reserve of the country, and to facilitate and improve the payments system. While these latter functions were seen as having beneficial economic consequences, the ability to share in the profits of seignorage and greater centralized control over the metallic (gold) reserve had obvious political attractions as well. In any case, prior to 1900, most economic analysis of the role of Central Banks concentrated on the question of whether the note issue, and the gold reserves of the country, should be centralized, and, if and when centralized, how controlled by the Central Bank.

Once such government-sponsored banks had been established, however, their central position within the system, their 'political' power as the government's bank, their command (usually) over the bulk of the nation's specie reserve, and, most important, their ability to provide extra cash, notes, by rediscounting commercial bills made them become the bankers' bank: commercial banks would not only hold a large proportion of their own (cash) reserves as balances with the Central Bank, but also rely on it to provide extra liquidity when in difficulties. In several early cases, such as the Bank of England's, this latter role had not been initially intended; in most cases of Central Banks founded in the 19th century the full ramifications of their role as bankers' bank were only dimly perceived at the time of their founding; these functions developed naturally from the context of relationships within the system.

Initially, indeed, the role of Central Banks in maintaining the convertibility of their notes, into gold or silver, was not different, nor seen as different, from that of any other bank. Their privileged legal position, as banker to the government and in note issue, then led naturally to a degree of centralization of reserves within the banking system in the hands of the Central Bank, so it became a banker's bank. It was the responsibility that this position was found to entail, in the process of historical experience, that led Central Banks to develop their particular art of discretionary monetary management and overall support and responsibility for the health of the banking system at large.

This management has had two (interrelated) aspects: a macro function and responsibility relating to overall monetary conditions in the economy, and a micro function relating to the health and wellbeing of the (individual) members of the banking system. Until 1914 such management largely consisted of seeking to reconcile the need to maintain the chosen metallic standard, usually the gold standard, on the one hand with concern for the stability and health of the financial system, and beyond that of the economy more widely, on the other. Thereafter, as the various pressures of the 20th century disrupted first the gold standard and thereafter the Bretton Woods' system of pegged exchange rates, the macro-economic objectives of monetary management have altered and evolved. Yet at all times concern for the health of the banking system has remained a paramount concern for the Central Bank.

This concern for the wellbeing of the banking system as a whole was, at least for those Central Banks founded in the 19th century or before, largely an evolutionary development and not one that they had been programmed to undertake from the start. Indeed in England the legislative framework of the 1844 Bank Charter Act was to prove something of a barrier to the development of the micro-supervisory functions of the Bank: for this Act divided the Bank into two Departments – the Issue Department, whose note issuing function was to be closely constrained by strict rules (to maintain the Gold Standard); and the Banking Department, which was intended to behave simply as an ordinary competitive, profit-maximizing, commercial bank.

Nevertheless the micro-functions of a Central Bank in providing a central (and therefore economical) source of reserves and liquidity to other banks, and hence both a degree of insurance and supervision, cannot be undertaken effectively by a commercial competitor, basically because of competitive conflicts of interest. The advantages of having some institutions providing such micro-Central Banking functions are such that even in those various countries initially without Central Banks there was some natural tendency towards their being provided, after a fashion, from within the private sector – for example by clearing houses in the United States, or by a large commercial bank providing quasi-Central Bank functions. Nevertheless, because of conflicts of interest, such functions were not, and cannot be, adequately provided by competing commercial institutions.

Some Central Banks, mainly those that began their existence under private ownership (e.g. the Bank of England, the Banca d'Italia, but also some that were subject to political oversight, e.g. the Banque de France, the Commonwealth Bank of Australia), retained for a considerable time a large role in ordinary commercial banking. It was, however, the metamorphosis from their involvement in commercial banking, as a competitive, profit-maximizing role that marked the true emergence in those countries of proper Central Banking. This metamorphosis occurred naturally, but with considerable difficulty in England, the difficulty arising in part from the existence of property rights in the profits of the Bank, and in part from concern about the moral hazards of the Bank consciously adopting a supervisory role (as evidenced in the arguments between Bagehot and Hankey, reported in Bagehot's *Lombard Street*).

Indeed, with the Central Bank coming to represent the ultimate source of liquidity and support to the individual commercial banks, this micro-function does bring with it naturally a degree of 'insurance'. Such insurance, in turn, does involve some risk of moral hazard: commercial banks, believing that they will be protected by their Central Bank from the consequences of their own follies, may adopt too risky and careless strategies. That concern has led Central Banks to become involved – to varying extents – in the regulation and supervision of their banking systems. In all countries the Central Bank plays *some* role in the support of its commercial banks, because it alone can provide 'lender of last resort' assistance; but the extent to which it shares the insurance, supervisory, and regulatory function, both for the banking system more narrowly and for the wider financial system, with government and private bodies set up specifically for such purposes, varies from country to country. With structural changes apparently breaking down the barriers between the banking system on the one hand and other financial intermediaries on the other in the course of the 1970s and 1980s, the question of the division of responsibility of the Central Bank on the one hand, and other supervisory government bodies and insurance agencies on the other, has become topical.

The Central Bank's more glamorous function is the conduct of macro-monetary policy. The main objective of this function in normal times has been to maintain the (internal and external) value, and reputation, of the national currency. At times of national crisis, notably during wars, however, the financial needs of the State have generally overridden the desire for financial stability, with the conduct of monetary policy then being mainly determined by questions of how the necessary finance can most effectively be mobilized to support the urgent needs of the State. Apart from such national emergencies, the desire to achieve financial stability became synonymous, during the 19th and early 20th centuries, with adherence to the Gold Standard.

The break-down of the Gold Standard in the interwar period left many countries with high unemployment, a falling price level, and international trade and capital flows increasingly constrained by direct controls. In this context it became widely felt that monetary policy was relatively powerless: once interest rates were brought down to low levels, there was little more, it was argued, that monetary policy could do. The management of aggregate demand would, therefore, have to be left to fiscal policy, with direct controls of various kinds used to constrain subsequent inflationary pressures (e.g. in World War II) and international disequilibria.

The erosion of direct controls in the late 1940s and 1950s, and the establishment of the Bretton Woods system of pegged, but adjustable, exchange rates, meant that Central Banks generally were able, during the 1950s and 1960s, to return to their accustomed policy of maintaining the value of their national currencies by seeking to hold these pegged to the US dollar and thence, until the late 1960s, to gold. With the US dollar at the centre of the world financial system, the Federal Reserve System had a different and special responsibility, to maintain the internal stability of the $. After many successful years, US monetary policy and the Bretton Woods system were overwhelmed by pressures arising from the Vietnam War, political strains within the Western Alliance, and, finally, the 1973 Oil Shock.

Up till then, most Western governments had sought to maximize employment and growth, along broadly Keynesian lines, subject to trying to maintain the exchange rate peg. With that peg no longer in place after 1972, governments then placed various emphases on supporting full employment on the one hand and monetary constraint on the other. In the event, however, there seemed no evidence that countries with more expansionary monetary policies, and thence more inflation, did achieve notably higher rates of growth or employment. This experience led directly to the adoption of 'pragmatic' monetarist policies by the Central Banks of the main industrialized countries, whereby they sought to achieve publicly announced, steadily declining rates of growth for certain domestic monetary intermediate target aggregates.

This policy shift has, in turn, had a chequered history. Monetarists claim that the commitment to, and technical execution of, monetary targetting has been unsatisfactory. Keynesians claim that it has involved no more than simple deflation, with the policy's success in reducing inflation in the early 1980s tarnished by a dramatic growth in unemployment and a poor rate of growth of real output. Moreover, the conduct of policy has been complicated by a generally growing instability, partly induced by structural change, in the relationship between money and nominal incomes, an unstable velocity of money; and also by serious and persistent volatility in exchange rates and interest rates, often leaving these seemingly way out-of-line with economic fundamentals.

As of 1985, it seems difficult to see how a fully international system of pegged exchange rates could be re-established, though this would provide the traditional, and simplest, milieu for Central Bank policy. (This, though, would still allow regional groupings of countries to seek to maintain a stable exchange rate system between themselves, such as the European Monetary System, generally based on a central key currency within the group). On the other hand, previous enthusiasm for rules, and for fixed targets for monetary growth, is dissipating, partly as the evolving structure of the financial system once again brings into question the appropriate definition, role, and essential properties, of money and banks. So for the moment, there seems no valid alternative to a discretionary conduct of monetary policy, with an eye not only both to monetary and exchange rate developments, but also to the broader evolution of the economy.

BIBLIOGRAPHY

Classical

Bagehot, W. 1873. *Lombard Street*. London: Henry S. King. Reprint of the 1915 edn, New York: Arno Press, 1969.

Fetter, F. 1965. *Development of British Monetary Orthodoxy, 1797–1875*. Cambridge, Mass.: Harvard University Press.

Thornton, H. 1802. *An Inquiry into the Nature and Effects of the Paper Credit of Great Britain*. London: Hatchard.

Evolution

Goodhart, C.A.E. 1985. *The Evolution of Central Banks*. ICERD Monograph, London School of Economics.

Hawtrey, R.G. 1932. *The Art of Central Banking*. London: Longmans.

Sayers, R. 1957. *Central Banking after Bagehot*. Oxford: Clarendon Press.

Smith, V. 1936. *The Rationale of Central Banking*. London: P.S. King & Son.

Timberlake, R., Jr. 1978. *The Origins of Central Banking in the United States*. Cambridge, Mass.: Harvard University Press.

US National Monetary Commission. 1910–11. (Twenty volumes of papers and original material on banking and Central Banking in all major industrialized countries). Washington, DC: Government Printing Office.

Veit, O. 1969. *Grundriss der Wahrungspolitik*. 3rd edn, Frankfurt: Fritz Knapp Verlag.

Contemporary

Bank of England. 1984. *The Development and Operation of Monetary Policy, 1960–1983*. Oxford: Clarendon Press.

Board of Governors of the Federal Reserve System. *The Federal Reserve System: Purposes and Functions*. Washington, DC: Federal Reserve Board.

Duwendag, D. et al. 1985. *Geldtheorie und Geldpolitik*. 3rd edn, Cologne: Bund-Verlag.

Federal Reserve Bank of New York. 1983. *Central Bank Views on Monetary Targeting*. New York: Federal Reserve Bank of New York.

Meek, P. 1982. *US Monetary Policy and Financial Markets*. New York: Federal Reserve Bank of New York.

Woolley, J. 1984. *Monetary Politics*. Cambridge: Cambridge University Press.

Cheap Money

SUSAN HOWSON

'By a long-established convention the rate of discount or the short-term rate of interest is called the "price" of money, so that "dear money" means a high rate, "cheap money" a low rate' (Hawtrey, 1938, p. 28n). By the time Hawtrey was writing, however, the meaning of cheap money was changing, as a result of changes in both economic theory and monetary policy, to include low *long*-term interest rates. In the late 20th century money has not often been cheap in either sense, so that cheap or cheaper money now usually refers simply to a fall in (real) interest rates.

In the late 19th century and early 20th century, 'cheap money' meant low money market rates of interest, the rate at which commercial bills could be discounted. Since in England these rates were strongly influenced by the Bank of England's rediscount rate (Bank Rate), which was generally higher than the market rate, a 3% Bank Rate could be regarded as the upper limit of cheap money (Hawtrey, 1938, p. 133). On this criterion there was cheap money for varying periods of time in all but nine years from 1844 to 1914 (Palgrave, 1903, p. 98; Hawtrey, 1938, Appendix I). The Bank of England, committed to maintaining the pound sterling on the gold standard with the aid of a relatively small gold reserve, varied its rate very frequently, so that these periods were of short duration, except for the spells of cheap money that followed upon the dear money of financial crises. In 1844–5, 1848–53, 1858–60, 1867–8, 1876–7, 1893–6, and 1908–9 Bank Rate was usually *below* 3% for a year or more. The most prolonged of these spells, occurring in the last years of the 'Great Depression', was permitted by a large inflow of American gold into Britain, at a time of increasing gold production, falling prices, and high unemployment (Hawtrey, 1938, pp. 110–12; Sayers, 1936, ch. 1; Sayers, 1976, p. 51). Bank Rate stood at 2% for $2\frac{1}{2}$ years, the longest period at its historical minimum before the 1930s. In the previous decade, though Bank Rate was more variable, interest rates had also been generally low. As they were to do again in the 1930s, the British government took advantage of falling long-term rates to reduce the interest paid on a large proportion of outstanding national debt: the famous 'Goschen conversion' of 1888 reduced the interest rate on 3% Consols to $2\frac{3}{4}$% until 1903 and $2\frac{1}{2}$% thereafter (Clapham, 1944, Vol. 2, pp. 318–21; Spinner, 1973, pp. 139–503; G.J. Goschen was Chancellor of the Exchequer).

After World War I Bank Rate changes were less frequent than before 1914, partly because a high Bank Rate was now associated with high unemployment (Committee on Currency and Foreign Exchanges after the War, 1918; Moggridge, 1972; Sayers, 1976, chs 6, 7 and 9; Howson, 1975, chs 2 and 3). At the same time Bank Rate was generally higher than before the war, having been raised and kept high to curb the postwar boom in 1919–20, and again as part of the attempts to return to and stay on the gold standard at prewar parity. It was 3% only twice in 1919–31, in 1922–3 and 1930–31, and $2\frac{1}{2}$% once, for 10 weeks in mid-1931. By the time Britain left the gold standard there was a widespread desire for 'cheap money', for the sake of both the economy and the budget. Developments in monetary theory in these years (for example, Robertson, 1926; Keynes, 1930) implied that low *long-term* interest rates would be needed to increase investment in fixed capital and hence income and employment, rather than just low short-term rates to boost investment in working capital (inventories) as in the older views of, say, Hawtrey (1913, 1919, 1938). In 1932 the British government embarked upon a 'cheap money policy' to provide a spell of low long-term rates as well as to enable the conversion of high interest bearing government debt contracted during World War I. This also involved the establishment of an Exchange Equalization Account (EEA) to manage the exchange rate and provide sterilization of the effects of reserve changes on the monetary base. The announcement of the conversion of £2000 million 5% War Loan 1929–47 to $3\frac{1}{2}$% War Loan 1952 or after was made on 30 June 1932, when Bank Rate was reduced to 2%. Apart from a short-lived rise at the outbreak of World War II, Bank Rate remained at 2% until 7 November 1951 (Nevin, 1953 and 1955, ch. 3; Howson, 1975, ch. 4, and 1980; Sayers, 1976, ch. 18).

Similar, although more complex, developments in monetary theory and policy had been taking place in the USA in the interwar years (Friedman and Schwartz, 1963, chs 6–9; Chandler, 1971, ch. 8). On both sides of the Atlantic the persistence of low interest rates and high unemployment in the 1930s induced considerable scepticism as to the efficacy of cheap money (however defined) as well as increased confidence in the monetary authorities' power to bring it about (Sayers, 1951 and 1957, chs 3 and 6; Keynes, 1936; Wallich, 1946; Morgan, 1944). The decisions to maintain cheap money during and immediately after World War II reflected the scepticism, the confidence, and the desire to avoid the high borrowing costs of World War I. Monetary policy became a matter of issuing sufficient quantities of suitable debt instruments to satisfy the public's asset preferences and allowing the money supply to expand to whatever extent was necessary to maintain the fixed pattern of interest rates (Sayers, 1956, chs 5 and 7; Friedman and Schwartz, 1963, ch. 10; Chandler, 1971, pp. 346–8). Interest rates ranged from $\frac{3}{8}$% on Treasury bills to $2\frac{1}{2}$% for long-term government bonds in the USA, and from 1% on Treasury bills to 3% for long-term government bonds in the UK. In

Britain after the war, Hugh Dalton, Chancellor of the Exchequer 1945–7, also tried to go further and pursue a 'cheaper money policy', specifically to lower interest rates for government debt by $\frac{1}{2}\%$ all the way along the yield curve. There was soon a reaction against the monetization of debt implied in these policies, and in 1947 official support of the markets for government securities was weakened in both countries, although the cheap money policies were not finally abandoned until 1951 (Paish, 1947; Sayers, 1957, ch. 2; Friedman and Schwartz, 1963, ch. 11; Dow, 1964, chs 2 and 9; Howson, 1985).

Monetary theory and practice have changed the concept of 'cheap money' again since 1951. In a more inflationary world the importance of controlling the money supply has been recognized – in the 1970s if not before – as have the inadequacies of interest rates (short or long) as an indicator of monetary conditions. When prices are rising rapidly, money can be 'cheap' even if nominal interest rates are at historically high levels. The stance of a central bank's monetary policy is now more often represented by the rate of the growth of the money supply, rather than by interest rates.

BIBLIOGRAPHY

Chandler, L.V. 1971. *American Monetary Policy 1928–1941*. New York: Harper & Row.
Clapham, J.H. 1944. *The Bank of England*. Cambridge: Cambridge University Press.
Committee on Currency and Foreign Exchanges after the War 1918. *First Interim Report*, Cd. 9182, London: HMSO.
Dow, J.C.R. 1964. *The Management of the British Economy 1945–60*. Cambridge: Cambridge University Press.
Friedman, M. and Schwartz, A.J. 1963. *A Monetary History of the United States 1867–1960*. Princeton: Princeton University Press.
Hawtrey, R.G. 1913. *Good and Bad Trade*. London: Constable & Co.
Hawtrey, R.G. 1919. *Currency and Credit*. London: Longmans, Green & Co.
Hawtrey, R.G. 1938. *A Century of Bank Rate*. London: Longmans, Green & Co.
Howson, S. 1975. *Domestic Monetary Management in Britain 1919–38*. Cambridge: Cambridge University Press.
Howson, S. 1980. *Sterling's Managed Float: The Operations of the Exchange Equalisation Account, 1932–39*. Princeton Studies in International Finance No. 46, November.
Howson, S. 1985. The origins of cheaper money, 1946–47. Economic History Workshop, University of Toronto.
Keynes, J.M. 1930. *A Treatise on Money*. London: Macmillan for the Royal Economic Society, 1971; New York: St. Martin's Press, 1971.
Keynes, J.M. 1936. *The General Theory of Employment, Interest and Money*. London: Macmillan for the Royal Economic Society, 1973; New York: Harcourt, Brace.
Moggridge, D.E. 1972. *British Monetary Policy 1924–1931*. Cambridge: Cambridge University Press.
Morgan, E.V. 1944. The future of interest rates. *Economic Journal* 54, December, 340–51.
Nevin, E. 1953. The origins of cheap money, 1931–32. *Economica* 20, February, 24–37.
Nevin, E. 1955. *The Mechanism of Cheap Money*. Cardiff: University of Wales Press.
Paish, F.W. 1947. Cheap money policy. *Economica* 14, August, 167–79.
Palgrave, R.H.I. 1903. *Bank Rate and the Money Market*. London: John Murray.
Robertson, D.H. 1926. *Banking Policy and the Price Level*. London: P.S. King & Son.
Sayers, R.S. 1936. *Bank of England Operations 1890–1914*. London: P.S. King & Son.

Sayers, R.S. 1951. The rate of interest as a weapon of economic policy. In *Oxford Studies in the Price Mechanism*, ed. T. Wilson and P.W.S. Andrews, Oxford: Clarendon Press.

Sayers, R.S. 1956. *Financial Policy 1939–45*. London: HMSO.

Sayers, R.S. 1957. *Central Banking after Bagehot*. Oxford: Clarendon Press.

Sayers, R.S. 1976. *The Bank of England 1891–1966*. Cambridge: Cambridge University Press.

Spinner, T.J., Jr. 1973. *George Joachim Goschen*. Cambridge: Cambridge University Press.

Wallich, H.C. 1946. The changing significance of the interest rate. *American Economic Review* 36, December, 761–87.

Credit

ERNST BALTENSPERGER

While the volume and complexity of credit transactions has grown immensely over the centuries, the act of credit extension and debt creation, or lending and borrowing, as such, is probably as old as human society. To extend credit means to transfer the property rights on a given object (e.g. a sum of money) in exchange for a claim on specified objects (e.g. certain sums of money) at specified points of time in the future. To take credit, or go into debt, is the other side of the coin. Credit and debt have always posed some special problems of understanding for economists, beyond those associated with the production, trade and consumption of 'ordinary' goods like wheat or cloth, or factors of production like labour services. There exists, of course, a wide array of different forms of credit contracts in today's economies. Classifications are customary; for example, according to types of debtors or creditors (domestic or foreign, public or private, etc.), length of contract duration, type of security put forward by the debtor, or the use of the loan by the borrower. However, this essay will attempt to concentrate on the essential features common to all or most groups of credit transactions, rather than enumerate and describe the differences between specific types and forms of credit.

THE ECONOMIC FUNCTION OF CREDIT. The credit market is essentially a market for intertemporal exchange. Something is given up in the present in exchange for something else in the future – or vice versa, if seen from the point of view of the borrower. The future 'repayment' typically includes a compensation in excess of the original 'payment'; that is, interest. The rate of interest represents the relative price in the market for intertemporal exchange.

The possibility of intertemporal exchanges allows market participants the realization of utility gains, just as voluntary exchange in general is mutually advantageous. The basic reason for this is that individuals are not normally indifferent about the distribution of their consumption over time but care about it. This notion of 'time preference' – used here in its most general and neutral sense, which does not necessarily imply a preference for present over future consumption – was first clearly formulated by Fisher (1930), who viewed *dated* consumption possibilities as the consumer's objects of choice; that is, as separate arguments of his utility function. This allowed the application of the standard tools of microeconomic analysis to problems of inter-temporal choice and proved to be the clue to a clear understanding and analytical treatment of credit and debt. Fisher's treatment still captures the essence of credit and the function it performs in the economy. The given time profile of income (endowments) faced by individuals will often not represent their most desired distribution of the given total consumption over time. The existence of a credit market (the possibility of intertemporal exchange) allows them to transfer a given stream into a preferred stream – either by anticipating future consumption via borrowing ('deficit units') or by transferring consumption into the future via saving and lending ('surplus units'). Transactions of this kind can be mutually advantageous, due to differences in endowments and/or differences in preferences between individuals.

Given real investment opportunities (capital accumulation), the existence of a credit market in general also allows the choice of superior investment decisions, ultimately leading to a higher level of utility. Thus the presence of a credit market, like any other market, permits a more efficient allocation of inputs and outputs, especially with respect to time.

This Fisherian view of the credit market makes clear that it constitutes part of the 'real' economy. That is, it performs a 'real' function by helping to determine the 'real' equilibrium of the economy and the levels of satisfaction reached by its members. It also makes clear that credit can play an important role even in a pure exchange economy with no production and capital formation, given sufficient divergence in individual tastes and/or endowments. On the other hand, production and capital formulation can, in principle, take place without credit. Resources can be set aside and invested directly by their owners (the savers). If the owners have no taste or ability for administering these investments, they can, in principle, hire labour (managers) to perform this job (wage, or equity, contracts instead of credit, or debt, contracts). That is, alternative contractual arrangements allowing capital formation and production are available. Of course, credit (debt) contracts, on the one hand, and work (equity) contracts, on the other hand, differ with respect to the way in which risks are shared between the parties involved and with respect to their incentive effects, and a credit market will in general, as already pointed out, be helpful in achieving an efficient allocation of resources and, ultimately, consumption.

CREDIT AND BUDGET CONSTRAINTS. A basic question arising with any credit transaction concerns the mechanisms which ensure that the debtor will meet his future payment obligations. As soon as he has obtained his credit, the borrower has, in principle, a strong incentive to 'run off'. This is linked to the question of the appropriate formulation of budget constraints in the presence of credit. What limits credit demand and present consumption (and the incentive to cheat)? Obviously, a credit market can come into existence and survive only if there exist disciplining mechanisms which serve to prevent, or at least severely restrict, dishonest behaviour. Penalties of one sort or another must be in force, be it through legal provisions (bankruptcy laws), social stigmatization or simply the exclusion from, or discrimination in, future credit market participation.

The appropriate formulation of intertemporal budget constraints, in view of a credit market, is comparatively unproblematic (1) as long as the future payment capacity of a potential debtor (his future income stream) is known with perfect certainty, and (2) if, due to social institutions guaranteeing complete enforceability, there is complete confidence in his willingness to fulfil his future payment obligations, as long as he objectively can. Under these conditions, the relevant magnitude serving to constrain an individual's lifetime consumption obviously is the present value of his lifetime income stream.

Matters are more complicated if the future is not perfectly foreseeable and/or contract enforceability is less than perfect. Unless credit extension is limited to the most pessimistic estimate of the debtor's future income or willingness to repay, there is then a possibility of default. Normally, creditors are willing to accept a certain positive probability of default in exchange for compensation in the form of a higher contractual rate of interest (a risk premium). However, the willingness to extend credit is affected, of course, by the possibility of default and its dependence on the amount of credit extended. Given a finite repayment capacity (finite future income), an increasing level of indebtedness increases the probability of default in two ways. First, for 'external' reasons: the possibility that the future payment obligations exceed the (uncertain) future repayment ability increases with increasing debt. Second, for 'internal' reasons (moral hazard): the incentive to 'run off' after credit has been obtained increases with an increasing repayment obligation; similarly, the incentive to produce future income may be lowered, since in case of partial default the debtor does not benefit from his own efforts. Given a finite repayment capacity, in fact, a point will be reached, sooner or later, where no increase in the contractual interest rate (no risk premium) can compensate the lender for the extra risk of non-payment resulting from a further increase in the level of debt, thus creating an absolute limit to the supply of credit to individuals. This was pointed out by Hodgman (1960), and has led him to speak of credit rationing.

An adequate level of trust in the implicit and explicit promises associated with outstanding debt contracts is an important prerequisite of a smoothly and efficiently operating financial system. Due to the intangible nature of 'trust', the danger of financial crises occuring whenever it is somehow weakened has always been inherent in a credit system. Institutional arrangements, such as a lender of last resort (usually the central bank) or an insurance system of one sort or another (e.g. deposit insurance) are important elements affecting the probability of such occurrences. They are traditionally seen as devices serving to eliminate, or at least contain, the risk of adverse chain reactions. Of course, one danger of institutions of this sort is that they may easily create a moral hazard problem themselves, by lowering the private costs of illiquidity and payment difficulties and thus reducing the private incentives to avoid excessive risks.

IMPERFECT INFORMATION AND THE CREDIT MARKET. In recent years the fact has been stressed that asymmetric information between market participants, and the resultant problems of adverse incentives and adverse selection, can lead to the breakdown of certain markets (incomplete markets) and to unusual types of market equilibria. These include equilibria with non-price rationing; that is, situations where the interest rate on a loan category is set by the lender at a given level and maintained there, even if there exists an excess demand for loans at this rate (Stiglitz and Weiss, 1981). Starting from the notion that the lender, due to asymmetric information, must, to a certain degree, lump heterogeneous loan customers together, the basic idea is that an increase in the loan rate (applying equally to all customers) will induce 'good' (high quality) customers to leave and 'bad' (low quality) customers to stay (adverse selection), or that individual customers will be induced by the higher loan rate to choose riskier investment projects (moral hazard). In either case, the average quality of loan customers is reduced. Thus an increase in the loan rate here has, in addition to its usual positive effect on lender return, a negative effect which may possibly dominate the former. If this is the case, it is not in the interest of the lender to raise the loan rate, even in the face of an excess demand for loans. The loan rate has then lost its traditional allocative role of bringing in line supply and demand, and instead serves as a device to limit the damages resulting from adverse selection and adverse incentives. Funds then must be allocated to customers in some other way.

This problem disappears again if creditors are able to overcome the underlying information asymmetries and identify different quality customers. Then they can offer different types of contracts (combinations of credit volumes and interest rates, possibly also of collateral levels and equity requirements) to different types of customers. One possibility which has been discussed, in analogy to similar problems in insurance and labour markets, concerns the feasibility of self-selection mechanisms. Under certain conditions it may be possible, by exploring the differences in preferences between high and low quality customers, to offer different types of contracts, so that each potential debtor has an incentive to choose of his own will the appropriate offer designed for his quality class. Another possibility concerns the ability of lenders to overcome the information deficiencies underlying the problems of adverse selection and incentives directly through information acquisition technologies of various sorts (direct screening and policing). Since this kind of information is customer-specific, this can encourage the development of long-term customer relationships. The empirical importance of the information-asymmetry models of credit-market behaviour referred to above thus will ultimately have to be judged in view of the empirical weight of these alternative response possibilities.

CREDIT AND CREDIT INSTITUTIONS. The role of credit as such must be clearly separated from the economic role of credit institutions, such as banks, playing the role of specialized intermediaries in the credit market by buying and simultaneously selling credit instruments (of a different type and quality). Since the ultimate borrowers and lenders can, in principle, do business with each other directly, without the help of such an intermediary, the function of these middlemen must be viewed as separate from that of credit as such.

Two main functions of institutions of this kind can be distinguished. The first is the function of risk consolidation or transformation. By dealing with a large number of creditors and debtors acting, to a considerable extent, independently of each other, the bank can, by exploiting the law of large numbers, achieve a consolidation of risks. In a world of subjective risk aversion, or if risk implies 'objective' costs of one sort or another (costs of adjusting to certain unfavourable states of the world), such a risk consolidation represents a utility gain for the individuals concerned, and this is a marketable service offered by these institutions to the public. Thus existence of risk and uncertainty (imperfect information) is fundamental for this first function of credit institutions.

The second major function of these institutions is that of a broker in the credit markets. As such, they specialize in producing intertemporal exchange transactions and owe their existence to their ability to bring together creditors and debtors at lower costs than the latter can achieve in direct transactions themselves. Transactions and information costs ('market imperfections') in the credit market, including the cost of evaluating credit risks as an especially important example, are fundamental for the financial intermediary in this second function. To summarize: the existence and function of credit institutions is linked in an essential way to the presence of uncertainty, imperfect information, and transactions costs in the credit market. In the absence of these elements, financial intermediaries would have no raison d'être (while credit as such can still perform an important function). Government, when issuing government bonds, can be viewed as an intermediary in a similar sense.

Another, basically similar, 'institutional' question concerns the marketability, or negotiability, of credit contracts and the existence of 'secondary' markets where they can be traded on a regular basis. This requires certain characteristics. In particular, the market cannot be too small, it must be comparatively homogeneous, and it must be possible to assess the quality of the traded contracts at reasonably low costs. The advantage to the creditor of such a resale market is, of course, its contribution to the liquidity of these assets.

CREDIT IN MACROECONOMIC THEORY. In macroeconomic theory, the credit market has frequently played the role of the 'hidden' market eliminated from explicit consideration via application of Walras's Law. Although not explicitly appearing, a credit market (in the form of a bond market) is, however, present in most traditional macromodels. This was clearly brought out, in particular, by Patinkin (1956). Credit has traditionally played a prominent role in some specific issues of macroanalysis, nevertheless. In particular, this is the case with respect to the question of wealth effects. To what extent does credit creation represent creation of net wealth (and in turn affect aggregate demand)? This became one of the dominant issues in monetary theory and macroeconomics during the 1950s and 1960s. See, in particular, Patinkin (1956). Aggregate demand for goods (as well as for money and other assets) was seen as depending on aggregate net wealth of the private sector, in addition to income and relative prices, and all assets were examined with regard to the existence of an equivalent and offsetting liability within the private sector. For most financial assets, such an offsetting liability obviously exists. The exceptions, in the traditional view, were money and – with less confidence, because of the question of the capitalization of future tax liabilities required to finance interest payments – government bonds. As Niehans (1978, p. 91) has argued, this emphasis on net wealth was misplaced in the sense that it failed to appreciate that demand effects arising from individual components of wealth can be powerful even if net wealth effects are negligible or nonexistent. That is, it is not just net wealth which affects the demand for goods and assets; rather, the stocks of the various wealth components given at any point in time, and their difference from the corresponding long-run desired levels, determine the economy's attempts to build up or reduce these components over time.

Another macroeconomic area where the credit market has traditionally played an important role is money supply theory or, more generally, aggregate models of the financial sector of the economy (e.g. Brunner and Meltzer, 1968; Tobin, 1969). Credit markets and credit creation are seen in these models in the light of their relation to money markets and money creation and nominal (price level) control of the system. Financial markets here are typically disaggregated into markets for assets serving as media of exchange (government money and bank demand deposits) and other (non-money) assets, such as bonds and other similar credit instruments. Models of this type have helped considerably to clarify the role of central bank policies in controlling monetary aggregates and, ultimately, the price level. In particular, they have shown that, as long as the degree of substitutability between money and other assets is less than perfect, central bank control over a comparatively narrow monetary aggregate, such as base money, is sufficient for nominal control of the system (price level control), a large menu and volume of private credit nothwithstanding.

BIBLIOGRAPHY

Brunner, K. and Meltzer, A.H. 1968. Liquidity traps for money, bank credit, and interest rates. *Journal of Political Economy* 76, January/February, 1–37.

Fisher, I. 1930. *The Theory of Interest*. New York: Macmillan.

Hodgman, D.R. 1960. Credit risk and credit rationing. *Quarterly Journal of Economics* 74(2), May, 258–78.

Niehans, J. 1978. Metzler, wealth, and macroeconomics: a review. *Journal of Economic Literature* 16(1), March, 84–95.

Patinkin, D. 1956. *Money, Interest, and Prices*. Evanston: Row & Peterson; 2nd edn, New York: Harper & Row, 1965.

Stiglitz, J. and Weiss, A. 1981. Credit rationing in markets with imperfect information. *American Economic Review* 71(3), June, 393–410.

Tobin, J. 1969. A general equilibrium approach to monetary theory. *Journal of Money, Credit, and Banking* 1(1), February, 15–29.

Credit Rationing

DWIGHT M. JAFFEE

Credit rationing is a condition of loan markets in which the lender supply of funds is less than borrower demand at the quoted contract terms. Credit rationing was briefly discussed in the context of usury ceilings by Adam Smith (1776) and was an issue in the bullion and currency controversies of 19th-century England (see Viner, 1937, pp. 256–7). Later, in his *Treatise on Money*, Keynes (1930, I, pp. 212–13; II, pp. 364–7) stressed the 'fringe of unsatisfied borrowers' as a factor influencing the volume of investment. Credit rationing came to prominence in the United States after World War II as part of the 'availability doctrine', first developed by Roosa (1951) and others in the Federal Reserve System. The focus of the availability doctrine, like Keynes's, is that credit rationing influences investment independently of variations in interest rates or in other factors that shift the demand schedules of borrowers.

MICROECONOMIC CREDIT RATIONING THEORY. The equivalent of credit rationing does not occur in well-functioning markets for goods and services because both suppliers and rationed demanders have incentive to raise the price. The price of a loan consists of the interest rate and possibly the non-rate terms such as collateral requirements. For rationing to exist on a continuing basis in loan markets, therefore, the interest rate must be maintained below the market-clearing level by special factors. Usury and other interest-rate ceilings represent an obvious case where exogenously imposed restrictions are the source of credit rationing. Such imposed restrictions aside, however, the goal of the theoretical credit-rationing literature is to identify as sufficient conditions those intrinsic factors that cause rational and unconstrained lenders to maintain loan rates below the market-clearing level on a continuing basis.

Hodgman (1960) was among the first to focus on the risk of default as a source of credit rationing, but he recognized that default risk *alone* is not a sufficient condition for credit rationing to occur. The basic reason is that, if the lender and borrower share and dependably act on the same information concerning default, then the interest rate can accurately reflect any expected default behaviour. Default risk thus does not remove the incentive to raise the loan rate if there is excess demand. Nevertheless, Freimer and Gordon (1965) developed a credit-rationing model with rational lenders in the special case where the loan repayment is set equal to the *best* possible outcome of the investment project. If there exists borrower excess demand in this circumstance, then credit rationing occurs, because a higher interest rate cannot provide the lender with additional loan revenue. It was later recognized, however, that this rationing result depends on a peculiar form of asymmetrical information, in that the borrower must maintain an optimistic appraisal of the anticipated outcomes, while the lender considers default a certainty; otherwise there would be no basis for the excess demand.

Modern theory identifies the market failures of moral hazard and adverse selection as much more general features of loan markets than can be the source of credit rationing when there is asymmetrical information. Moral hazard and adverse selection occur when the interest rate or the loan size chosen by the lender affect borrower behaviour (moral hazard) or the riskiness of the applicant pool (adverse selection). There is also a class of customer-relationship models, based on the premise that long-standing customers receive priority access to credit, but it appears that these models also require a basis in asymmetrical information to generate credit rationing (Kane and Malkiel, 1965, and Fried and Howitt, 1980).

Jaffee and Russell (1976) developed a model of credit rationing based on moral hazard in the context of a consumer loan model with competitive lenders. The key feature of the model is that the propensity for default by certain borrowers rises as they are offered larger loans. The zero-profit, loan-contract, locus is therefore rising, with higher rates necessary to compensate lenders for the higher default experience on contracts with larger loans. The market-clearing contract is one point on this locus, but there also exists an alternative rationing contract with a lower interest rate, a lower loan size, and thereby a lower average default rate. Borrowers with low default propensities prefer and are able to enforce this rationing contract as the market equilibrium.

Stiglitz and Weiss (1981) developed an investment loan model of credit rationing that includes both moral hazard and adverse selection. The moral hazard feature of the model arises because individual borrowers choose to operate riskier projects at higher loan rates. The adverse selection feature arises because the relatively safe investments of some borrowers become unprofitable at higher loan rates, causing the remaining pool of loan applicants to become riskier. Thus, while higher loan rates increase the lender's expected revenue on any given project, higher rates may create moral hazard and adverse selection effects that reduce the lender's expected revenue for all borrowers. Given that the risk character of individual borrowers and projects cannot be identified *a priori*, it may be optimal policy for the lender to set the loan rate below the market-clearing level and to ration credit.

Lenders also have incentive to screen applicants, to set non-price terms such as collateral requirements, and to offer loan contracts that cause borrowers to identify their risk attributes as a function of their contract selection. The rationing propositions based on asymmetrical information have been criticized for ignoring lender use of such devices (Barro, 1976; Bester, 1985). In fact, however, while such devices may reduce the magnitude of credit rationing, they generally will not eliminate it. The key point is that the lender must control an additional independent instrument for each dimension of loan risk in order to eliminate the moral hazard and adverse selection that are the source of credit rationing. In practice, loan default is a complex, multi-dimensional process, and lenders have access to only relatively crude or costly devices for gaining information. It is thus unrealistic to assume that cost-effective use of these devices will reveal the precise risk attributes of individual borrowers.

EMPIRICAL AND MACROECONOMIC ASPECTS OF CREDIT RATIONING. Empirical tests of the existence and effects of credit rationing generally use indirect methods based on proxies and other measures with an assumed relationship to actual rationing. Direct measures of credit rationing are uncommon because they require data on applications and rejections, as well as loans made, and these are rarely available. The indirect methods used include survey data, proxy measures, and cross-section and time-series analysis. Jaffee (1971) provides a discussion of the various techniques and the evidence up to 1970.

Borrower surveys are made occasionally on an *ad hoc* basis, usually to study the determinants of investment demand. Interest rates are consistently rated the most important financial variable, but credit rationing is noted by about one-quarter of the firms, with a higher incidence among smaller firms. Lender surveys of loan rates and non-rate terms on business and mortgage loans are made on a continuing basis by the Federal Reseve and Federal Home Loan Bank systems, and some data are available for consumer loan markets as well. Studies of these data show that loan demand and corresponding real expenditures are negatively related to higher levels of the non-rate terms, such as higher collateral requirements, as well as to higher loan-rate levels.

These results confirm that non-rate terms can be treated symmetrically with loan rates as components of the vector that determine the price of a loan (Baltensperger, 1974 and 1978; Harris, 1974). There are alternative interpretations, however, with regard to the implications of this for credit rationing. In one view, the variability of non-price terms provides an *offset to credit rationing*, in that an excess demand for loans and thereby the need for credit rationing can be reduced by higher levels of non-price terms. In another view, the variability of non-price terms is considered a *form of credit rationing*, in that higher values of non-rate terms are used to ration the available supply of funds. This difference in view is a matter of definition, but it is important for monetary policy that the variability of non-price terms and the related 'credit rationing' provide a channel of impact on the real sectors of the economy that does not require variations in interest-rate levels.

Credit rationing proxy measures provide another empirical technique based on the theoretically expected effects of credit rationing. Most credit rationing theories imply that identifiably risk-free borrowers will not be rationed, and therefore that a higher proportion of total loans made to risk-free borrowers can be associated with greater rationing of risky borrowers, given that the ratio of demand between risk-free and risky borrowers has no corresponding variation. Jaffee and Modigliani (1969) implemented this technique, and tests of the proxy variable confirmed the existence of *dynamic* credit rationing, which occurs in the short-run as the loan rate adjusts to the market-clearing or equilibrium level, but did not consider *equilibrium* credit rationing, which occurs in a continuing equilibrium with the loan rate maintained below the market-clearing level.

A variety of time-series studies using special econometric methods for markets in disequilibrium have been carried out to test for the effects of credit rationing in mortgage and business loan markets (Fair and Jaffee, 1972; Sealey, 1979). Most studies have found some statistical evidence of credit rationing, but the quantitative magnitudes are generally inconsequential. Thus, while credit rationing may be a consistent feature of lender behaviour, an important impact on real investment expenditures has not been confirmed.

A basic explanation is that rationed firms may have access to alternative forms of credit. Trade credit, provided between non-financial firms, is particularly important in this respect because the amount outstanding in the US is of the same order of magnitude as business loans. There is the question, however, of why the problems of asymmetrical information do not cause lending firms, just as they cause lending banks, to ration credit. Theory on this point has been slow to develop, but it is plausible that the degree of asymmetrical information may be less between two firms acting as buying and seller of the same commodity than between one firm and a lending institution.

Credit rationing activity in mortgage and consumer loan markets in the US has been dominated by interest-rate ceilings. *Usury law ceilings* (Goudzwaard, 1968) become restrictive if the ceilings are not adjusted in line with rapidly rising market rates of interest, and lending activity is reduced in areas with the lowest ceilings. *Deposit rate ceilings* indirectly affect loan markets by restricting the flow of funds to depository institutions during high rate periods; the effect of these ceilings on mortgage lending and housing activity is especially clear (see Jaffee and Rosen, 1979). Most usury and deposit rate ceilings in the US were removed during the early 1980s, and it is anticipated that credit rationing in these markets will decline.

Recent discussions regarding credit rationing and monetary policy are taking place in the context of the major financial market innovations and deregulation of the early 1980s. The competitive and innovative forces in financial markets are expanding rapidly, with the result that loan markets, which specialize in originating risky instruments, and capital markets, which traditionally trade low-risk securities, are becoming integrated. This process includes the entry of capital market firms directly into loan markets, and the development of new capital market securities that consist of individual loans and that carry insurance of other guarantees against default. A possible result is that credit rationing and the availability channel of monetary policy will become less important features of the financial markets.

At the same time, the unique role played by loan markets and lending institutions in allocating capital to risky borrowers has received renewed attention (Bernanke, 1983; Blinder and Stiglitz, 1983; Stiglitz, 1985). Also, it has been argued that credit flows may provide a better indicator for monetary policy than traditional money supply measures (Friedman, 1983). Consequently, while the recent innovations and deregulation may change the location and reduce the magnitude of credit rationing, they do not change the fundamental problems of market failure under asymmetrical information, and credit rationing in one form or another is likely to continue.

BIBLIOGRAPHY

Baltensperger, E. 1976. The borrower-lender relationship, competitive equilibrium, and the theory of hedonic prices. *American Economic Review* 66, June, 401–5.

Baltensperger, E. 1978. Credit rationing: issues and questions. *Journal of Money, Credit, and Banking* 10(2), May, 170–83.

Barro, R. 1976. The loan market, collateral, and the rate of interest. *Journal of Money, Credit and Banking* 8(4), November, 439–56.

Bernanke, B. 1983. Nonmonetary effects of the financial collapse in the propagation of the Great Depression. *American Economic Review* 73(3), June, 257–76.

Bester, H. 1985. Screening versus rationing in credit markets with imperfect information. *American Economic Review* 75(4), September, 850–55.

Blinder, A. and Stiglitz, J. 1983. Money, credit constraints, and economic activity. *American Economic Review* 73(2), May, 297–302.

Fair, R. and Jaffee, D. 1972. Methods of estimation for markets in disequilibrium. *Econometrica* 40(3), May, 497–514.

Freimer, M. and Gordon, M. 1965. Why bankers ration credit. *Quarterly Journal of Economics* 79(3), August, 397–416.

Fried, J. and Howitt, P. 1980. Credit rationing and implicit contract theory. *Journal of Money, Credit and Banking*, August, 305–14.

Friedman, B. 1983. The roles of money and credit in macroeconomic analysis. In *Macroeconomics, Prices and Quantities: Essays in Memory of Arthur Okun*, ed. J. Tobin, Washington, DC: Brookings Institution.

Goudzwaard, M. 1968. Price ceilings and credit rationing. *Journal of Finance* 23, March, 177–85.

Harris, D. 1974. Credit rationing at commercial banks: some empirical evidence. *Journal of Money, Credit, and Banking* 6(2), May, 227–40.

Hodgman, D. 1960. Credit risk and credit rationing. *Quarterly Journal of Economics* 74, May, 258–78.

Jaffee, D. 1971. *Credit Rationing and the Commercial Loan Market*. New York: John Wiley.

Jaffee, D. and Modigliani, F. 1969. A theory and test of credit rationing. *American Economic Review* 59(5), December, 850–72.

Jaffee, D. and Rosen, K. 1979. Mortgage credit availability and residential construction activity. *Brookings Papers on Economic Activity* No. 2, 333–76.

Jaffee, D. and Russell, T. 1976. Imperfect information, uncertainty, and credit rationing. *Quarterly Journal of Economics* 90(4), November, 651–66.

Kane, E. and Malkiel, B. 1965. Bank portfolio allocation, deposit variability, and the availability doctrine. *Quarterly Journal of Economics* 79(2), February, 113–34.

Keynes, J.M. 1930. *A Treatise on Money*. London: Macmillan; New York: St. Martin's Press, 1971.

Rosa, R.V. 1951. Interest rates and the central bank. In *Money, Trade, and Economic Growth: Essays in Honor of John H. Williams*, ed. H.L. Waitzman, New York: Macmillan.

Sealey, C. 1979. Credit rationing in the commercial loan market: estimates of a structural model under conditions of disequilibrium. *Journal of Finance* 34(3), June, 689–702.

Smith, A. 1776. *An Inquiry into the Nature and Causes of the Wealth of Nations*. Ed. E. Cannan, London: Methuen, 1961; New York: Modern Library, 1937.

Stiglitz, J. 1985. Credit markets and the control of capital. *Journal of Money, Credit, and Banking* 17(2), May, 133–52.

Stiglitz, J. and Weiss, A. 1981. Credit rationing in markets with imperfect information. *American Economic Review* 71(3), June, 393–410.

Viner, J. 1937. *Studies in the Theory of International Trade*, New York: Harper & Brothers.

Currency Boards

ALAN WALTERS

Once ubiquitous in the colonial regimes of Africa, Asia and the Caribbean, currency boards now survive only in such small countries as Singapore, Brunei and Hongkong. The main characteristic of the currency board system is that the board stands ready to exchange domestic *currency* for the foreign reserve currency at a specified and fixed rate. To perform this function the board is required to hold realizable financial assets in the reserve currency at least equal to the value of the domestic currency outstanding. Hence in the currency board system there can be no fiduciary issue. The backing to the currency must be at least 100 per cent. Although in principle it is the currency board that is required to convert on demand all offers of domestic or reserve currency, in practice, where there is a banking system, however elementary, it is the banks that have carried out most of the exchange business. The buying and selling rates for both currencies have a sufficient spread so that the costs of exchange are covered. This convertibility of currencies in the currency board system does not extend to bank deposits or any other financial assets. If a person has a bank deposit and wishes to use the currency board to convert it to foreign currency then the deposit must be first converted into domestic currency and then presented to the currency board.

These disciplines of convertibility and the avoidance of deficit financing were characteristic of much of 19th-century Britain and France. The principle of the currency board was enshrined in the provisions of the (British) Bank Charter Act of 1844. The Issue Department of the Bank of England was to act like a currency board. It is not surprising that this principle was considered proper for the newly acquired colonies. At first, settlers and officials used the notes and coin of the imperial power as a normal extension of imperial trade. The metropolitan currency and coin, since it was widely accepted and considered 'as good as gold', served as a stable means of exchange and as a store of value in those largely inflation-free days of colonial occupation.

There were disadvantages of circulating the metropolitan currency, for example sterling notes and gold sovereigns, in the colonies. First, there was a high risk

109

of destruction or loss. Second, real resources were locked into the circulating media and produced no return. Any loss of currency notes would be to the benefit of the issuer (e.g. the Bank of England) and the colony would correspondingly lose the real value of the notes. The institution of a currency board enabled the colony to avoid such loss. The Bank of England note could be stored in the currency board's vaults and local currency issued to the same value. Thus the accidental loss of a domestic note would not diminish the net assets of the colony. In addition, the currency board would find it efficient to replace worn notes from its stock without having its assets tied up in sending battered Bank of England notes back to London for reissue.

In practice the currency board did not need to hold all its reserves in Bank of England notes. It could buy interest-bearing financial assets of suitable liquidity. Provided these assets could be converted at sufficiently short notice without significant loss into bank notes (or provided the currency board could borrow notes on such security), the principles of convertibility, 100 per cent reserves and no fiduciary issue were satisfied. This more sophisticated currency board system could be used to earn at least some of the profits of seignorage for the benefit of the colony.

Most colonies developed a currency board system, although a few continued to circulate some foreign notes and coins as parallel currencies. The non-colonial countries of Liberia and Panama, however, have used the United States dollar as a circulating medium. In the case of Liberia it was argued that there were doubts whether the people would have confidence in a currency board supervised by the government of Liberia. In particular, there were fears – alas not groundless – that the monetary system would be used improperly to finance government spending.

As colonies became independent states in the 1950s and 1960s they generally eschewed the currency board system and formed Central Banks to manage their currencies, ostensibly for 'development' purposes. The central banks, as distinct from the currency boards that they replaced, required the commercial banks to hold reserves as deposits at the Central Bank. And the government could create money and finance government deficits by borrowing from the newly created Central Bank. Some countries, such as Singapore, continued to operate a sophisticated currency board system. And Hong Kong, after experimenting with an unpegged currency from 1972, returned to a currency board system based on the United States dollar in October 1983.

The financial experience of countries which departed from currency board systems has not been auspicious. Increasing inflation, generated largely by deficit financing through Central Bank credit and note issue, has been characteristic of most of the two or three decades since independence. The objective of promoting growth and development has not been generally achieved; indeed, in Africa the experience and the forecast is one of degeneration. It is difficult to avoid the conclusion that the financial instability brought in train by the abrogation of the currency board system has played a considerable role in this process. Nevertheless, it is unlikely that, whatever the arguments in favour of the currency board system, there will ever be a resuscitation of what is wrongly regarded as a manipulative monetary mechanism of colonialism or neo-imperialism.

The claims for a currency board system are many, some clearly dubious. One main claim is that the currency board system provides an annual increment of the money supply which is simply the mirror image of the surplus on the current balance of payments. If there were no banks, or if the banks acted only as depositories or 'cloakrooms' for currency, and if there were no imports or exports of capital in the form of foreign currency, then this assertion would be correct. The only way in which the residents could acquire foreign currency, and so swap for domestic currency, would be through net earnings from trade. When there is a surplus on the current account the money supply grows by that amount, and when a deficit appears the money stock contracts by the value of the deficit. This one-to-one relationship was thought to provide an automatic system which ensured that monetary behaviour always moved to eliminate a deficit or a surplus.

With notes and coin as the sole form of money and with no capital imports of foreign currency this one-to-one model was clearly valid. However, with the additional elements of bank deposits and credit the issue becomes much less clear cut. A proportional relation still holds even with a fully developed system of bank deposits acting as money and bank credit, provided first that there were no foreign capital movements, second that the banks maintain domestic currency in their reserves as a constant fraction of their deposit liabilities, and third that the public hold a constant ratio of domestic currency to bank deposits. All these fixed ratios would ensure that the M_1 definition of the money supply (currency plus checking accounts) would expand proportionally, but not one-to-one with the current balance.

If there are capital flows other than those required to settle the net bills of the trade account, then the proportionality disappears. A flow of capital, such as a colonial branch bank borrowing from its parent, will entail the acquisition of a foreign financial asset (as well as the corresponding liability). The branch bank, if required to hold reserves in domestic currency, will exchange its foreign financial asset (or strictly currency) at the currency board and acquire domestic currency reserves. So, keeping the reserve fraction constant, it will extend loans and expand deposits, thus increasing the deposit component of the money supply. The limit to such borrowing and domestic credit creation is set by the demand for credit in the colony, which in turn depends on the marginal profitability of credit in the colony relative to the interest rate. (This rate will normally be at a slight premium over the metropolitan interest rate.) In practice, the limit to such borrowings will be set by judgements of bankers and businessmen of the capacity and willingness of domestic borrowers to pay the servicing charges.

There is one set of circumstances which would insulate the monetary system from external capital flows. This would be the case where the importation of capital is effected only to supply the foreign exchange component of a domestic investment which would otherwise not occur. The insulation is complete if the investment generates profits in foreign exchange which just offset the servicing charges. These conditions of foreign capital flows were probably a fair approximation to reality for the period covered by the currency board era. But with the dominance of Western commercial bank lending to Third World governments, they are hardly characteristic of modern capital flows. Capital flows normally do affect monetary conditions.

The proportionality proposition is also upset by changes in the reserve–deposit ratios and by any changes in the fraction of the money stock which the public desires to hold in the form of currency. Prudential control of banks, often the responsibility of the Central Bank in the parent bank's country, usually takes the form of specifying *minimum* reserves which may be less than the prudential reserves held normally by banks. The branch banks may thus decide to extend credit and deposits, when conditions of confidence and credibility change, by running down their reserve to deposit ratio to somewhere near the specified minimum. The ability of branch banks generally to borrow from the head office in London gives considerable latitude to their liquidity requirements and virtually guarantees the solvency of the branch in the colony.

In the long run, much more important than the reserve–deposit ratio are changes in the currency-deposit ratio of the public. The modern process of financial innovation economizes on cash. The use of the cheque rather than cash is the predominant financial trend in all countries. For any given quantity of currency and other bank reserves the choice of the public for a larger ratio of deposits to currency has provided the main impetus for an expansion of the money supply (M_1) in currency board systems. The stability and confidence generated by the currency board system undoubtedly much encouraged the use of deposits.

This phenomenon nullifies one of the main criticisms of the currency board system, namely that it provides a stultifying monetary constraint on development and inhibits growth in the colony. It is perhaps ironic that the countries that have retained their currency board arrangements, Singapore and Hongkong, have been the highest growth economies in the oil-importing Third World. Their money supply has expanded partly through current balance surpluses and capital imports, but mainly through the increased use of deposits associated with the financial stability of the currency board system. Both Singapore and Hong Kong inflated during the late 1960s and 1970s at roughly the same relatively low rates as the currencies on which they were based. Thus they avoided the excessive inflation which affected many Third World countries which had adopted more 'advanced' systems of central bank finance.

Another important criticism was thought to be not only the preclusion of counter-cyclical monetary and budgetary policy, but also the promotion of an actually pro-cyclical policy. Many curency board colonies produced export crops which were sold in markets with widely fluctuating prices. The collapse of commodity prices in a world recession generally gave rise to a large deficit on the current balance and so induced the currency board to contract the money supply. The isomorphic case of a boom in export prices was thought to be less onerous. Under a liberal trade regime the increase in foreign exchange receipts from exports could be offset in part by an expansion of imports which would damp down the inflationary pressure generated by the rise in export prices. Although no monetary manipulation can turn a one-commodity export economy into a nicely diversified recession-proof system, there was no reason, apart from extraneous regulations, why the authorities as well as firms and persons could not hold or transfer foreign assets as a precaution against such oscillations. In the case of the Hong Kong currency board, the freedom to hold assets in any form and any currency is the *sine qua non* of the financial system. And, for many decades, the government of Hong Kong has held a large portfolio of foreign financial assets which can be used to expand or contract the money supply and hence influence the currency board issue.

It has been thought that the currency board system is likely to exacerbate liquidity shortages and even the solvency of the domestic banking system, and so make it difficult to contain runs on banks and all the fear and instability that inevitably follows. Again, this criticism has proven largely invalid. Since most banking business was carried out by the branches of metropolitan banks, there was little fear of a run on a particular branch causing solvency problems, and liquidity shortages could be covered quickly by transfer. Moreover the knowledge that the resources of the parent banks lay behind the branch gave rise to a singular confidence and so nipped any incipient run in the bud. For the local banks, which have no such recourse, the ebb and flow of confidence were much more serious (as in the United States in 1931–3 and Hong Kong in 1983 and 1985). Insofar as the currency board system promotes international branch banking, so it promotes stability.

Although the currency board system did not have all the virtues or faults which were attributed to it, it did have some singular advantages. To some extent it depoliticized the monetary system and insulated the public purse from plundering politicians. There was no resort to the printing press to reward political allies or ruin one's opponents. It gave a real credibility to the fixed exchange rate so that people willingly held both currency and deposits knowing that they would maintain their value. Similarly it precluded the possibility that the exchange rate would be used to attempt to solve political and social problems. These constraints, once thought to be vices, are now widely regarded as virtues. The evident failure of trying to promote growth or equality by inflationary finance may create a new respect for currency boards. The return of Hong Kong in 1983 to a full currency board system based on the US dollars was in response to political uncertainties as well as the realization that such financial stability was sorely needed.

It would be rash, however, to imagine that currency boards are the wave of the future. One suspects that they may be used rather more frequently in small economies that are heavily dependent on large trading partners. Similarly they are likely to remain the basic system for the great trading centres such as Singapore and Hong Kong where they have worked so well. The most demanding requirement of a currency board system is that, even under the most trying conditions, the financial community have faith that the board will honour its exchange obligations at the specified parity. Few Third World governments command such credibility. Thus, the currency board is unlikely to be the main vehicle for monetary and fiscal rectitude in the Third World.

BIBLIOGRAPHY

Drake, P.J. (ed.) 1966. *Money and Banking in Malaya and Singapore.* Singapore: Malayan Publications.

Greaves, I.C. 1953. *Colonial Monetary Conditions.* London: HMSO.

Greenwood, J.G. 1984. Why the HK$/US$ linked rate system should not be changed. *Asian Monetary Monitor* 8(6), November–December.

Newlyn, W.T. and Rowan, D.C. 1954. *Money and Banking in British Colonial Africa.* London: Oxford University Press.

Dear Money

SUSAN HOWSON

The obverse of cheap money, 'dear money' is also used to denote episodes in which central banks have raised (short-term) interest rates deliberately to bring about a contraction of money or credit, often in order to preserve a fixed exchange rate. The historical episodes are memorable for their effects on economic activity and on subsequent monetary theory and policy.

The major financial crises of the 19th century were accompanied by the Bank of England's raising of its discount rate (Bank rate) to at least 5% (the maximum permitted under the usury laws until 1833) in order to protect the gold reserve from an internal or external drain. The tradition as it developed after the Bank Charter Act of 1844 was for the Bank to act as a lender of last resort even when that involved an expansion of the fixed fiduciary note issue imposed by the Act, but at a penal rate. Hence Bank rate went to 8% in 1847, 10% in 1857 and again in 1866, 9% in 1873, but only 6% in the Baring crisis of 1890, the smooth handling of which was seen as a success for the Bank's methods (Hawtrey, 1938, chs 1 and 3; Morgan, 1943, chs 7–9; Clapham, 1944, Vol. 2, ch. 6; Sayers, 1976, pp. 1–3). In the early 20th century the events of the crisis of 1907 seemed to confirm the utility of central banks in general and the efficacy of Bank rate in particular. When the American stock exchange boom broke, Bank rate was quickly raised to 7% in response to gold outflows from London. The outflows were swiftly reversed while a banking panic in the US turned into a severe though short-lived slump. The outcome in the US was the establishment of the National Monetary Commission in 1908 and the Federal Reserve System which it recommended, in 1914. In Britain, belief in the power of interest rates to influence economic activity was reinforced, and lasted for a generation (Hawtrey, 1938, pp. 115–18; Friedman and Schwartz, 1963, pp. 156–74; Sayers, 1957, pp. 62–4; Sayers, 1976, pp. 54–60; Keynes, 1930, Vol. I, ch. 13).

After World War I dear money was applied again, vigorously but after some hesitation, in both Britain and America to curb the postwar boom: Bank rate went to 6% in November 1919, 7% in April 1920, the Federal Reserve Bank of

New York rediscount rate to 6% in January 1920. In both countries the rises came too late and were too strong: the restocking boom was already breaking and the subsequent slump was severe and (in the UK) prolonged (Friedman and Schwartz, 1963, pp. 221–39; Howson, 1974, and 1975, ch. 2). The Federal System continued to experiment in the 1920s with the use of interest rates to control the domestic economy (Chandler, 1958; Friedman and Schwartz, 1963, ch. 6), but elsewhere, with many countries struggling to return to or maintain the international gold standard, dear money, in the sense of high (short-term) interest rates was frequently and widely used for balance of payments reasons (Clarke, 1967; Moggridge, 1972). It was with considerable relief that countries falling off the gold standard in the 1930s took advantage of their new-found monetary independence to promote cheap money. The revival of monetary policy on both sides of the Atlantic after 1951 did not involve the use of dear money in traditional ways: concern with price stability was initially tempered by the objective of 'full employment' and in Britain at least interest rate rises for the sake of external balance were usually employed only as one element in 'packages' of deflationary measures; by the time the reduction of inflation became an important objective dear money as a target or as an indicator of monetary policy had been replaced by the rate of growth of the money supply (Dow, 1964, ch. 3; OECD, 1974; Blackaby, 1978, chs 5 and 6).

BIBLIOGRAPHY

Blackaby, F.T. (ed.) 1978. *British Economic Policy 1960–74.* Cambridge: Cambridge University Press.

Chandler, L.V. 1958. *Benjamin Strong: Central Banker.* Washington, DC: Brookings Institution.

Clapham, Sir John. 1944. *The Bank of England.* Cambridge: Cambridge University Press.

Clarke, S.V.O. 1967. *Central Bank Cooperation 1924–31.* New York: Federal Reserve Bank of New York.

Dow, J.C.R. 1964. *The Management of the British Economy 1945–60.* Cambridge: Cambridge University Press.

Friedman, M. and Schwartz, A.J. 1963. *A Monetary History of the United States 1867–1960.* Princeton: Princeton University Press.

Hawtrey, R.G. 1938. *A Century of Bank Rate.* London: Longmans Green & Co.

Howson, S. 1974. The origins of dear money, 1919–20. *Economic History Review* 27(1), February, 88–107.

Howson, S. 1975. *Domestic Monetary Management in Britain 1919–38.* Cambridge: Cambridge University Press.

Keynes, J.M. 1930. *A Treatise on Money.* London: Macmillan for the Royal Economic Society, 1971; New York: St. Martin's Press, 1971.

Moggridge, D.E. 1972. *British Monetary Policy 1924–1931.* Cambridge: Cambridge University Press.

Morgan, E.V. 1943. *The Theory and Practice of Central Banking 1797–1913.* Cambridge: Cambridge University Press.

OECD. 1974. *Monetary Policy in the United States.* Paris: OECD.

Sayers, R.S. 1957. *Central Banking After Bagehot.* Oxford: Clarendon Press.

Sayers, R.S. 1976. *The Bank of England 1891–1944.* Cambridge: Cambridge University Press.

Demand for Money:
Theoretical Studies

BENNETT T. McCALLUM AND
MARVIN S. GOODFRIEND

In any discussion of the demand for money it is important to be clear about the concept of money that is being utilized; otherwise, misunderstandings can arise because of the various possible meanings that readers could have in mind. Here the term will be taken to refer to an economy's *medium of exchange*: that is, to a tangible asset that is generally accepted in payment for any commodity. Money thus conceived will also serve as a store of value, of course, but may be of minor importance to the economy in that capacity. The monetary asset will usually also serve as the economy's medium of account – that is, prices will be quoted in terms of money – since additional accounting costs would be incurred if the unit of account were a quantity of some asset other than money. The medium-of-account role is, however, not logically tied to the medium of exchange (Wicksell, 1906; Niehans, 1978).

Throughout much of Western history, most economies have adopted as their principal medium of exchange a commodity that would be valuable even if it were not used as money. Recently, however, fiat money – intrinsically worthless tokens made of paper or some other cheap material – has come to predominate. Under a commodity money arrangement, the exchange value of money will depend upon the demand for the monetary commodity in its non-monetary as well as its monetary uses. But in a discussion of money demand, as distinct from a discussion of the price level, any possible non-monetary demand for the medium of exchange – which will be absent anyhow in fiat money system – can legitimately be ignored.

The quantity of money demanded in any economy – indeed, the set of assets that have monetary status – will be dependent upon prevailing institutions, regulations and technology. Technical progress in the payments industry will, for instance, tend to alter the quantity of money demanded for given values of determinants such as income. This dependence does not, however, imply that the demand for money is a nebulous or unusable concept, any more than the existence of technical progress and regulatory change in the transportation industry does so for the demand for automobiles. In practice, some lack of clarity pertains to the operational measurement of the money stock, as it does to the stock of automobiles or other commodities. But in an economy with a well-established national currency, the principle is relatively clear: assets are part of the money stock if and only if they constitute *claims* to currency, unrestricted (at par). This principle rationalizes the common practice of including demand deposits in the money stock of the United States, while excluding time deposits and various other assets.

The rapid development during the 1960s and 1970s of computer and tele-communications technologies has led some writers (e.g. Fama, 1980) to contemplate economies – anticipated by Wicksell (1906) – in which virtually all purchases are effected not by the transfer of a tangible medium of exchange, but by means of signals to an accounting network, signals that result in appropriate debits and credits to the wealth accounts of buyers and sellers. If there were literally *no* medium of exchange, the wealth accounts being claims to some specified bundle of commodities, the economy in question would be properly regarded and analysed as a non-monetary economy, albeit one that avoids the inefficiencies of crude barter. If, by contrast, the accounting network's credits were claims to quantities of a fiat or commodity medium of exchange, then individuals' credit balances would appropriately be included as part of the money stock (McCallum, 1985).

BASIC PRINCIPLES. An overview of the basic principles of money demand theory can be obtained by considering a hypothetical household that seeks at time t to maximize

$$u(c_t, l_t) + \beta u(c_{t+1}, l_{t+1}) + \beta^2 u(c_{t+2}, l_{t+2}) + \cdots \tag{1}$$

where c_t and l_t are the household's consumption and leisure during t and where $\beta = 1/(1 + \delta)$, with $\delta > 0$ the rate of time preference. The within-period utility function $u(\cdot, \cdot)$ is taken to be well behaved so that unique position values will be chosen for c_t and l_t. The household has access to a productive technology described by a production function that is homogeneous of degree one in capital and labour inputs. But for simplicity we assume that labour is supplied inelastically, so this function can be written as $y_t = f(k_{t-1})$, where y_t is production during t and k_{t-1} is the stock of capital held at the end of period $t - 1$. The function $f(\cdot)$ is well behaved, so a unique positive value of k_t will be chosen for the upcoming period. Capital is unconsumed output, so its price is the same as that of the consumption good and its rate of return between t and $t + 1$ is $f'(k_t)$.

Although this set-up explicitly recognizes the existence of only one good, it is intended to serve a simplified representation – one formally justified by the analysis of Lucas (1980) – of an economy in which the household sells its specialized output and makes purchases (at constant relative prices) of a large number of distinct consumption goods. Carrying out these purchases requires *shopping time*, s_t, which subtracts from leisure: $l_t = 1 - s_t$, where units are chosen so that there is 1 unit of time per period available for shopping and leisure together. (If labour were elastically supplied, then labour time would have to be included in the expression.) In a monetary economy, however, the amount of shopping time required for a given amount of consumption will depend negatively upon the quantity of real money balances held by the household (up to some satiation level). For concreteness, we assume that

$$s_t = \psi(c_t, m_t) \tag{2}$$

where $\psi(\cdot, \cdot)$ has partial derivatives $\psi_1 > 0$ and $\psi_2 \leqslant 0$. In (2), $m_t = M_t/P_t$, where M_t is the nominal stock of money held at the end of t and P_t is the money price of a consumption bundle. (A variant with M_t denoting the start-of-period money stock will be mentioned below.) The transaction variable is here specified as c_t rather than $c_t + \Delta k_t$ to reflect the idea than only a few distinct capital goods will be utilized, so that the transaction cost to expenditure ratio will be much lower than for consumption goods.

Besides capital and money, there is a third asset available to the household. This asset is a nominal bond; i.e., a one-period security that may be purchased at the price $1/(1 + R_t)$ in period t and redeemed for one unit of money in $t + 1$. The symbol B_t will be used to denote the number (possibly negative) of these securities purchased by the household in period t, while $b_t = B_t/P_t$.

In the setting described, the household's budget constraint for period t may be written as follows:

$$f(k_{t-1}) + v_t \geqslant c_t + k_t - k_{t-1} + m_t - (1 + \pi_t)^{-1} m_{t-1} + (1 + R_t)^{-1} b_t$$
$$- (1 + \pi_t)^{-1} b_{t-1} \tag{3}$$

Here v_t is the real value of lump-sum transfers (net of taxes) from the government, while π_t is the inflation rate, $\pi_t = (P_t - P_{t-1})/P_{t-1}$. Given the objective of maximizing (1), first-order conditions necessary for optimality of the household's choices include the following, in which ϕ_t and λ_t are Lagrangian multipliers associated with the constraints (2) and (3), respectively:

$$u_1(c_t, 1 - s_t) - \phi_t \psi_t(c_t, m_t) - \lambda_t = 0 \tag{4}$$

$$- u_2(c_t, 1 - s_t) + \phi_t = 0 \tag{5}$$

$$- \phi_t \psi_2(c_t, m_t) - \lambda_t + \beta \lambda_{t+1}(1 + \pi_{t+1})^{-1} = 0 \tag{6}$$

$$- \lambda_t + \beta \lambda_{t+1}[f'(k_t) + 1] = 0 \tag{7}$$

$$- \lambda_t(1 + R_t)^{-1} + \beta \lambda_{t+1}(1 + \pi_{t+1})^{-1} = 0. \tag{8}$$

These conditions, together with the constraints (2) and (3), determine current and planned values of c_t, s_t, m_t, k_t, b_t, ϕ_t, and λ_t for given time paths of v_t, R_t, and π_t (which are exogenous to the household) and the predetermined values of k_{t-1}, m_{t-1}, and b_{t-1}. (There is also a relevant transversality condition, but it can be ignored for the issues at hand.) Also l_t values can be obtained from $l_t = 1 - s_t$ and, with P_{t-1} given, P_t, M_t, and B_t values are implied by the π_t, m_t, and b_t sequences.

The household's optimizing choice of m_t can be described in terms of two distinct concepts of a money-demand function. The first of these is a proper demand function; that is, a relationship giving the chosen quantity as a function of variables that are either predetermined or exogenous to the economic unit in question. In the present context, the money-demand function of that type will be of the form:

$$m_t = \mu(k_{t-1}, m_{t-1}, b_{t-1}, v_t, v_{t+1}, \dots, R_t, R_{t+1}, \dots, \pi_t, \pi_{t+1}, \dots) \tag{9}$$

where the variables dated $t + 1, t + 2, \dots$ must be understood as anticipated values. Now, it will be obvious that this relationship does not closely resemble those normally described in the literature as 'money demand functions'. There is a second type of relationship implied by the model, however, that does have such a resemblance. To obtain this second expression, one can eliminate $\beta\lambda_{t+1}(1 + \pi_{t+1})^{-1}$ between equations (6) and (8), then eliminate λ_t and finally ϕ_t from the resultant by using (4) and (5). These steps yield the following:

$$-u_2(c_t, 1 - s_t)\psi_2(c_t, m_t) = [u_1(c_t, 1 - s_t) - u_2(c_t, 1 - s_t)\psi_1(c_t, m_t)]$$

$$[1 - (1 + R_t)^{-1}]. \tag{10}$$

Then $\psi(c_t, m_t)$ can be used in place of s_t, and the result is a relationship that involves *only* m_t, c_t, and R_t. Consequently, (10) can be expressed in the form:

$$h(m_t, c_t, R_t) = 0 \tag{11}$$

and if the latter is solvable for m_t one can obtain:

$$M_t/P_t = L(c_t, R_t). \tag{12}$$

Thus the model at hand yields a *portfolio-balance* relationship between real money-balances demanded, a variable measuring the volume of transactions conducted, and the nominal interest rate (which reflects the cost of holding money rather than bonds). It can be shown, moreover, that for reasonable specifications of the utility and shopping-time functions, $L(\cdot, \cdot)$ will be increasing in its first argument and decreasing in the second.

There are, of course, two problems in moving from a demand function (of either type) for an individual household to one that pertains to the economy as a whole. The first of these involves the usual problem of aggregating over households that many have different tastes and/or levels of wealth. It is well known that the conditions permitting such aggregation are extremely stringent in the context of any sort of behavioural relation; but for many theoretical purposes it is sensible to pretend that they are satisfied. The second problem concerns the existence of economic units other than households – 'firms' being the most obvious example. To construct a model analogous to that above for a firm, one would presumably posit maximization of the present value of real net receipts rather than (1), and the constraints would be different. In particular, the shopping-time function (2) would need to be replaced with a more general relationship depicting resources used in conducting transactions as a function of their volume and the real quantity of money held. The transaction measure would not be c_t for firms or, therefore, for the economy as a whole. But the general aspects of the analysis would be similar, so we shall proceed under the presumption that the crucial issues are adequately represented in a setting that recognizes only economic units like the 'households' described above.

The distinction between the proper money-demand funcction (9) and the more standard portfolio-balance relation (12) is important in the context of certain issues. As an example, consider the issue of whether wealth or income should appear as a 'scale variable' (Meltzer, 1963). From the foregoing, it is clear that wealth is an important determinant of money demand in the sense that k_{t-1}, m_{t-1}, and b_{t-1} are arguments of the demand function (9). Nevertheless, formulation (12) indicates that there is no separate role for wealth in a portfolio-balance relation if appropriate transaction and opportunity-cost variables are included.

An issue that naturally arises concerns the foregoing discussion's neglect of randomness. How would the analysis be affected if it were recognized that future values of variables cannot possibly be known with certainty? In answer, let us suppose that the household knows current values of all relevant variables including P_t, R_t, and v_t when making decisions on m_t and c_t, but that its views concerning variables dated $t+1, t+2, \ldots$ are held in the form of non-degenerate probability distributions. Suppose also that there is uncertainty in production, so that the marginal product of capital in $t+1$, $f'(k_t)$, is viewed as random. Then the household's problem becomes one of maximizing the expectation of (1), with $u(\cdot,\cdot)$ a von Neumann-Morgenstern utility function, given information available in period t. Consequently, the first-order conditions (4)–(8) must be replaced with ones that involve conditional expectations. For example, equation (7) would be replaced with:

$$-\lambda_t + \beta E_t\{\lambda_{t+1}[f'(k_t)+1]\} = 0 \qquad (7')$$

where $E_t(\cdot)$ denotes the expectation of the indicated variable conditional upon known values of P_t, R_t, v_t, and so on. With this modification, the nature of the proper demand function becomes much more complex – indeed, for most specifications no closed form solution analogous to (9) will exist. Nevertheless, the portfolio-balance relation (12) will continue to hold exactly as before, for the steps described in its derivation above remain the same except that it is $E_t[\beta\lambda_{t+1}(1+\pi_{t+1})^{-1}]$ that is eliminated between equations corresponding to (6) and (8). From this result it follows that, according to our model, the relationship of M_t/P_t to the transaction and opportunity-cost variables is invariant to changes in the probability distribution of future variables.

Another specification variant that should be mentioned reflects the assumption that it is money held at the start of a period, not its end, that facilitates transactions conducted during the period. If that change in specification were made and the foregoing analysis repeated, it would be found that the household's concern in period t would be to have the appropriate level of real money balances at the start of period $t + 1$. The portfolio-balance relation analogous to (12) that would be obtained in the deterministic case would relate $m_t + 1$ to c_{t+1} and R_t, where $m_{t+1} = M_{t+1}/P_{t+1}$ with M_{t+1} reflecting money holdings at the end of period t. Consequently, M_{t+1}/P_t would be related to R_t, planned c_{t+1}, and P_t/P_{t+1}. Thus the theory does not work out as cleanly as in the case considered above even in the absence of randomness, and is complicated further by the recognition of the latter. The fundamental nature of the relationships are, however, the same as above.

Another point deserving of mention is that if labour is supplied elastically, the portfolio-balance relation analogous to (12) will include the real wage-rate as an additional argument. This has been noted by Karni (1973) and Dutton and Gramm (1973). More generally, the existence of other relevant margins of substitution can bring in other variables. If stocks of commodities held by households affect shopping-time requirements, for example, the inflation rate will appear separately in the counterpart of (12) (see Feige and Parkin, 1971).

Finally, it must be recognised that the simplicity of the portfolio-balance relation (12) would be lost if the intertemporal utility function (1) were not time-separable. If, for example, the function $u(c_t, l_t)$ in (1) were replaced with $u(c_t, l_t, l_{t-1})$ or $u(c_t, c_{t-1}, l_t)$, as has been suggested in the business cycle literature, then the dynamic aspect of the household's choices would be more complex and a relation like (12) – i.e. one that includes only contemporaneous variables – could not be derived.

HISTORICAL DEVELOPMENT. The approach to money-demand analysis outlined above, which features intertemporal optimization choices by individual economic agents whose transactions are facilitated by their holdings of money, has evolved gradually over time. In this section we briefly review that evolution.

While the earlier literature on the quantity theory of money contained many important insights, its emphasis was on the comparison of market equilibria rather than individual choice; that is, on 'market experiments' rather than 'individual experiments', in the language of Patinkin (1956). Consequently, there was little explicit consideration of money-demand behaviour in pre-1900 writings in the quantity theory tradition. Indeed, there was little emphasis on money demand *per se* even in the classic contributions of Mill (1848), Wicksell (1906) and Fisher (1911), despite the clear recognition by those analysts that some particular quantity of real money holdings would be desired by the inhabitants of an economy under any specified set of circumstances. Notable exceptions, discussed by Patinkin (1956, pp. 386–417), were provided by Walras and Schlesinger.

In the English language literature, the notion of money demand came forth more strongly in the 'cash balance' approach of Cambridge economists, an approach that featured analysis organized around the concepts of money demand and supply. This organizing principle was present in the early (c1871) but unpublished writings of Marshall (see Whitaker, 1975, p. 165–8) and was laid out with great explicitness by Pigou (1917). The Cambridge approach presumed that the quantity of money demanded would depend primarily on the volume of transactions to be undertaken, but emphasized volition on the part of money-holders and recognized (sporadically) that the ratio of real balances to transaction volume would be affected by foregone 'investment income' (i.e., interest earnings). In this regard Cannan (1921), a non-Cambridge economist who was influenced by Marshall, noted that the quantity of money demanded should be negatively related to anticipated inflation – an insight previously expressed by Marshall in his testimony of 1886 for the Royal Commission on the Depression of Trade and Industry (Marshall, 1926). In addition, Cannan developed very clearly the point that the relevant concept is the demand for a *stock* of money.

Although the aforementioned theorists developed several important constituents of a satisfactory money-demand theory, none of them unambiguously cast his explanation in terms of marginal analysis. Thus a significant advance was provided by Lavington (1921, p. 30), in a chapter entitled 'The Demand for Money', who attempted a statement of the marginal conditions that must be satisfied for optimality by an individual who consumes, holds money, and holds interest-bearing securities. But despite the merits of his attempt, Lavington confused – as Patinkin (1956, p. 418) points out – the subjective sacrifice of permanently adding a dollar to cash balances with that of adding it for only one period. Thus it was left for Fisher (1930, p. 216) to provide a related but correct statement. The discussions of both Lavington and Fisher are notable for identifying the interest rate as a key determinant of the marginal opportunity cost of holding money.

In a justly famous article, Hicks (1935) argued persuasively that progress in the theory of money would require the treatment of money demand as a problem of individual choice at the margin. Building upon some insightful but unclear suggestions in Keynes's *Treatise on Money* (1930), Hicks investigated an agent's decision concerning the relative amounts of money and securities to be held at a point in time. He emphasized the need to explain why individuals willingly hold money when its return is exceeded by those available from other assets and – following Lavington and Fisher – concluded that money provides a service yield not offered by other assets. Hicks also noted that the positive transaction cost of investing in securities makes it unprofitable to undertake such investments for very short periods. Besides identifying the key aspects of marginal analysis of money demand. Hicks (1935) pointed out that an individual's total wealth will influence his demand for money. All of these points were developed further in chapters 13 and 19 of Hicks's *Value and Capital* (1939). The analysis in the latter is, some misleading statements about the nature of interest notwithstanding, substantively very close to that outlined in the previous section of this article. Hicks did not, however, provide formal conditions relating to money demand in his mathematical appendix.

The period between 1935 and 1939 witnessed, of course, the publication of Keynes's *General Theory* (1936). That work emphasized the importance for macroeconomic analysis of the interest-sensitivity of money demand – 'liquidity preference', in Keynes's terminology – and was in that respect, as in many others, enormously influential. Its treatment of money demand *per se* was not highly original, however, in terms of fundamentals. (This statement ignores some peculiarities resulting from a presumably inadvertent attribution of money illusion; on this topic, again see Patinkin, 1956, pp. 173–4.)

The importance of several items mentioned above – payments practices, foregone interest and transaction costs – was explicitly depicted in the formal optimization models developed several years later by Baumol (1952) and Tobin (1956). These models, which were suggested by mathematical inventory theory, assume the presence of two assets (money and an interest-bearing security), a fixed cost of making transfers between money and the security, and a lack of synchronization between (exogenously given) receipt and expenditure streams. In addition, they assume that all payments are made with money. Economic units are depicted as choosing the optimal frequency for money-security transfers so as to maximize interest earnings net of transaction costs.

In Baumol's treatment, which ignores integer constraints on the number of transactions per period, the income and interest-rate elasticities of real money demand are found to be $\frac{1}{2}$ and $-\frac{1}{2}$, respectively. Thus the model implies 'economies of scale' in making transactions. Tobin's (1956) analysis takes account of integer constraints, by contrast, and thus implies that individuals respond in a discontinuous fashion to alternative values of the interest rate. In his model it appears entirely possible for individual economic units to choose corner solutions in which none of the interest-bearing security is held. A number of extensions of the Baumol–Tobin approach have been made by various authors; for an insightful survey the reader is referred to Barro and Fischer (1976).

Miller and Orr (1966) pioneered the inventory approach to money demand theory in a stochastic context. Specifically, in their analysis a firm's net cash inflow is generated as a random walk, and the firm chooses a policy to minimize the sum of transaction and foregone-interest costs. The optimal decision rule is of the (S, s) type: when money balances reach zero or a ceiling, S, the firm makes transactions to return the balance to the level s. In this setting there are again predicted economies of scale, while the interest-rate elasticity is $-\frac{1}{3}$. For extensions the reader is again referred to Barro and Fischer (1976).

The various inventory models of money demand possess the desirable feature of providing an explicit depiction of the *source* of money's service yield to an individual holder. It has been noted (e.g. by Friedman and Schwartz, 1970) that the type of transaction demand described by these models is unable to account for more than a fraction of the transaction balances held in actual economies. Furthermore, their treatment of expenditure and receipt streams as exogenous is unfortunate and they do not generalize easily to fully dynamic settings. These points imply, however, only that the inventory models should not be interpreted too literally. In terms of fundamentals they are closely related to the basic model outlined in the previous section.

A quite different approach was put forth by Tobin (1958), in a paper that views the demand for money as arising from a portfolio allocation decision made under conditions of uncertainty. In the more influential of the paper's models, the individual wealth-holder must allocate his portfolio between a riskless asset, identified as money, and an asset with an uncertain return whose expected value exceeds that of money. Tobin shows how the optimal portfolio mix depends, under the assumption of expected utility maximization, on the individual's degree of risk aversion, his wealth, and the mean-variance characteristics of the risky asset's return distribution. The analysis implies a negative interest sensitivity of money demand, thereby satisfying Tobin's desire to provide an additional rationalization of Keynes's (1936) liquidity-preference hypothesis. The approach has, however, two shortcomings. First, in actuality money does not have a yield that is riskless in real terms, which is the relevant concept for rational individuals. Second, and more seriously, in many actual economies there exist assets 'that have precisely the same risk characteristics as money and yield higher returns' (Barro and Fischer, 1976, p. 139). Under such conditions, the model implies that no money will be held.

Another influential item from this period was provided by Friedman's well-known 'restatement' of the quantity theory (1956). In that paper, as in Tobin's, the principal role of money is as a form of wealth. Friedman's analysis emphasized margins of substitution between money and assets other than bonds (e.g. durable consumption goods and equities). The main contribution of the paper was to help rekindle interest in monetary analysis from a macroeconomic perspective, however, rather than to advance the formal theory of money demand.

A model that may be viewed as a formalization of Hicks's (1935, 1939) approach was outlined by Sidrauski (1967). The main purpose of Sidrauski's paper was to study the interaction of inflation and capital accumulation in a dynamic context, but his analysis gives rise to optimality conditions much like those of equations (4)–(8) of the present article and thus implies money-demand functions like (9) and (12). The main difference between Sidrauski's model and ours is merely due to our use of the 'shopping time' specification, which was suggested by Saving (1971). That feature makes real balances an argument of each individual's utility function only indirectly, rather than directly, and indicates the type of phenomenon that advocates of the direct approach presumably have in mind. Thus Sidrauski's implied money-demand model is the basis for the one presented above, while a stochastic version of the latter, being fundamentally similar to inventory or direct utility-yield specifications, is broadly representative of current mainstream views.

ONGOING CONTROVERSIES. Having outlined the current mainstream approach to money-demand analysis and its evolution, we now turn to matters that continue to be controversial. The first of these concerns the role of uncertainty. In that regard, one point has already been developed; i.e., that rate-of-return uncertainty on other assets cannot be used to explain why individuals hold money in economies – such as that of the US – in which there exist very short-term assets that yield positive interest and are essentially riskless in nominal terms. But this does not imply that uncertainty is unimportant for money demand in a more general sense, for there are various ways in which it can affect the analysis. In the basic model outlined above, uncertainty appears explicitly only by way of the assumption that households view asset returns as random. In that case, if money demand and consumption decisions for a period are made simultaneously then the portfolio-balance relation (12) will be – as shown above – invariant to changes in the return distributions. But the same is not true for the proper demand function (9). And the arguments c_t and R_t of (12) will themselves be affected by the extent of uncertainty, for it will affect households' saving, as well as portfolio, decisions. The former, of course, impact not only on c_t but also on the economy's capital stock and thus, via the equilibrium real return on capital, on R_t. In addition, because R_t is set in nominal terms, its level will include a risk differential for inflation uncertainty (Fama and Farber, 1979).

Furthermore, the invariance of (12) to uncertainty breaks down if money must be held at the start of a period to yield its transaction services during that period. In this case, the money demand decision temporally precedes the related consumption decision so the marginal service yield of money is random with moments that depend on the covariance matrix of forecast errors for consumption and the price level. Thus the extent of uncertainty, as reflected in this covariance matrix, influences the quantity of real balances demanded in relation to R_t and plans for c_{t+1}.

There is, moreover, another type of uncertainty that is even more fundamental than rate-of-return randomness. In particular, the existence of uncertainty regarding exchange opportunities available at an extremely fine level of temporal and spatial disaggregation – uncertainties regarding the 'double coincidence of wants' in meetings with potential exchange partners – provides the basic *raison d'être* for a medium of exchange. In addition, the ready verifiability of money enhances the efficiency of the exchange process by permitting individuals to economize on the production of information when there is uncertainty about the reputation of potential trading partners. Thus uncertainty is crucial in explaining why it is that money holdings help to facilitate transactions – to save 'shopping time' in our formalization. In this way randomness is critically involved, even when it does not appear explicitly in the analysis. (Alternative treatments of uncertainty in the exchange process have been provided by Patinkin, 1956; Brunner and Meltzer, 1971; King and Plosser, 1986.)

An important concern of macroeconomists in recent years has been to specify models in terms of genuinely structural relationships; that is, ones that are invariant to policy changes. This desire has led to increased emphasis on explicit analysis of individuals' dynamic optimization problems, with these expressed in terms of basic taste and technology parameters. Analysis of that type is especially problematical in the area of money demand, however, because of the difficulty of specifying rigorously the precise way – at a 'deeper' level than (2), for example – in which money facilitates the exchange process. One prominent attempt to surmount this difficulty has featured the application of a class of overlapping-generations models – i.e. dynamic equilibrium models that emphasize the differing perspectives on saving of young and old individuals – to a variety of problems in monetary economics. The particular class of overlapping-generations models in question is one in which, while there is an analytical entity termed 'fiat money', the specification deliberately excludes any shopping-time or related feature that would represent the transaction-facilitating aspect of money. Thus this approach, promoted most prominently in the work of Wallace (1980), tries to surmount the difficulty of modelling the medium-of-exchange function of money by simply ignoring it, emphasizing instead the asset's function as a store of value.

Models developed under this overlapping-generations approach typically possess highly distinctive implications, of which the particularly striking examples will be mentioned. First, if the monetary authority causes the stock of money to grow at a rate in excess of the economy's rate of output growth, no money will be demanded and the price level will be infinite. Second, steady-state equilibria in which money is valued will be Pareto optimal if and only if the growth rate of the money stock is non-positive. Third, open-market changes in the money stock will have no effect on the price level. It has been shown, however, that these implications result from the model's neglect of the medium-of-exchange function of money. Specifically, McCallum (1983) demonstrates that all three implications vanish if this neglect is remedied by recognition of shopping-time considerations as above. That conclusion suggests that the class of overlapping-generations models under discussion provides a seriously misleading framework for the analysis of monetary issues. This weakness, it should be added, results not from the generational structure of these models, but from the overly restrictive application of the principle that assets are valued solely on the basis of the returns that they yield; in particular, the models fail to reflect the non-pecuniary return provided by holdings of the medium of exchange. On these points see also Tobin (1980).

Recognizing this problem but desiring to avoid specifications like (2), some researchers have been attracted to the use of models incorporating a *cash-in-advance* constraint (e.g. Lucas, 1980; Svensson, 1985). In these models, it is assumed that an individual's purchases in any period cannot exceed the quantity of money brought into that period. Clearly, imposition of this type of constraint gives a medium-of-exchange role to the model's monetary asset and thereby avoids the problems of the Wallace-style overlapping-generations models. Whether it does so in a satisfactory manner is, however, more doubtful. In particular, the cash-in-advance formulation implies that start-of-period money holdings place a *strict* upper limit on purchase during the period. This is a considerably more stringent notion than that implied by (2), which is that such purchases are possible but increasingly expensive in terms of time and/or other resources. Thus the demand for money will tend to be less sensitive to interest-rate changes with the cash-in-advance specification than with one that ties consumption and money holding together less rigidly. More generally, the cash-in-advance specification can be viewed as an extreme special case of the shopping-time function described in (2), in much the same way as a fixed-coefficient production function is a special case of a more general neoclassical technology. For some issues, use of the special case specification will be convenient and not misleading, but care must be exerted to avoid inappropriate applications. It seems entirely unwarranted, moreover, to opt for the cash-in-advance specification in the hope that it will be more nearly structural and less open to the Lucas critique (1976) than relations such as (2). Both of these specificational devices – and probably any that will be analytically tractable in a macroeconomic context – should be viewed not as literal depictions of technological or social constraints, but as potentially useful metaphors that permit the analyst to recognize in a rough way the benefits of monetary exchange. (On the general topic, see Fischer, 1974.)

A final controversy that deserves brief mention pertains to an aspect of money demand theory that has not been formally discussed above, but which is of considerable importance in practical applications. Typically, econometric estimates of money-demand functions combine 'long run' specifications such as (12) with a *partial adjustment* process that relates actual money-holdings to the implied 'long run' values. Operationally, this approach often results in a regression equation that includes a lagged value of the money stock as an explanatory variable. (Distributed-lag formulations are analytically similar.) Adoption of the partial adjustments mechanism is justified by appeal to portfolio-adjustment costs. Specifically, some authors argue that money balances serve as a 'buffer stock' that temporarily accommodates unexpected variations in income, while others attribute sluggish adjustments to search costs.

From the theoretical perspective, however, the foregoing interpretation for the role of lagged-money balances (or distributed lags) appears weak. If is difficult to believe that tangible adjustment costs are significant, and in their absence there is no role for lagged money balances, in formulations such as (12) when appropriate transaction and opportunity-cost variables are included. Furthermore, typical estimates suggest adjustment speeds that are too slow to be plausible.

These points have been stressed by Goodfriend (1985), who offers an alternative explanation for the relevant empirical findings. A model in which there is full contemporaneous adjustment of money-holding to transaction and opportunity-cost variables is shown to imply a positive coefficient on lagged money when these determinants are positively autocorrelated and contaminated with measurement error. Under this interpretation, the lagged variable is devoid of behavioural significance; it enters the regression only because it helps to explain the dependent variable in a mongrel equation that mixes together relations pertaining to money-demand and other aspects of behaviour. (This particular conclusion is shared with the 'buffer stock' approach described by Laidler (1984), which interprets the conventional regression as a confounding of money-demand with sluggish price-adjustment behaviour.) Furthermore, the measurement error hypothesis can account for positive auto-correlation of residuals in the conventional regression and, if measurement errors are serially correlated, the *magnitude* of the lagged-money coefficient typically found in practice.

BIBLIOGRAPHY

Barro, R.J. and Fischer S. 1976. Recent developments in monetary theory. *Journal of Monetary Economics* 2(2), April, 133–67.

Baumol, W.J. 1952. The transactions demand for cash: an inventory theoretic approach. *Quarterly Journal of Economics* 66, November, 545–56.

Brunner, K. and Meltzer, A. 1971. The uses of money: money in the theory of an exchange economy. *American Economic Review* 61(5), December, 784–805.

Cannan, E. 1921. The application of the theoretical apparatus of supply and demand to units of currency. *Economic Journal* 31, December, 453–61.

Dutton, D.S. and Gramm, W.P. 1973. Transactions costs, the wage rate, and the demand for money. *American Economic Review* 63(4), September, 652–65.

Fama, E.F. 1980. Banking in the theory of finance. *Journal of Monetary Economics* 6(1), January, 39–57.

Fama, E.F. and Farber, A. 1979. Money, bonds, and foreign exchange. *American Economic Review* 69(4), September, 639–49.

Feige, E. and Parkin, M. 1971. The optimal quantity of money, bonds, commodity inventories, and capital. *American Economic Review* 61(3), June, 335–49.

Fischer, S. 1974. Money and the production function. *Economic Inquiry* 12(4), December, 517–33.

Fisher, I. 1911. *The Purchasing Power of Money.* New York: Macmillan.

Fisher, I. 1930. *The Theory of Interest.* New York: Macmillan.

Friedman, M. 1956. The quantity theory of money: a restatement. In *Studies in the Quantity Theory of Money*, ed. M. Friedman, Chicago: University of Chicago Press.

Friedman, M. and Schwartz, A.J. 1970. *Monetary Statistics of the United States.* New York: Columbia Press for the National Bureau of Economic Research.

Goodfriend, M. 1985. Reinterpreting money demand regressions. *Carnegie-Rochester Conference Series on Public Policy* 22, Spring, 207–42.

Hicks, J.R. 1935. A suggestion for simplifying the theory of money. *Economica* 2, February, 1–19.

Hicks, J.R. 1939. *Value and Capital.* Oxford: Oxford University Press; 2nd edn, New York: Oxford University Press, 1946.

Karni, E. 1973. The transactions demand for cash: incorporation of the value of time into the inventory approach. *Journal of Political Economy* 81(5), September-October, 1216–25.

Keynes, J.M. 1930. *A Treatise on Money.* 2 vols, London: Macmillan; New York: St. Martin's Press, 1971.

Keynes, J.M. 1936. *The General Theory of Employment, Interest and Money.* London: Macmillan; New York: Harcourt, Brace.

King, R.G. and Plosser, C.I. 1986. Money as the mechanism of exchange. *Journal of Monetary Economics* 17(1), January, 93–115.

Laidler, D. 1984. The 'buffer stock' notion in monetary economics. *Economic Journal* 94, supplement, 17–34.

Lavington, F. 1921. *The English Capital Market.* London: Methuen.

Lucas, R.E., Jr. 1976. Econometric policy evaluation: a critique. *Carnegie-Rochester Conference Series on Public Policy* 5, Autumn, 19–46.

Lucas, R.E. Jr. 1980. Equilibrium in a pure currency economy. In *Models of Monetary Economies*, ed. J.H. Kareken and N. Wallace, Minneapolis: Federal Reserve Bank of Minneapolis.

McCallum, B.T. 1983. The role of overlapping-generations models in monetary economics. *Carnegie-Rochester Conference Series on Public Policy* 18, Spring, 9–44.

McCallum, B.T. 1985. Bank deregulation, accounting systems of exchange, and the unit of account: a critical review. *Carnegie-Rochester Conference Series on Public Policy* 23, Autumn, 13–45.

Marshall, A. 1926. *Official Papers by Alfred Marshall.* Ed. J.M. Keynes, London: Macmillan; reprinted, New York: A.M. Kelley, 1965.

Meltzer, A.H. 1963. The demand for money: the evidence from the time series. *Journal of Political Economy* 71, June, 219–46.

Mill, J.S. 1848. *Principles of Political Economy.* 2 vols. London: John W. Parker.

Miller, M.H. and Orr, D. 1966. A model of the demand for money by firms. *Quarterly Journal of Economics* 80, August, 413–35.

Niehans, J. 1978. *The Theory of Money.* Baltimore: Johns Hopkins University Press.

Patinkin, D. 1956. *Money, Interest, and Prices.* New York: Harper and Row.

Pigou, A.C. 1917. The value of money. *Quarterly Journal of Economics* 32, November, 38–65.

Saving, T.R. 1971. Transactions costs and the demand for money. *American Economic Review* 61(3), June, 407–20.

Sidrauski, M. 1967. Rational choice and patterns of growth in a monetary economy. *American Economic Association Papers and Proceedings* 57, May, 534–44.

Svensson, L.E.O. 1985. Money and asset prices in a cash-in-advance economy. *Journal of Political Economy* 93(5), October, 919–44.

Tobin, J. 1956. The interest-elasticity of transactions demand for cash. *Review of Economics and Statistics* 38, August, 241–7.

Tobin, J. 1958. Liquidity preference as behavior toward risk. *Review of Economic Studies* 25, February, 65–86.

Tobin, J. 1980. Discussion. In *Models of Monetary Economics*, ed. J.H. Kareken and N. Wallace, Minneapolis: Federal Reserve Bank of Minneapolis.

Wallace, N. 1980. The overlapping generations model of fiat money. In *Models of Monetary Economies*, ed. J.H. Kareken and N. Wallace, Minneapolis: Federal Reserve Bank of Minneapolis.

Whitaker, J.K. (ed.) 1975. *The Early Economic Writings of Alfred Marshall, 1867–1890.* 2 vols, New York: Free Press.

Wicksell, K. 1906. *Lectures on Political Economy.* Trans. E. Classen, London: Routledge & Kegan Paul, 1935, Vol. II; New York: A.M. Kelley, 1967.

Demand for Money: Empirical Studies

STEPHEN M. GOLDFELD

The relation between the demand for money balances and its determinants is a fundamental building block in most theories of macroeconomic behaviour and is a critical component in the formulation of monetary policy. Indeed, a stable demand function for money has long been perceived as a prerequisite for the use of monetary aggregates in the conduct of policy. Not surprisingly, then, the demand for money has been subjected to extensive empirical scrutiny.

Several broad factors have shaped the evolution of this research. First, there is the evolving nature of theories of the demand for money. The simple versions of the so-called quantity theory were followed by the Keynesian theory of liquidity preference and then by more modern variants. As theory evolved, so did empirical research. A second factor is the growing arsenal of econometric techniques that has permitted more sophisticated examinations of dynamics, functional forms, and expectations. These techniques have also provided researchers with a wide variety of diagnostic tests to evaluate the adequacy of particular specifications.

Finally, and perhaps most importantly, research has been spurred by the apparent breakdown of existing empirical models in the face of newly emerging data. These difficulties have been particularly evident since the mid-1970s. In many countries this period has been marked by unusual economic conditions including severe bouts of inflation, record-high interest rates, and deep recessions. This period also coincided with the widespread adoption of floating exchange rates and, in a number of major industrial countries, with substantial institutional changes brought about by financial innovation and financial deregulation. The period since 1974 thus provided a very severe test of empirical money demand relationships. As we shall see, this period succeeded in exposing a number of shortcomings in existing specifications of money demand functions. Where institutional change was particularly marked, it also led to a change in what we think of as 'money'.

It is perhaps ironic that the emergence of these shortcomings roughly coincided with the adoption by a number of central banks of policies aimed at targeting monetary aggregates. Some have argued that this association is more than mere coincidence. In any event, given the vested interest of policy-makers in the existence of a reliably stable money demand function, it is hardly surprising that employees of central banks were among the most active contributors to the most recent literature on money demand. The Federal Reserve System of the United States, with its dominant market share of monetary economists, was particularly active in this regard.

As noted, appreciation of empirical research on money demand requires a bit of background on monetary theory and it is with this that we begin our discussion. We next consider some measurement issues and then turn to the early empirical results. After briefly documenting the emerging difficulties with these results, we finally consider recent reformulations of the demand for money.

I. THEORETICAL OVERVIEW. One of the earliest approaches to the demand for money, the *quantity theory of money* starts with the *equation of exchange*. One version of the equation can be written

$$MV \equiv PT \tag{1}$$

where M is the quantity of money, V is the velocity of circulation, P is the price level, and T is the volume of transactions. While M, P and T are directly measurable, V is implicitly defined by (1) so (1) is merely an identity. However, if we add the key assumption that velocity, V, is determined by technological and/or institutional factors and is therefore relatively constant, one can recast (1) as a demand function for money in which the demand for real balances, M/P, is proportional to T.

This simple demand for money function was modified by Keynes's (1936) analysis which introduced the speculative motive for holding money along with the transactions motive embodied in (1). The speculative motive views money and bonds as alternative assets with bond holding, in turn, viewed as depending on the rate of return on bonds. This introduction of the interest rate into the demand for money, where it joined the transactions variable suggested by the quantity theory is the main empirical legacy of Keynes. Once the interest rate is introduced, there is no presumption that velocity will be constant from period to period.

Post-Keynesian developments moved in several different directions. One is represented by Friedman (1956), whose restatement of the quantity theory dispensed with the individual motives posited by Keynes and treated money like any other asset yielding a flow of services. This view emphasized the level of wealth as one of the major determinants of money demand. Friedman also suggested that a quite broad range of opportunity cost variables including the expected rate of inflation have theoretical relevance in a money demand function. (Given this emphasis, it is ironic that Friedman's early empirical results

(Friedman, 1959) seemed to suggest that interest rates were unimportant in explaining velocity movements.)

While Friedman's approach sidestepped the explicit role of money in the transactions process, other influential post-Keynesian developments reconsidered and expanded on the transactions motive. William Baumol (1952) and James Tobin (1956) both applied inventory-theoretic considerations to the transactions demand for money. This led to the so-called *square-root law* with average money holdings given by

$$M = (2bT/r)^{1/2} \tag{2}$$

where r is the interest rate on bonds and b is the brokerage charge or transactions cost for converting bonds into cash. Dividing both sides of equation (2) by the price level, makes the real transactions demand for money depend on 'the' interest rate, real brokerage charges and the level of real transactions. Miller and Orr (1966) extended this analysis to allow for uncertainty in cash flows, providing the insight and a firm's average money holdings depends on the variance of its cash flow viewed as a measure of the uncertainty of the flow of receipts and expenditures.

Keynes's speculative motive has also been reformulated – largely in terms of portfolio theory (Tobin, 1958). However, given the menu of assets available in most countries, this approach actually undermines the speculative demand for money. The reason is that if there is a riskless asset (e.g. a savings deposit) paying a higher rate of return than money (presumed to be zero in most models), then money is a dominated asset and will not be held. One can resurrect an asset demand for money by combining the portfolio approach with transaction costs but this has yet to be done in a fully general way. One partial attempt in this direction (Ando and Shell, 1975) demonstrates that in a world with a riskless and a risky asset the demand for money will not depend on the rate of return on the risky asset. This approach suggests using only a small number of interest rates, pertaining to riskless assets, in empirical work.

II. SOME MEASUREMENT ISSUES. Empirical estimation of money demand function requires choosing explicit variables measuring both money and its determinants. Even if guided by a particular theory, such choices are often less than clear-cut. Given the diversity of theories, the range of possible variables is wider yet. This is immediately evident when one considers how to measure 'money'; the sharp distinction between money and other assets turns out to be a figment of the textbook. Moreover, what passes for money can be readily altered by changing financial institutions.

In general, theories based on the transactions motive provide the most guidance and lead to a so-called *narrow* definition of money that includes currency and deposits transferable by cheque (also called checkable deposits). In some institutional settings a plausible measure of checkable deposits is readily apparent. In the United States, for example, for many years only demand deposits at commercial banks were checkable. In other settings, there may well be a spectrum of checkable assets without any clear-cut dividing line. For example, a deposit account may limit the number of cheques per month or may have a minimum cheque size. Other accounts may permit third-party transfers only if regular periodic payments are involved or may permit cheque writing only with substantial service charges. When such deposit accounts should be included in a transactions-based definition of money is not obvious.

Furthermore, even in a world in which the definition of checkable deposits is relatively unambiguous, it is not clear that currency and checkable deposits should be regarded as perfect substitutes, a view that is implicit in simply adding them together to produce a measure of money. Currency and checkable deposits may differ in transactions costs, risk of loss, and ease of concealment of illegal or tax-evading activities. It may thus be preferable to estimate separate demand functions for currency and checkable deposits.

Once one moves away from a transactions view of the world, the appropriate empirical definition of money is even less clear. A theory that simply posits that money yields some unspecified flow of services must confront the fact that many assets may yield these services in varying degrees. Such theories have typically relied on a relatively broad definition of money but the definitions utilized are inevitably somewhat arbitrary. (This issue is taken up again in section IV.)

As with the definition of money, alternative theories have different implications for the relevant set of explanatory variables. As we have seen, the most prominent variables suggested by theory include the level of transactions, wealth, the opportunity cost of holding money, and transaction costs. Each of these involves measurement problems, even in a world of certainty. When uncertainty is allowed for, and expectational issues therefore arise, matters are even worse.

The level of transactions (T in equation (2)) is typically measured by the level of income or gross national product (GNP). While the term 'gross' in GNP makes it sound comprehensive, GNP is much less inclusive than a general measure of transactions. In particular, it excludes all sales of intermediate goods, purchases of existing goods, and financial transactions, all of which may contribute to a demand for money. The empirical use of GNP as a proxy for T therefore presumes that GNP and T move in a proportionate way. Unfortunately, this key assumption is extremely difficult to test because reliable data on T are nonexistent. (Moreover, it is not the case that all transactions are equally 'money intensive'. To cope with this empirically might require separately introducing the various components of T or, as an approximation, of GNP.)

As an alternative to GNP, some researchers have used permanent income, typically measured as an exponentially weighted average of current and past-values of GNP. This is generally done in the spirit of the modern quantity theory where permanent income is a proxy for wealth. As an empirical matter, given the high correlation of GNP and permanent income, a permanent income variable could easily 'work' even if money demand is dominated by transactions considerations. One can, of course, use a measure of wealth directly (only non-human wealth is readily available). This is certainly consistent with the quantity theory view and, given that financial transactions may generate a demand for money, can fit into a transactions view.

Before leaving measures of transactions, we should note one further problem that arises because of issues of aggregation. Most theories of the demand for money apply to an individual behavioural unit but are generally estimated with aggregate data without much attention to the details of aggregation. This failure may lead to the omission of potentially important variables. For example, in the context of a transactions variable, aggregation may suggest that the distribution of income as well as the level of income matters. However, with a few exceptions discussed below, we shall not focus on problems of aggregation.

Another set of measurement issues is presented by the opportunity cost of holding money. We consider in turn the two parts to this story: the rate of return on assets alternative to money; and the own rate of return on money. Under the transactions view, the relevant alternative is a 'bond' that is used as a temporary repository of funds soon to be disbursed. As a practical matter this has led to the use of one or more of the following rates: the yield on short-term government securities; the yield on short-term commercial paper; and the yield on time or savings deposits. As we have seen, the relevant set of alternatives under the modern quantity theory is much broader and empirical research in this spirit has also used long-term bond rates, either government or corporate. Indeed, a few studies have attempted to use proxies for the entire term structure of interest rates. In addition, some investigators use the rate of return on corporate equities and/or the expected rate of inflation.

The own rate of return on money obviously depends on the concept of money chosen for analysis. The seemingly simplest case occurs with a narrow definition of money that bears an explicit zero rate of return. In such cases, most investigators have treated the own rate of return as zero. This, however, is not precisely correct since holders of deposits may earn an implicit rate of return, either because they receive services or because service charges may be foregone as the level of deposits rises. Measuring this implicit return is no easy matter. Matters are considerably more complicated when broader definitions of money are used and some components of money bear explicit interest, especially when there are several components each carrying a different rate of return. The aggregate own rate of return would then be a complex function of the interest rates, shares, and elasticities of each of the components. For the most part, researchers have not faced this issue squarely. However, the advent of interest-bearing checkable deposits that exist alongside zero-return demand deposits means that even those using narrow definitions of money must address this issue.

A final variable that appears prominently in equation (2) is the transactions cost, b. This is sometimes interpreted as the brokerage charge for selling 'bonds' or as the 'shoe-leather' cost of going to the bank. Whatever the interpretation, however, such variables have generally been conspicuous by their absence from empirical work. Researchers have thus implicitly assumed that real transactions costs are constant. The validity of this assumption has grown increasingly

135

questionable as innovation and technical change have spread through the financial sector. Unfortunately, there are only highly imperfect proxies available to measure b. The consequences of this are examined below.

III. EMPIRICAL FINDINGS: THE EARLY RESULTS. Before considering empirical results, a word needs to be said about the types of data that have been used. While there have been some cross-section studies using data at a variety of levels of aggregation, the vast majority of available studies employ highly aggregated time series data. Initially these were confined to annual observations, but increasingly the focus has been on shorter periods such as quarterly, monthly, or even weekly data. In part this shift stems from the availability of short-period data but, more importantly, from the related perception that the quarterly or monthly time frame is more useful for guiding monetary policy.

The earliest empirical work in monetary economics primarily involved producing estimates of velocity, characterizing its behaviour over time and identifying the institutional factors responsible for longer-run movements in velocity. (For a discussion of this literature, see Selden, 1956.) Modern empirical studies of money demand first appeared a few years after the publication of Keynes's *General Theory* in 1936. Not surprisingly, these studies focused on testing the prediction of the hypothesis of liquidity preference that there was an inverse relationship between the demand for money and the interest rate. One approach to this problem was to establish a positive correlation between interest rates and velocity.

A second approach involved distinguishing between 'active' and 'idle' balances and then relating idle balances to the interest rate. Conceptually this amounted to posting a demand function for money of the form

$$M/P = ky + f(r) \tag{3}$$

where y is income or GNP. With k assumed known, idle balances, given by $(M/P - ky)$, can then be related to r. Tobin (1947), using data from 1922 to 1945, calculated k by assuming idle balances were zero in 1929 and found a relatively close relationship between idle balances and r of a roughly hyberbolic shape. Of course, as was recognized at the time, there is an element of arbitrariness in the definition of idle balances, and it is a short step to estimate question (3) directly, obviating the necessity of distinguishing between active and idle balances. Indeed, this approach had already been suggested in 1939 by A. J. Brown who estimated a variant of (3). (Brown's paper, which is surprisingly modern, both conceptually and statistically, is also noteworthy for the inclusion of the rate of inflation in the demand for money.)

Initially at least, typical estimates of the demand-for-money function were based on annual data and used a log-linear specification, which has constant elasticities. Thus, a typical equation used in empirical work was of the form

$$\ln(M_t/P_t) = \beta_0 + \beta_1 \ln y_t + \beta_2 \ln r_t. \tag{4}$$

As before, y is a scale variable such as income or wealth and r represents the interest rate. Sometimes several scale variables or interest rates were used; additional variables were also included on occasion. From the late 1950s on many studies estimated equations like (4) for a number of countries. These studies differed in terms of the sample period (sometimes going back as far as the late 1800s) and the specific choice of dependent and independent variables. While these studies hardly produced identical conclusions, at least through the early 1970s a number of common findings did emerge. For the United States (see Laidler, 1977): (1) Various interest rates – sometimes several at once – proved to be of statistical significance in (4) with elasticities of short-term and long-term rates generally ranging from -0.1 to -0.2 and -0.2 to -0.8, respectively. (2) Income, either measured or permanent, and non-human wealth all achieved statistical significance, although typically only when these variables were included one at a time. Some studies viewed the matter as a contest between these several variables, the winner often depending on the sample period, the definition of M, and econometric details. Estimated scale elasticities ranged from about $\frac{1}{2}$ to nearly 2, but most estimates were in the lower end of the range. (3) As judged by a variety of procedures, both formal and informal, the demand function for money exhibited a reasonable amount of stability over time.

While many of the early studies using annual data tended to ignore dynamic aspects of the specification, a number did address this issue, most frequently by the simple device of including a lagged dependent variable in the money demand equation. One rationale for this is the partial adjustment model, which posits the existence of a 'desired' level of real money balances $M*/P$, and further assumes that the actual level of money balances adjusts in each period only part of the way toward its desired level. This idea is captured in the logarithmic adjustment equation

$$\ln(M_t/P_t) - \ln(M_{t-1}/P_{t-1}) = \gamma[\ln(M_t^*P_t) - \ln(M_{t-1}/P_{t-1})] \qquad (5)$$

where M_t/P_t denotes the actual value of real money balances. The parameter y governs the speed of adjustment; $y = 1$ corresponds to complete adjustment in one period (i.e. $M_t = M_t^*$). Implementation of (5) is achieved by expressing M_t^*/P_t as a function of y_t and r_t as in (4) and substituting into (5). The resulting equation gives M_t/P_t as a function of y_t, r_t, and M_{t-1}/P_{t-1}. As we shall see below, the partial adjustment model is not without its shortcomings.

Not surprisingly, allowance for dynamics proved of particular importance once investigators began using quarterly data. Dynamics aside, results obtained with quarterly data generally confirmed the findings with annual data. Quarterly data did suggest it was preferable to work with narrow definitions of the money stock. Indeed, some studies suggested there was a further payoff to disaggregating the narrow money stock, either into its components (i.e. currency and checkable deposits) or by type of holder (e.g. household vs. business). On the whole, however, these refinements were not necessary to yield a serviceable quarterly money demand function. A simple specification in which real narrow money balances depended on GNP, a short-term market interest rate, a savings deposit rate, and lagged money balances appeared to be adequate for most purposes (Goldfeld, 1973).

As the 1970s unfolded, however, this happy state of affairs unravelled. Difficulties were particularly pronounced with United States data, but instabilities appeared with equations for other countries as well (Boughton, 1981; Goldfeld, 1976). In the United States these difficulties first surfaced around 1974. Had past behaviour held up, the behaviour of real GNP and interest rates from the end of 1973 to the end of 1975 should have produced a mild decline in money demand in 1974 followed by a recovery of 1975. Instead, real money balances steadily declined, falling by about 7 per cent during this period. The economy seemed to be making do with less money. Or put another way, conventional money demand functions made sizeable and unprecedented overprediction errors. From 1974 to 1976 the cumulative drift was about 9 per cent. Another indication of the difficulty emerged when the post-1973 data were added to the estimation sample. Inclusion of the recent data tended to change the parameter estimates in the conventional money demand function, generally yielding quite unsatisfactory estimates. For example, the parameter y tended to hover close to zero, implying implausibly long adjustment lags. These same difficulties were picked up by formal econometric tests that rejected the hypothesis that the structure of the money demand function had remained constant. Prior to 1974 these tests had given no indication of instability.

Stimulated by these difficulties, the last decade has witnessed a veritable outpouring of research on money demand. The primary emphasis has been on 'fixing' matters by improving the specification and/or using more appropriate econometric techniques. While progress has been made, even improved specifications have not proved immune from episodes of apparent instability.

IV. RECENT REFORMULATIONS. A substantial part of recent research has focused on the United States, but the issues are of general relevance for other countries. It should be noted that open-economy considerations, which have received only limited attention in the literature on the United States, would be more relevant for many other countries. On the other hand, the emphasis on financial innovation and deregulation in the case of the United States is probably of lesser importance for many countries.

The idea that financial innovation contributed to the instability of money demand in the United States stemmed from two observations: (1) the errant behaviour of money demand in the mid-1970s appeared to be concentrated in business holdings of checkable deposits; and (2) marked improvements were evident in business cash management techniques. These improvements, including such arcane-sounding devices as cash concentration accounts, lockboxes and zero balance accounts, altered the nature of the transactions process and permitted firms to economize on the need for transactions balances. These improvements stemmed both from exogenous technological innovations (e.g. in telecommunications) and from endogenous decisions whereby firms, stimulated by the high opportunity cost of holding cash, invested in new transactions technologies. In the context of the Baumol–Tobin inventory-theoretic model of money demand. those changes can be modelled as a reduction in transactions costs, b, while in the Miller–Orr variant one can view these innovations as reducing the uncertainty of receipts and expenditures. While early innovations in the United States appeared concentrated in the business sector, more recent innovations – such as money market mutual funds – and financial deregulation have affected households as well. (As an aside, it should be noted that the constraints of regulation stimulated financial innovation that in turn forced deregulation. To the extent that innovation and deregulation contributed to instability in money demand, regulation, which was in part aimed at improving the workings of monetary policy, sowed the seeds of later difficulties for policy.)

Explicit consideration of financial innovation in an econometric specification has, however, proved extremely difficult. The basic problem is that there are no reliable direct data on transactions costs. What indirect evidence there is stems from the use of time trends to capture exogenous technical change or of some function of previous peak interest rates as a proxy for endogenous reductions in transactions costs. The idea behind the latter variable is that high interest rates create an incentive to incur the fixed costs necessary to introduce a new technology but that once interest rates decline the technology remains in place. The use of a previous peak variable is meant to capture this irreversibility and researchers using such a variable have found that it improves the fit of money demand functions. Unfortunately, however, the resulting estimates do not appear very robust, either to small changes in specification or to the use of additional data. Some economists have played down the potential importance of financial innovations, pointing to the fact that high interest rates did not appear to stimulate the same degree of innovation in other countries. Nevertheless, most empirical researchers remain quite uneasy with their inability to capture adequately relevant changes in transactions costs since it raises the possibility of a continuing source of specification error.

Of course, financial innovation is not the only conceivable source of specification error, and when money demand functions began misbehaving, other elements of the conventional specification were re-examined. In particular, researchers again considered the use of alternative measures of transactions, wealth, and interest rates. They also relaxed the assumption of a constant elasticity implicit in equation (4) and re-examined the benefits of disaggregating money holdings by type of holder (e.g. business vs. households). In contrast with earlier work, these efforts suggested a greater role for wealth and some evidence on the importance of allowing for a nonconstant interest elasticity and for introducing a measure of the own rate of return on money. They also reconfirmed that there are gains to disaggregation by types of holder. Nevertheless, these improvements still left unexplained much of the aberrant behaviour of money demand.

Another approach was to reconsider the definition of money. Since a substantial volume of monetary data is available, economists who are unhappy with the official definitions are free to construct their own. Research along these lines has been in two diametrically opposed directions. The first has regarded the official definitions of even 'narrow' money as too broad, at least from a purely transactions point of view. This concern has led some to suggest using a disaggregated approach in which separate empirical demand functions are estimated for each monetary asset. This sidesteps the definitional issue and at the same time permits the use of econometric techniques that take account of the interrelated nature of the demand functions. In practice, however, the application of this approach has been complicated by the appearance of new financial instruments brought about by deregulation, and such efforts have not been fully successful.

The second approach, noting that the line between transactions and other motives has become empirically murky, has considered whether relatively broad definitions of money could yield a stable demand function. However, conventional broad monetary aggregates obtained by simply adding together quantities of different assets are subject to the criticism that they combine components that offer differing degrees of monetary services. Consequently, most recent research along these lines has involved the weighting of the various components of a broad measure of money by the degree of 'moneyness' or 'liquidity' of each component. Although, the way in which this is done is inevitably somewhat aribtrary, in recent years some progress has been made in applying index-number theory to this issue (Barnett, 1982). Indeed, the Federal Reserve now regularly publishes a number of such weighted money measures, sometimes called Divisia indexes. Thus far, this research seems to suggest that only the broadest of such monetary measures appear to yield a stable demand function. Even this result, however, is not without its difficulties. For one, a complete understanding of this result requires an economic explanation of the behaviour of the weights used to construct the measures. (Especially where the weights are based on relative velocity or turnover data, there appears to be some circularity in the construction of the measures that will give the appearance of stability.) Second, it is important for the results to be useful in formulating policy that these weights be forecastable. On the whole, while promising, the verdict on the Divisia approach is still out, either as an explanation of instability or for use in the policy process.

Yet another feature of money demand that has received recent attention is the dynamics of the adjustment process. As noted above, the so-called real partial adjustment model of equation (5) formed the basis of much early work. However, this model has come in for a wide variety of criticism. One aspect of this can be seen by rewriting (5) as follows:

$$\ln M_t - \ln M_{t-1} = \gamma [\ln(M_t^*/P_t) - \ln(M_{t-1}/P_{t-1})] + \Delta \ln P_t. \qquad (6)$$

As (6) shows, since the coefficient of Δ in P_t is unity, the specification presumes as immediate adjustment to changes in the price level. As this assumption seems unwarranted, more recent research has used the so-called nominal adjustment model given by

$$\ln M_t - \ln M_{t-1} = \gamma(\ln M_t^* - \ln M_{t-1}). \qquad (7)$$

Estimation of (7) is quite similar to (5) except that the variable M_{t-1}/P_t replaces the variable M_t/P_{t-1}. A variety of empirical tests suggest that the nominal model is to be preferred, but also indicate clearly that this change does not repair the money demand function.

Other re-examinations of dynamics have suggested that the simple partial adjustment model, either nominal or real, is more fundamentally flawed. Some writers point to the fact that the Miller–Orr transactions model predicts that money holders, facing a fixed cost of adjusting, will either make no adjustment or a complete adjustment. Partial adjustment would not be observed for an individual money holder. However, the applicability of this feature of the Miller–Orr model to aggregate data is not fully clear. Other attempts to derive an adjustment model from an optimizing framework have suggested models with a variable speed of adjustment with the speed parameter y depending on income or interest rates. However, there has been only limited empirical work with such models.

Considerably more empirical work has been done with models where the speed of response of money holdings to some shock depends on which variable is producing the change in desired money holdings. This would accommodate the suggestion that changes in real income, especially when such changes are paid in the form of money, should yield quicker adjustments of money holdings than changes in interest rates. To allow for these effects, one must relax the rigid geometrically distributed lag specification. Data for the United States do seem to provide some support for this more general adjustment model but, as with other suggested improvements, this change is not sufficient to yield a single acceptable function that fits the post-World War II data.

A final attack on the partial adjustment model involves a more general reconsideration of the adjustment process. The point can be seen most clearly if we assume that the monetary authorities exogenously fix the nominal money supply. In such a world the desired nominal stock of money must adjust to the given stock, presumably by adjustments to variables influencing desired holdings. A particularly simple version of this idea would dispense with the partial adjustment model of (7) and replace it with an adjustment equation for prices as in

$$\ln P_t - \ln P_{t-1} = \lambda(\ln M_t - \ln M_t^*) \tag{8}$$

While this obviates the need for a short-run money demand function, long-run money demand appears in (8) via M_t^*.

A variant of this approach would estimate the money demand function by imposing the assumption of rationality on price expectations. For example, one could begin with (4) or even (7) and use it to solve for the price level. Then, via the Fisher equation expressing the nominal rate of interest as the sum of the real rate and the expected rate of inflation, one can use the hypothesis of rational expectations to express the actual price level (or the rate of inflation) as a function of income, the money stock, and the real rate of interest. If we further posit the stochastic process for income, for the money stock (e.g. via a money supply rule) and for the real rate (e.g. the real rate is constant), we can use the resulting equation to estimate the parameters of the money demand function.

The estimation of money demand via (8) or its rational expectations variant is, however, not without its difficulties. One problem is that this approach implies that the inflation rate reacts quickly to changes in output or the money supply. Put another way, it assumes that the rate of inflation moves like an asset price determined in financial markets. This approach conflicts with the evidence of the stickiness of prices in response to shocks of various sorts. One way around this difficulty is to posit that the adjustments to 'disequilibrium' in the money market are effected in interest rates and/or output. (See Laidler and Bentley (1983), for a small model with these features.)

A second difficulty is the assumption that the money supply is exogenously set. For the United States, at least, the assumption seems most relevant for the period October 1979 to October 1982, the three years during which the Federal Reserve officially adopted monetary targeting. However, stated official policy notwithstanding, some have argued that the Federal Reserve never really pursued a policy of monetary targeting while others have suggested that such a policy began well before October 1979. This suggests that it is not always easy to identify changing monetary regimes. Nevertheless, it is clear that changes in the rules governing monetary policy can have implications for the proper specification and estimation of a money demand function. That is, conventional specifications may work in some circumstances but not others. Indeed, it has been suggested that failure to allow for this accounts for at least part of the apparent instability of conventional money demand functions (Gordon, 1984).

While it is undoubtedly important to view the money demand function as part of a more complete system, to date this has not been empirically done in a satisfactory way. Part of the problem stems from the need to specify the money supply process in some detail; a task made difficult by changing policy strategies and deregulation. Moreover, there is yet another complication, the question of the time unit of the analysis. Practitioners of monetary policy tend to have a relatively short decision-making horizon so that capturing the money supply process may require weekly or monthly data. In contrast, most money demand estimation has used quarterly or annual data. Put another way, proper attention to the dynamics of the monetary sector may require more care in the choice of the time unit of analysis. It may also require some sophisticated econometric techniques to perform estimation in the face of changing monetary regimes.

V. CONCLUSION. The current state of affairs finds the empirical money demand function to be in a bit of disarray, especially if one judges success by our ability to specify a single function that appears stable over the postwar period. To be sure, there are ample potential explanations – perhaps embarrassingly many – for the observed difficulties with conventional models. However, data inadequacies or econometric problems mean that it is not always easy to incorporate these explanations into an empirical demand function for money. Some have concluded from this that greater instability in money demand is a fact, not to be repaired in any simple way. It is the challenge of future research to overcome these difficulties. Given progress to date, it seems likely that further research will yield a more satisfactory statistical explanation of money demand. However, the flimsy nature of past apparent successes and the theoretical and empirical difficulties alluded to above alert us to the need for substantial scrutiny in evaluating new models. Ultimately, of course, such models need to stand the forward-looking test of time; that is, they need to continue to hold outside the period of estimation.

BIBLIOGRAPHY

Ando, A. and Shell, K. 1975. Demand for money in a general portfolio model. In *The Brookings Model: Perspectives and Recent Developments*, Amsterdam: North-Holland.

Barnett, W. 1982. The optimum level of monetary aggregation. *Journal of Money, Credit and Banking* 14(4), Part II, November, 687–710.

Baumol, W.J. 1952. The transactions demand for cash: an inventory theoretic approach. *Quarterly Journal of Economics* 66, November, 545–56.

Boughton, J.M. 1981. Recent instability of the demand for money: an international perspective. *Southern Economic Journal* 47(3), January, 579–97.

Brown, A.J. 1939. Interest, prices, and the demand schedule for idle money. *Oxford Economic Papers* 2, May, 46–69. Reprinted, in *Oxford Studies in the Price Mechanism*, ed. T. Wilson and P. Andrews, Oxford: Clarendon Press, 1951.

Friedman, M. 1956. The quantity theory of money – a restatement. In M. Friedman (ed.), *Studies in the Quantity Theory of Money*, Chicago: University of Chicago Press.

Friedman, M. 1959. The demand for money: some theoretical and empirical results. *Journal of Political Economy* 67, August, 327–51.

Goldfeld, S.M. 1973. The demand for money revisited. *Brookings Papers on Economic Activity* No. 3, 577–638.

Goldfeld, S.M. 1976. The case of the missing money. *Brookings Papers on Economic Activity* No. 3, 683–730.

Gordon, R.J. 1984. The short-run demand for money: a reconsideration. *Journal of Money, Credit and Banking* 16(4), Part I, November, 403–34.

Keynes, J.M. 1936. *The General Theory of Employment, Interest, and Money*. London: Macmillan; New York: Harcourt, Brace.

Laidler, D.E.W. 1977. *The Demand for Money: Theories and Evidence*. New York: Dun-Donnelley.

Laidler, D.E.W. and Bentley, B. 1983. A small macro-model of the post-war United States. *Manchester School of Economics and Social Studies* 51(4), December, 317–40.

Miller, M.H. and Orr, D. 1966. A model of the demand for money by firms. *Quarterly Journal of Economics* 80, August, 413–35.

Selden, R. 1956. Monetary velocity in the United States. In *Studies in the Quantity Theory of Money*, ed. M. Friedman, Chicago: University of Chicago Press.

Tobin, J. 1947. Liquidity preference and monetary policy. *Review of Economics and Statistics* 29, May, 124–31.

Tobin, J. 1956. The interest-elasticity of transactions demand for cash. *Review of Economics and Statistics* 38, August, 241–7.

Tobin, J. 1958. Liquidity preference as behaviour towards risk. *Review of Economic Studies* 25, February, 65–86.

Disintermediation

CHARLES GOODHART

'Intermediation' generally refers to the interposition of a financial institution in the process of transferring funds between ultimate savers and ultimate borrowers. The forms of services that such financial intermediaries provide, the characteristics of their liabilities and assets, and the rationale for their existence is described elsewhere. For this purpose, we only need to assume that a certain pattern of financial intermediation is given, say by actual historical development, or is theoretically optimal.

Disintermediation is then said to occur when some intervention, usually by government agencies for the purpose of controlling, or regulating, the growth of financial intermediaries, lessens their advantages in the provision of financial services, and drives financial transfers and business into other channels. In some cases the transfers of funds that otherwise would have gone through the books of financial intermediaries now pass directly from saver to borrower. An example of this is to be found when onerous reserve requirements on banks leads them to raise the margin (the spread) between deposit and lending rates, in order to maintain their profitability, so much that the more credit-worthy borrowers are induced to raise short-term funds directly from savers, for example, in the commercial paper market. Another, more recent, example arises when stringent capital adequacy requirements lead banks to provide funds to borrowers in a form that can be packaged into securities of a kind that can be on-sold to ultimate savers, rather than kept on the books of the banks involved, and thereby need larger capital backing.

Disintermediation not only refers to those instances where financial flows are constrained by intervention to pass more directly from saver to borrower (than in an unconstrained context), but also where such flows pass through different, and generally less efficient, channels than would otherwise be the case. This latter is just as common in practice. For example, where constraints and regulations are imposed on some sub-set of domestic financial institutions, substitute services of a similar kind will become provided by 'fringe' financial institutions that are not so constrained. More generally, in the absence of exchange control, constraints and burdens on the provision of domestic financial services will encourage financial institutions to provide these same services abroad, notably in the international Euro-markets. Indeed, the development of the Euro-markets provides a case study of the power of disintermediation out of more rigorously controlled domestic financial markets into an international milieu not subject to such controls.

The likelihood of such disintermediation imposes a limit on the authorities' ability to impose controls and regulations on financial intermediaries. If such controls are to be effective, they presumably force financial intermediaries to behave in a way that they would not voluntarily do, and hence represent a burden on them. There will then be an incentive for the controlled financial intermediary to seek to escape such a burden, for example through disintermediation. This represents a perennial problem for the monetary authorities. Logically, it might seem to lead to a tendency for the authorities to be forced to extremes, either to prevent disintermediation altogether by extending the ambit of controls to all forms and kinds of financial intermediation, or alternatively to allow complete laissez-faire within the financial system, despite the dangers of financial instability that might ensue. In practice, however, the authorities try to seek a compromise in the form of regulations sufficiently well-designed to maintain monetary control and financial stability, without being sufficiently burdensome to cause large-scale disintermediation. This is not, however, an easy exercise and requires continuous adjustment by the authorities as the financial system evolves.

Endogenous and Exogenous Money

MEGHNAD DESAI

The issue of endogeneity or exogeneity of money is one that runs through the history of monetary theory, with prominent authors appearing to hold views on either side. Narrowly put, those who plug for the exogeneity view take one or all among the cluster of variables – price level, interest rate or real output – as being determined by movements in the stock of money. Those who hold the endogeneity view consider that the stock of money in circulation is determined by one or all of the variables mentioned above. This narrow definition begs several questions. The variables price level (P), interest rate (R), real output (Y) and money stock (M) are all at the macroeconomic level, i.e. in the context of a one-good economy. Some part of the continuing debate can be traced to the view held by various participants in the controversy about whether such a high level of aggregation is appropriate, e.g. is there *a* rate of interest? Another part of the debate refers to the choice of money stock variable. Is it commodity money (gold), fiat (paper) money, bank deposits or a larger measure of liquidity that is to stand for *the* money stock? The problem can be dealt with even at a one-good level either in the context of a closed economy or an open economy and either in an equilibrium or a disequilibrium context, static or dynamic, short run or long run. The basic issue is about the direction of causality-money to other variables or other variables to money. But as our understanding of the underlying statistical theory concerning causality and exogeneity has advanced in recent years, it must also be added that participants in the controversy conflate the exogeneity of a variable (especially of money) with its *controllability* by policy. Strictly speaking one can have exogeneity without any presumption that the variable can be manipulated by policy, for example rainfall. Also once posed in a dynamic context, we should distinguish between weak exogeneity, which allows for feedback from the endogenous to the exogenous variables over time, and strong exogeneity, which does not allow such a feedback (Hendry, Engle and

146

Richard, 1983). Endogeneity or exogeneity are notions that only make sense in such a model, which has then allowed the controversy to continue.

SOME DEFINITIONS. To simplify matters, at the risk of putting off readers, let us begin by specifying a small model within whose context endogeneity and exogeneity can be defined. This macroeconomic model will consist of four variables P, Y, R and M whose exogenous/endogenous status is at debate. We subdivide them into the three non-monetary variables P, Y, R labelled X and money M. There are of course other truly exogenous variables – tastes, technology, international variables – which we label Z. Now we observe that the variables X and M are correlated, i.e. jointly distributed conditional upon the set of variables Z. The question of endogeneity or exogeneity of money is as to whether the correlation between X and M can be written in terms of X being a function of M and Z, or M being a function of X and Z. In econometric terms, we can partition the joint distribution of X and M into a *conditional* distribution of X on M, Z and a marginal distribution of M on Z (the exogenous money case) or a conditional distribution of M on X and Z and a marginal distribution of X on Z. Thus when we say money is exogenous it is exogenous with respect to X variables but it could still be determined by Z variables; symmetrically for the X variables being exogenous. If M is influenced by the past values of X as well as by Z though not by the current values of X, then M is said to be weakly exogenous. Thus M may be controlled by monetary authorities but they may be reacting to past behaviour of X variables. Then M is determined by a reaction function and is only weakly exogenous. The same definition of weak exogeneity extends to the Z variables. Thus even international variables, such as capital inflow, may be determined by past values of X variables in which case they are weakly exogenous (for further detail, see Desai, 1981). The best way to consider the issue of exogeneity of money is to specify the type of money economy envisaged – commodity money, paper money, credit money and look at the variables likely to influence the supply of money and its relation with other variables.

COMMODITY MONEY. Historically the argument about exogeneity is constructed around the Quantity Theory of Money, which stated that the amount of money in circulation at any time determined the volume of trade and if the amount went on increasing it would lead sooner or later to an increase in price. In the context of commodity money, the proposition concerned attempts by coining authorities to debase coinage by clipping or alloying it with inferior metal. These were ways in which the amount of money could be altered by policy manipulation and then exogenously act upon prices. But in a commodity money regime, the stock of money could also be altered by influx of precious metal through gold discoveries and greater influx. These were exogenous variations not susceptible to policy manipulation but presumed an open economy. The first statement of the quantity theory of money by David Hume starts with an illustration of an influx of gold from outside and traces its effects first on real economic activity and eventually on prices. In Hume's quantity theory, money is exogenous but

147

not subject to policy manipulation. The opposite view (argued by James Steuart for instance) was that it was the volume of activity that elicited the matching supply of money. This could be done partly by dis-hoarding on the parts of those who now expected a better yield on their stock. It could also be altered if banks were willing to 'accommodate' a larger volume of bills (see Desai, 1981). Dis-hoarding implies that a portion of the money supply *in circulation* is endogenously determined in a commodity money economy. It could be argued that even the influx of gold could have been caused by the discrepancy between the domestic and the world gold price, which in the 18th century before a world gold market existed could be substantial. In the latter case money would be weakly exogenous as long as there were lags between the appearance of discrepancy and the inflow of gold.

INSIDE MONEY. Once however one introduces banks into the scheme of things, the issue of exogeneity becomes complex. Till very recently we have lacked a theory of banking behaviour of any degree of sophistication, although in terms of institutional description we have much knowledge. If banks are willing to 'accommodate' a greater volume of trade, this can only be because they find it profitable to do so. This increased profitability may be actual or perceived but it must be a result of an increase in differential between the interest (discount) rate borrowers are willing to pay and the rate at which banks can acquire liquidity. Banks can then choose to expand the ratio of credit to the cash base and sustain a higher volume. Banks create inside money and inside money can only be regarded as endogenous. But the extent to which a single bank can create money will depend on the behaviour of the *banking system*. The banking system can by the cloakroom mechanism choose any ratio of credit to cash base. It is conceivable though not likely that in such a system of inside money, banks could arbitrarily, i.e. exogenously, increase money supply. They must however base such an action on considerations of expected profitability. We can envisage a situation in which banks guided by 'false' expectations can sustain a credit boom by a bootstraps mechanism. This is the way in which a Wicksellian cumulative process could sustain itself. An arbitrary, exogenous increase in inside money by the banking system though possible is not very likely. It runs into the problems caused by the leakage of cash either internally (finite limits to the velocity of circulation of cash) or abroad. It was the international leakage that was normally regarded as the most likely constraint since it caused outflow of gold – the International Gold Standard which provided the context for 19th-century theories in this imposed exogenous constraints on money supply by imposing a uniform gold price in all countries. In such a case, money is exogenous and not subject to policy manipulation. In as much as gold movements are triggered by internal variables, it is weakly exogenous.

OUTSIDE FIAT MONEY. It is the case of fiat money printed as the state's liability, i.e. as outside money, that provides the best illustration of exogenous money not subject to any constraint. In a world where only paper currency was used and it was printed by the monetary authorities, the stock of money could be exogenously determined. This would be additionally so even if there was inside money as long as the monetary authorities could insist that banks obeyed a strict cash to deposit ratio and there were no substitutes for cash available beyond the control of the monetary authorities. It is this view of money that most closely corresponds to Keynes's assumption in the *General Theory* and it is also in the monetarist theory of Milton Friedman. The banking system is a passive agent in this view and given the cash base is always fully loaned up. Thus given the amount of high powered money in the system providable only by the monetary authorities, the supply of money is determined. Even if the stock of money were exogenous, its impact on the non-monetary variables X can be variable. This is because the velocity of circulation which translates the stock of money into money in circulation need not be constant but variable. If the velocity of circulation were not only a variable but also a function of the X variables, then although the monetary authorities can determine the stock of money the influence of money on real variables is not as predicted by the Quantity Theory. Thus it is not the exogeneity of money issue that divides monetarists and Keynesians but the determinants of the velocity of circulation. For the monetarist, the velocity of circulation $(M/P \cdot Y)$ has to be independent of P, Y, R and M. For Keynesians, the demand for money depends on the rate of interest crucially and the interest elasticity of demand for money is a variable tending to infinity in a liquidity trap.

MODERN CREDIT ECONOMY. In a world with inside and outside money with a sophisticated banking system as well as a non-banking financial sector, the question of exogeneity is the most complex. In the previous case of outside fiat money, we assumed that the cash ratio was fixed and adhered to by banks. It is when the banks' reserve base contains government debt instruments – treasury bills, bonds, etc. – that the profit-maximizing behaviour of the banks renders a greater part of the money stock endogenous. Thus while the narrow money base – currency in circulation and in central bank reserves – can be regulated by the monetary authority, the connection between money base and total liquidity in the economy becomes highly variable. Banks will expand their loan portfolio as long as the cost of replenishing their liquidity does not exceed the interest rate they can earn on loans. The relation between broad money (M_3) and narrow money (M_0) becomes a function of the funding policy concerning the budget deficit and the structure of interest rates. Thus the stock of narrow money can be exogenous and policy determined. But the stock of broad money is endogenous. A crucial recent element has been the financial revolution of the last decade (De Cecco, 1987). A variety of financial instruments – credit cards, charge cards, money market funds, interest-bearing demand deposits, electronic cash transfer – has made the ratio of cash to volume of financial transactions variable though with a steep downward trend. It has also increased the number of money substitutes and made the cost of liquidity lower. The non-banking financial system thus can create liquidity by 'accommodating' a larger volume of business, advancing trade credit, allowing consumer debt to increase etc. The velocity of circulation of cash increases very sharply in such a world and liquidity, a broader concept that even broad money, becomes endogenous. Here again profitability of liquidity creation becomes the determining variable. But the financial revolution has also integrated world financial markets and economies are increasingly open. Thus capital flows are rapid and respond to minute discrepancies in the covered interest parity. In such a world money is at best weakly exogenous but more usually endogenous. The issue of exogeneity or endogeneity of money thus crucially depends on the type of money economy that one is considering – commodity money, paper money, credit (mobile) money. It also depends on the sophistication of the banking and financial system within which such money is issued. Debates over the last two hundred years have used the word money to cover a variety of situations. It has also not been clarified whether the issue is exogeneity of money or its controllability and whether it is merely the stock of money or its velocity as well which is being considered. Once these issues have been clarified, the notion of exogeneity needs to be defined in the modern econometric fashion, relative to a model in order to decide whether money can be exogenous. It seems likely that the narrower the definition of money stock, the more likely is it to fulfil the requirement of (weak) exogeneity. Such exogeneity is necessary but not sufficient to demonstrate that money determines the price level or the real economy.

BIBLIOGRAPHY

De Cecco, M. 1987. *Changing Money: Financial Innovations in Developed Countries.* Oxford: Blackwell.

Desai, M. 1981. *Testing Monetarism.* London: Frances Pinter; New York: St. Martin's Press, 1982.

Hendry, D., Engle, R. and Richard, J.L. 1983. Exogeneity. *Econometrica* 51(2), March, 227–304.

Equation of Exchange

MICHAEL D. BORDO

The equation of exchange (often referred to as the quantity equation) is one of the oldest formal relationships in economics, early versions of both verbal and algebraic forms appearing at least in the 17th century. Perhaps the best known variant of the equation of exchange is that expressed by Irving Fisher (1922):

$$MV = PT \qquad (1)$$

Equation (1) represents a simple accounting identity for a money economy. It relates the circular flow of money in a given economy over a specified period of time to the circular flow of goods. The left-hand side of equation (1) stands for money exchanged, the right-hand side represents the goods, services and securities exchanged for money during a specified period of time. M is defined as the total quantity of money in the economy, T as the total physical volume of transactions, where a transaction is defined as any exchange of goods, including physical capital, services and securities for money, P is an appropriate price index representing a weighted average of the prices of all transactions in the economy. Finally, to make the stock of money comparable with the flow of the value of transactions (PT), and to make the two sides of the equation balance, it is multiplied by V, the transactions velocity of circulation, defined as the average number of times a unit of currency turns over (or changes hands) in the course of effecting a given year's transactions.

An alternative variant of the Equation of Exchange is the income version by Pigou (1927). Empirical difficulties in measuring an index of transactions, and the special price index related to it, led, with the development of national income accounting, to the formulation of equation (2):

$$MV = PY \qquad (2)$$

where y represents national income expressed in constant dollars, P the implicit price deflator and V the income velocity of circulation defined as the average number of times a unit of currency turns over in the course of financing the year's final activity.

Equations (1) and (2) differ from each other because the volume of transactions in the economy includes intermediate goods and the exchange of existing assets, in addition to final goods and services. Thus vertical integration and other factors which affect the ratio of transactions to income would also alter the ratio of transactions velocity to income velocity.

A third version of the Equation of Exchange, the Cambridge Cash Balance Approach (Pigou, 1917: Marshall, 1923; Keynes, 1923), converts the flow of spending into units comparable to the stock of money

$$M = kPY \tag{3}$$

where $k = 1/V$ is defined as the time duration of the flows of goods and services money could purchase, for example, the average number of weeks income held in the form of money balances.

Equations (2) and (3) are arithmetically equivalent to each other but they rest on fundamentally different notions of the role of money in the economy. Both equations (2) and (1) view money primarily as a medium of exchange and the quantity of money is represented as continually 'in motion' – constantly changing hands from buyer to seller in the course of a time period. Equation (3) views money as a temporary abode of purchasing power (an asset) forming part of a cash balance 'at rest'. Consequently, the items included in the definition of money in the transactions and income versions of the Equation of Exchange are assets used primarily to effect exchange – currency and checkable deposits, whereas the Cash Balance approach includes, in addition to these items, non-checkable deposits and possibly other liquid assets.

The Equation of Exchange is useful both as a classification scheme for analysing the underlying forces at work in a money economy and as a building block or engine of analysis for monetary theory and in particular for the Quantity Theory of Money.

As a classification scheme, the equation as a basic accounting identity of a money economy demonstrates the two-sided nature of the circular flow of income – that the sum of expenditures must equal the sum of receipts. The left-hand side of the equation shows the market value of goods and services purchased (dollar value of goods exchanged) and the money received. The equation also relates the stock of money to the circular flow of income by multiplying M by its velocity. Finally, the equation is useful in creating definitional categories – M, V, P, T – amenable both to empirical measurement and to theoretical analysis.

The Equation of Exchange is best known as a building block for the Quantity Theory of Money. The traditional approach has been to make behavioural assumptions about each of the variables in the equation, converting it from an identity to a theory. The simplest application, dubbed the 'Naive Quantity Theory' (Locke, 1691) treated V and T in equation (1) as constants, with P varying in direct proportion to M.

A more sophisticated version (Fisher, 1911) treats each of M, V and T as being normally determined by independent sets of forces, with V as determined by slowly changing factors such as those affecting the payments process and the community's money holding habits.

The Cambridge Cash Balance approach, based on equation (3), views the Quantity Theory as encompassing both a theory of money demand and money supply. In this approach the nominal money supply is determined by the monetary standard and the banking system while the nominal quantity of money demanded is proportional to nominal income, with k the factor of proportionality, representing the community's desired holding of real cash balances. k in turn is determined by economic variables such as the rate of interest in addition to the factors stressed by the Fisher approach. The price level (value of money) is then determined by the equality of money supply and demand.

The Equation of Exchange can also be regarded as a building block for a macro theory of aggregate demand and supply (Schumpeter, 1966). If we view MV as aggregate demand and T or y as aggregate supply, then P would be determined in the familiar Marshallian way.

Finally, the equation can be used to construct a theory of nominal income. According to this approach (Friedman and Schwartz, 1982), nominal income is determined by the interaction of the money supply and a stable demand for real cash balances. The decomposition of a given change in nominal income into a change in the price level and in real output is determined in the short run by inflation (deflation) forecast errors and in the long run by the natural rate of output.

The Equation of Exchange both as a classification scheme and as a building block for the Quantity Theory of Money can be traced back to the earliest development of economic science.

The pre-Classical writers of the 17th and 18th centuries viewed the Equation in both senses. Locke (1691), Hume (1752) and Cantillon (1735) each organized his approach to monetary issues using the Equation. Locke had a clear statement of the naive quantity theory assuming both V and T to be immutable constants. Hume followed Locke but made a clear distinction between long run statics and short run dynamics. In the long run the price level would be proportional to M but in the short run or transition period, changes in M would produce changes in T. Cantillon had a clear understanding of the relationship between the stock of money and the circular flow of income. Indeed, he was the first to define explicitly the concept of velocity of circulation, viewing V not as a constant but as a variable influenced in a stable way by both technological and economic variables. Furthermore, like Hume, Cantillon distinguished between the long run equilibrium nature of the quantity theory and short run disequilibrium. Both Locke and Hume viewed the Equation from the perspective of money 'at rest' forming a cash balance whereas Cantillon viewed money as continuously in 'motion'.

John Law (1705) understood the Equation of Exchange but used it to derive a link between changes in the quantity of M and changes in T.

The Classical economists, Thornton, Ricardo, Mill, Senior and Cairnes followed the Locke/Hume/Cantillon tradition of the quantity theory of money using a verbal version of the Equation of Exchange in their monetary analysis.

Algebraic versions of the Equation first appeared in the 17th and 18th centuries (see Marget, 1942; Humphrey, 1984). The British writers Briscoe (1694) and Lloyd (1771) both expressed a rudimentary version of equation (1), unfortunately omitting a term for velocity. Turner (1819) formulated the equation without breaking PT into separate components. The most complete early statement of the equation was by Sir John Lubbock (1840) who not only included all the items of the Equation but (preceding Fisher) distinguished between the quantities and velocities of hard currency, bank notes and bills of exchange. Similar complete algebraic statements of the Equation were made by the German writers Lang (1811) and Rau (1841); the Italian Pantaleoni (1889); the Frenchmen Levasseur (1858), Walras (1874) and de Foville (1907); and the Americans Newcomb (1885), Hadley (1896), Norton (1902) and Kemmerer (1907). Of this group Newcomb presented the clearest statement. Newcomb started with the concept of exchange as involving the transfer of money for wealth. Summing up all exchanges in the economy he arrived at his Equation of Societary Circulation:

$$VR = KP \qquad (4)$$

where V represents the total value of currency, R the rapidity (velocity) of circulation, K the volume of real transactions, P a price index.

The clearest and best known algebraic expressions of the Equation were by the neoclassical economists Irving Fisher (1922) and A.C. Pigou (1917). Fisher (1911), directly following Newcomb, defined the Equation of Exchange as

> a statement, in mathematical form, of the total transaction: effected in a certain period in a given community. ... [I]n the grand total of all exchanges for a year, the total money paid is equal to the total value of goods bought. The equation thus has a money side and a goods side. The money side is the total money paid, and may be considered as the product of the quantity of money multiplied by its rapidity of circulation. The goods side is made up of the products of quantities of goods exchanged multiplied by their respective prices (pp. 15–17).

This statement expressed as in equation (1) or in an expanded version distinguishing between currency and deposits payable by check,

$$MV + M'V' = PT \qquad (5)$$

where M' is defined as checkable deposits and V' their velocity, Fisher then used to analyse the forces determining the price level.

Fisher's approach followed the 'motion' theory tradition of Cantillon with velocity determined primarily by technological and institutional factors. In contrast Pigou (1917) and other writers in the Cambridge tradition, Marshall (1923) and Keynes (1923), followed the 'rest' approach of Locke and Hume expressing the Equation as

$$1/P = kR/M \qquad (6)$$

where R represents total resources enjoyed by the community, k the proportion of resources the community chooses to keep in the form of titles to legal tender, M the number of units of legal tender and P a price index. For Pigou the fundamental difference between his approach and that of Fisher was that by focusing

attention on the proportion of their resources that people *choose* to keep in the form of titles to legal tender instead of focusing on the 'velocity of circulation'... it brings us... into relation with *volition* – an ultimate *cause of demand* – instead of with something that seems at first sight *accidental and arbitrary* (p. 174, emphasis added).

The Cambridge Cash Balance Version of the Equation of Exchange, by focusing on the demand for money and volition rather than emphasizing mechanical aspects of the circular flow of money, can be viewed as the starting point for the Keynesian approach to the demand for money (Keynes, 1936), for modern choice theoretic approaches to money demand (Hicks, 1935) and for the Modern Quantity Theory of Money (Friedman, 1956).

BIBLIOGRAPHY

Bordo, M.D. 1983. Some aspects of the monetary economics of Richard Cantillon. *Journal of Monetary Economics* 12, 234–58.

Briscoe, J. 1694. *Discourse on the Late Funds....* London.

Cantillon, R. 1755. *Essai sur la nature du commerce en général.* Ed. H. Higgs, London: Macmillan, 1931; reprinted New York: Augustus M. Kelley, 1964.

Fisher, I. 1911. *The Purchasing Power of Money.* 2nd edn, 1922. Reprinted, New York: Augustus M. Kelley, 1963.

Foville, A. de. 1907. *La monnaie.* Paris.

Friedman, M. 1956. The quantity theory of money – a restatement. In *Studies in the Quantity Theory of Money,* ed. M. Friedman, Chicago: University of Chicago Press.

Friedman, M. and Schwartz, A.J. 1982. *Monetary Trends in the United States and the United Kingdom: their relation to income, prices and interest rates, 1867–1975.* Chicago: University of Chicago Press for the National Bureau of Economic Research.

Hadley, A.T. 1896. *Economics.* New York.

Hicks, J.R. 1935. A suggestion for simplifying the theory of money. *Economica* 2, February, 1–19.

Holtrop, M.W. 1929. Theories of the velocity of circulation of money in earlier economic literature. *Economic Journal* 39, January, 503–24.

Hume, D. 1752. Of money. In *Essays, Moral, Political and Literary,* Vol. I of *Essays and Treatises,* a new edition, Edinburgh: Bell and Bradfute; Cadell and Davies, 1804.

Humphrey, T.M. 1984. Algebraic quantity equations before Fisher and Pigou. *Federal Reserve Bank of Richmond Economic Review* 70(5), September/October, 13–22.

Kemmerer, E.W. 1907. *Money and Credit Instruments in Their Relation to General Prices.* New York: H. Holt & Co.

Keynes, J.M. 1923. *A Tract on Monetary Reform.* Reprinted, London: Macmillan for the Royal Economic Society, 1971; New York: St. Martin's Press, 1971.

Keynes, J.M. 1936. *The General Theory of Employment, Interest and Money.* Reprinted,

London: Macmillan for the Royal Economic Society, 1973; New York: St. Martin's Press, 1971.

Lang, J. 1811. *Gundlineien der politischen Arithmetik*. Kharkov.

Levasseur, E. 1858. *La question de l'or: les mines de Californie et d'Australie*. Paris.

Lloyd, H. 1771. *An Essay on the Theory of Money*. London.

Locke, J. 1691. *The Works of John Locke*, Vol. 5. London, 1823.

Lubbock, J. 1840. *On Currency*. London.

Marget, A.W. 1942. *The Theory of Prices*. New York: Prentice-Hall.

Marshall, A. 1923. *Money, Credit and Commerce*. London: Macmillan. Reprinted, New York: Augustus M. Kelley, 1965.

Newcomb, S. 1885. *Principles of Political Economy*. New York: Harper & Brothers.

Norton, J.P. 1902. *Statistical Studies in the New York Money Market*. New York.

Pantaleoni, M. 1889. *Pure Economics*. Trans. T.B. Bruce, London: Macmillan, 1898.

Pigou, A.C. 1917. The value of money. *Quarterly Journal of Economics* 32, November. Reprinted in *Readings in Monetary Theory*, ed. F.A. Lutz and L.W. Mints for the American Economic Assocation, Homewood, Ill.: Irwin, 1951.

Pigou, A.C. 1927. *Industrial Fluctuations*. 2nd edn, London: Macmillan, 1929; reprinted, New York: A.M. Kelley, 1967.

Rau, K.H. 1842. *Grundsätze der Volkswirtschaftslehre*. 4th edn, Leipzig and Heidelberg.

Schumpeter, J.A. 1954. *History of Economic Analysis*. New York: Oxford University Press.

Turner, S. 1819. *A Letter Addressed to the Right Hon. Robert Peel with Reference to the Expediency of the Resumption of Cash Payments at the Period Fixed by Law*. London.

Walras, L. 1874–7. *Eléments d'économie politique pure*. Lausanne: Corbaz. Definitive edn. 1926, Trans. by W. Jaffé as *Elements of Pure Economics*, New York: Orion, 1954.

Financial Intermediaries

JAMES TOBIN

The tangible wealth of a nation consists of its natural resources, its stocks of goods, and its net claims against the rest of the world. The goods include claims against the rest of the world. The goods include structures, durable equipment of service to consumers or producers, and inventories of finished goods, raw materials and goods in process. A nation's wealth will help to meet its people's future needs and desires; tangible assets do so in a variety of ways, sometimes by yielding directly consumable goods and services, more often by enhancing the power of human effort and intelligence in producing consumable goods and services. There are many intangible forms of the wealth of a nation, notably the skill, knowledge and character of its population and the framework of law, convention and social interaction that sustains cooperation and community.

Some components of a nation's wealth are appropriable; they can be owned by governments, or privately by individuals or other legal entities. Some intangible assets are appropriable, notably by patents and copyrights. In a capitalist society most appropriable wealth is privately owned, more than 80 per cent by value in the United States. Private properties are generally transferable from owner to owner. Markets in these properties, *capital markets*, are a prominent feature of capitalist societies. In the absence of slavery, markets in 'human capital' are quite limited.

A person may be wealthy without owning any of the assets counted in appropriable *national wealth*. Instead, a personal wealth inventory would list paper currency and coin, bank deposits, bonds, stocks, mutual funds, cash values of insurance policies and pension rights. These are paper assets evidencing claims of various kinds against other individuals, companies, institutions or governments. In reckoning personal *net worth*, each person would deduct from the value of his total assets the claims of others against him. In 1984 American households' gross holdings of financial assets amounted to about 75 per cent of their net worth, and their net holdings to about 55 per cent (Federal Reserve, 1984). If the net worths of all economic units of the nation are added up, paper claims and obligations cancel each other. All that remains, if valuations are consistent and the census is complete, is the value of the national wealth.

If the central government is excluded from this aggregation, *private net worth* – the aggregate net worth of individuals and institutions and subordinate governments (included in the 'private sector' because, lacking monetary powers, they have limited capacities to borrow) – will count not only the national-wealth assets they own but also their net claims against the central government. These include coin and currency, their equivalent in central bank deposit liabilities, and interest-bearing Treasury obligations. If these central government debts exceed the value of its real assets, *private net worth* will exceed national wealth. (However, in reckoning their net worth, private agents may subtract something for the future taxes they expect to pay to service the government's debts. Some economists argue that the subtraction is complete, so that public debt does not count in aggregate private wealth (Barro, 1974) while others give reasons the offset is incomplete (Tobin, 1980). The issue is not crucial for this essay.)

OUTSIDE ASSETS, INSIDE ASSETS AND FINANCIAL MARKETS

Private net worth, then, consists of two parts: privately owned items of national wealth, mostly tangible assets, and government obligations. These *outside* assets are owned by private agents not directly but through the intermediation of a complex network of debts and claims. *inside* assets.

Empirical magnitudes. For the United States at the end of 1984, the value of tangible assets, land and reproducible goods, is estimated at $13.5 trillion, nearly four times the Gross National Product for the year. Of this, $11.2 trillion were privately owned. Adding net claims against the rest of the world and privately owned claims against the federal government gives private net worth of $12.5 trillion, of which only $1.3 trillion represent outside financial assets. The degree of intermediation is indicated by the gross value of financial assets, nearly $14.8 trillion; even if equities in business are regarded as direct titles to real property and excluded from financial assets, the outstanding stock of inside assets is $9.6 trillion. Of these more than half, $5.6 trillion, are claims on financial institutions. The $9.6 million is an underestimate, because many inside financial transactions elude the statisticians. The relative magnitudes of these numbers have changed very little since 1953, when private net worth was $1.27 trillion, gross financial assets $1.35 trillion, $1.05 excluding equities, and GNP was $0.37 trillion (Federal Reserve, 1984).

Raymond Goldsmith, who has studied intermediation throughout a long and distinguished career and knows far more about it than anyone else, has estimated measures of intermediation for many countries over long periods of time (1969, 1985). Here is his own summary:

> The creation of a modern financial superstructure, not in its details but in its essentials, was generally accomplished at a fairly early stage of a country's economic development, usually within five to seven decades from the start of

modern economic growth. Thus it was essentially completed in most now-developed countries by the end of the 19th century or the eve of World War I, though somewhat earlier in Great Britain. During this period the financial interrelations ratio, the quotient of financial and tangible assets, increased fairly continuously and sharply. Since World War I or the Great Depression, however, the ratio in most of these countries has shown no upward trend, though considerable movements have occurred over shorter periods, such as sharp reductions during inflations; and though significant changes have taken place in the relative importance of the various types of financial institutions and of financial instruments. Among less developed countries, on the other hand, the financial interrelations ratio has increased substantially, particularly in the postwar period, though it generally is still well below the level reached by the now-developed countries early in the 20th century.

Goldsmith finds that a ratio of the order of unity is characteristic of financial maturity, as is illustrated by the figures for the United States given above (1985, pp. 2–3).

Goldsmith finds also that the relative importance of financial institutions, especially non-banks, has trended upwards in most market economies but appears to taper off in mature systems. Institutions typically hold from a quarter to a half of all financial instruments. Ratios around 0.40 were typical in 1978, but there is considerably more variation among countries than in the financial interrelations ratio. The United States, at 0.27, is on the low side, probably because of its many well-organized financial markets (1985, Table 47, p. 136).

The volume of gross financial transactions is mind-boggling. The GNP velocity of the money stock in the United States is 6 or 7 per year; if intermediate as well as final transactions for goods and services are considered, the turnover may be 20 or 30 per year. But demand deposits turn over 500 times a year, 2500 times in New York City banks, indicating that most transactions are financial in nature. The value of stock market transactions alone in the United States is one third of the Gross National Product; an average share of stock changes hands every nineteen months. Gross foreign exchange transactions in United States dollars are estimated to be hundreds of billions of dollars every day. 'Value added' in the financial services industries amounts to 9 per cent of United States GNP (Tobin, 1984).

Outside and inside money. The outside/inside distinction is most frequently applied to money. *Outside money* is the monetary debt of the government and its central bank, currency and central bank deposits, sometimes referred to as 'base' or 'high-powered' money. *Inside money*, 'low-powered', consists of private deposit obligations of other banks and depository institutions in excess of their holdings of outside money assets. Just which kinds of deposit obligations count as 'money' depends on definitions, of which there are several, all somewhat arbitrary. Outside money in the United States amounted to $186 billion at the end of 1983, of which $36 billion was held as reserves by banks and other depository institutions; the remaining $150 billion was held by other private agents as currency. The total money stock M1, currency in public circulation plus checkable deposits, was \$480 billion. Thus inside M1 was \$294 billion, more than 60 per cent of the total.

Financial markets, organized and informal. Inside assets and debts wash out in aggregative accounting; one person's asset is another's debt. But for the functioning of the economy, the inside network is of great importance. *Financial markets* allow inside assets and debts to be originated and to be exchanged at will for each other and for outside financial assets. These markets deal in paper contracts and claims. They complement the markets for real properties. Private agents often borrow to buy real property and pledge the property as security; households mortgage new homes, businesses incur debt to acquire stocks of materials or goods-in-process or to purchase structures and equipment. The term *capital markets* covers both financial and property markets. *Money markets* are financial markets in which short-term debts are exchanged for outside money.

Many of the assets traded in financial markets are promises to pay currency in specified amounts at specified future dates, sometimes conditional on future events and circumstances. The currency is not always the local currency; obligations denominated in various national currencies are traded all over the world. Many traded assets are not denominated in any future monetary unit of account: equity shares in corporations, contracts for deliveries of commodities – gold, oil, soy beans, hog bellies. There are various hybrid assets: preferred stock gives holders priority in distributions of company profits up to specified pecuniary limits; convertible debentures combine promises to pay currency with rights to exchange the securities for shares.

Capital markets, including financial markets, take a variety of forms. Some are highly organized auction markets, the leading real-world approximations to the abstract perfect markets of economic theory, where all transactions occurring at any moment in a commodity or security are made at a single price and every agent who wants to buy or sell at that price is accommodated. Such markets exist in shares, bonds, overnight loans of outside money, standard commodities, and foreign currency deposits, and in future contracts and opinions for most of the same items.

However, many financial and property transactions occur otherwise, in direct negotiations between the parties. Organized open markets require large tradable supplies of precisely defined homogeneous commodities or instruments. Many financial obligations are one of a kind, the promissory note of a local business proprietor, the mortgage on a specific farm or residence. The terms, conditions, and collateral are specific to the case. The habit of referring to classes of heterogeneous negotiated transactions as 'markets' is metaphorical, like the use of the term 'labour market' to refer to the decentralized processes by which wages are set and jobs are filled, or 'computer market' to describe the pricing and selling of a host of differentiated products. In these cases the economists' faith is that the outcomes are 'as if' the transaction occurred in perfectly organized auction markets.

FINANCIAL ENTERPRISES AND THEIR MARKETS

Financial intermediaries are enterprises in the business of buying and selling financial assets. The accounting balance sheet of a financial intermediary is virtually 100 per cent paper on both sides. The typical financial intermediary owns relatively little real property, just the structures, equipment, and materials necessary to its business. The equity of the owners, or the equivalent capital reserve account for mutual, cooperative, nonprofit, or public institutions, is small compared to the enterprises' financial obligations.

Financial intermediaries are major participants in organized financial markets. They take large asset positions in market instruments; their equities and some of their liabilities, certificates of deposit or debt securities, are traded in those markets. They are not just middlemen like dealers and brokers whose main business is to execute transactions for clients.

Financial intermediaries are the principal makers of the informal financial markets discussed above. Banks and savings institutions hold mortgages, commercial loans, and consumer credit; their liabilities are mainly checking accounts, savings deposits, and certificates of deposit. Insurance companies and pension funds negotiate private placements of corporate bonds and commercial mortgages; their liabilities are contracts with policy-holders and obligations to future retirees. Thus financial intermediaries do much more than participate in organized markets. If financial intermediaries confined themselves to repackaging open market securities for the convenience of their creditors, they would be much less significant actors on the economic scene.

Financial businesses seek customers, both lenders and borrowers, not only by interest rate competition but by differentiating and advertising their 'products'. Financial products are easy to differentiate, by variations in maturities, fees, auxiliary services, office locations and hours of business, and many other features. As might be expected, non-price competition is especially active when prices, in this case interest rates, are fixed by regulation or by tacit or explicit collusion. But the industry is by the heterogeneous nature of its products monopolistically competitive; non-price competition flourishes even when interest rates are free to move. The industry shows symptoms of 'wastes of monopolistic competition'. Retail offices of banks and savings institutions cluster like competing gasoline stations. Much claimed product differentiation is trivial and atmospheric, emphasized and exaggerated in advertising.

Financial intermediaries cultivate long-term relationships with customers. Even in the highly decentralized financial system of the United States, local financial intermediaries have some monopoly power, some clienteles who will stay with them even if their interest rates are somewhat less favourable than those elsewhere. Since much business is bilaterally negotiated, there are ample opportunities for price discrimination. The typical business customer of a bank is both a borrower and a depositor, often simultaneously. The customer 'earns' the right for credit accommodation when he needs it by lending surplus funds to the same bank when he has them. The same reciprocity occurs between credit unions and mutual savings institutions and some of their members. Close ties frequently develop

161

between a financial intermediary and non-financial businesses whose sales depend on availability of credit to their customers, for example between automobile dealers and banks. Likewise, builders and realtors have funded and controlled many savings and loan associations in order to facilitate mortgage lending to home buyers.

Financial intermediaries balance the credit demands they face with their available funds by adjusting not only interest rates but also the other terms of loans. They also engage in quantitative rationing, the degree of stringency varying with the availability and costs of funds to the intermediary. Rationing occurs naturally as a by-product of lending decisions made and negotiated case by case. Most such loans require collateral, and the amount and quality of the collateral can be adjusted both to individual circumstances and to overall market conditions. Borrowers are classified as to riskiness and charged rates that vary with their classification.

United States commercial banks follow the 'prime rate convention'. One or another of the large banks acts as price leader and sets a rate on six-month commercial loans for its prime quality borrowers. If other large banks agree, as is usually the case, they follow, and the rate becomes standard for the whole industry until one of the leading banks decides another change is needed to stay in line with open-market interest rates. Loan customers are rated by the number of half-points above prime at which they will be accommodated. Of course, some applications for credit are just turned away. One mechanism of short-term adjustment to credit market conditions is to stiffen or relax the risk classifications of customers, likewise to deny credit to more or fewer applicants. Similar mechanisms for rationing help to equate demands to supplies of home mortgage finance and consumer credit.

THE FUNCTIONS OF FINANCIAL MARKETS AND INTERMEDIARY INSTITUTIONS
Intermediation, as defined and described above, converts the outside privately owned wealth of the economy into the quite different forms in which its ultimate owners hold their accumulated savings. Financial markets alone accomplish considerable intermediation, just by facilitating the origination and exchange of inside assets. Financial intermediaries greatly extend the process, adding 'markets' that would not exist without them, and participating along with other agents in other markets, organized or informal.

What economic functions does intermediation in general perform? What do inside markets add to markets in the basic outside assets? What functions does institutional intermediation by financial intermediaries perform beyond those of open markets in financial instruments? Economists characteristically impose on themselves questions like these, which do not seem problematic to lay practitioners. Economists start from the presumption that financial activities are epiphenomena, that they create a veil obscuring to superficial observers an underlying reality which they do not affect. The celebrated Modigliani-Miller theorem (1958), generalized beyond the original intent of the authors, says so. With its help the sophisticated economist can pierce the veil and see that the values of financial assets are just those of the outside assets to which they are ultimately claims, no matter how circuitous the path from the one to the other.

However, economists also understand how the availability of certain markets alters, usually for the better, the outcomes prevailing in their absence. For a primitive illustration, consider the functions of inside loan markets as brilliantly described by Irving Fisher (1930). Each household has an inter-temporal utility function in consumptions today and at future times, a sequence of what we now would call dated 'endowments' of consumption, and an individual 'backyard' production function by which consumption less than endowment at any one date can be transformed into consumption above endowment at another date. Absent the possibility of intertemporal trades with others, each household has to do its best on its own; its best will be to equate its marginal rate of substitution in utility between any two dates with its marginal rate of transformation in production between the same dates, with the usual amendments for corner solutions. The gains from trade, i.e., in this case from auction markets in inter-household lending and borrowing, arise from differences among households in those autarkic rates of substitution and transformation. They are qualitatively the same as those from free contemporaneous trade in commodities between agents or nations.

The introduction of consumer loans in this Fisherian model will alter the individual and aggregate paths of consumption and saving. It is not possible to say whether it will raise or lower the aggregate amount of capital, here in the sense of labour endowments in process of producing future rather than current consumable output. In either case it is likely to be a Pareto-optimal improvement, although even this is not guaranteed *a priori*.

Similar argument suggests several reasons why ultimate savers, lenders, creditors prefer the liabilities of financial intermediaries not only to direct ownership of real property but also to the direct debt and equity issues of investors, borrowers and debtors:

Convenience of denomination. Issuers of securities find it costly to cut their issues into the variety of small and large denominations savers find convenient and commensurate to their means. The financial intermediary can break up large-denomination bonds and loans into amounts convenient to small savers, or combine debtors' obligations into large amounts convenient to the wealthy. Economies of scale and specialization in financial transactions enable financial intermediaries to tailor assets and liabilities to the needs and preferences of both lenders and borrowers. This service is especially valuable for agents on both sides whose needs vary in amount continuously; they like deposit accounts and credit lines whose use they can vary at will on their own initiative.

Risk pooling, reduction and allocation. The risks incident to economic activities take many forms. Some are nation-wide or world-wide – wars and revolutions, shifts in international comparative advantage, government fiscal and monetary policies, prices and supplies of oil and other basic materials. Some are specific

163

to particular enterprises and technologies – the capacity and integrity of managers, the qualities of new products, the local weather. A financial intermediary can specialize in the appraisal of risks, especially specific risks, with expertise in the gathering and interpretation of information costly or unavailable to individual savers. By pooling the funds of its credits, the financial intermediary can diversify away risks to an extent that the individual creditors cannot, because of the costs of transactions as well as the inconvenience of fixed lumpy denominations.

According to Joseph Schumpeter ([1911] 1934, pp. 72–4), bankers are the gatekeepers – Schumpeter's word is 'ephor' – of capitalist economic development; their strategic function is to screen potential innovators and advance the necessary purchasing power to the most promising. They are the source of purchasing power for investment and innovation, beyond the savings accumulated from past economic development. In practice, the cachet of a banker often enables his customer also to obtain credit from other sources or to float paper in open markets.

Maturity shifting. A financial intermediary typically reconciles differences among borrowers and lenders in the timing of payments. Bank depositors want to commit funds for shorter times than borrowers want to have them. Business borrowers need credit to bridge the time gap between the inputs to profitable production and their output and sales. This source of bank business is formally modeled by Diamond and Dybvig (1983). The bank's scale of operations enables it to stagger the due dates of, say, half-year loans so as to accommodate depositors who want their money bank in three months or one month or on demand. The reverse maturity shift may occur in other financial intermediaries. An insurance company or pension fund might invest short-term the savings its policy-owners or future pensioners will not claim for many years.

Transforming illiquid assets into liquid liabilities. Liquidity is a matter of degree. A perfectly liquid asset may be defined as one whose full present value can be realized, i.e., turned into purchasing power over goods and services, immediately. Dollar bills are perfectly liquid, and so for practical purposes are demand deposits and other deposits transferable to third parties by check or wire. Liquidity in this sense does not necessarily mean predictability of value. Securities traded on well organized markets are liquid. Any person selling at a given time will get the same price whether he decided and prepared to sell a month before or on the spur of the moment. But the price itself can vary unpredictably from minute to minute. Contrast a house, neither fully liquid nor predictable in value. Its selling proceeds at this moment are likely to be greater the longer it has been on the market. Consider the six-month promissory note of a small business proprietor known only to his local banker. However sure the payment on the scheduled date, the note may not be marketable at all. If the lender wants to realize its value before maturity, he will have to find a buyer and negotiate. A financial intermediary holds illiquid assets while its liabilities are liquid, and holds assets unpredictable in value while it guarantees the value of its liabilities. This is the traditional business of commercial banks, and the reason for the strong and durable relations of banks and their customers.

SUBSTITUTION OF INSIDE FOR OUTSIDE ASSETS

What determines the aggregate liabilities and assets of financial intermediaries? What determines the gross aggregate of inside assets generated by financial markets in general, including open markets as well as financial intermediaries? How can the empirical regularities found by Goldsmith, cited above, be explained?

Economic theory offers no answers to these questions. The differences among agents that invite mutually beneficial transactions, like those discussed above, offer opportunities for inside markets. Theory can tell us little *a priori* about the size of such differences. Moreover, markets are costly to operate, whether they are organized auction markets in homogeneous instruments or the imperfect 'markets' in heterogeneous contracts in which financial intermediaries are major participants. Society cannot afford all the markets that might exist in the absence of transactions costs and other frictions, and theory has little to say on which will arise and survive.

The macroeconomic consequence of inside markets and financial intermediaries generally to provide substitutes for outside assets and thus to economize their supplies. That is, the same microeconomic outcomes are achievable with smaller supplies of one or more of the outside assets than in the absence of intermediation. The way in which intermediation mobilizes the surpluses of some agents to finance the deficits of others is the theme of the classical influential work of Gurley and Shaw (1960).

Consider, for example, how commercial banking diminishes the need of business firms for net worth invested in inventories, by channeling the seasonal cash surpluses of some firms to the contemporaneous seasonal deficits of others. Imagine two firms A and B with opposite and complementary seasonal zigzag patterns. A needs $2 in cash at time zero to buy inputs for production in period 1 sold for $2; the pattern repeats in 3, 4, ... B needs $2 in cash at time 1 to buy inputs for production in period 2 sold for $2 in period 3, and so on in 4, 5, ... In the absence of their commercial bank, A and B each need $2 of net worth to carry on business; from period to period each alternates holding it in cash and in goods-in-process. Between them the two firms always are holding $2 of currency and $2 of inventories. Enters the bank and lends A half the $2 he needs to carry his inventory in period 1; A repays the loan from sales proceeds the next period, 2; the bank now lends $1 to B, ... A and B now need only $1 of currency; each has on average net worth of $1.50 – $2 and $1 alternating; as before they are together always holding $2 of inventories. Moreover, with a steady deposit of $2 from a third party, the bank could finance both businesses completely; they would need no net worth of their own. The example is trivial, but commercial banking proper can be understood as circulation of deposits and loans among businesses and as a revolving fund assembled from other sources and lent to businesses.

As a second primitive example, consider the effects of introducing markets that enable risks to be borne by those households more prepared to take them. Suppose that of two primary outside assets, currency and tangible capital, the return on the latter has the greater variance. Individuals who are risk neutral will hold all their wealth (possibly excepting minimal transactions balances of currency) in capital as long as its expected return exceeds the expected real return on currency. If these more adventurous households are not numerous and wealthy enough to absorb all the capital, the expected return on capital will have to exceed that on currency enough to induce risk-averse wealth-owners to hold the remainder. In this equilibrium the money price of capital and its mean real return are determined so as to allocate the two assets between the two kinds of households. Now suppose that risk-neutral households can borrow from the risk-averse types, most realistically via financial intermediaries, and that the latter households regard those debts as close substitutes for currency, indeed as inside money if intermediation by financial intermediaries is involved. The inside assets do double duty, providing the services and security of money to those who value them while enabling the more adventurous to hold capital in excess of their own net worth. As a result, the private sector as a whole will want to hold a larger proportion of its wealth in capital at any given expected real return on capital. In equilibrium, the aggregate capital stock will be larger and its expected return, equal to its marginal productivity in a steady state, will be lower than in the absence of intermediation.

Intermediation can diminish the private sector's need not just for outside money but for net worth and tangible capital. These economies generally require financial markets in which financial intermediaries are major participants, because they involve heterogeneous credit instruments and risk pooling. In the absence of home mortgages, consumer credit, and personal loans for education, young households would not be able to spend their future wages and salaries until they receive them. Constraints on borrowing against future earnings make the age-weighted average net non-human wealth of the population greater, but the relaxation of such liquidity constraints increases household welfare. Financial intermediaries invest the savings of older and more affluent households in loans to their younger and less wealthy contemporaries; otherwise those savings would go into outside assets. Likewise insurance makes it unnecessary to accumulate savings as precaution against certain risks, for example the living and medical expenses of unusual longevity. It is an all too common fallacy to assume that arrangements that increase aggregate savings and tangible wealth always augment social welfare.

DEPOSIT CREATION AND RESERVE REQUIREMENTS

The substitution of inside money for outside money is the familiar story of deposit creation, in which the banking system turns a dollar or base or 'high-powered' money into several dollars of deposits. The extra dollars are inside or 'low-powered' money. The banks need to hold only a fraction k, set by law or convention or prudence, of their deposit liabilities as reserves in base money. In an equilibrium in which they hold no excess reserves their deposits will be a multiple $1/k$ of their reserves; they will have created $(1 - k)/k$ dollars of substitute money.

A key step in this process is that any bank with excess reserves makes a roughly equal amount of additional loans, crediting the borrowers with deposits. As the borrowers draw checks, these new deposits are transferred to other accounts, most likely in other banks. As deposits move to other banks, so do reserves, dollar for dollar. But now those banks have excess reserves and act in like manner. The process continues until all banks are 'loaned up', i.e. deposits have increased enough so that the initial excess reserves have become reserves that the banks require or desire.

The textbook fable of deposit creation does not do justice to the full macroeconomics of the process. The story is incomplete without explaining how the public is induced to borrow more and to hold more deposits. The borrowers and the depositors are not the same public. No one borrows at interest in order to hold idle deposits. To attract additional borrowers, banks must lower interest rates or relax their collateral requirements or their risk standards. The new borrowers are likely to be businesses that need bank credit to build up inventories of materials or goods in process. The loans lead quickly to additional production and economic activity. Or banks buy securities in the open market, raising their prices and lowering market interest rates. The lower market rates may encourage businesses to float issues of commercial paper, bonds or stocks, but the effect of investment in inventories or plant and equipment are less immediate and less potent than the extension of bank credit to a business otherwise held back by illiquidity. In either case, lower interest rates induce other members of the public, those who indirectly receive the loan disbursements or those who sell securities to banks, to hold additional deposits. They will be acquiring other assets as well, some in banks, some in other financial intermediaries, some in open financial markets. Lower interest rates may also induce banks themselves to hold extra excess reserves.

Interest rates are not the only variables of adjustment. Nominal incomes are rising at the same time, in some mixture of real quantities and prices depending on macroeconomic circumstances. The rise in incomes and economic activities creates new needs for transactions balances of money. Thus the process by which excess reserves are absorbed entails changes in interest rates, real economic activity, and prices in some combination. It is possible to describe scenarios in which the entire ultimate adjustment is in one of these variables. Wicksell's cumulative credit expansion, which in the end just raises prices, is a classic example.

Do banks have a unique magic by which asset purchases generate their own financing? Is the magic due to the 'moneyness' of the banks' liabilities? The preceding account indicates it is not magic but reserve requirements. Moreover, a qualitatively similar story could be told if reserve requirements were related to bank assets or non-monetary liabilities and even if banks happened to have no monetary liabilities at all. In the absence of reserve requirements aggregate bank assets and liabilities, relative to the size of the economy, would be naturally limited by public supplies and demands at interest rates that cover banks' costs and normal profits. If, instead of banks, savings institutions specializing in

167

mortgage lending were subject to reserve requirements, their incentives to minimize excess reserves would inspire a story telling how additional mortgage lending brings home savings deposits to match (Tobin, 1963).

RISKS, RUNS AND REGULATIONS

Some financial intermediaries confine themselves to activities that entail virtually no risk either to the institution itself or to its clients. An open-end mutual fund or unit trust holds only fully liquid assets traded continuously in organized markets. It promises the owners of its shares payment on demand at their pro rata net value calculated at the market prices of the underlying assets – no more, or less. The fund can always meet such demands by selling assets it holds. The shareowners pay in one way or another an agreed fee from the fund – the convenience and flexibility of denomination, the bookkeeping, the transactions costs, the diversification, the expertise in choosing assets. The shareowners bear the market risks on the fund's portfolio – no less and, assuming the fund is honest, no more. Government regulations are largely confined to those governing all public security issues, designed to protect buyers from deceptions and insider manipulations. In the United States regulation of this kind is the province of the federal Securities and Exchange Commission.

Most financial intermediaries do take risks. The risks are intrinsic to the functions they serve and to the profit opportunities attracting financial entrepreneurs and investors in their enterprises. For banks and similar financial intermediaries, the principal risk is that depositors may at any time demand payments the institution can meet, if at all, only at extraordinary cost. Many of the assets are illiquid, unmarketable. Others can be liquidated at short notice only at substantial loss. In some cases, bad luck or imprudent management brings insolvency; the institution could never meet its obligations no matter how long its depositors and other creditors wait. In other cases, the problem is just illiquidity; the assets would suffice if they could be held until maturity, until buyers or lenders could be found, or until normal market conditions returned.

Banks and other financial intermediaries hold reserves, in currency or its equivalent, deposits in central banks, or in other liquid foims as precaution against withdrawals by their depositors. For a single bank, the withdrawal is usually a shift of deposits to other banks in interbank clearings of checks or other transfers to third parties at the initiative of depositors. For the banking system, as a whole, withdrawal is a shift by the public from deposits to currency.

'Withdrawals' may in practice include the exercise of previously agreed borrowing rights. Automatic overdraft privileges are more common in other countries, notably the United Kingdom and British Commonwealth nations, than in the United States. They are becoming more frequent in the United States as an adjunct of bank credit cards. Banks' business loan customers often have explicit or implicit credit lines on which they can draw on demand.

Unless financial intermediaries hold safe liquid assets of predictable value matched in maturities to their liabilities – in particular, currency or equivalent against all their demand obligations – they and their creditors can never be completely protected from withdrawals. The same is true of the banking system as a whole, and of all intermediaries other than simple mutual funds. 'Runs', sudden, massive, and contagious withdrawals, are always possible. They destroy prudent and imprudent institutions alike, along with their depositors and creditors. Of course, careful depositors inform themselves about the intermediaries to which they entrust their funds, about their asset portfolios, policies and skills. Their choices among competing depositories provide some discipline, but it can never be enough to rule out disasters. What the most careful depositor cannot foresee is the behaviour of other depositors, and it is rational for the well-informed depositor of a sound bank to withdraw funds if he believes that others are doing so or are about to do so.

Governments generally regulate the activities of banks and other financial intermediaries in greater detail than they do nonfinancial enterprises. The basic motivations for regulation appear to be the following.

It is costly, perhaps impossible, for individual depositors to appraise the soundness and liquidity of financial institutions and to estimate the probabilities of failures even if they could assume that other depositors would do likewise. It is impossible for them to estimate the probabilities of 'runs'. Without regulation, the liabilities of suspect institutions would be valued below par in check collections. Prior to 1866 banks in the United States were allowed to issue notes payable to bearers on demand, surrogates for government currency. The notes circulated at discounts varying with the current reputations of the issuers. A system in which transactions media other than government currency continuously vary in value depending on the issuer is clumsy and costly.

The government has an obligation to provide at low social cost an efficient system of transactions media, and also a menu of secure and convenient assets for citizens who wish to save in the national monetary unit of account. Those transactions media and saving assets can be offered by banks and other financial intermediaries, in a way that retains most of the efficiencies by decentralization and competition, if and only if government imposes some regulations and assumes some residual responsibilities. The government's role takes several forms.

Reserve requirements. An early and obvious intervention was to require banks to hold reserves in designated safe and liquid forms against their obligations, especially their demand liabilities. Left to themselves, without such requirements, some banks might sacrifice prudence for short-term profit. Paradoxically, however, required reserves are not available for meeting withdrawals unless the required ratio is 100 per cent. If the reserve requirement is 10 per cent of deposits, then withdrawal of one dollar from a bank reduces its reserve holdings by one dollar but its reserve requirement by only ten cents. Only excess reserves or other liquid assets are precautions against withdrawals. The legal reserve requirement just shifts the bank's prudential calculation to the size of these secondary reserves. Reserve requirements serve functions quite different from their original motivation. In the systems that use them, notably the United States, they are the fulcrum for central bank control of economy-wide monetary conditions. (They are also

169

an interest-free source of finance of government debt, but in the United States today this amounts to only $45 billion of a total debt to the public of $1700 billion.)

Last-resort lending. Banks and other financial intermediaries facing temporary shortages of reserves and secondary reserves of liquid assets can borrow them from other institutions. In the United States, for example, the well-organized market for 'federal funds' allows banks short of reserves to borrow them overnight from other banks. Or banks can gain reserves by attracting more deposits, offering higher interest rates on them than depositors are getting elsewhere. These ways of correcting reserve positions are not available to troubled banks, suspected of deep-rooted problems of liquidity or solvency or both, for example bad loans. Nor will they meet a system-wide run from liabilities of banks and other financial intermediaries into currency.

Banks in need of reserves can also borrow from the central bank, and much of this borrowing is routine, temporary, and seasonal. Massive central bank credit is the last resort of troubled banks which cannot otherwise satisfy the demands of their depositors without forced liquidations of their assets. The government is the ultimate supplier of currency and reserves in aggregate. The primary *raison d'être* of the central bank is to protect the economy from runs into currency. System-wide shortages of currency and reserves can be relieved not only by central bank lending to individual banks but by central bank purchases of securities in the open market. The Federal Reserve's inability or unwillingness – which it was is still debated – to supply the currency bank depositors wanted in the early 1930s led to disastrous panic and epidemic bank failures. No legal or doctrinal obstacles would now stand in the way of such a rescue.

Deposit insurance. Federal insurance of bank deposits in the United States has effectively prevented contagious runs and epidemic failures since its enactment in 1935. Similar insurance applies to deposits in savings institutions. In effect, the federal government assumes a contingent residual liability to pay the insured deposits in full, even if the assets of the financial intermediary are permanently inadequate to do so. The insured institutions are charged premiums for the service, but the fund in which they are accumulated is not and cannot be large enough to eliminate possible calls on the Treasury. Although the guarantees are legally limited to a certain amount, now $100,000, per account, in practice depositors have eventually recovered their full deposits in most cases. Indeed the guarantee seems now to have been extended *de facto* to all deposits, at least in major banks.

Deposit insurance impairs such discipline as surveillance by large depositors might impose on financial intermediaries; instead the task of surveillance falls on the governmental insurance agencies themselves (in the United States the Federal Deposit Insurance Corporation and the Federal Savings and Loan Insurance Corporation) and on other regulatory authorities (the United States Comptroller of the Currency, the Federal Reserve, and various state agencies). Insurance transfers some risks from financial intermediary depositors and owners to taxpayers at large, while virtually eliminating risks of runs. Those are risks we generate ourselves; they magnify the unavoidable natural risks of economic life. Insurance is a mutual compact to enable us to refrain from *sauve qui peut* behaviour that can inflict grave damage on us all. Formally, an uninsured system has two equilibria, a good one with mutual confidence and a bad one with runs. Deposit insurance eliminates the bad one (Diamond and Dybvig, 1983).

One hundred per cent reserve deposits would, of course, be perfectly safe – that is, as safe as the national currency – and would not have to be insured. Those deposits would in effect *be* currency, but in a secure and conveniently checkable form. One can imagine a system in which banks and other financial intermediaries offered such accounts, with the reserves behind them segregated from those related to the other business of the institution. That other business would include receiving deposits which required fractional or zero reserves and were insured only partially, if at all. The costs of the 100 per cent reserve deposit accounts would be met by service charges, or by government interest payments on the reserves, justified by the social benefits of a safe and efficient transactions medium. The burden of risk and supervision now placed on the insuring and regulating agencies would be greatly relieved. It is, after all, historical accident that supplies of transactions media in modern economies came to be byproducts of banking business and vulnerable to its risks.

Government may insure financial intermediaries loans as well as deposits. Insurance of home mortgages in the United States not only has protected the institutions that hold them and their depositors but has converted the insured mortgages into marketable instruments.

Balance sheet supervision. Government surveillance of financial intermediaries limits their freedom of choice of assets and liabilities, in order to limit the risks to depositors and insurers. Standards of adequacy of capital – owners' equity at risk in the case of private corporations, net worth in the case of mutual and other nonprofit forms of organization – are enforced for the same reasons. Periodic examinations check the condition of the institution, the quality of its loans, and the accuracy of its accounting statements. The regulators may close an institution if further operation is judged to be damaging to the interest of the depositors and the insurers.

Legislation which regulates financial intermediaries has differentiated them by purpose and function. Commercial banks, savings institutions, home building societies, credit unions, and insurance companies are legally organized for different purposes. They are subject to different rules governing the nature of their assets. For example, home building societies – savings and loan associations in the United States – have been required to keep most of their asset portfolios in residential mortgages. Restrictions of this kind mean that when wealth-owners shift funds from one type of financial intermediary to another, they alter relative demands for assets of different kinds. Shifts of deposits from commercial banks to building societies would increase mortgage lending relative to commercial lending. Regulations have also restricted the kinds of liabilities allowed various types of financial intermediary. Until recently in the United States, only banks were permitted to have liabilities payable on demand to third parties by check or wire. Currently deregulation is relaxing specialized restrictions on financial intermediary assets and liabilities and blurring historical distinctions of purpose and function.

Interest ceilings. Government regulations in many countries set ceilings on the interest rates that can be charged on loans and on the rates that can be paid on deposits, both at banks and at other financial intermediaries. In the United States the Banking Act of 1935 prohibited payment of interest on demand deposits. After the second world war effective ceilings on savings and time deposits in banks and savings institutions were administratively set, and on occasion changed, by federal agencies. Under legislation of 1980, these regulations are being phased out.

The operating characteristics of a system of financial intermediaries in which interest rates on deposits of various types, as well as on loans, are set by free competition are quite different from those of a system in which financial intermediary rates are subject to legal ceilings or central bank guidance, or set by agreement among a small number of institutions. For example, when rates on deposits are administratively set, funds flow out of financial intermediaries when open market rates rise and return to financial intermediaries when they fall. These processes of 'disintermediation' and 're-intermediation' are diminished when financial intermediary rates are free to move parallel to open market rates. Likewise flows between different financial intermediaries due to administratively set rate differences among them are reduced when they are all free to compete for funds.

A regime with market-determined interest rates on moneys and near-moneys has significantly different macroeconomic characteristics from a regime constrained by ceilings on deposit interest rates. Since the opportunity cost of holding deposits is largely independent of the general level of interest rates, the 'LM' curve is steeper in the unregulated regime. Both central bank operations and exogenous monetary shocks could be expected to have larger effects on nominal income, while fiscal measures and other shocks to aggregate demand for goods and services would have smaller effects (Tobin, 1983).

Entry, branching, merging. Entry into regulated financial businesses is generally controlled, as are establishing branches or subsidiaries and merging of existing institutions. In the United States, charters are issued either by the federal government or by state governments, and regulatory powers are also divided. Until recently banks and savings institutions, no matter by whom chartered, were not allowed to operate in more than one state. This rule, combined with various restrictions on branches within states, gave the United States a much larger number of distinct financial enterprises, many of them very small and very local, than is typical in other countries. The prohibition of interstate operations is now being eroded and may be effectively eliminated in the new few years.

Deregulation has been forced by innovations in financial technology that made

172

old regulations either easy hurdles to circumvent or obsolete barriers to efficiency. New opportunities not only are breaking down the walls separating financial intermediaries of different types and specializations. They are also bringing other businesses, both financial and nonfinancial, into activities previously reserved to regulated financial institutions. Mutual funds and brokers offer accounts from which funds can be withdrawn on demand or transferred to third parties by check or wire. National retail chains are becoming financial supermarkets – offering credit cards, various mutual funds, instalment lending, and insurance along with their vast menus of consumer goods and services; in effect, they would like to become full-service financial intermediaries. At the same time, the traditional intermediaries are moving, as fast as they can obtain government permission, into lines of business from which they have been excluded. Only time will tell how these commercial and political conflicts are resolved and how the financial system will be reshaped (*Economic Report of the President*, 1985, ch. 5).

PORTFOLIO BEHAVIOUR OF FINANCIAL INTERMEDIARIES
A large literature has attempted to estimate econometrically the choices of assets and liabilities by financial intermediaries, their relationships to open market interest rates and to other variables exogenous to them. Models of the portfolio behaviour of the various species of financial intermediary also involve estimation of the supplies of funds to them, and the demands for credit, from other sectors of the economy, particularly households and nonfinancial businesses. Recent research is presented in Dewald and Friedman (1980).

Difficult econometric problems arise in using time series for these purposes because of regime changes. For example, when deposit interest rate ceilings are effective, financial intermediaries are quantity-takers in the deposit markets; when the ceilings are non-constraining or non-existent, both the interest rates and the quantities are determined jointly by the schedules of supplies of deposits by the public and of demands for them by the financial intermediary. Similar problems arise in credit markets where interest rates, even though unregulated, are administered by financial intermediaries themselves and move sluggishly. The prime commercial loan rate is one case; mortgage rates in various periods are another. In these cases and others, the markets are not cleared at the established rates. Either the financial intermediary or the borrowers are quantity-takers, or perhaps both in some proportions. Changes in the rates follow, dependent on the amount of excess demand or supply. These problems of modelling and econometric estimation are discussed in papers in the reference above. The seminal paper is Modigliani and Jaffee (1969).

BIBLIOGRAPHY
Barro, R. 1974. Are government bonds net wealth? *Journal of Political Economy* 82(6), November–December, 1095–117.
Dewald, W.G. and Friedman, B.M. 1980. Financial market behavior, capital formation, and economic performance. (A conference supported by the National Science Foundation.) *Journal of Money, Credit and Banking*, Special Issue 12(2), May.

Diamond, D.W. and Dybvig, P.H. 1983. Bank runs, deposit insurance, and liquidity. *Journal of Political Economy* 91(3), June, 401–19.

Economic Report of the President. 1985. Washington, DC: Government Printing Office, February.

Federal Reserve System, Board of Governors. 1984. *Balance Sheets for the US Economy 1945–83*. November, Washington, DC.

Fisher, I. 1930. *The Theory of Interest*. New York: Macmillan.

Goldsmith, R.W. 1969. *Financial Structure and Development*. New Haven: Yale University Press.

Goldsmith, R.W. 1985. *Comparative National Balance Sheets: A Study of Twenty Countries, 1688–1978*. Chicago: University of Chicago Press.

Gurley, J.G. and Shaw E.S. 1960. *Money in a Theory of Finance*. Washington, DC: Brookings Institute.

Modigliani, F. and Miller, M.H. 1958. The cost of capital, corporation finance and the theory of investment. *American Economic Review* 48(3), June, 261–97.

Modigliani, F. and Jaffee, D.M. 1969. A theory and test of credit rationing. *American Economic Review* 59(5), December, 850–72.

Schumpeter, J.A. 1911. *The Theory of Economic Development*. Trans. from the German by R. Opie, Cambridge, Mass.: Harvard University Press, 1934.

Tobin, J. 1963. Commercial banks as creators of 'money'. In *Banking and Monetary Studies*, ed. D. Carson, Homewood, Ill.: Richard D. Irwin.

Tobin, J. 1980. *Asset Accumulation and Economic Activity*. Oxford: Blackwell.

Tobin, J. 1983. Financial structure and monetary rules. *Kredit und Kapital* 16(2), 155–71.

Tobin, J. 1984. On the efficiency of the financial system. *Lloyds Bank Review* 153, July, 1–15.

High-powered Money and the Monetary Base

KARL BRUNNER

The concept of high-powered money or a monetary base appears as an important term in any analysis addressing the determinants of a nation's money stock in regimes exhibiting financial intermediation. Two types of money can be distinguished in such institutional contexts. One type only occurs as a 'monetary liability' of financial intermediaries. It characteristically offers a potential claim on another type of money. The contractual situation between customers and intermediaries reveals that this potential claim, to be exercised any time at the option of the owner, forms a crucial condition for the marketability of the intermediaries' monetary liabilities. This second type offers in contrast no such potential claim. While it is exchangeable for other objects, it is a sort of 'ultimate money' without regress to other types of money.

This characterization differs from the widely used classification 'outside-inside' money. 'Inside money' matches in a consolidated balance sheet of 'money-producers' a corresponding amount of private debt. Money which cannot be matched in this way forms the outside money. But outside money does not necessarily coincide with the monetary base. The latter magnitude exceeds the volume of outside money by the amount of private debt acquired by the Central Bank in fiat regimes. The two concepts refer, however, to the same magnitude in pure commodity regimes and even in some possible Central Bank regimes with specific arrangements. It follows that the monetary base covers a somewhat wider range than outside money. This difference corresponds to the different analytic purposes of the two concepts. The 'monetary' base is designed for explanations of the behaviour of a nation's money stock, whereas 'outside money' was advanced to express the monetary system's contributions to the economy's net wealth.

The distinction between monetary base and the nation's money stock is hardly informative or relevant for pure commodity money regimes. The distinction becomes important with the emergence of intermediation. Financial intermediation inserts a wedge between the monetary base and the money stock (see article on

175

money supply). But regimes with intermediation cover a wide range of arrangements bearing on the nature of the monetary base. High-powered money may consist of commodity money with or without fiat component or of pure fiat money. These differences are characteristically associated with significant differences in the supply conditions of high-powered money.

The measurement of the monetary base for any country involves, at this stage of monetary evolution, the consolidated balance sheet of the Central Bank system. But the Central Bank is usually not the only producer of 'ultimate money'. The balance sheet of other agencies may also have to be considered. This extension covers in the USA a special Treasury monetary account summarizing the Treasury's money creating activity. In other cases, a balance sheet of the mint or an exchange equalization account may have to be added. But whatever the range of ultimate money producers may be, we need to consolidate their respective balance sheets into a single statement. The monetary 'liabilities' of this consolidated statement, i.e., all items listed on the right-side of the consolidated statement which are money, constitute the monetary base.

The consolidated statement determines that the monetary base can be expressed in two distinct ways. It can be exhibited as the sum of its uses by banks and public. The 'uses statement' thus presents the monetary base as the sum of bank reserves in form of base money and currency held by the public. A 'source statement' complements the uses statement. The sources statement can be immediately read from the balance sheet. The monetary base appears thus as the sum of all assets listed on the left-side of the consolidated statement minus the sum of all non-monetary liabilities. Both statements can be easily derived from the published data in the USA. More difficulties may be encountered for other countries.

The comparatively simple case of the USA may be used to exemplify the sources statement needed for the subsequent discussion. We can write the following expression:

$$\text{Monetary Base} = \text{Federal Reserve Credit}$$

(i.e., earning assets of Central Bank consisting of government securities and advances to banks) + gold stock (including SDR's) minus treasury cash (i.e. free gold) + treasury currency (mostly coin) + a mixture of other assets minus other liabilities (including net worth).

Both uses and sources statement refer to important aspects of the money supply process. The uses statement refers in particular to the allocation of base money, determined by the public's and the bank's behaviour, between bank reserves and currency held by the public. This allocation contributes to shape the link between monetary base and money stock. The sources statement on the other hand directs our attention to an examination of possible (or relevant) supply conditions of base money.

The measurement, but not the definition, of the base clearly depends on prevailing institutions. One particular institution, viz. the imposition of variable reserve requirements on financial intermediaries, suggests a useful extension of the money base. Changes in reserve requirements release or absorb reserves similar to transactions between banks and Central Bank, e.g., an open-market operation. Similar consequences follow with respect to both money stock and 'bank credit'. Thus appeared an extension of the monetary base beyond the 'sources base' (or the volume of high-powered money) defined by the sources statement. The monetary base is understood as the sum of the 'sources base' and a reserve adjustment magnitude (RAM). This magnitude is the cumulated sum of all past releases and absorption of reserves due to changes in reserve requirements. This practice has become the standard procedure in the reports published by the Federal Reserve Bank of St Louis. The extended concept of the base offers the further advantage that the resulting magnitude only reflects actions of the monetary authorities and also reflects all the most important actions proceeding within a given institutional framework.

The sources statement offers a useful starting point for an analysis of the supply conditions of the monetary base. The study of these conditions is motivated by the systematic relation between base and money supply. Changes in the monetary base are a necessary condition for persistently large or substantially accelerated monetary growth in most countries for most of the time. Substantial changes in the monetary base are frequently also a sufficient condition for corresponding changes in the money supply.

The sources statement yields a means to examine the sources of all changes in the base. We can thus investigate which of the sources dominate the trend, the variance of cyclical movements and the variances of middle range or very short-run movements. The patterns shift over time with the monetary regime and vary substantially between countries. Trend and longer-term variance in the USA are dominated, for instance, by the behaviour of the Federal Reserve Credit (i.e., the earning assets of the Central Bank system). We find in contrast for the Swiss case that trend and variance of the base are dominated by the behaviour of the gold stock and foreign exchange holdings. The portfolio of government securities play a comparatively small role. Such examination can also be exploited in order to judge whether movements in the base are essentially temporary or can reasonably be expected to persist with a longer duration.

The stochastic structure of the major and minor source components constitute the supply conditions of the monetary base. These conditions are sensitively associated with a variety of institutional arrangements under the control of legislative bodies or policymakers. The procedures instituted, for instance, by the Federal Reserve system to offer check collection services to banks contribute to the shortest run variance of the monetary base. Reserve requirements imposed on the liabilities of financial institutions offer policy-makers an opportunity to raise the proportion of outstanding government debt held by the Central Bank. Higher reserve requirements raise the level of the monetary base required to produce a given money supply. Correspondingly a larger volume of government securities can be held by the Central Bank.

The supply conditions may disconnect the behaviour of the base from the economy. This will happen whenever the processes governing the source components operate essentially independently of the economy's movements. In general some dependence may be produced by the prevailing institutions and policies. Such a feedback creates a role for the interaction within asset markets, and also between asset markets and output markets in the determination of the monetary base. The supply conditions of the monetary base acquire thus a central role in our monetary affairs. This is most particularly the case as these conditions emerge from legislative decisions and policy strategies. They fully characterize under the circumstances an important component of a monetary regime. Different monetary regimes are reflected by variations in the supply conditions. The growing dissatisfaction with the discretionary regime, which produced the Great Depression and the inflation of the 1970s, initiated in recent years much public debate about the nature of an adequate monetary regime. A rational examination requires in this case an evaluation of the consequences associated with alternative supply conditions governing the monetary base. This programme still needs some attention by the professions and ultimately (and very hopefully) even by politicians.

Hyperinflation

PHILLIP CAGAN

Hyperinflation is an extremely rapid rise in the general level of prices of goods and services. It typically lasts a few years or in the most extreme cases much less before moderating or ending. There is no well-defined threshold. It is best described by a listing of cases, which vary enormously. The numerous cases have provided a testing ground for theories of monetary dynamics reported in a vast literature.

HISTORICAL SURVEY. The world's record occurred in Hungary after World War II when an index of prices rose an average 19,800 per cent per month from August 1945 to July 1946 and 4.2×10^{16} per cent in the peak month of July. Also in the aftermath of World War II extreme price increases occurred in China, Greece, and Taiwan. Hyperinflations followed World War I in Austria, Germany, Hungary, Poland and Russia. If we measure the total increase in prices from the first to last month in which the monthly increase exceeded 50 per cent and afterwards stayed below that rate for a year or more, a price index rose from 1 to 3.8×10^{27} in the record Hungarian episode, 10^{11} in China, 10^{10} in Germany, and ranged down to 70 in Austria and 44 in the first Hungarian episode after World War I. In the last, the mildest of those cited above, the rise in prices averaged 46 per cent per month.

Prior to World War I extreme inflations were rare. A price index rose from 1 to about 18 from mid-1795 to mid-1796 at the height of the *assignats* inflation in France, from 1778 to 1780 in the American War of Independence, to 12 from 1863 to 1865 in the Confederacy during the American Civil War, and comparable inflation rates were reported for Columbia in 1902. The oft-cited currency depreciations of the ancient and medieval world and of Europe in the 17th century from the influx of precious metals were mild by modern experience. Earlier extreme inflations were rare because of the prevalence of commodity monies and convertibility. Only inconvertible paper currencies can be expanded rapidly without limit to generate hyperinflation.

Although the greatest hyperinflations have occurred in countries devastated by war, non-war-related inflation rates of several hundred per cent were reached briefly in 1926 in Belgium and France. Since World War II to the time of writing (1985) the frequency of both mild and extreme inflations unrelated to war has increased throughout the world. While rates of several hundred per cent per year or more for short periods have become common since World War II, few cases have exceeded 1000 per cent per year for even a few months (Meiselman, 1970), and hence they fall far short of the great hyperinflations. The rate of over 10,000 per cent per year in Bolivia in 1985 is a major exception.

MONETARY CHARACTERISTICS. Extreme increases in the price level cannot occur without commensurate increases in the money stock, which are usually less than proportionate because of decreases in the demand for real money balances. Governments resort to issuing money rapidly when they are unable to contain expanding budget expenditures and to raise sufficient funds by conventional taxation and borrowing from the public. Money creation is a special form of taxation which is levied on the public's holdings of money. It is administratively easy to impose and collect. Excessive money issues to finance the government budget add to aggregate spending and raise prices; the resulting depreciation in the purchasing power of outstanding money balances imposes the tax. Bailey (1956) finds the social costs of this tax to be high compared with other forms of taxation.

Escalations of inflation at any level tend to stimulate economic activity temporarily. Since high rates of inflation tend to distort relative prices, however, much of the economic activity is socially wasteful. Many businesses and workers are dependent on prices and wages that lag behind the general inflation, and thus suffer severe declines in real income. In addition, unanticipated depreciations in financial and monetary assets in real terms produce major redistributions of wealth. These effects are socially and politically disruptive (Bresciani-Turroni, 1931). Yet the de-escalation of inflation temporarily contracts aggregate demand, which is also disruptive and therefore politically difficult to undertake.

THEORETICAL ISSUES. The depreciation of money during inflation greatly increases the cost of holding it. Although depreciating currencies are not abandoned completely, testifying to the great benefits of a common medium of exchange, the public undertakes costly efforts to reduce holdings of a rapidly depreciating money, including barter arrangements and the use of more stable substitutes such as foreign currencies (Barro, 1970). These efforts result in a large reduction in money balances in real terms and a large rise in monetary velocity.

A study of this result by Cagan (1956) estimated the demand for real money balances in hyperinflation as inversely dependent on the *expected* rate of inflation. Expectations about future developments can differ from concurrent conditions and determine the public's response to inflation. Cagan hypothesized that expectations are formed adaptively, whereby expected values are adjusted in proportion to their discrepancy from actual values. The theoretical implication is that expected inflation can be estimated as an exponentially weighted average of past inflation rates.

Such adaptive expectations lag behind the changes in actual values, which can explain why hyperinflations characteristically tend to escalate. As the inflation tax extracts revenue from real money balances, the expected inflation rate increases to match the higher actual rate and the revenue declines in real terms, but with a lag. The real revenue can be increased by speeding up money creation, but only until expectations adjust to the higher inflation rate. If the inflation rate were to remain constant so that the expected rate eventually matched it, the real revenue from money creation would be sustainable at a constant level. Among such constant levels a maximum real revenue is obtainable by a particular constant inflation rate, which depends on the elasticity of demand for real money balances with respect to the inflation rate. This revenue can be raised further by continually increasing monetary growth and the inflation rate. The hyperinflations kept escalating well beyond the maximizing constant rate to obtain more revenue.

Inflation also usually reduces the real value of other tax revenues because of lags between the imposition of a tax and its collection. A tax on money balances must exceed the reduced real collections of other taxes in order to prevent a decline in total government real revenue. This is often true initially under civil disorder, but hyperinflation reduces all taxes in real terms and in a short time largely destroys its revenue justification.

Adaptive expectations can be a 'rational' way for people to distinguish between transitory and one-time permanent changes in a variable (Muth, 1960). But if the inflation rate is continually rising, adaptive expectations as a weighted average of past rates are always too low, and such a series of correlated expectational errors is inconsistent with rational behaviour. The theory of rational expectations argues that the public uses all available information in predicting the inflation rate, including economic models of the process. This implies in particular that expectations of inflation, taking into account the importance of money, will focus on the money creating policies of the monetary authorities. If the government is after a certain amount of revenue, the public may be able to estimate the rate of money creation, which can be translated into a path for prices. Usually, however, the amount of money issued may change unpredictably or otherwise not be knowable with much precision.

Rational expectations have two important empirical implications for hyperinflation. First, if money is consistently issued to raise a certain revenue in real terms, monetary growth will depend on the inflation rate (Webb, 1984). The money stock is then statistically endogenous to the inflationary process. Sargent and Wallace (1973) and Frenkel (1977) presented statistical evidence that money depends on prices in the German hyperinflation, though such evidence has been contested (Protopapadakis, 1983).

To find that the money supply is endogenous does not mean that money demand is no longer dependent on the expected rate of inflation. But the finding discredits econometric regressions of real money balances on inflation rates. Other variables are needed to measure the expected cost of holding money.

Frenkel (1977) used the forward premium on foreign exchange in the German hyperinflation, which reflected the market's estimate of future depreciation of the foreign exchange rate and presumably was dominated by expectations of inflation. (This also helps avoid possible spurious correlation when a price series for calculating real money balances is used in the same regression to derive the rate of price change.) The forward premium does explain movements in real money balances and confirms as a proxy the effect of the expected inflation rate. The forward premium in Germany was also found to be uncorrelated with past inflation, which satisfies the rational expectations requirement that the premium should not depend on past information and not involve lagged adjustments. This leaves unexplained, however, why the German inflation rate escalated beyond the revenue-maximizing constant rate, since rational expectations prevent anticipated escalation from increasing the revenue. Sargent (1977) suggests that the revenue-maximizing rate, when properly estimated under the hypothesis of rational expectations, was not exceeded by actual inflation rates. Another possibility is that public behaviour did not fully anticipate the successive increases in inflation rates, which thus temporarily added to the government's inflation revenue.

STABILIZATION REFORM. Hyperinflation, if driven by rising expectations of inflation rather than rising money growth, can become a self-generating process. This has never occurred, however, except conceivably for very brief periods. Hyperinflations can always be stopped, therefore, by ending the monetary support. But the revenue from money creation is often difficult for governments to replace or survive without explaining why some countries are subjected to high inflation for long periods.

Yet many hyperinflations have been stopped all at once with a programme of reform and without prolonged economic disruption. After a short period the economy usually recovers and prospers. These stabilization programmes have been studied to determine the necessary conditions for success (Sargent, 1982; Bomberger and Makinen, 1983). Some attempted reforms have failed, notably twice in Greece after World War II (Makinen, 1984). First of all, it is critical to gain control over monetary growth, and this requires an end to the government's dependence on money creation to finance its budget. Successful reforms involve a reorganization of government finances, both to cut expenditures and to raise taxes, and legal authority for the central bank to refuse to create money to lend to the government. Although a new currency unit is often issued to replace the depreciated one, this is symbolic only. Foreign loans or financial aid to bolster foreign exchange reserves and to finance government deficits for a while help to inspire confidence in the success of stabilization, but have not always been necessary. Convertibility of the new currency into gold or a key foreign currency assures the reform but is not always introduced immediately. Such convertibility to end a severe inflation has proven difficult in the post-Bretton Woods environment in which the key foreign currency (usually the dollar) floats in value. Fixing the foreign exchange rate can then produce massive trade deficits (if the key currency appreciates) which are impossible to maintain. Chile in the early 1980s is a notable example (Edwards, 1985).

Most reforms are initially popular, promising to bring back the benefits of a well-functioning monetary system. A resurgence of public confidence in the currency usually occurs, which produces a substantial increase in money demand from low hyperinflation levels. This allows a one-time increase in the money supply without raising prices. The monetary expansion must not continue beyond the demand increase, however, or it will set off a new round of inflation, and the stabilization will fail. Many reforms that eventually failed gained credibility initially and had an increase in money demand, but then subsequently over issued money and returned to high inflation rates. To avoid this outcome there must be a commitment to maintain a stable price index or convertibility.

Stabilization reforms that have achieved an immediate end to hyperinflations contrast with the protracted efforts to subdue many moderate inflations. One difference is that in hyperinflations long-term contracts specifying prices or interest rates and wage agreements are no longer entered into because of great uncertainty over the inflation rate. Consequently, few parties are injured by such contracts when hyperinflation suddenly ends, and inflexibilities in the price system do not impede the required substantial readjustment of relative prices. Contracts that index financial and wage contracts to previous price movements impart a momentum to inflation that makes it more disruptive to end the process. The wide use of indexing, as in Brazil and Israel in the early 1980s, reduces differential price and wage movements but creates an obstacle to successful reform.

Hyperinflations on the order of those following the two World Wars remain rare and, when they occur, soon escalate to levels that necessitate an ending by drastic measures. Inflations on the order of 50 to several hundred per cent a year have been difficult to end, though they often subside for varying periods. These inflations despite their serious economic consequences give no indication of disappearing.

BIBLIOGRAPHY

Bailey, M. 1956. The welfare cost of inflationary finance. *Journal of Political Economy* 64, April, 93–110.

Barro, R.J. 1970. Inflation, the payments period and the demand for money. *Journal of Political Economy* 78, November/December, 1228–63.

Bomberger, W.A. and Makinen, G.E. 1983. The Hungarian hyperinflation and stabilization of 1945–46. *Journal of Political Economy* 91, October, 801–24.

Bresciani-Turroni, C. 1931. *The Economics of Inflation: A Study of Currency Depreciation in Post-War Germany: 1914–1923.* Trans., London: Allen & Unwin, 1937.

Cagan, P. 1956. The monetary dynamics of hyperinflation. In *Studies in the Quantity Theory of Money*, ed. M. Friedman, Chicago: University of Chicago Press.

Edwards, S. 1985. Stabilization with liberalization: an evaluation of ten years of Chile's experiment with free-market policies, 1973–1983. *Economic Development and Cultural Change* 33, January, 223–54.

Frenkel, J.A. 1977. The forward exchange rate, expectations, and the demand for money: the German hyperinflation. *American Economic Review* 67, September, 653–70.

Makinen, G.E. 1984. The Greek stabilization of 1944–46. *American Economic Review* 74, December, 1067–74.

Meiselman, D. (ed.) 1970. *Varieties of Monetary Experience*. Chicago: University of Chicago Press.

Muth, J. 1960. Optimal properties of exponentially weighted forecasts. *Journal of the American Statistical Association* 55, June, 299–306.

Protopapadakis, A. 1983. The endogeneity of money during the German hyperinflation: a reappraisal. *Economic Inquiry* 21, January, 72–92.

Sargent, T.J. 1977. The demand for money during hyperinflation under rational expectations I. *International Economic Review* 18, February, 59–82.

Sargent, T.J. 1982. The ends of four big inflations. In *Inflation: Causes and Effects*, ed. R. Hall, Chicago: University of Chicago Press.

Sargent, T.J. and Wallace, N. 1973. 'Rational' expectations and the dynamics of hyperinflation. *International Economic Review* 14, June, 328–50.

Webb, S.B. 1984. The supply of money and Reichsbank financing of government and corporate debt in Germany, 1919–1923. *Journal of Economic History* 44, June, 499–507.

Liquidity

A.B. CRAMP

Liquidity is a highly complex phenomenon. Its concrete manifestation is powerfully affected by changes in financial institutions and practices, which have been occurring with extraordinary rapidity in recent decades. It calls for analysis both at the microeconomic and the macroeconomic level, with unusually strong dangers of committing fallacies of composition. It needs to be conceptualized both *ex ante* and *ex post*, involving recognition that the latter perspective alone facilitates statistical estimation, while the former is more relevant to transactors' wealth-holding and expenditure decisions. Together, these factors render extremely difficult a definitive answer to the major policy-related issue, namely the extent to which liquidity weakens the Quantity Theory link between 'money' stocks and expenditure flows.

As this statement of the issue implies, debate focuses initially mainly at the macroeconomic level, and mainly on financial (as opposed to 'real') assets. These have been classified by Hicks (1967) into the categories of (1) *running assets*, required by transactors for the maintenance of their activity; (2) *reserve assets*, held to facilitate flexibility of response to ill-foreseen change in economic stimuli; (3) *investment assets*, held for their yield.

Category (1) includes 'money' balances needed to satisfy Keynes's transactions motive to liquidity. But in addition to these claims on (primarily?) banks, it also includes claims on non-financial entities in the form of trade credit, representing goods which have been sold but not yet paid for. Category (2) includes money balances held to satisfy Keynes's precautionary motive to liquidity, along with a familiar spectrum of liquid assets which are mostly short-term claims on the public sector (e.g. Treasury Bills) or on non-bank financial institutions (e.g. building society deposits). Category (3) includes Keynes's speculative money balances, as well as the whole gamut of long-term claims in the form of bonds and so on.

This classification of financial assets, though heroically simplified, is adequate to facilitate discussion and assessment of the three main conceptualizations of

185

liquidity which have emerged in the course of efforts at clarification (see Newlyn, 1962). The first of these has been labelled *maturity*. Treating 'money' as an asset having zero life to maturity, and on the (strong) simplifying assumption that all assets possess specific maturity dates, one may notionally construct a 'maturity curve' showing the cumulative total of assets due to mature by various future dates (Figure 1). For a given asset total, the higher is the intercept of this curve, and the shallower the gradient, the more liquid is the economy's position – because the closer assets are to maturity, the greater in general is the possibility of realizing them before maturity without risk of significant capital loss. It would follow that the more liquid an economy is in this sense, the greater is its capacity to sustain varying output levels without inhibition from interest-rate volatility and associated changes in the market value of a given asset stock.

Such an account presumes that 'money' plays no unique role in the process of acquisition and disposal of financial assets. But in reality, of course, non-money assets are not normally realized, and used to finance spending, without first being exchanged for money balances. This pivotal intermediary role of money is recognized by the second of the three major liquidity concepts, namely *easiness*: this has been defined as the ratio of the stock of money balances (not to the stock of wealth but) to the flow of output, that is, M/Y. The apparent implication is that a high ratio would facilitate expansion of output if adequate incentive existed, while a low ratio would tend to inhibit expansion and possibly enforce contraction. Such an implication is consonant, of course, with the Quantity Theory tradition. In assessing its practical validity, it is necessary to indicate doubts arising from a 'Liquidity Theory' perspective of the kind adumbrated most powerfully, perhaps, by Gurley and Shaw (1960).

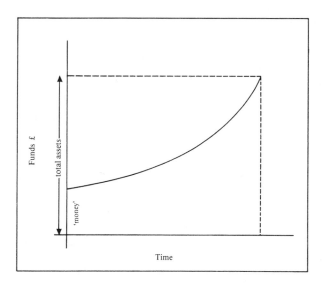

Figure 1

These doubts are of three main kinds. First, it has proved impossible to define money in a manner that commands universal (or even widespread) assent, and enables it to be distinguished clearly from what have been variously labelled liquid assets, near-moneys, or money substitutes (see Sayers, 1960). This is true of the situation in (financially sophisticated) economies at any particular time, and the difficulty is compounded when attention is directed to changes in institutional structures and practices, changes always occurring, more rapidly or less. Historically, bank notes and bank deposits were initially regarded as a means of economizing on holdings of balances of 'real money', or metallic coin. First bank notes then demand deposits, were admitted to the money category. But what of bank time deposits, holders of which could normally suppose that banks would honour their cheques, in effect treating the deposits as belonging to the demand category, usually without substantial penalty? And if bank time deposits be regarded as money, how do they differ fundamentally from, say, building society deposits normally held on similar terms and for similar purposes? And if money is so ineradicably slippery conceptually, can it be so important an entity, in developed economies at least, as Quantity Theory reasoning suggests?

These considerations are closely related to the second kind of doubt, which concentrates on the notion, central to modern Quantity Theory reasoning, of a firm and identifiable demand for money, functionally related to a relatively small number of identifiable variables (e.g. wealth stocks, asset yields). If monetary assets are held in each of Hicks's three categories already mentioned, and within each category are grouped with alternative assets which may be more or less closely substitutable, there would seem in principle to be considerable scope for portfolio adjustment by transactors, to offset any potential effects of monetary stringency on spending plans.

The force of these two kinds of doubt might be weakened, were it true that the supply of particular classes of asset, to which the label 'money' might be affixed, proved to be unresponsive to changing private sector demand, or in other words was determined 'exogenously'. It might then follow that this supply, particularly if its 'givenness' were reinforced by restrictive monetary policy measures, would act as a significant brake on the possibilities of portfolio reshuffling mentioned in the previous paragraph, because a situation might be reached in which wealth-holders were unable to switch into 'money' assets on non-penalty terms, or even at all. In fact, however, our third kind of doubt centres precisely on the claim that the supply of *all* assets, including those which might be called 'money', is essentially subject to endogenous rather than exogenous determination. Before investigating this claim, however, it will be well to introduce our third major liquidity concept, known as *financial strength*.

The explication of this concept calls for recognition of two further complications for financial analysis, largely avoided so far in this article. The first of these is the distinction between the public and the private sectors of the economy. The second is the recognition, perhaps rather belated, that financial claims which represent assets to their holders also represent liabilities to their issuers. With

187

these points in mind, we may approach a simple analysis of the financial strength of, initially, an individual private sector 'transactor' – whether person/family, company/organization, or other entity.

Beginning on the asset side of such a transactor's balance sheet, we may regard holdings of claims on the government (g), and on other private sector entities (a_p), both measured at market rather than nominal values, as unambiguously contributing to the transactor's financial strength (Z) – which can thus be represented by $g + a_p$.

However, it is necessary to make some offset on account of the transactor's liabilities, presumed for simplicity to be entirely due to private sector bodies, and which we may label l_p. So we have $Z = g + a_p - l_p$. But the offset arguably need not include *all* such liabilities, for the transactor may be regarded as being content to incur some volume of liabilities, as having a 'propensity to owe', ω. This propensity, however, must be limited by reference (*inter alia*) to the size of the (present and prospective) income streams from which debt may be serviced; it may thus be expressed as a proportion of income, ωY. So the final expression for Z is given by $g + a_p - (l_p - \omega Y)$.

This, to repeat, is the expression for the individual transactor. Aggregating for the whole economy, on the (debatable) assumption that asset-holders' and liability-issuers' reactions to growth of claims are equal and opposite, we arrive by cancellation at an expression for the financial strength of the private sector as $g - \omega Y$. (It will be noted that this approach treats g as being, in Gurley and Shaw's terminology, 'outside money', on the assumption – again debatable but probably often roughly valid – that *government* spending is not inhibited by the size of its existing liabilities.)

But just one more layer of complexity is unavoidable if we are to achieve even provisional approximation to an extraordinarily confusing reality. We must recognize that much, perhaps the bulk, of private-sector debt will be owed to financial institutions, so that the picture is seriously incomplete unless we incorporate some notion, however simplified, of the conditions on which financial institutions will lend, and in particular of the elasticity of supply of credit – in response to changes in demand for credit, and in interest rates.

It is the contention of many theorists that financial intermediaries typically give priority to meeting the demands of their private sector customers, absorbing volatility in credit demand by (a) attracting new deposits at interest rates which rise only gently because of a high elasticity of substitution among reserve assets; and (b) permitting their reserves, largely in the form of holdings of g, to fluctuate. The result is that credit supply is seen as being highly elastic to private sector demand. Moreover, according to the so-called 'new view' of banking theory, on which see Tobin (1963), point (b) at least is true of banks as well as of other financial institutions. The conclusion is that the supply of bank deposits, the stock residue of previous bank credit flows, is also essentially determined 'endogenously' rather than 'exogenously'. The implication is that the supply of money does *not* automatically act as a significant brake on possibilities of portfolio reshuffling indicated above, and that monetary policy operating through market methods as opposed to direct controls would be hard-pressed to change the situation significantly. This implication would, however, be liable to break down in the case of a liquidity crisis following a strong boom; but such conditions in any case enforce relaxation of tight money policies.

Putting together the rather complex considerations we have outlined, the case for believing that liquidity in modern economies does weaken the Quantity Theory is arguably very strong. In the face of monetary stringency, transactors can sustain spending flows by reshuffling asset portfolios. Some part of this reshuffling will provide financial intermediaries with increased lending powers. Banks tend to maintain private sector lending flows by lending less to the public sector. In Quantity Theory language, money is in quite elastic supply, the velocity of circulation is volatile enough to offset such monetary restriction as the authorities may achieve, and the much-derided argument of the Radcliffe Report (1959) concerning the liquidity-related weakness of reasonably gentle monetary policy using market methods is essentially correct.

BIBLIOGRAPHY

Gurley, J.G and Shaw, E.S. 1960. *Money in a Theory of Finance.* Washington, DC: Brookings Institution.

Hicks, J.R. 1967. *Critical Essays in Monetary Theory.* Oxford: Oxford University Press.

Newlyn, W.T. 1962. *The Theory of Money.* Oxford: Oxford University Press.

Report of the Committee on the Working of the Monetary System. 1959. (The Radcliffe Report) London: HMSO, Cmnd. 827.

Sayers, R.S. 1960. Monetary thought and monetary policy in England. *Economic Journal* 70, December, 710–24.

Tobin, J. 1963. Commercial banks as creators of 'money'. In *Banking and Monetary Studies,* ed. D. Carson, Homewood, Ill.: Richard D. Irwin.

Loanable Funds

S.C. TSIANG

The term 'loanable funds' was used by the late D.H. Robertson, the chief advocate of the loanable funds theory of the interest rate, in the sense of what Marshall used to call 'capital disposal' or 'command over capital', (Robertson, 1940, p. 2). In a money-using economy where money is the only accepted means of payment, however, loanable funds are simply sums of money offered and demanded during a given period of time for immediate use at a certain price.

The loanable funds theory of interest is the theory which maintains that the interest rate, i.e. the price for the use of such funds per unit of time, must be determined by the supply and demand for such funds.

The insistence on the *flow* nature of loanable funds is based upon the crucial conception that in a money-using world the major bulk of money normally exists in a continuous circular flow. It is constantly passing out of the hands of one person as the means of payment for his expenditures into the hands of others as the embodiment of their incomes and sales proceeds, which will in turn be expended, and so on *ad infinitum*. A part of the money in this endless circular flow, however, is observed to be constantly being diverted into a side stream leading to the money market, where it constitutes the supply of loanable funds. From there borrowers of loanable funds would then take them off and in general would put them back into the main circular flow of expenditures and incomes (receipts).

This emphasis on the flow nature of loanable funds does not imply that the loanable funds theory would be unaware that there are sometimes money balances held inactive, like stagnant puddles lying off the main stream of the money flow. The loanable funds theory, however, would maintain that the stocks of money off the circular flow, as well as the stock of money inside the circular flow, have no direct influence on the money market. It is only when people attempt to divert money from the circular flow into the money market (saving), or into the stagnant puddles (hoarding), or conversely try to withdraw the inactive money from the stagnant puddles for re-injection into the circular flow or into the money market (boarding or dishoarding), that the interest rate will be directly affected. In other words, only *adjustments* in the idle balances (hoarding or dishoarding) together with the flows of savings and investment exert direct influences on the interest rate.

Since flows must be measured over time, we must choose a convenient unit to measure time. To take account of the fact that money does not circulate with infinite velocity, Robertson defined the unit period as one 'during which, at the outset of our inquiry, the stock of money changes hands once in final exchange for the constituents of the community's real income or output' (Robertson, 1940, p. 65). In my opinion, however, it would be more consistent and convenient to define the unit period as one during which, at the outset, the stock of money changes hands once in exchange for all commodities and services instead of restricting the objects of exchange to final products only (Tsian, 1956, esp. pp. 545–7). The reason for this will be clear later. Based on our new definition of the unit period, all gross incomes and sales proceeds from goods and services received during the current period cannot be spent on anything until the next period when they are then said to be 'disposable'.

The definition of the unit period, however, does not preclude the funds borrowed or realized from sales of financial assets from being expendable during the same period. This differential treatment of the proceeds of sales of financial assets as distinguished from the proceeds of sales from goods and services is also an attempt to simulate the real situation in our present world; for the velocity of circulation of money against financial assets is in fact observed to be many times faster than that against goods and services. Assuming that there is a fixed unit period in our short period analysis does not necessarily imply that we are *ipso facto* assuming the invariability of the velocity of circulation of money; for short period variations in the velocity of money can be taken care of in terms of increases or decreases in the idle balances held.

Under this definition of the unit period and the implicit assumptions behind it, each individual, therefore, faces a financial constraint in that during a given unit period he can spend only his disposable income and his idle balances (the sum of the two constitutes the entire stock of money he possesses at the beginning of the period) plus the money he can currently borrow on the money market. Buying on credit is to be treated as first borrowing the money and then spending it. Thus when he plans to spend more than his disposable income and the amount he is willing to dishoard from his idle balances, he must borrow the excess from the money market to satisfy his total demand for finance. Since additions to the demand side are equivalent to deductions from the supply side, and vice versa, we need not dispute with Robertson when he classifies the demand for, and the supply of, loanable funds on the money market as follows (Robertson, 1940, p. 3):

On the demand side, he lists, with terminology slightly changed:

D1 funds required to finance current expenditures on investment of fixed or working capital;

D2 funds required to finance current expenditures on maintenance or replacement of existing fixed or working capital (note here that if our unit period were defined in the way Robertson defined it, i.e., as the period during which the total stock of money changes hands only once in the final exchange for the constituents of the community's real income, then the current expenditure on maintenance and replacement, i.e., on intermediate products, cannot be said to require a dollar for dollar provision of finance as would expenditures on final products);

D3 funds to be added to inactive balances held as liquid reserves;

D4 funds required to finance current expenditures on consumption in excess of disposable income. Correspondingly, on the supply side, he gives:

S1 current savings defined as disposable income minus planned current consumption expenditure;

S2 current depreciation or depletion allowances for fixed and working capital taken out of the gross sales proceeds of the preceding period;

S3 dishoarding withdrawn from previously held inactive balances of money;

S4 net creation of additional money by banks.

The function of the money market is to match the flow demands for loanable funds to the flow supplies, and the instrument with which it operates to achieve equilibrium between the two sides is the vector of interest rates. It is to be noted that in the flow equilibrium condition the total stock of money does not figure at all.

Nevertheless, it must be pointed out that the flow equilibrium condition of the money market as conceived by the loanable funds theorists can imply the stock equilibrium condition as conceived by the liquidity preference theorists, provided two necessary conditions are satisfied. Of the four demands for loanable funds listed above, D1, D2 and D4 are the additional demands for transactions balances (or what Keynes in 1937 called the finance demand for liquidity) needed by some firms and consumers to finance their current planned expenditures. And of the four sources of supply of loanable funds, S1 and S2 are but the reductions in demand for finance which other consumers of firms can spare during the current period. Therefore, D1, D2 and D4 minus S1 and S2 must be equal to the net aggregate increase which the community as a whole would want to add to their transactions balances.

Similarly, D3 minus S3 is the net increase which the community would want to add to their inactive balances (including precautionary, speculative, and investment balances).

Thus the equilibrium condition of the demand for and supply of loanable funds, i.e.,

$$D1 + D2 + D3 + D4 = S1 + S2 + S3 + S4,$$

which can be rearranged as:

$$[D1 + D2 + D4 - (S1 + S2)] + (D3 - S3) = S4,$$

implies that the total increases in aggregate demand for transactions balances (finance) and for inactive balances equal the net current increases in money supply created by banks. Provided it may be presumed (a) that the previous stock supply of and demand for money were originally equal to each other, and

(b) that the current increases (or decreases) in supply and demand for money (treated above as flow supply and demand for loanable funds) represent the full unlagged adjustments of the previous stock supply and demand to their new equilibrium values, the flow equilibrium of the loanable funds should necessarily imply a new stock equilibrium (Tsiang, 1982).

The two necessary provisos used to be taken for granted by the liquidity preference theorists, who generally think that full stock equilibrium can be achieved instantaneously at any point in time. Recently, however, Professor James Tobin, in his Nobel lecture given in 1981 (Tobin, 1982), has come to recognize that the money market cannot operate within a dimensionless point of time, but must operate in finite time periods, which he called slices of time. Furthermore, he recognized that the equilibrium which can be expected in such a short slice of time can only be that between the adjustments in the stock demanded and in the stock supplied during the period. Since adjustments in stocks per time period are flows, Tobin's new approach is thus really a sort of flow equilibrium analysis.

Moreover, Tobin, at the same time, also admitted that in such a short period as a slice of time, portfolios of individual agents cannot adjust fully to new market information. Lags in response are inevitable and rational in view of the costs of transactions and decisions. Thus neither of the two necessary conditions is satisfied in the real world. Consequently, even when the money market has brought the flow demand for and supply of loanable funds to equality, the stock demand for money and the total money stock need not have reached mutual equilibrium, which the Keynesians and the stock-approach economists used to assume as being attainable at every point of time.

Finally, it should be realized that the demand for finance for planned investment expenditure, which Keynes (1937, p. 667) admitted he should not have overlooked in his *General Theory*, is of the nature of a flow generated by a flow decision to invest. It is not just a partial adjustment of the stock demand for money towards its new equilibrium value as treated in Tobin's new theory (Tobin, 1982). As Keynes put it in his reply to Ohlin (1937), '"Finance" is a revolving fund, ... As soon as it is used in the sense of being expended, the lack of liquidity is automatically made good and the readiness to become temporarily unliquid is available to be used over again' (Keynes, 1937, p. 666). This is essentially a reaffirmation of the traditional conception of the circular flow of money, which loanable funds theorists had emphasized from the outset, but which Keynes himself had pushed into the dark background with his emphasis that the entire stock of money is being held voluntarily in portfolio allocation.

The rediscovery of the demand for finance by Keynes and the more recent unheralded switch on the part of Tobin towards the flow approach from his usual stock approach indicate that the loanable funds theory is perhaps the more appropriate approach at least for short period dynamic analysis.

BIBLIOGRAPHY
Keynes, J.M. 1937. The ex-ante theory of the rate of interest. *Economic Journal* 47, December, 663–9.

Ohlin, B. 1937. Some notes on the Stockholm theory of savings and investment, I. *Economic Journal* 47, March, 53–69.

Ohlin, B. 1937. Some notes on the Stockholm theory of savings and investment, II. *Economic Journal* 47, June, 221–40.

Robertson, D.H. 1940. *Essays in Monetary Theory.* London: P.S. King.

Tobin, J. 1982. Money and finance in the macroeconomic process. *Journal of Money, Credit and Banking* 14, May, 171–204.

Tsiang, S.C. 1956. Liquidity preference and loanable funds theories, multiplier and velocity analysis: a synthesis. *American Economic Review* 46, September, 539–64.

Tsiang, S.C. 1982. Stock or portfolio approach to monetary theory and the neo-Keynesian school of James Tobin. *IHS-Journal* 6, 149–71.

Monetarism

PHILLIP CAGAN

Monetarism is the view that the quantity of money has a major influence on economic activity and the price level and that the objectives of monetary policy are best achieved by targeting the rate of growth of the money supply.

BACKGROUND AND INITIAL DEVELOPMENT. Monetarism is most closely associated with the writings of Milton Friedman who advocated control of the money supply as superior to Keynesian fiscal measures for stabilizing aggregate demand. Friedman (1948) had proposed that the government finance budget deficits by issuing new money and use budget surpluses to retire money. The resulting countercyclical variations in the money stock would stabilize the economy, provided that the government set its expenditures and tax rates to balance the budget at full employment. In his *A Program for Monetary Stability* (1960), however, Friedman proposed that constant growth of the money stock, divorced from the government budget, would be simpler and equally effective for stabilizing the economy.

In their emphasis on the importance of money, these proposals followed a tradition of the Chicago School of economics. Preceding Friedman at the University of Chicago, Henry Simons (1936) had advocated control of the money stock to achieve a stable price level, and Lloyd Mints (1950) laid out a specific monetary programme for stabilizing an index of the price level. These writers rejected reliance on the gold standard because it had failed in practice to stabilize the price level or economic activity. Such views were not confined to the University of Chicago. In the 1930s James Angell of Columbia University (1933) advocated constant monetary growth, and in the post-World War II period Karl Brunner and Allan Meltzer were influential proponents of monetarism. The term 'monetarism' was first used by Brunner (1968). He and Meltzer founded the 'Shadow Open Market Committee' in the 1970s to publicize monetarist views on how the Federal Reserve should conduct monetary policy. Monetarism gradually gained adherents not only in the US but also in Britain (Laidler, 1978) and other Western European countries, and subsequently around the world. The growing prominence of monetarism led to intense controversy among economists over the desirability of a policy of targeting monetary growth.

The roots of monetarism lie in the quantity theory of money which formed the basis of classical monetary economics from at least the 18th century. The quantity theory explains changes in nominal aggregate expenditures – reflecting changes in both the physical volume of output and the price level – in terms of changes in the money stock and in the velocity of circulation of money (the ratio of aggregate expenditures to the money stock). Over the long run changes in velocity are usually smaller than those in the money stock and in part are a result of prior changes in the money stock, so that aggregate expenditures are determined largely by the latter. Moreover, over the long run growth in the physical volume of output is determined mainly by real (that is, nonmonetary) factors, so that monetary changes mainly influence the price level. The observed long-run association between money and prices confirms that inflation results from monetary overexpansion and can be prevented by proper control of the money supply. This is the basis for Friedman's oft-repeated statement that inflation is always and everywhere a monetary phenomenon.

The importance of monetary effects on price movements had been supported in empirical studies by classical and neo-classical economists such as Cairnes, Jevons and Cassel. But these studies suffered from limited data, and the widespread misinterpretation of monetary influences in the Great Depression of the 1930s fostered doubts about their importance in business cycles. As Keynesian theory revolutionized thinking in the late 1930s and 1940s, it offered an influential alternative to monetary interpretations of business cycles.

The first solid empirical support for a monetary interpretation of business cycles came in a series of studies of the US by Clark Warburton (e.g. 1946). Subsequently Friedman and Anna J. Schwartz compiled new data at the National Bureau of Economic Research in an extension of Warburton's work. In 1962 they demonstrated that fluctuations in monetary growth preceded peaks and troughs of all US business cycles since the Civil War. Their dates for significant steps to higher or lower rates of monetary growth showed a lead over corresponding business cycle turns on the average by about a half year at peaks and by about a quarter year at troughs, but the lags varied considerably. Other studies have found that monetary changes take one to two years or more to affect the price level.

In *A Monetary History of the United States, 1867–1960* (1963) Friedman and Schwartz detailed the role of money in business cycles and argued in particular that severe business contractions like that of 1929–33 were directly attributable to unusually large monetary contractions. Their monetary studies were continued in *Monetary Statistics of the United States* (1970) and *Monetary Trends in the United States and the United Kingdom* (1982). A companion National Bureau study *Determinants and Effects of Changes in the Stock of Money* (1965) by Phillip Cagan presented evidence that the reverse effect of economic activity and prices on money did not account for the major part of their observed correlation, which therefore pointed to an important causal role of money.

The monetarist proposition that monetary changes are responsible for business cycles was widely contested, but by the end of the 1960s the view that monetary policy had important effects on aggregate activity was generally accepted. The obvious importance of monetary growth in the inflation of the 1970s restored money to the centre of macroeconomics.

MONETARISM VERSUS KEYNESIANISM. Monetarism and Keynesianism differ sharply in their research strategies and theories of aggregate expenditures. The Keynesian theory focuses on the determinants of the components of aggregate expenditures and assigns a minor role to money holdings. In monetarist theory money demand and supply are paramount in explaining aggregate expenditures.

To contrast the Keynesian and monetarist theories, Friedman and David Meiselman (1963) focused on the basic hypothesis about economic behaviour underlying each theory: for the Keynesian theory the consumption multiplier posits a stable relationship between consumption and income, and for the monetarist theory the velocity of circulation of money posits a stable demand function for money. Friedman and Meiselman tested the two theories empirically using US data for various periods by relating consumption expenditures in one regression to investment expenditures, assuming a constant consumption multiplier, and in a second regression to the money stock, assuming a constant velocity. They reported that the monetarist regression generally fitted the data much better. These dramatic results were not accepted by Keynesians, who argued that the Keynesian theory was not adequately represented by a one-equation regression and that econometric models of the entire economy, based on Keynesian theory, were superior to small-scale models based solely on monetary changes.

The alleged superiority of Keynesian models was contested by economists at the Federal Reserve Bank of St Louis (see Andersen and Jordan, 1968). They tested a 'St Louis equation' in which changes in nominal GNP depended on current and lagged changes in the money stock, current and lagged changes in government expenditures, and a constant term reflecting the trend in monetary velocity. When fitted to historical US data, the equation showed a strong permanent effect of money on GNP and a weak transitory (and in later work, nonexistent) effect of the fiscal variables, contradicting the Keynesian claim of the greater importance of fiscal than monetary policies. Although the St Louis equation was widely criticized on econometric issues, it was fairly accurate when first used in the later 1960s to forecast GNP, which influenced academic opinion and helped bring monetarism to the attention of the business world.

Although budget deficits and surpluses change interest rates and thus can affect the demand for money, monetarists believe that fiscal effects on aggregate demand are small because of the low interest elasticity of money demand. Government borrowing crowds out private borrowing and associated spending, and so deficits have little net effect on aggregate demand. The empirical results of the St Louis equation are taken as confirmation of weak transitory effects. The debate over the effectiveness of fiscal policy as a stabilization tool has produced a large literature.

197

In their analysis of the transmission of monetary changes through the economy, Brunner and Meltzer (1976) compare the effects of government issues of money and bonds. If the government finances increased expenditures in a way that raises the money supply, aggregate expenditures increase and nominal income rises. Moreover, the increased supply of money adds to the public's wealth, and greater wealth increases the demand for goods and services. This too raises nominal income. The rise in nominal income is at first mainly a rise in real income and later a rise in prices. They compare this result with one in which the government finances its increased expenditures by issuing bonds rather than money. Again wealth increases, and this raises aggregate expenditures. As long as the government issues either money or bonds to finance a deficit, nominal income must rise due to the increase in wealth. Brunner and Meltzer therefore agree with Keynesians that in principle a deficit financed by bonds as well as by new money is expansionary. However, they show that the empirical magnitudes of the economy are such that national income rises more from issuing a dollar of money that a dollar of bonds.

POLICY IMPLICATIONS OF MONETARISM. Because monetary effects have variable lags of one to several quarters or more, countercyclical monetary policy actions are difficult to time properly. Friedman as well as Brunner and Meltzer argued that an active monetary policy, in the absence of an impossibly ideal foresight, tends to exacerbate, rather than smooth, economic fluctuations. In their view a stable monetary growth rate would avoid monetary sources of economic disturbances, and could be set to produce an approximately constant price level over the long run. Remaining instabilities in economic activity would be minor and, in any event, were beyond the capabilities of policy to prevent. A commitment by the monetary authorities to stable monetary growth would also help deflect constant political pressures for short-run monetary stimulus and would remove the uncertainty for investors of the unexpected effects of discretionary monetary policies.

A constant monetary growth policy can be contrasted with central bank practices that impart pro-cyclical variations to the money supply. It is common for central banks to lend freely to banks at times of rising credit demand in order to avoid increases in interest rates. Although such interest-rate targeting helps to stabilize financial markets, the targeting often fails to allow rates to change sufficiently to counter fluctuations in credit demands. By preventing interest rates from rising when credit demands increase, for example, the policy leads to monetary expansion that generates higher expenditures and inflationary pressures. Such mistakes of interest-rate targeting were clearly demonstrated in the 1970s, when for some time increases in nominal interest rates did not match increases in the inflation rate, and the resulting low rates of interest in real terms (that is, adjusted for inflation) overstimulated investment and aggregate demand.

The same accommodation of market demands for bank credit results from the common practice of targeting the volume of borrowing from the central bank. Attempts to keep this volume at some designated level require the central bank to supply reserves through open market operations as an alternative to borrowing by banks when rising market credit demands tighten banks reserve positions, and to withdraw reserves in the opposite situation. The resulting procyclical behaviour of the money supply could be avoided by operations designed to maintain a constant growth rate of money.

Brunner and Meltzer (1964a) developed an analytic framework describing how monetary policy should aim at certain intermediate targets as a way of influencing aggregate expenditures. The intermediate targets are such variables as the money supply or interest rates. (Since the Federal Reserve does not control long-term interest rates or the money stock directly, it operates through instrumental variables, such as bank reserves or the federal funds rate, which it can affect directly.) The question of the appropriate intermediate targets of monetary policy soon became the most widely-discussed issue in monetary policy.

In recognition of the deficiencies of interest-rate targeting, some countries turned during the 1970s to a modified monetary targeting in which annual growth ranges were announced and adhered to, though with frequent exceptions to allow for departures deemed appropriate because of disturbances from foreign trade and other sources. Major countries adopting some form of monetary targeting included the Federal Republic of Germany, Japan, and Switzerland, all of which kept inflation rates low and thus advertised by example the anti-inflationary virtues of monetarism. In the US the Federal Reserve also began to set monetary target ranges during the 1970s but generally did not meet them and continued to target interest rates. In October 1979, when inflation was escalating sharply, the Federal Reserve announced a more stringent targeting procedure for reducing monetary growth. Although the average growth rate was reduced, the large short-run fluctuations in monetary growth were criticized by monetarists. In late 1982 the Federal Reserve relaxed its pursuit of monetary targets.

By the mid-1980s the US and numerous other countries were following a partial form of monetary targeting, in which relatively broad bands of annual growth rates are pursued but still subject to major departures when deemed appropriate. These policies are monetarist only in the sense that one or more monetary aggregates are an important indicator of policy objectives; they fall short of a firm commitment to a steady, let along a noninflationary, monetary growth rate.

MONETARIST THEORY. Monetarist theory of aggregate expenditures is based on demand function for monetary assets that is claimed to be stable in the sense that successive residual errors are generally offsetting and do not accumulate. Given the present inconvertible-money systems, the stock of money is treated as under the control of the government. Although a distinction is made in theory between the determinants of household and business holdings of money, money demand is usually formulated for households and applied to the total. In these formulations the demand for money depends on the volume of transactions, the fractions of income and of wealth the public wishes to hold in the form of money balances, and the opportunity costs of holding money rather than other income-producing assets (that is, the difference between yields on money and on alternative assets). The alternative assets are viewed broadly to include not only financial instruments but also such physical assets as durable consumer goods, real property, and business plant and equipment. The public is presumed to respond to changes in the amount of money supplied by undertaking transactions to bring actual holdings of both money and other assets into equilibrium with desired holdings. As a result of substitutions between money and assets, starting with close substitutes, yields change on a broad range of assets, including consumer durables and capital goods, in widening ripples that affect borrowing, investment, consumption, and production throughout the economy.

The end result is reflected in *aggregate* expenditures and the average level of prices. Independently of this monetary influence on aggregate expenditures and the price level, developments specific to particular sectors determine the distribution of expenditures among goods and services and relative prices. Thus monetarist theory rejects the common technique for forecasting aggregate output by adding up the forecasts for individual industries or the common practice of explaining changes in the price level in terms of price changes for particular goods and services.

Monetarists were early critics of the once influential Keynesian theory of a highly elastic demand for money with respect to short-run changes in the interest rate on liquid short-term assets, which in extreme form became a 'liquidity trap'. Empirical studies have found instead that interest rates on savings deposits and on short-term market securities have elasticities smaller even than the $-\frac{1}{2}$ implied by the simple Baumol-Tobin cash balance theory (Baumol, 1952; Tobin, 1956).

In empirical work a common form of the demand function for money includes one or two interest rates and real GNP as a proxy for real income. A gradual adjustment of actual to desired money balances is allowed for, implying that a full adjustment to a change in the stock is spread over several quarters. The lagged adjustment is subject to an alternative interpretation in which money demand reflects 'permanent' instead of current levels of income and interest rates. This interpretation de-emphasizes the volume of transactions as the major determinant of money demand in favour of the monetarist view of money as a capital asset yielding a stream of particular services and dependent on 'permanent' values of wealth, income, and interest rates (in most studies captured empirically by a lagged adjustment). Treatment of the demand for money as similar to demands for other asset stocks is now standard practice.

The monetarist view of money as a capital asset suggests that the demand for it depends on a variety of characteristics, and not uniquely on its transactions services. The definition of money for policy purposes depends on two considerations: the ability of the monetary authorities to control its quantity, and the empirical stability of a function describing the demand for it. In their study of the US Friedman and Schwartz used an early version of M2, which included time and savings deposits at commercial banks, but they argued that minor changes in coverage would not greatly affect their findings. Subsequently the quantity of transactions balances M1 has become the most widely used definition of money for most countries, though many central banks claim to pay attention also to broader aggregates in conducting monetary policy.

In view of the wide range of assets into which the public may shift any excess money balances, the transmission of monetary changes through the economy to affect aggregate expenditures and other variables can follow a variety of paths. Monetarists doubt that these effects can be adequately captured by a detailed econometric model which prescribes a fixed transmission path. Instead they prefer models that dispense with detailed transmission paths and focus on a stable overall relationship between changes in money and in aggregate expenditures.

In both the monetarist model and large-scale econometric models, changes in the money stock are usually treated as exogenous (that is, as determined outside the model). It is clear that money approaches a strict exogeneity only in the long run. The US studies by Friedman and Schwartz and by Cagan established that the money supply not only influences economic activity but also is influenced by it in turn. This creates difficulties in testing empirically for the monetary effects on activity because allowance must be made for the feedback effect of economic activity on the money supply. Econometric models of the money supply can allow for feedback through the banking system (Brunner and Meltzer, 1964b). Under modern systems of inconvertible money, however, the feedback is dominated by monetary policies of the central banks, and attempts to model central bank behaviour have been less than satisfactory. Statistical tests of the exogeneity of the money supply using the Granger-Sims methodology have given mixed results. Although the concurrent mutual interaction between money and economic activity remains difficult to disentangle, the longer the lag in monetary effects the less likely that the feedback from activity to money can account for the observed association. In the St Louis equation, for example, while the correlation between changes in GNP and in money concurrently could largely reflect feedback from GNP to money, the correlation between changes in GNP and lagged changes in money are less likely to be dominated by such feedbacks.

OPPOSITION TO MONETARY TARGETING. While monetarism refocused attention on money and monetary policy, there is widespread doubt that velocity is sufficiently stable to make targeting of monetary growth desirable. Movements in velocity when monetary growth is held constant produce expansionary and contractionary effects on the economy. In the US the trend of velocity was fairly stable and predictable from the early 1950s to the mid-1970s, but money demand equations based on that period showed large overpredictions after the mid-1970s (Judd and Scadding, 1982). Financial innovations providing new ways of making payments and close substitutes for holding money were changing the appropriate definition of money and the parameters of the demand function. In the US the gradual removal of ceilings on interest rates banks could pay on deposits played a major role in these developments by increasing competition in banking. In Great Britain the removal of domestic controls over international financial transactions led to unusual movements in money holdings in 1979–80. Germany and

Switzerland also found growing international capital inflows at certain times a disruptive influence on their monetary policies.

The 'monetary theory of the balance of payments' (Frenkel and Johnson, 1976) is an extension of monetarism to open economies where money supply and demand are interrelated among countries through international payments. A debated issue is whether individual countries, even under flexible exchange rates, can pursue largely independent monetary policies. The growing internationalization of capital markets is often cited as an argument against the monetarist presumption that velocity and the domestic money supply under flexible foreign exchange rates are largely independent of foreign influences.

Uncertainties over the paper definition of money and instability in the velocity of money as variously defined led to monetarist proposals to target the monetary liabilities of the central bank, that is, the 'monetary base' consisting of currency outstanding and bank reserves. The monetary base has the advantage of not being directly affected by market innovations and so of not needing redefinitions when innovations occur. Monetarists have proposed maintaining a constant growth rate of the base also because it would simplify – indirectly virtually eliminate – the monetary policy function of central banks and governments. Some of the European central banks have found targeting the monetary base preferable to targeting the money supply, though not without important discretionary departures from the target.

Yet financial market developments can also produce instabilities in the relationship between the monetary base and aggregate expenditures. Economists opposed to monetarism propose instead that stable growth of aggregate expenditures be the target of monetary policy and that it be pursued by making discretionary changes as deemed appropriate in growth of the base. This constrasts sharply with the monetarist opposition to discretion in the conduct of policy.

THE PHILLIPS CURVE TRADE-OFF. The inflationary outcome of discretionary monetary policy since World War II can be explained in terms of the Phillips curve trade-off between inflation and unemployment. Along the Phillips curve lower and lower unemployment levels are associated with higher and higher inflation rates. Such a relationship, first found in historical British data, was shown to fit US data for the 1950s and 1960s and earlier. The trade-off depends on sticky wages and prices. As aggregate demand increases, the rise in wages and prices trails behind, inducing an expansion of output to absorb part of the increase in demand. US experience initially suggested that any desired position on the Phillips curve could be maintained by the management of aggregate demand. Thus a lower rate of unemployment could be achieved and maintained by tolerating an associated higher rate of inflation. Given this presumed trade-off, policy makers tended to favour lower unemployment at the cost of higher inflation.

In the 1970s, however, the Phillips curve shifted toward higher rates of inflation for given levels of unemployment. Friedman (1968) argued that the economy gravitates toward a 'natural rate of unemployment' which in the long run is largely independent of the inflation rate and cannot be changed by monetary policy. Wages and prices adjust sluggishly to unanticipated changes in aggregate demand but adjust more rapidly to maintained increases in demand and prices that are anticipated. Consequently, the only way to hold unemployment below the natural rate is to keep aggregate demand rising faster than the anticipated rate of inflation. Since the anticipated rate tends to follow the actual rate upward, this leads to faster and faster inflation. This 'acceleration principle' implies that there is no permanent trade-off between inflation and unemployment. The existence of a natural rate of unemployment also implies that price stability does not lead to higher unemployment in the long run.

Monetarist thought puts primary emphasis on the long-run consequences of policy actions and procedures. It rejects attempts to reduce short-run fluctuations in interest rates and economic activity as usually beyond the capabilities of monetary policy and as generally inimical to the otherwise achievable goals of long-run price stability and maximum economic growth. Monetarists believe that economic activity, apart from monetary disturbances, is inherently stable. Much of their disagreement with Keynesians can be traced to this issue.

RATIONAL EXPECTATIONS. One version of the rational expectations theory goes beyond monetarism by contending that there is little or no Phillips curve trade-off between inflation and unemployment even in the short run, since markets are allegedly able to anticipate any systematic countercyclical policy pursued to stabilize the economy. Only unanticipated departures from such stabilization policies affect output; all anticipated monetary changes are fully absorbed by price changes. Since unsystematic policies would have little countercyclical effectiveness or purpose, the best policy is to minimize uncertainty with a predictable monetary growth.

This theory shares the monetarist view that unpredictable fluctuations in monetary growth are an undesirable source of uncertainty with little benefit. But the two views disagree on the speed of price adjustments to predictable monetary measures and on the associated effects on economic activity. Monetarists do not claim that countercyclical policies have no real effects, but they are sceptical of our ability to use them effectively. It is the ill-timing of countercyclical policies as a result of variable lags in monetary effects that underlies the monetarist preference for constant monetary growth to avoid uncertainty and inflation bias.

INTEREST IN PRIVATE MONEY SUPPLIES. Monetarism is the fountainhead of a renewed interest in a subject neglected during the Keynesian revolution: the design of monetary systems that maintain price-level stability. Scepticism that price-level stability can be achieved even by a constant growth rate of money however defined or of the monetary base has led to proposals for a strict gold standard or for a monetary system in which money is supplied by the private sector under competitive pressures to maintain a stable value. While monetarists are sympathetic to proposals to eliminate discretionary monetary policies, they view such alternative systems as impractical and believe that a nondiscretionary government policy of constant monetary growth is the best policy.

ASSOCIATED VIEWS OF THE MONETARIST SCHOOL. Monetarism is associated with various related attitudes toward government (see Mayer, 1978). Monetarism shares with laissez faire a belief in the long-run benefits of a competitive economic system and of limited government intervention in the economy. It opposes constraints on the free flow of credit and on movements of interest rates, such as the US ceilings on deposit interest rates (removed by the mid-1980s except on demand deposits). The disruptive potential of such ceilings became evident in the 1970s when financial innovations, partly undertaken to circumvent the ceilings, produced the transitional shifts in the traditional money-demand functions that created difficulties for the conduct of monetary policy. Government control over the quantity of money is viewed as a justifiable exception to laissez faire, however, in order to ensure the stability of the value of money.

BIBLIOGRAPHY

Andersen, L.C. and Jordan, J.L. 1968. Monetary and fiscal actions: a test of their relative importance in economic stabilization. Federal Reserve Bank of St Louis *Review* 50, November, 11–24.

Angell, J. 1933. Monetary control and general business stabilization. In *Economic Essays in Honour of Gustav Cassel*, London: Allen and Unwin.

Baumol, W.J. 1952. The transactions demand for cash: an inventory theoretic approach. *Quarterly Journal of Economics* 66, November, 545–56.

Brunner, K. 1968. The role of money and monetary policy. *Federal Reserve Bank of St Louis Review* 50, July, 8–24.

Brunner, K. and Meltzer, A. 1964a. The federal reserve's attachment to the free reserve concept. U.S. Congress House Committee on Banking and Currency, Subcommittee on Domestic Finance, April.

Brunner, K. and Meltzer, A. 1964b. Some further investigations of demand and supply functions for money. *Journal of Finance* 19, May, 240–83.

Brunner, K. and Meltzer, A. 1976. An aggregative theory for a closed economy. In *Studies in Monetarism*, ed. J. Stein, Amsterdam: North Holland.

Cagan, P. 1965. *Determinants and Effects of Changes in the Stock of Money 1875–1960*. New York: Columbia University Press for the National Bureau of Economic Research.

Frenkel, J.A. and Johnson, H.G. Eds. 1976. *The Monetary Approach to the Balance of Payments*. Toronto: University of Toronto Press.

Friedman, M. 1948. A monetary and fiscal framework for economic stability. *American Economic Review* 38, June, 256–64.

Friedman, M. 1960. *A Program for Monetary Stability*. New York: Fordham University Press.

Friedman, M. 1968. The role of monetary policy. *American Economic Review* 58, March, 1–17.

Friedman, M. and Meiselman, D. 1963. The relative stability of monetary velocity and the investment multiplier in the United States, 1897–1958. In Commission on Money and Credit, *Stabilization Policies*, Englewood Cliffs, NJ: Prentice-Hall.

Friedman, M. and Schwartz, A.J. 1963. Money and business cycles. *Review of Economics and Statistics* 45(1), part 2, Supplement, February, 32–64.

Friedman, M. and Schwartz, A. 1963. *A Monetary History of the United States 1867–1960*. Princeton: Princeton University Press for the National Bureau of Economic Research.

Friedman, M. and Schwartz, A. 1970. *Monetary Statistics of the United States Estimates, Sources, Methods*. New York: National Bureau of Economic Research.

Friedman, M. and Schwartz, A. 1982. *Monetary Trends in the United States and the United Kingdom Their Relation to Income, Prices and Interest Rates, 1867–1975*. Chicago: University of Chicago Press.

Judd, J.P. and Scadding, J.L. 1982. The search for a stable money demand function: a survey of the post-1973 literature. *Journal of Economic Literature* 20, September, 993–1023.

Laidler, D. 1978. Mayer on monetarism: comments from a British point of view. In *The Structure of Monetarism*, ed. T. Mayer, New York: W.W. Norton & Co. New York.

Mayer, T. (ed.) 1978. *The Structure of Monetarism*. New York: W.W. Norton & Co.

Mints, L.W. 1950. *Monetary Policy for a Competitive Society*. New York: McGraw-Hill.

Simons, H. 1936. Rules versus authorities in monetary policy. *Journal of Political Economy* 44, February, 1–30.

Tobin, J. 1956. The interest elasticity of transactions demand for cash. *Review of Economics and Statistics* 38, August, 241–7.

Warburton, C. 1946. The misplaced emphasis in contemporary business-fluctuation theory. *Journal of Business*, October.

Monetary Base

CHARLES GOODHART

A key characteristic of bank deposits is that they carry a guarantee of convertibility at sight, or after due notice, into cash. In order to maintain such convertibility, a bank needs to hold reserves of cash. Historically such cash mostly took the form of metallic coin, that is, gold, silver or copper. Nowadays the cash base mostly consists of the liabilities of the Central Bank, primarily notes, but also bankers' balances at the Central Bank which the bankers can, if they wish, withdraw in note form to add to their own cash holdings. The monetary base, mostly consisting of Central Bank notes in the hands of the public and in the tills of the banks, is so called because it provides the cash base on which the much larger superstructure of convertible deposits is erected.

Such cash holdings have generally not paid any interest; indeed it would be difficult to devise a technical method of paying interest on notes and coins. Accordingly commercial banks have had an incentive to economize on their holdings of such zero-yielding cash assets, restricting them to the minimum required in order to satisfy the convertibility requirements, while protecting themselves against large-scale deposit withdrawals by holding a range of liquid (near-cash) assets, which could be rapidly transformed into cash (liquified) at short notice, but which nevertheless offered a reasonable yield. The main component of such second-line liquidity has historically been short-term commercial or Treasury bills; the liquidity of such bills has, in turn, been enhanced by the willingness of the Central Bank always to re-discount, and to maintain a market in, such bills, though on occasions at a penalty price.

Although most banking panics have actually been caused by growing concern about some banking institutions' solvency, the actual event that forces closure in such cases, at any rate in the earlier years of banking, was the inability of the bank to continue paying out its depositors, when the bank was faced with a 'run' of deposit withdrawals, in cash. Accordingly, to show how strong the bank was, banks tended to window-dress their balance sheets on publication dates, with more cash and liquid assets than they in reality normally held. Meanwhile, the monetary authorities, noting that the proximate cause of failure was a shortage of cash reserves, often imposed requirements, whether backed by legal force or through moral suasion, that the banks should hold a certain percentage of their assets in cash form, and, in some cases, an additional percentage in some specified set of liquid assets. This latter policy had certain inherent deficiencies. First, to the extent that such balances were actually *required* to be held, they could not then be legally used to meet withdrawals, so the effective available reserves became the margin of 'free reserves' in excess of requirements. Moreover, any, even temporary, decline of reserve holdings below the required level was taken as a signal of weakness and distress in itself. Second, the requirements for banks to hold larger zero-yielding and low-yielding balances, than they would have voluntarily done, adversely affected their profitability. This not only weakened their ability to compete, but in some cases may have encouraged the banks to undertake a riskier strategy in order to restore their profitability, thereby negating the initial intentions of the authorities.

Still, the banks *had* to hold a certain proportion of cash reserves, in order to remain in business: indeed there was often a certain observed regularity and stability in the ratio of their cash reserves to deposits – though this was sometimes the consequence either of window-dressing or of official requirements. Such stability in the banks' reserve deposit ratio, combined with the fact that the cash base largely represented the liabilities of the Central Bank, led economists to construct a theory of the determination, and control, of the money stock. This is based on certain simple accounting identities. The money stock (M) is defined as comprising two main components, being respectively currency (C) and bank deposits (D) held by the general public. It is, therefore, possible to set down the identity

$$M = D + C$$

which must hold exactly by definition. Similarly it is possible to define the sum of currency held by the general public (C) and the cash reserves of the banking sector (R) as 'high-powered money' or 'monetary base' (H). Again, the additional identity can be formed

$$H = R + C$$

By algebraic manipulation of these two identities it is possible to arrive at a third identity

$$M = H(1 + C/D)(R/D + C/D)$$

describing the money stock in terms of the level of high-powered money and two ratios, R/D, the banks' reserve/deposit ratio, and C/D, the general public's currency/deposit ratio. Since this relationship is also an identity, it always holds true by definition; changes in the money stock can therefore be expressed in terms of these three variables alone. To be able to express changes in the money stock in terms of only three variables has considerable advantages of brevity and simplicity. Nevertheless, the use of such an identity does not in any sense provide a behavioural theory of the determination of the stock of money.

The associated behavioural story rests upon a supposed 'multiplier' process, the monetary base multiplier. On this thesis, the Central Bank undertakes open-market operations, in order to vary its own liabilities, and, in the process, the reserve base of the banking system. When, for example, the Central Bank sells an asset, the purchaser, probably a non-bank, pays for the purchase by a cheque on her own bank, so that bank's balance with the Central Bank is reduced. Then, on this story, that bank sells an asset itself in order to restore its depleted cash balance. This second purchaser, again probably a non-bank, paying again by cheque, will by so doing transfer cash reserves from his own bank to the first bank in order to pay for the purchase, but in the process the cash shortage will be transferred to this second bank. And so the multiplier process will continue. So long as the Central Bank does not re-enter the market in order to buy assets, its initial open market sale will cause a multiple fall in bank assets and deposits, the size of which multiplier will depend on the C/D and the R/D ratios described above.

In practice, however, the banking system has virtually *never* worked in that manner. Central Banks have, indeed, made use of their monopoly control over access to cash and their power to enforce that by open market operations, but for the purpose of making effective a desired level of (short-term) interest rates, not to achieve a pre-determined quantity of monetary base or of some monetary aggregate. The various influences, external forces and objectives that have affected the authorities' views of the appropriate level of interest rates have varied over time, including such considerations as a desire to maintain a fixed exchange rate, for example on the Gold Standard, or to encourage investment, or, more recently, to influence the pace of monetary growth itself.

Indeed, Central Banks have historically been at some pains to assure the banking system that the institutional structure is such that the system as a whole can *always* obtain access to whatever cash the system may require in order to meet its needs, though at a price of the Central Bank's choosing: and there has been a further, implicit corollary that that interest rate will not be varied capriciously. The whole structure of the monetary system has evolved on this latter basis, that is, that the untrammelled force of the monetary base multiplier will *never* be unleashed. Furthermore, recent institutional developments, notably the growth of the wholesale inter-bank liability market, imply that the monetary base multiplier no longer would, or could, work in the textbook fashion. The development of liability management, through such wholesale markets, means that commercial banks now respond to a loss of liquidity, whether from a Central Bank open-market sale or some other source, by bidding for additional funds in such liability markets, rather than by selling assets. In these circumstances, a loss of cash reserves to the banking system, driving these below an acceptable minimum, will simply have the effect of driving interest rates upwards, both in liability markets, and more generally on deposit and asset rates, without having initially any direct effect on monetary quantities. In the short run, then, interest rates can rise, in a virtually limitless spiral until extra reserves are attracted into the system, whether from the Central Bank, or elsewhere. In the somewhat longer run, however, the rise in interest rates will subsequently bring about a reallocation by both bank depositors and bank borrowers of their funds, which will, in general, have the effect of bringing about a transfer of funds from non-interest-bearing narrow monetary aggregates, and also leading to a reduction of now more expensive bank borrowing.

In short, the behavioural process runs from an initial change in interest rates, whether administered by a Central Bank or determined by market forces, to a subsequent readjustment in monetary aggregate quantities: the process does *not* run from a change in the monetary base, working via the monetary base multiplier, to a change in monetary aggregates, and thence only at the end of the road to a readjustment of interest rates. In reality, the more exogenous, or policy-determined, variable is the change in (short-term) interest rates, while both the monetary base and monetary aggregates are endogenous variables. This reality is, unfortunately, sharply in contrast with the theoretical basis both of many economists' models, and also of their teaching. The fact that it is commonplace to find economists treating the monetary base and/or the money stock as exogenously determined in their models does not mitigate the error; the fact is that this approach is simply incorrect. Moreover, when it comes to a practical, historical account of how Central Banks have *actually* behaved, most economists, even including those who treat the money stock as exogenously determined in their own theoretical models, accept the reality that Central Banks have generally sought to set interest rates, according to various objectives, and that the monetary base and money stock has, therefore, been endogenously determined. The argument then switches from an analysis of how the money stock is determined, to the normative question of whether the present techniques of monetary control adopted by most Central Banks are appropriate and reasonable, or whether the Central Banks should, instead, adopt monetary base control, and thenceforth actually seek to operate the kind of control technique, which is to be found in textbook and theory, but very rarely operated in practice.

The arguments against Central Bank discretionary control of interest rates are several. First, that the authorities do not have sufficient understanding to be able to adjust interest rates in a stabilizing fashion. The second, is that the authorities would be under (political) pressures to hold interest rates down, since rising interest rates are politically unpopular. Such pressures could cause interest rates to be adjusted too little and too late, with the consequence that monetary growth would have, and indeed can be shown to have empirically, a pro-cyclical bias, so that monetary policy would act in a de-stabilizing fashion.

The positive argument for monetary base control is that this would provide a clear and accountable guide for Central Banks. It would remove the political element in the determination of interest rates and give market forces a greater role in setting this key price. Moreover, the medium and longer term stability of the relationship between monetary growth and nominal incomes would allow adherence to closer monetary control, via operating through the monetary base multiplier, to result in greater long term stability of nominal incomes and inflation.

In recent years, many Central Banks have accepted, in part, the argument that (political) pressures have led to some bias to delay, and have adopted publicly announced monetary targets as a main intermediate objective for their policies. They maintain, however, that structural changes and other unforeseeable forces can change the relationship between any monetary aggregate and nominal incomes quite markedly, even over short periods, so that a degree of discretion in maintaining monetary control remains essential. Furthermore, and more closely related to the question of monetary base control, they believe that their present techniques, mostly involving direct interest rate adjustments, remain sufficient to the task.

In particular Central Banks assert that, given the present institutional structure, the attempt to enforce and impose a certain predetermined level of monetary base on the banking system, irrespective of that system's requirements at the time for cash reserves, would lead to a devastating increase in the volatility of interest rates. Moreover, with the resulting effect on the monetary aggregates occurring after a lag, which could be quite long as individual agents adjusted to the rapidly changing level of interest rates, the ultimate effect of the initial shock would itself be unpredictable, and not necessarily desirable. In this context, the experience of the Federal Reserve in the US, which in October 1979 adopted a moderated version of monetary base control, whose potential extreme effects were alleviated by allowing the system access to the discount window, is instructive. The volatility of short-term interest rates increased four-fold during the period of the experiment, lasting from October 1979 until September 1982; moreover this volatility also passed through into the long-term bond market and the foreign exchange market. Despite trying to control the reserve base of the monetary system, the exercise resulted in even greater short-term volatility in the rate of growth of the targeted monetary aggregate, M1. The result, therefore, was much greater market volatility, without any particular success in achieving a more stable path for the monetary aggregates.

Proponents of the switch to monetary base control often accept that the present institutional structure is, indeed, geared to present Central Bank operating techniques, and would, perhaps, be likely to suffer greater interest rate volatility, were monetary base control methods to be adopted. But they then claim that the commitment to, and experience with, monetary base control methods would lead the institutional structure to adapt reasonably quickly so as to moderate such interest rate volatility. There was little sign of that occurring in the United States by 1982. Be that as it may, the opponents of monetary base control argue that those same institutional changes would, inter alia, probably lead institutions to hold larger cash reserve balances on average, but be prepared to allow these to adjust much more in response to the authorities' actions to change the cash base. If so, the new institutional structure would cause changes that would not only lead to much greater variability in the R/D ratio, which would itself lessen the reliability and predictability of the money multiplier, but could also well lead to disintermediation to other financial intermediaries, might be better placed to protect themselves from the instability to the system caused by the authorities' actions. Under such circumstances, therefore, the advantages that are now posited for monetary base control on the basis of calculations of the money multiplier constructed in the present institutional setting, might well erode, if not vanish entirely, should the policy regime actually change.

BIBLIOGRAPHY

Classical.
Keynes, J.M. 1930. *A Treatise on Money.* London: Macmillan; New York: St. Martin's Press, 1971.
Phillips, C.A. 1920. *Bank Credit.* New York: Macmillan.

Historical.
Cagan, P. 1965. *Determinants and Effects of Changes in the Stock of Money, 1875–1960.* New York: Columbia University Press for the National Bureau of Economic Research.
Friedman, M. and Schwartz, A.J. 1963. *A Monetary History of the United States, 1867–1960.* Princeton: Princeton University Press.
Frowen, S.F. et al. 1977. *Monetary Policy and Economic Activity in West Germany.* Stuttgart and New York: Gustav Fischer Verlag.

Contemporary.
Aschheim, J. 1961. *Techniques of Monetary Control.* Baltimore: Johns Hopkins Press.
Bank for International Settlements. 1980. *The Monetary Base Approach to Monetary Control.* Basle: BIS.
Burger, A.E. 1971. *The Money Supply Process.* Belmont: Wadsworth.
Dudler, H.-J. 1984. *Geldpolitik und ihre theoretischen Grundlagen.* Frankfurt: Fritz Knapp Verlag.
Federal Reserve Bank of Boston Conference Series. 1972. *Controlling Monetary Aggregates. II: The Implementation.* Boston: FRB.
Federal Reserve Staff Studies. 1981. *The New Monetary Control Procedures.* Washington, DC: Board of Governors of the Federal Reserve System.
Goodhart, C.A.E. 1984. *Monetary Theory and Practice.* London: Macmillan.
H.M. Treasury and The Bank of England. 1984. *Monetary Control.* Cmd 7858, London: HMSO.
Meigs, A.J. 1962. *Free Reserves and the Money Supply.* Chicago: University of Chicago Press.
Tobin, J. 1963. Commercial banks as creators of 'money'. In *Banking and Monetary Studies,* ed. D. Carson, Homewood, Ill.: Richard, D. Irwin.

Monetary Cranks

DAVID CLARK

The history of ideas tends to concentrate on the successful ideas – ideas which appear to have been precursors of the orthodoxy of the day. As a result, ideas which had large followings but which are later considered 'cranky' tend to be ignored. This is especially true of the ideas of those who we can loosely call the monetary cranks.

These persons have placed money at the centre of their economic analysis, have usually placed major blame for society's evils on alleged financial conspiracies and bankers' ramps – on the 'Money Power' – and have advocated a variety of monetary experiments. Over the past century particularly, such concerns can be found in all Western countries, on both the Left and the Right of politics. This entry can only provide the broadest of overviews of the voluminous literature in this field.

Opposition to financial oligarchies has a long history. The Medicis of 15th-century Florence aroused suspicion and hostility. In *Lombard Street* (1873), Walter Bagehot described the streets around the Bank of England in London as 'by far the greatest combination of power and economic oligarchy that the world has every seen'. But it was the fiery late-19th-century American populist, William Jennings Bryan, who popularized the term 'Money Power' (cited in Douglas, 1924, Preface):

> The Money Power preys upon the nation in times of peace and conspires against it in times of adversity. It is more despotic than monarchy, more insolent than autocracy, more bureaucratic than bureaucracy. It denounces, as public enemies, all who question its methods, or throw light upon its crimes. It can only be overthrown by the awakened conscience of the nation.

Monetary parables have a long history, ranging from David Hume's 1752 hope that 'by miracle, every man in Great Britain should have five pounds slipped into his pocket in one night', through to Milton Friedman's 1969 postulated helicopter miracle, whereby dollars would be dropped from the heavens. (These are discussed in Clayton, 1971, p. 6.) Over the past three centuries, however, actual monetary experiments have taken two main forms: attempts to overcome economic fluctuations by means of adjusting note issue; and attempts to achieve a more stable price level through the formulation and adoption of a new or different monetary standard.

Such experiments were first undertaken in the North American colonies. The first paper money issued by any government in Europe or the Americas was printed by Massachusetts to pay the wages of its soldiers engaged in conflict with the French in Canada at the end of the 17th century. Other New England colonies followed suit and a competitive depreciation of the individual currencies followed. The French Canadians even used playing cards as a form of money.

In 1721, a Mr Wise of Chebacco, Massachusetts, concerned at the depreciation of the notes admonished his fellow colonists (cited in Lester, 1939):

> Gentlemen! You must do by your Bills, as all Wise Men do by their Wives; Make the Best of them... Wise Men Love their Wives; and what ill-conveniences they find in them they bury; and what Vertues they are inrich't with they Admire and Magnifie. And thus you must do by your Bills for there is not doing without them; if you Divorce or Dissieze yourselves of them you are undone.

Hence the American colonies developed the practice of adjusting note issue to stimulate business or countervail a recession. They believed that there is a very close relationship between money, prices and business conditions and that the appropriate note issue would greatly stimulate business. Their efforts were made easier by the fact that there was no bank issued money.

In England, after the Napoleonic Wars, the first great debate about monetary reform occurred, with persons such as Joseph Lowe, John Rooke and Poulett Scrope, proposing a 'managed currency', the volume of which was to be controlled according to changing prices in such a way as to keep the price level steady. Similarly, Henry Thornton's *Paper Credit* (1802) argued that contraction or expansion of the money supply had real effects on the level of economic activity. In the 1840s, Thomas Attwood claimed that if Britain's coinage 'were accommodated to man and man to our coinage then world would be capable of multiplying its production to an unlimited extent'. However, David Ricardo's and John Stuart Mill's failure to appreciate that credit expansion might stimulate the level of economic activity, rather than just increase prices, dominated economic thinking for the rest of the 19th century (see Viner, 1937).

This opened the door for the monetary cranks, who argued that money did matter. Their main inspiration came from the underconsumptionist tradition. A number of authorities have emphasized that underconsumptionist literature is difficult to categorize (e.g., Schumpeter, 1954, p. 740; Haberler, 1937, ch. 5; Bleaney, 1976, ch. 1). Still, the argument that there is a permanent deficiency of purchasing power produced all kinds of suggestions as to how such a deficiency could be remedied.

In the interwar period, underconsumptionist ideas fell on particularly receptive ears. Many persons, particularly those concerned with high unemployment, were prepared to believe that the schemes of the monetary cranks would increase demand and hence create jobs. The quantity of pamphlet literature on monetary reform over this era is thus enormous. A common argument was that because World War I was financed by printing money, the same method could be used to eliminate unemployment. Opposition to the Gold Standard usually accompanied this argument.

Academic discussion of monetary matters was disparate and disputatious (see, for example the famous debate between F.A. von Hayek and P. Srraffa in the *Economic Journal*, March-June 1932) and this was seized upon by the monetary reformers, who sought to penetrate what they claimed were the obfuscations of the academics. They also pointed to the fact that discussion of money and banking tended to be confined to tendentious tomes written for bank employees, while economic theory textbooks devoted little space to arguments against Say's Law.

Major C.H. Douglas was probably the best-known reformer in English-speaking countries in this era (see Douglas, 1924) but there were many, many others who wrote on monetary reform. These included: A.H. Abbati, who attracted the interest of John Maynard Keynes and D.H. Robertson; Sir Normal Angel, whose set of cards *The Money Game* was widely used in high schools in Britain and the US; W.T. Foster and W. Catchings, who were probably the best known US reformers; and Frederick Soddy of Oxford University, who, after being awarded the Nobel Prize for Chemistry, set out to solve the money problem inspired by John Ruskin's *Unto this Last* (1862) and an Australian invention. Soddy argued that the Gold Standard could be replaced with a machine based on the automatic totalizator at Sydney's Randwick Racecourse (Soddy, 1931). Cole (1933) discusses some of this literature.

Strangely, Schumpeter (1954) contains no reference to Douglas but he does mention (pp. 1090–91) G.F. Knapp's *The State Theory of Money* (1924), which promoted similar ideas and had considerable impact in interwar Germany. For example, in the dying days of the Weimar Republic, at the suggestion of H.J. Rustow and W. Lavtenbach of the Ministry of Economics, interest-bearing tax certificates were issued in lieu of treasury bills and exchequer bonds. Employers were given these certificates if they employed additional employees and reduced the wages of existing employees (see Rustow, 1978).

With the Keynesian Revolution and the increased emphasis given to monetary theory by academic economists in recent decades, the monetary cranks have largely disappeared from public debate, although underconsumptionist ideas will probably have supporters while there is unemployment.

Any explanation of the appeal of these ideas over generations would have to invoke sociology and psychology. Such ideas found strong support because they enabled persons to impress their peers with their apparent understanding of economics, even though they had no formal training in the discipline. They offered the false hope that there were simple solutions to the complexities of modern economic life. They also transcended party political allegiances – similar passages about 'credit slavery' and 'Shylocks' can be found in Hitler's *Mein Kampf* and left-wing pamphlets of the same era. A very wide range of individuals can be opposed to private banks and the 'Money Power' without their opposition leading to more sophisticated political analysis. In fact, as the history of populism shows, 'Funny Money' beliefs provided a kind of ideological release valve.

The history of ideas contains numerous examples of the power of the phrase-monger. The simpler the panacea, the greater the chance the agitator will have of attracting a following. As the Chartist agitator Ernest Jones once advised (cited in Martin and Rubinstein, 1979, p. 43): 'We say to the great minds of the day, come among the people, write for the people and your fame will live forever'.

BIBLIOGRAPHY

Angell, N. 1936. *The Money Mystery: an Explanation for Beginners.* London: J.M. Dent & Sons. (*The Money Game*, a set of cards for teaching purposes, was sold in conjunction with this book.)

Bleaney, M. 1976. *Underconsumption Theories: a History and Critical Analysis.* London: Lawrence & Wishart; New York: International Publishers.

Clayton, G. et al. 1971. *Monetary Theory and Policy in the 1970s.* Oxford: Oxford University Press.

Cole, G.D.H. 1933. *What Everybody Wants to Know about Money: a Planned Outline of Monetary Problems.* London: Victor Gollancz.

Douglas, C.H. 1924. *Social Credit.* London: Eyre & Spottiswoode.

Durbin, E.F.M. 1934. *Purchasing Power and Trade Depression.* London: Chapman & Hall.

Haberler, G. 1937. *Prosperity and Depression.* Cambridge, Mass.: Harvard University Press.

Lester, R.A. 1939. *Monetary Experiments: Early American and Recent Scandinavian.* Princeton: Princeton University Press.

Martin, D. and Rubinstein, D. (eds) 1979. *Ideology and the Labour Movement.* London: Croom Helm.

Rustow, H.J. 1978. The economic crisis of the Weimar Republic and how it was overcome. *Cambridge Journal of Economics* 2(4), December, 409–21.

Schumpeter, J.A. 1954. *A History of Economic Analysis.* London: George Allen & Unwin; New York: Oxford University Press, 1954.

Soddy, F. 1931. *Money versus Man.* London: Elkin Mathews & Marrot.

Viner, J. 1937. *Studies in the Theory of International Trade.* London: George Allen & Unwin; New York: Harper.

Monetary Disequilibrium and Market Clearing

HERSCHEL I. GROSSMAN

Conventional wisdom interprets the empirical relation between monetary aggregates and measures of real aggregate economic activity primarily as reflecting the effect of monetary policy on real activity. A host of historical episodes apparently accord with this interpretation. It is, for example, hard to deny that disinflationary monetary policy contributed to the 1982 recession in the United States.

Some theorists, such as King and Plosser (1984), have questioned this interpretation and have developed real business cycle models that attempt to explain the observed correlations of money and real activity as solely a result of the common influences of other factors, such as disturbances to tastes, technology, and resources or disturbances to monetary velocity. These theorists, however, have not been able to identify an alternative set of impulses that does not contain disturbances to monetary aggregates and that does have appropriate structural characteristics, sufficient magnitude, and requisite regularity to be responsible for the bulk of observed fluctuations in real activity. This inability to identify alternative causal factors reinforces the standard reading of history that monetary policy influences real activity. (See McCallum (1986) for a thorough critique of real business cycle models.)

Given the conventional interpretation of the observed relation between money and real activity, a satisfactory theoretical and empirical analysis of macroeconomic fluctuations must account for an effect of monetary policy on real activity as well as for an effect of monetary policy on inflation. This account must be consistent with the following general features of the data: (1) current realizations of monetary aggregates are correlated with subsequent realizations of both real activity and inflation; (2) the correlations of money with real activity are strong in the short run but weaken in the long run whereas the correlations of money with inflation are weak in the short run but become stronger in the long run;

216

and (3) the correlations with real activity are stronger for unanticipated realizations of monetary aggregates. The main attraction of monetary-disequilibrium theory, whch is the useful name that Leland Yeager (1986) uses for what is often called the Keynesian or non-market-clearing approach, is that it provides an explanation for the effects of monetary policy on real activity and inflation that in its modern versions, which incorporate the natural-rate hypothesis and the rational-expectations hypothesis, seems to be broadly consistent with these general features of the data.

An explanation for the effect of monetary policy on real activity also must satisfy criteria of logical consistency. Most importantly, aggregate economic activity is merely a statistical summary of a multitude of individual productive decisions, which are the same individual decisions that determine resource allocation and income distribution. Accordingly, the assumptions about economic behaviour used to account for the relation between money and real activity should be consistent with the assumptions used to explain resource allocation and income distribution. Moreover, we cannot avoid this consistency requirement by asserting that macroeconomic fluctuations are a short-run phenomenon, whereas questions about resource allocation and income distribution involve the long run. In fact, economists routinely apply standard microeconomic analysis to the short run – that is, to a time horizon shorter than the typical business cycle.

The distinguishing feature of conventional economic analysis of resource allocation and income distribution is the assumption that producers in free markets exhaust perceived opportunities for mutually advantageous exchange. Standard microeconomic analysis takes this assumption to be a corollary of the basic economic postulate of maximization. The most unattractive aspect of monetary-disequilibrium theory is that, as yet, its proponents (who include most macroeconomists) have been unable to reconcile it with the postule of maximization and the corollary that perceived gains from trade are exhausted.

A frequent claim is that the existence of coordination problems reconciles monetary disequilibrium with the postule of maximization. Various authors argue that, even with producers behaving as rational maximizers, perception and coordination of the wage and price adjustments necessary to clear markets in the face of unanticipated monetary disturbances takes time. For example, Yeager (1986) points out that 'one cannot consistently both suppose that the price system is a communication mechanism – a device for mobilizing and coordinating knowledge dispersed in millions of separate minds – and suppose that people *already* have the knowledge that the system is working to convey'. This observation is correct, but it seems irrelevant for the analysis of monetary disequilibrium because the values of monetary aggregates are public information. In contrast to truly private information, the monetary aggregates are not information that the price system has to convey.

A further frequent claim is that even with complete information, strategic considerations would cause individual rationality to diverge from the collective rationality implicit in monetary equilibrium. In his Presidential Address to the American Economic Association, Charles Schultze (1985) invokes the analogy of the prisoner's dilemma to argue that the unwillingness of any producer 'to go first' would inhibit wage and price adjustments. This analysis is confusing because it seems to imply too much – namely, that wages and prices are rigid rather than merely sticky. In any event, the usefulness of the prisoner's dilemma analogy for understanding market behaviour seems limited because the prisoner's dilemma relates to a hypothetical game played by a small number of agents who cannot communicate with each other during the game.

For a monopolist or collusive oligopoly, individual and collective optimality of wage and price adjustments obviously coincide. In a market of many imperfectly competitive producers, however, optimal individual wage and price responses to some disturbances can differ from optimal collective responses. But observed changes in monetary aggregates are not such a disturbance. Unless price adjustments are prohibitively costly, optimal individual price setting behaviour requires responding to an observed disturbance of monetary aggregates even if the individual thinks that other individuals are ignoring the disturbance. The 'initial' response, of course, might not be an equiproportionate price adjustment but, even without rational expectations, subsequent responses culminate in an equiproportionate adjustment. Moreover, if we assume either that expectations are rational or that price-adjustment costs are small, the theory suggests that the full adjustment is essentially instantaneous.

Schultze and Yeager also refer to models of efficient long-term contracts and implicit buyer-seller understandings. This reference is puzzling, because, although these models suggest that real or relative wages and prices would be less flexible than models of spot markets imply, models of efficient contracts also suggest, if anything, that rational wage setters would fully index nominal wages and prices to observed monetary disturbances. Schultze recognizes this point, but claims that the complexity of the relation between monetary aggregates and market-clearing nominal wages precludes indexation. It is not clear, however, why this problem results in zero indexation. Even if producers cannot easily determine the optimal degree of indexation, they surely know that some positive indexation would be better than zero indexation. Similarly, currently popular models of efficiency wages, whatever their ability to explain the equilibrium structure of real wages and employment, also have no apparent relevance for the problem of rationalizing stickiness of nominal wages and resulting monetary disequilibrium.

In the early 1970s, theorists like Robert Lucas (1972, 1973) and Robert Barro (1976) responded to the problem of reconciling monetary disequilibrium with the postulate of maximization by utilizing advances in the theory of expectations and general economic equilibrium under incomplete information to formulate 'equilibrium' models of macroeconomic fluctuations. These equilibrium models assume that all perceived gains from trade are realized and that expectations are rational, and they rely on assumed lack of information about monetary aggregates in order to generate an effect of monetary aggregates on real activity. In recent years, interest in these equilibrium models has waned largely because more extensive theoretical and econometric analysis has shown these models to be unable to account for the observed relation between monetary aggregates and real activity.

218

The empirical problem with equilibrium models, it should be stressed, does not involve direct evidence that perceived gains from trade are actually not realized. In fact, contractual versions of equilibrium models – see, for example, Azariadis (1978) and Grossman (1981) – readily account for prominent observed features of macroeconomic fluctuations that would seem inconsistent with market clearing if market clearing were narrowly interpreted in a framework of spot markets. These observed features include lack of correlation between aggregate employment and real wage rates and the use of layoffs to effect employment separations.

The empirical rejection of equilibrium models is based on rejection of an essential testable implication of the combined assumptions that all perceived gains are realized and that expectations are rational. This implication is that disturbances to monetary aggregates affect real aggregates only to the extent that currently available information does not permit agents to infer current monetary aggregates accurately. The testable form of this implication, derived by Boschen and Grossman (1982) following the lead of King (1981), is that the current innovation in real activity is uncorrelated with contemporaneous measures of current and past changes in monetary aggregates. Not surprisingly, econometric analysis of data for the United States reported by Boschen and Grossman not only unambiguously rejects this hypothesis, but also finds no correlation between the innovation in real activity and revisions in preliminary estimates of monetary aggregates, these revisions being measures of the unperceived part of monetary policy.

The early equilibrium models of Lucas and Barro obscured the problem of reconciling equilibrium assumptions with the observed relation between monetary aggregates and real activity because they abstracted from the existence of contemporaneously available monetary data. Barro himself was among the first to recognize the consequences of relaxing this abstraction. An empirical study by Barro and Hercovitz (1980) anticipated the subsequent and more formal theoretical and econometric analysis of King and Boschen and Grossman. In an early reassessment of equilibrium theories, Barro wrote,

> A significant weakness of the [equilibrium] approach is the dependence of some major conclusions on incomplete contemporaneous knowledge of monetary aggregates, which would presumably be observed cheaply and rapidly if such information were important. The role of incomplete current information on money in equilibrium business cycle theory parallels the use of adjustment costs to explain sticky wages and prices with an associated inefficient determination of quantities in Keynesian models. The underpinning of the two types of macroeconomic models are both vulnerable on a priori grounds... (Barro, 1981, ch. 2, p. 74).

On the same page, however, Barro is quick to emphasize that doubts about the explanatory value for business cycles of currently available equilibrium theories do not constitute support for Keynesian disequilibrium analysis. The disequilibrium theories are essentially incomplete models that raise even larger questions about the consistency of model structure with underlying rational behaviour. It remains a fair observation that existing macroeconomic theories – including new and old approaches – provide only limited knowledge about the nature of business cycles.

Lucas also has recognized the consequences for the implications of equilibrium models of taking contemporaneous monetary information into account. In a recent lecture Lucas (1985) acknowledges that 'insofar as the monetary information necessary to permit agents to correct for what are, or ought to be, units changes is public... then one would expect this information to be used, independent of the form of interaction among agents'. Nevertheless, Lucas still seems willing to defend abstracting from contemporaneous monetary data as an 'as-if' assumption, although apparently he can only vaguely conjecture why rational agents would ignore information that is important and freely available. In the same lecture, he offers only the thought that 'it seems to me most unlikely that it would be in the private interest of individual agents to specialize their individual information systems so as to be well-equipped to adapt for units changes of monetary origin'.

As an alternative to the formulations of equilibrium models, other theorists have reacted to the difficulty of reconciling monetary disequilibrium with the postulate of maximization by appealing, either implicitly or explicitly, to concepts of near rationality. The seminal work of Stanley Fischer (1977), incorporating rational expectations into a non-market-clearing framework, is an important example of this approach. In Fischer's model, although nominal wages are sticky, these predetermined nominal wages are equal to rational expectations of market-clearing wages.

Econometric testing of these nearly rational, monetary-disequilibrium models with rational expectations encounters the difficult problem of realistically dating the formation of the expectations relevant for the determination of current nominal wages and current real activity. As explained in Grossman (1983), Barro's empirical results on the relation between real activity and unanticipated monetary disturbances, summarized in Barro (1981b), provide qualified support for Fischer's model. In another study, Grossman and Haraf (1985), by taking advantage of the fact that wage setting in Japan is both decentralized and synchronized, were able to examine empirically some detailed implications of Fischer's model and to show that the model, if suitably elaborated, seems to fit the Japanese data.

More recent theoretical work by Akerlof and Yellen (1985) focuses on the possibility that near rationality can account for monetary disequilibrium. This analysis directly confronts the problem that the postulate of maximization is inconsistent with an effect of monetary policy on real activity. It poses the questions of how much non-maximizing behaviour is necessary, and what form this behaviour must take, in order for the effects of monetary disturbances on real activity to have a realistic order of magnitude. Akerlof and Yellen show that minor deviations from maximization by a subset of producers, who individually suffer only second-order consequences, are sufficient to produce first-order macroeconomic effects.

These recent developments still leave us without a fully unified theoretical framework applicable to the analysis of macroeconomic fluctuations and to the analysis of resource allocation and income distribution. Apparently, economic theory in its present state has to rely on empirical regularities to identify the sets of questions for which either near rationality of full rationality are more useful 'as if' assumptions.

BIBLIOGRAPHY

Akerlof, G. and Yellen, J. 1985. A near-rational model of the business cycle with wage and price inertia. *Quarterly Journal of Economics* 100(402), Supplement, 823–38.

Azariadis, C. 1978. Escalation clauses and the allocation of cyclical risks. *Journal of Economic Theory* 18(1), June, 119–55.

Barro, R.J. 1976. Rational expectations and the role of monetary policy. *Journal of Monetary Economics* 2(1), January, 1–32. Reprinted as ch. 3 in R.J. Barro, *Money, Expectations, and Business Cycles*, New York: Academic Press, 1981; also reprinted in *Rational Expectations and Econometric Practice*, ed. R.E. Lucas, Jr. and T.J. Sargent, Minneapolis: University of Minnesota Press, 1981.

Barro, R.J. 1981a. The equilibrium approach to business cycles. Ch. 2 in *Money, Expectations, and Business Cycles*, New York: Academic Press.

Barro, R.J. 1981b. Unanticipated money growth and economic activity in the United States. Ch. 5 in *Money, Expectations, and Business Cycles*, New York: Academic Press.

Barro, R.J. and Hercovitz, Z. 1980. Money stock revisions and unanticipated money growth. *Journal of Monetary Economics* 6(2), April, 257–67.

Boschen, J. and Grossman, H.I. 1982. Tests of equilibrium macroeconomics using contemporaneous monetary data. *Journal of Monetary Economics* 10(3), November, 309–33.

Fischer, S. 1977. Long-term contracts, rational expectations, and the optimal money supply rule. *Journal of Political Economy* 85(1), February, 191–205. Reprinted in *Rational Expectations and Econometric Practice*, ed. R.E. Lucas, Jr. and T.J. Sargent, Minneapolis: University of Minnesota Press, 1981.

Grossman, H.I. 1981. Incomplete information, risk shifting, and employment fluctuations. *Review of Economic Studies* 48(2), April, 189–97.

Grossman, H.I. 1983. The natural-rate hypothesis, the rational-expectations hypothesis, and the remarkable survival of non-market-clearing assumptions. *Carnegie-Rochester Conference Series on Public Policy* 19, Autumn, 225–45.

Grossman, H.I. and Haraf, W.S. 1985. Shunto, rational expectations, and output growth in Japan. NBER Working Paper No. 1144, revised July 1985.

King, R.G. 1981. Monetary information and monetary neutrality. *Journal of Monetary Economics* 7(2), March, 195–206.

King, R.G. and Plosser, C.I. 1984. Money, credit, and prices in a real business cycle. *American Economic Review* 74(3), June, 363–80.

Lucas, R.E., Jr. 1972. Expectations and the neutrality of money. *Journal of Economic Theory* 4(2), April, 103–24. Reprinted in R.E. Lucas, Jr., *Studies in Business Cycle Theory*, Cambridge, Mass.: MIT Press, 1981.

Lucas, R.E., Jr. 1973. Some international evidence on output-inflation tradeoffs. *American Economic Review* 63(3), June, 326–34. Reprinted in R.E. Lucas, Jr., *Studies in Business-Cycle Theory*, Cambridge, Mass.: MIT Press, 1981.

Lucas, R.E., Jr. 1985. Models of Business Cycles. Yrjö Jahnsson Lectures, Helsinki, May.

McCallum, B.T. 1986. On 'real' and 'sticky-price' theories of the business cycle. *Journal of Money, Credit and Banking* 17, November.

Schultze, C.L. 1985. Microeconomic efficiency and nominal wage stickiness. *American Economic Review* 75(1), March, 1–15.

Yeager, L. 1986. The significance of monetary disequilibrium. *Cato Journal* 6, Fall.

Monetary Equilibrium

OTTO STEIGER

The concept of monetary equilibrium is the fundamental feature of the macro-economic theory originally formulated by Knut Wicksell (1898, 1906) and corrected, clarified and improved in the 1930s by Erik Lindahl (1930, 1934 and 1939b) and Gunnar Myrdal (1932, 1933 and 1939). Wicksell's approach was the first attempt to link the analysis of *relative prices* with the analysis of *money prices* (Shackle, 1945, p. 47).

In the Wicksell–Lindahl–Myrdal theoretical structure the idea of a monetary equilibrium – the term stemmed from Myrdal (1932, p. 193) – was designed to analyse the conditions for equality of certain relations in a monetary economy which guarantee *macroeconomic equilibrium*, with the emphasis on a *stable price level*, as well as the implications of their non-fulfilment, that is, the consequences of *monetary disequilibrium*. In this analysis the notion of monetary equilibrium served not only as a theoretical tool, but also as an operational goal for economic policy.

Although frequently confused with the concept of *monetary neutrality* or *neutral money*, it has to be emphasized that the notion of monetary equilibrium is conceptually distinct from this idea. The doctrine of neutral money – which also originated from Wicksell (Hayek, 1931) – aimed to indicate the conditions under which the tendencies towards equilibrium in a barter economy, i.e. the equilibrium of relative prices according to neoclassical value theory 'are to remain operative in a monetary economy' (Hayek, 1933, p. 160; cf. Koopmans, 1933, p. 228). The theory of monetary equilibrium did not relate to these condtiions, but to conditions of an equilibrium which the proponents of neutral money never intended to explain, still less to being regarded as a norm for economic policy.

The starting point of Wicksell's investigation into the conditions of monetary equilibrium, first presented in *Interest and Prices* (1898) and restated in *Lectures on Political Economy, Vol. II: Money* (1906), was his critical analysis of the attempts of both the dominating theories of value and the quantity theory of money to explain the value of money. These attempts had resulted in (i) a

223

dichotomy of economic theory with entirely different laws for the value of money and the value of commodities and (ii) a theory of money which was unable to explain its postulated proportionality between changes in the quantity of money and the price level as the inverse of the value of money.

With regard to the first point, Wicksell (1903, p. 486f) had no difficulty in explaining the failure of both classical and neoclassical value theory to integrate monetary theory because of the impossibility of treating money as a commodity like all other commodities; therefore, they had to rely on the quantity theory to explain the value of money. This theory however – Wicksell's second point – holds true only under the assumption of a constant velocity of circulation as in the extreme case of 'a pure cash system without credit' (1898, p. 59). With credit, the velocity of circulation becomes a variable, and it is impossible to prove satisfactory and exact relationship between the quantity of money and the price level.

To solve the complications arising from money given or received as credit, Wicksell made the 'assumption' of a *pure credit economy* (Ohlin, 1936, p. xiv). By this device the quantity of money was determined exogenously by the demand for money and, therefore, abandoned as a direct price-determining force – a feature also common to the development of Wicksell's theory by Lindahl and Myrdal. Thus, freed from the tyranny of the quantity of money, Wicksell had to look for other forces determining the value of money.

To reveal these forces, he replaced the relation of the quantity theory between the quantity of money and the price level by a theory of the relation between the *interest on money loans* and the price level, which he analysed in the framework of two approaches: (i) the relation of the money or loan rate of interest as determined on 'the money market' to the 'natural' or real rate of interest as determined by the physical marginal productivity of capital (later replaced by value productivity); and (ii) the relation of aggregate monetary demand for and supply of commodities linked in the same manner as demand for and supply of an individual commodity. In his analysis Wicksell connected both approaches by showing that in a closed, competitive economy with a pure credit system, a deviation between the loan rate and the real rate of interest, by means of credit expansion or contraction, will serve as an incentive for entrepreneurs to invest or disinvest leading to a shift in the relation between aggregate monetary demand and supply which, under the assumption of given output, must result in a rise or fall in all money prices that due to anticipations of their initial changes becomes indefinite – Wicksell's famous *cumulative process*.

It becomes clear from this analysis that the cumulative process describes a system where the movements in money prices set no forces in operation towards an equilibrium. Wicksell considered, therefore, the nature of this monetary equilibrium as fundamentally distinct from the equilibrium of relative prices with its inherent tendency towards stability. Once disturbed, monetary equilibrium could be restored, however, by means of a special equilibrium rate, the so-called *normal rate of interest* on loans. Wicksell thought that under the more realistic premise of a mixed cash/credit system the changes in money prices as 'the connecting link' (1898, p. 109) between the money market and the commodity market would force the monetary authority to establish this rate.

However, Wicksell's concept of the normal rate was far from being clear and precise because it implied, as first shown by Lindahl (1930; cf. 1939a), three different conditions for monetary equilibrium: (i) to equal the natural or real rate, (ii) to equalize expected investment and saving and (iii) to preserve a stable price level, primarily of consumption goods. In their development of Wicksell's analysis both Lindahl and Myrdal attacked the consistency of this triple condition leading more or less to an abandonment of the notion of the normal rate by Lindahl and its reformulation by Myrdal.

With regard to the first condition Lindahl rejected to regard the loan rate as 'normal', since the level of the real rate could not be determined independently of it. Lindahl's concept of the real rate was characterized, in contrast to Wicksell (1898) but – as he later had to concede (1939b, p. 261) – in accordance with Wicksell's 'prospective profit rate' (1906), not by physical but by exchange *value* productivity, i.e. he defined the real rate as 'the relation between anticipated future product values... and the values invested' (1930, p. 124; 1939a, p. 248). As the demand for investment and, thereby, its price is influenced by the loan rate, the real rate will always have a tendency to adjust to the former. Therefore, the real rate could only have a meaning as that level of the loan rate which secures equilibrium between the expected values of investment and saving – Wicksell's second condition.

However, even this level of the loan rate is not 'normal' in the sense that it represents a unique equilibrium rate, since a change in investment, due to *any* shift in the loan rate, will always be balanced by a subsequent variation in the distribution of income between borrowers and lenders via changes in the price level. Thus, the second condition is fulfilled for different loan rates associated with different changes in the price level, and Lindahl abandoned, therefore, the concept of the normal rate in Wicksell's third condition for the notion of the '*neutral* rate of interest', that is a loan rate which is neutral in relation to *expected* changes in the price level, not to its constancy. However, as Lindahl realized that even this concept would still suffer from certain weaknesses, due to the difficulties of defining the price level with regard to different expectations as well as the many possible combinations of short and long term loan rates that are neutral in respect to the price level, he eventually decided not to employ the notion of a normal rate at all, confining himself to show 'that different interest levels... lead to different developments of the price level' (1930, p. 134; 1939a, p. 260).

Lindahl's position was immediately attacked by Myrdal in the original Swedish version of *Monetary Equilibrium* (1932), where the latter interpreted Lindahl's analysis as an attempt to get rid of the concept of monetary equilibrium. To prove this assertion Myrdal, like Lindahl, discussed Wicksell's three conditions – an analysis which led to a reconstruction of the concept of the normal rate and to 'a refutation of Lindahl's criticism of Wicksell' (Hansson, 1982, p. 148).

With regard to Wicksell's first condition Myrdal tried to show that the real rate, contrary to Lindahl, could be treated as an independent entity determining the normal loan rate. In a response to Myrdal's criticism, Lindahl (1939b; cf. Hammarskjöld, 1933) conceded that the different real rates, as visualized by an investment schedule in the capital market, could be considered indeed as independent of the current loan rate. However, it would be impossible from this schedule alone 'to single out any definite real rate as having a decisive influence on the loan rate', i.e. to determine the normal rate unless the corresponding saving schedule is known. Thus, Wicksell's first condition could be inferred only from his second. However, in the final English edition of *Monetary Equilibrium* Myrdal had already changed his mind (cf. Palander, 1941). He now considered the determination of the first condition as being dependent on the second.

Myrdal's analysis of the first condition revealed the insight, that equality of the real and the loan rate as the condition, not for monetary equilibrium but for the determination of investment, could be used 'to explain *why* and *how* equilibrium is or is not maintained in the capital market' (Myrdal, 1939, p. 87), that is, whether Wicksell's second condition is or is not fulfilled which now became the sole criterion for monetary equilibrium and which Myrdal formulated in an *ex ante/ex post* framework (1939, ch. V; cf. 1932, pt. III; 1933, ch. V). This reformulation of the second condition was immediately accepted by Lindahl (1934; cf. 1939b, pp. 264–8) who, however, did *not* consider the equilibrium rate in the capital market as a *sufficient* condition for monetary equilibrium and developed instead a modified version of his concept of the 'neutral' rate as the normal rate.

In his investigation of Wicksell's third condition, Myrdal (1939, ch. VI; cf. 1932, pt. IV; 1933, ch. VI) concluded that monetary equilibrium is determined by the more fundamental first second conditions, not by a stable price level. A uniform change in all money prices would neither change investment nor disturb equilibrium in the capital market, since monetary aggregates would vary in the same proportion. However, as price level changes are not uniform in reality where some money prices, like capital values, are highly flexible, while others, especially wages, are very sticky, the latter would 'act as a restraint on the price system' (1939, p. 134). Therefore, even if the third condition was deprived its significance for the determination of monetary equilibrium, it could be used as a *norm for monetary policy* aiming to restore a disrupted monetary equilibrium. As Myrdal emphasized, this does not mean a stabilization of the general price level but a *mitigation of the business cycle* brought about by an adaption of the flexible prices to the more sticky ones. This could be achieved by a stabilization of 'an index of those prices which are sticky in themselves' and which in practice would mean a stabilization of wages permitting capital values to move. For the case of monetary disequilibrium characterized by decreasing investment and increasing unemployment, Myrdal showed that such a depressive process could be stopped and reverted by a monetary policy supported by fiscal policy which first of all increases capital values to the level of the sticky wages, thereby preventing a fall of the latter which otherwise would aggravate depression – as would a stabilization of capital values or any index of flexible prices. In spite of Myrdal's emphasis that 'the concept of monetary equilibrium has ... central importance for the whole

Wicksellian monetary theory' (1939, p. 30), both his and Lindahl's approaches are characterized by an obvious disinterest in equilibrium analysis and a preference for casuistic disequilibrium analysis (Siven, 1985) – a feature also common to the subsequent theories of the Stockholm School which, with the exception of Bent Hansen (1951, ch. 9), eventually discarded 'the conception of a monetary equilibrium as a tool for analysing economic development' (Lundberg, 1937, p. 246; cf. Ohlin, 1937, p. 224).

BIBLIOGRAPHY

Hammarskjöld, D. 1933. Utkast till en algebraisk metod för dynamisk prisanalys. *Ekonomisk* Tidskrift 34(5–6), 1932 (printed 1933), 157–76.

Hansen, B. 1951. *A Study in the Theory of Inflation*. London: Allen & Unwin; New York: Rinehart.

Hansson, B. 1982. *The Stockholm School and the Development of Dynamic Method*. London Croom Helm.

Hayek, F.A. 1931. *Prices and Production*. London: Routledge & Sons. 2nd edn, 1935, 2nd ed, New York: Augustus M. Kelley, 1967.

Hayek, F.A. 1933. Über 'neutrales' Geld. *Zeitschrift für Nationalökonomie* 4(5), October, 659–61. Quoted from and trans. as 'On "neutral" money', in F.A. Hayek, *Money, Capital & Fluctuations. Early Essays*, ed. R. McCloughry, London: Routledge & Kegan Paul, 1984, 159–62.

Koopmans, F.G. 1933. Zum Problem des 'neutralen' Geldes. In *Beiträge zur Geldtheories*, ed. F.A. Hayek, Vienna: Springer, 211–359.

Lindahl, E. 1930. *Penningpolitikens medel*. Lund: Gleerup; enlarged version of 1st edn, 1929. Revised version trans. as Lindahl (1939a).

Lindahl, E. 1934. A note on the dynamic pricing problem. Mimeo, Gothenburg, 13 October. Quoted from the corrected version published in Steiger (1971), 204–11.

Lindahl, E. 1939a. The rate of interest and the price level. In E. Lindahl, *Studies in the Theory of Money and Capital*, London: Allen & Unwin, 139–260. New York: Holt, Rinehart & Winston. Revised version of Lindahl (1930).

Lindahl, E. 1939b. Additional note (1939). Appendix to Lindahl (1939a), 260–68.

Lundberg, E. 1937. *Studies in the Theory of Economic Expansion*. Stockhölm: Norstedt & Söner.

Myrdal, G. 1932. Om penningteoretisk jämvikt. En studie över den 'normala räntan' i Wicksells penninglära. *Ekonomisk Tidskrift* 33(5–6), 1931 (printed 1932), 191–302. Revised version trans. as Myrdal (1933).

Mydral, G. 1933. Der Gleichgewichtsbegriff als Instrument der geldtheoretischen Analyse. In *Beiträge zur Geldtheorie*, ed. F.A. Hayek. Vienna: J. Springer, 361–487. 1st revised version of Myrdal (1932); 2nd revised version trans. as Myrdal (1939).

Myrdal, G. 1939. *Monetary Equilibrium*. London: Hodge. Revised version of Myrdal (1933).

Ohlin, B. 1936. Introduction to K. Wicksell, *Interest and Prices. A Study of the Causes Regulating the Value of Money*, London: Macmillan, vii–xxi.

Ohlin, B. 1937. Some notes on the Stockholm theory of savings and investment, II. *Econommic Journal* 47, June, 221–40.

Palander, T. 1941. Om 'Stockholmsskolans' begrepp och metoder. Metodologiska reflexioner kring Myrdals 'Monetary Equilibrium'. *Ekonomisk Tidskrift* 43(1), March, 88–143. Quoted from and trans. as 'On the concepts and methods of the 'Stockholm School'. Some methodological reflections on Myrdal's 'Monetary Equilibrium', *International Economic Papers* No. 3, 1953, 5–57.

Shackle, G.L.S. 1945. Myrdal's analysis of monetary equilibrium. *Oxford Economic Papers*, OS 7, March, 47–66.

Siven, C.-H. 1985. The end of the Stockholm School. *Scandinavian Journal of Economics* 87(4), 577–93.

Steiger, O. 1971. *Studien zur Entstehung der Neuen Wirtschaftslehre in Schweden. Eine Anti-Kritik.* Berlin: Duncker & Humblot.

Wicksell, K. 1898. *Gelzins und Güterpreise. Eine Studie über die den Tauschwert des Geldes bestimmenden Ursachen.* Jena: G. Fischer. Quoted from and trans. as *Interest and Prices. A Study of the Causes Regulating the Value of Money*, London: Macmillan, 1936; New York: A.M. Kelley, 1965.

Wicksell, K. 1903. *Den dunkla punkten i penningteorien. Ekonomisk Tidskrift* 5(12), 484–507.

Wicksell, K. 1906. *Förreläsningar i nationalekonomi.* Vol. II: *Om penningar och kredit.* Stockholmand Lund: Fritzes and Berlinska. Quoted from the trans. of the 3rd Swedish edn (1929), *Lectures on Political Economy.* Vol. II: *Money*, London: Routledge & Sons, 1935; New York: A.M. Kelley, 1967.

Monetary Policy

DAVID E. LINDSEY AND HENRY C. WALLICH

The term *monetary policy* refers to actions taken by central banks to affect monetary and other financial conditions in pursuit of the broader objectives of sustainable growth of real output, high employment, and price stability. The average rate of growth of the stock of money in circulation has been viewed for centuries as the decisive determinant of overall price trends in the long run. General financial conditions associated with money creation or destruction, including changes in interest rates, also have been considered for some time an important factor of business cycles.

In the modern era, the bulk of money in developed economies consists of bank deposits rather than gold and silver or government-issued currency and coin. Accordingly, governments have authorized central banks today to guide monetary developments with instruments that afford control over deposit creation and affect general financial conditions. Central banks' actions are deliberately aimed at influencing the performance of the nation's economy and not based on ordinary business considerations, such as profit. The guide-posts and degree of discretion central banks should use in implementing monetary policy remain controversial issues, as are questions of the coordination of monetary policy with fiscal policy and with policies abroad.

THE INSTRUMENTS OF MONETARY POLICY. The instruments available to central banks vary from country to country, depending on institutional structure, political system, and stage of development. In most developed capitalist economies, central banks basically use one or more of three main instruments to control deposit creation and affect financial conditions. *Required reserve ratios* set minimum fractions of certain deposit liabilities that commercial banks and in some countries thrift institutions must hold on reserve as assets in the form of cash in their vaults or deposits at the central bank. *The discount or official rate* is the interest charged by the central bank for providing reserve deposits directly to the banking system either through lending at a 'discount window' or through rediscounting or purchases of financial assets held by banks.

Open market operations are the third instrument. They involve either outright or temporary purchases and sales, typically of government securities, by the central bank with the market in general. The central bank pays for a securities purchase by crediting the reserve deposit account of the seller's bank, which in turn credits the deposit account of the seller. The central bank receives payment for a sale of securities by debiting the reserve account of the buyer's bank, which in turn debits the account of the buyer. In this way, open market operations that alter the amount of securities held in the central bank's asset portfolio have as their counterpart a change in the nonborrowed reserves held by banks, that is, the reserves that do not originate through bank discount borrowings. The amount of these nonborrowed reserves also is changed by variations in other, noncontrolled items on the asset or liability side of the central bank's balance sheet, such as gold holdings that were important historically or the deposits of domestic and foreign governments that can vary considerably today. Still, central banks routinely monitor these items and can prevent them from having sizeable undesired impacts on nonborrowed reserves by engaging in offsetting open market operations.

The sum of borrowed and nonborrowed reserves constitutes the total reserves available to the banking system. The central bank can exercise considerable control over these two sources of total reserve availability. Open market operations, as noted, provide for fairly close control of overall non-borrowed reserves. The level of the discount rate as well as other administrative procedures affect the amount of borrowed reserves. Given the interest rates on other sources of short-term bank funding, a change in the discount rate, or commonly in some countries in other lending terms and conditions, alters the incentives banks face to borrow reserves at the discount window. A discount rate increase, for example, would tend to induce banks to reduce their discount borrowing and turn to other sources of funds. Banks would attempt to replace the funds by borrowing reserves from other banks, or by issuing large-sized certificates of deposit, or even by selling liquid financial assets in secondary markets. These actions would transmit upward tendencies to the interest rates on these instruments.

The control by central banks over the availability of total reserves to private banks gives central banks at one remove a decisive influence over the availability of deposits to the public as well as over conditions in the money market. Given total reserves, the required reserve ratio sets an upper limit on the amount of deposits that can be created. In practice, this upper limit is not reached because private banks desire to hold a portion of total reserves not as required reserves but in the form of a cushion of reserves in excess of requirements. But since excess reserves are assets that typically earn no interest, unlike loans and investments, banks seek to hold them to minimal levels.

If reserves represent the level central banks can use to control deposits, then the required reserve ratio represents the fulcrum. A given increase in the supply of total reserves has an amplified effect on deposits. This is the case whether it is brought about through an open market operation that tends to raise non-borrowed reserves or a cut in the discount rate that tends to raise borrowed reserves. Banks initially receiving the new reserves could immediately attempt to loan their surfeit of reserves to other banks, thus depressing the interest rate on overnight loans of reserves between banks. The easing of conditions in this market puts downward pressure on rates on other money market instruments, such as Treasury bills or large certificates of deposit. This general reduction in short-term interest rates encourages the public to hold more transactions and savings deposits, because the incentive to economize on such money balances is reduced by the narrower opportunity cost (in terms of foregone interest income) of holding low-return deposits instead of other interest-bearing assets. Deposits will rise, boosting required reserves, until required reserves have risen enough to exhaust all unwanted excess reserves, which necessitates an expansion in deposits that is some multiple of the original increase of reserves.

Required reserve ratios also represent a potentially active, alternate instrument for varying supplies of money and credit. Changes in these requirements alter the amount of bank deposits that a given quantity of total reserves can support. However, reserve requirement variations are a blunt instrument at best, as even relatively small changes in them produce large effects on the amount of deposits that can be supported by reserves outstanding. Accordingly, central banks infrequently resort to changes in these required reserve ratios.

Some countries do not impose reserve requirements. In those cases, the central bank's liabilities to banks are represented by voluntarily held vault cash and clearing or working balances. These central banks can still use open-market-type operations to influence deposit creation and money market conditions by varying reserve supply relative to these voluntary demands for reserves. However, the relationship between reserves and deposits, which in these countries depends on the average of the banks' desired ratios of reserve assets to deposits of the public, is less predictable than is the case with binding reserve requirements.

Whether the banking system's vault cash and deposits at the central bank are held predominantly as required or voluntary reserves, total reserves plus currency outside banks represent the nation's total monetary base. This aggregate also is potentially controllable by the central bank. Since currency has traditionally been supplied to meet the demands of the public, as a practical matter, however, central banks have found it more advisable to exercise direct control over reserves than over the monetary base.

Variations in the supply of reserves relative to the demand for them, with associated impacts on the cost of reserves, other interest rates, and the stock of money, are the initial channels through which most central banks of developed capitalist countries use their policy instruments to affect the macroeconomy. Some countries with less developed securities markets rely more heavily on policies focused on bank lending, including in some cases direct controls on bank credit through ceilings or reserve requirements against bank assets. The activities of these central banks in controlling aggregate credit and its allocation are conceptually separate from monetary policy *per se* and are not considered in this article.

231

THE DISTINCTIONS BETWEEN MONETARY POLICY, DEBT MANAGEMENT, AND FISCAL POLICY. Monetary policy can be distinguished from debt management and fiscal policy. Debt management and monetary policy are similar only in the limited sense that both change the composition of the public's holdings of financial assets and the public's liquidity position through shifts between short- and longer-term assets. More liquidity is provided if the government shortens the average maturity of its debt outstanding. Similarly, if a central bank purchases government debt from a member of the public, liquidity is enhanced because the public has traded a less liquid security for a more liquid deposit. Nonetheless, an open market purchase by the central bank of government securities in effect retires the debt, by replacing securities outstanding in the hands of the banks or the public with bank reserves and associated public deposits, both of which earn no or below-market returns on the margin. The injection of this kind of reserve liability of the central bank from outside the private economy brings about widespread portfolio adjustments that lower market interest rates generally as an aspect of the expansion in money. A debt management operation of the federal government, by contrast, just replaces one security in the hands of the public with another, affecting the term structure of oustanding debt and possibly the term structure of interest rates but not the general level of interest rates.

Monetary policy is clearly distinguishable from fiscal policy because each affects the economy through a different role. Fiscal policy has a direct effect on spending through government outlays and a direct effect on income available for spending through tax rates. Fiscal policy also has a financial aspect because budgetary deficits or surpluses imply changes in government debt that presumably influence total credit demands and interest rates. (On the other hand, to the debatable extent that the public views government debt as entailing an ultimate tax liability, a larger government deficit indirectly would tend to encourage an equal and offsetting increase in private saving to finance future tax payments and hence discourage private spending.) In contrast to the direct spending and income effects of fiscal policy, the impact of monetary policy is wholly indirect and depends on the response of spenders and borrowers to the changes in monetary and financial conditions brought about by policy actions.

THE MACROECONOMIC EFFECTS AND OBJECTIVES OF MONETARY POLICY. Monetary policy responsibilities of central banks today go far beyond the role originally seen for central banks, which involved ensuring the stability of the banking system and the convertibility of deposits, especially in time of financial panics. Early in their history, central banks assumed the role of 'the lender of last resort', meaning that they would provide a source of funds for financially troubled banks to forestall liquidity crises. Subsequent experience indicated the need for central banks to provide an 'elastic currency' to accommodate seasonal variations in the demands for reserve assets. By doing so, central banks could avoid periodic reserve shortages that had disturbed market conditions and also, on occasion, confidence as well, giving rise to runs on banks. Deposit insurance, bank supervision with on-site examinations, and bank regulation ranging from circumscribing certain risky activities to setting minimum requirements for bank capital or certain bank assets or liabilities also have been introduced to help assure a stable banking system. In some countries, responsibility for many of these functions has been granted to other governmental agencies.

A major role for central banks in maintaining the safety and soundness of the financial system has continued to the present day, even though it has been joined in this century by a responsibility for overall macroeconomic stabilization. Macroeconomic stability requires a sound financial system; a weak financial system may not be able to withstand the effects of exogenous shocks to the economy or of restrictive policy actions that otherwise would be appropriate.

The dominant influence of monetary policy over time on the price level traditionally has elevated long-term price stability to a paramount position among the macroeconomic objectives of central banks. Under a gold standard historically, the world stock of gold provided a longer-term anchor to the world's average price level. But the commitment of central banks to buy and sell gold at a fixed price in terms of the domestic currency automatically gave rise to substantial inflows or outflows of gold to individual countries in the process of international adjustment. Large impacts on domestic economic activity and prices resulted in cyclical instability and sustained inflationary or deflationary episodes. The demise of the gold standard lessened the constraints on central banks in pursuing shorter-term domestic stabilization goals, but the discipline of the outstanding gold stock over long-term international price trends also was lost. In the modern era, central banks have been given the charge of exercising self-discipline in seeking the objective of longer-term price stability. Meanwhile, the widely recognized short-run impact of monetary policy on economic activity and employment has fostered increased emphasis on countercyclical objectives as well.

Over extended periods, the effects of monetary policy are concentrated almost wholly on nominal magnitudes, that is, those measured in terms of the monetary unit. As noted, central banks are able to control the nominal stock of bank reserves and, at one remove, the money stock. Average price trends become established as the nominal quantity of money interacts over time with the private sector's demand for real money balances, that is, the value of money after adjustment for the impact of inflation or deflation of prices. Thus, monetary policy has considerable influence over the long run on the average price level. In addition, factors that affect demands for real money balances, such as financial innovation, and more generally, that affect demands or supplies of aggregate output also play a role in price level determination.

The supply of output is determined in the long run mainly by real factors such as population growth, participation in the labour force, capital accumulation, and productivity trends. Real values for wages, interest rates, and currency exchange rates also respond secularly to fundamental real forces. The influence of monetary policy over the level and trend rate of change of the nominal price level carries over indirectly as an influence on the nominal values of these other variables but not on their real values. The real values of wages, interest rates, and exchange rates that are ground out by the market economy interact over time with nominal price behaviour to determine their nominal values. In the very long run, then, a change in the nominal quantity of money will be neutral as all nominal prices and wages tend to adjust proportionally, *ceteris paribus*.

While the influence of monetary policy on the behaviour of real values is widely agreed to be minor over the long pull, it is also recognized that monetary policy can affect real variables significantly in a shorter run, cyclical context. Doubts about the effectiveness of expansive monetary policy under conditions of a domestic depression raised during the Keynesian revolution have since been largely resolved. The views of today's mainstream macroeconomists with regard to the impact of monetary impulses on real economic activity are not far from those expressed in the following passage from David Hume:

> Though the high prices of commodities be a necessary consequence of the encrease in gold and silver, yet it follows not immediately upon that encrease; but some time is required before the money circulates through the whole state and makes it effect be felt on all ranks of people. At first no alteration is perceived; by degrees the price rises, first of one commodity then another; till the whole at last reaches a just proportion with the new quantity of specie.... In my opinion, it is only this interval, or intermediate situation, between the acquisition of money and rise of prices, that the encreasing quantity of gold and silver is favourable to industry (David Hume, 'Of Money', 1752; reprinted in *Writings on Economics*, edited by Eugene Rotwein, Madison: University of Wisconsin Press, 1955).

The proposition that monetary policy actions necessarily have a short-run effect on real variables is not universally accepted. In the last decade, the macro rational expectations school has argued that changes in monetary policy may not alter real variables, even in the short run. If a policy-induced movement in the nominal money stock is expected by the public in advance, then the public will have the incentive to adjust accordingly the actual, as well as expected, levels of all nominal values. Such a public response in principle would neutralize even the short-run impact of the expected policy change on real variables.

This recent challenge to the traditional view concedes, though, that unexpected policy actions can alter real variables, if only temporarily. Unanticipated policy actions can cause the outcomes for various nominal, and thus real, magnitudes to diverge, at least for a time, from their expected values. But the rational expectations school stresses that the public will come to expect policy actions that respond systematically to economic developments. Only policy actions that were purely random, or based on information not shared by the public, would then be unexpected, in which case the scope for effective countercyclical policy would be greatly narrowed.

In recent years, however, considerable counterevidence has been marshalled to the view that only unexpected policy moves can affect real values. Most empirical studies suggest that even systematic and expected changes in the direction of monetary policy do not show through fully right away in nominal values but have short-run impacts on real economic values.

234

The evident lagged effects on nominal values have been explained by various frictions, adjustment costs, and information imperfections. While prices may adjust minute-by-minute in auction markets, in other markets explicit or implicit longer-term contracts impart rigidities to nominal prices and wages, preventing a complete short-run adjustment to even expected changes in nominal policy variables. Costs of changing certain prices also can give rise to gradual adjustment of nominal magnitudes over time. In addition, the buffer role of inventories keeps even an expected change in nominal spending on goods and services from being felt by all producers simultaneously. Finally, because firms and workers get information about demands for their own goods and services more rapidly than information about economy-wide demands, they can misperceive as only local events what really are generalized phenomena ultimately affecting all nominal values. Economic agents can be induced in the short-run to change their real behaviour in supplying goods and services, rather than fully altering the nominal prices or wages they offer as would actually be called for by overall developments.

THE CHANNELS THROUGH WHICH MONETARY POLICY AFFECTS THE ECONOMY. Even though economists now better understand these general behaviour patterns, the precise channels through which monetary policy actions are transmitted to the economy at large and the specific variables that best indicate the stance of monetary policy remain unresolved issues. The immediate effects of changes in the instruments controlled by central banks on the supply and cost of reserves are clear. Both an open market purchase of government securities that raises nonborrowed reserves and a cut in the discount rate augment reserve availability relative to demands for excess and required reserves. This places interest rates on money market instruments under downward pressure. After that, an almost infinite sequence of 'ripple effects' ensues, and analysts still differ in sorting out the most important of these in affecting the economy. Their differing views reflect the complexity of the linkages between the modern financial system and economic activity and the alternative simplifications various schools have adopted in an effort to capture the essential elements.

The mainstream view derives from the Keynesian tradition and highlights induced movements in market interest rates across the maturity spectrum as the primary linkage between monetary policy actions and private spending. An 'easing' or 'tightening' of monetary policy is indexed by decreases or increases in market rates. Of course, the distinction between nominal and real interest rates is recognized; a change in market interest rates that simply compensates for an accompanying change in inflationary expectations may have minimal real economic effects.

These Keynesian channels of influence have been worked out in some detail, both theoretically and in large-scale econometric models. With an easing monetary policy action, for example, the initial fall in money market rates induces market participants to revise downward their expected levels of future short-term rates as well, causing a softening in long-term rates. Inflation expectations are thought to adjust sluggishly in lagged response to actual inflation and to be largely unresponsive to the monetary easing itself. Thus, any tendency for inflation expectations to rise is viewed as minor. More administered interest rates, such as the prime rate and consumer credit and mortgage rates also come under downward pressure over time, and credit terms and conditions tend to become less restrictive.

Spending in the interest-sensitive sectors, such as housing, consumer durables, and business investment, are most affected at first, as lowered borrowing costs stimulate demand. Some second-round effects also begin to come into play. The associated increase in income and production further stimulates consumption and investment spending. Also, the fall in interest rates is mirrored by a rise in financial asset values, and this gain in wealth encourages even more consumption spending.

Prices come under delayed upward pressure in part because tighter labour markets reduce the unemployment rate, at least transitionally, below its 'natural' level consistent with the realization of wage and price expectations. Such a fall in unemployment is associated with an acceleration of wage rates. Higher capacity utilization also may boost price markups over costs. As the actual inflation rate picks up, inflation expectations begin to increase as well, imparting a separate upward thrust to price and wage setting.

An internationally related channel also can become important, especially in countries with a significant external sector and flexible exchange rates. A more accommodative monetary policy action that reduces domestic interest rates is likely to diminish the demand for assets denominated in the home currency. Under flexible exchange rates, the resulting depreciation of the exchange value of the currency will lower export prices in world markets and raise import prices. These developments will work over time to bolster spending on net exports. But as the associated rise in import prices feeds through the domestic price structure, broad price indexes also will tend to move higher.

Monetarists adopt a somewhat different viewpoint, asserting that monetary policy stimulus is best measured by the growth of the money stock. A sustained speed-up in money growth after some lag leads to a temporary strengthening in real economic activity and even later to faster inflation. The process is set in motion as an injection of reserves supports more money than the public desires to hold given prevailing levels of real income, prices and interest rates. As the extra balances 'burn a hole in people's pockets', purchases of a wide variety of goods and services as well as financial assets are stimulated. Short-term market interest rates may fall initially, but more importantly, prices across a broad spectrum of financial and real assets are bid up, stimulating demand for and production of investment and consumer goods. Monetarists, like Keynesians, contend that in the long run the impact on real activity dissipates as the monetary stimulus becomes fully reflected in inflation. People end up needing the extra money just to carry out normal transactions at inflated prices, leaving no more extra stimulus to real spending.

GUIDES FOR MONETARY POLICY. With a wide variety of financial and non-financial measures affected in the process of economic adjustment to a monetary policy action, the question remains as to which variable represents the best indicator of the stance of policy, that is, the variable providing the most reliable indication of the future effects of monetary policy on the economy. Moreover, with policy decisions having lagged effects and policymakers necessarily uncertain about economic linkages and trends, such a variable presumably also could be used to keep policymakers' judgement from going astray by serving as an intermediate guide to monetary policy actions. An intermediate guide is a variable that the central bank would attempt to keep in line with a prespecified target, and thus it would need to be reasonably controllable by the central bank. The central bank would adjust the level of the intermediate target less frequently than the settings of the policy instruments.

Central banks over time have used, with evolving emphasis, alternative primary policy guides. Historically, the price at which gold or some other metal was convertible into the domestic currency played this role. Subsequently, market interest rates and foreign exchange rates received more emphasis as policy guides. In recent decades, targets for overall money and debt have been adopted in many industrial countries. Other candidates have been proposed, including the monetary base, indexes of commodity prices or the general price level, nominal GNP, and real interest rates.

Unfortunately, both macroeconomic analysis and experience suggest that no single variable can consistently serve as a reliable policy guide, so no hard-and-fast answer as to the best one can be given that holds under all conditions. All variables beyond non-borrowed reserves and the discount rate are influenced by factors other than monetary policy actions, and it turns out that the degree of stimulus to the economy involved in movements in any of them will depend on the nature of the other factors at work. Summarizing the advantages and disadvantages of several variables demonstrates this dilemma.

Monetary aggregates represent collections of financial assets, grouped according to their degree of 'moneyness'. Narrow measures of money comprise currency and fully checkable deposits to encompass the public's primary transactions balances. Broader measures also include other highly liquid accounts with additional savings features. Sharp lines of demarcation separating the various aggregates are difficult to draw as the characteristics of various assets often shade into one another over a wide spectrum, especially in countries with developed, deregulated, and innovative financial markets.

Monetary aggregates serve well as policy guides when the public's demands for them are stably related to nominal spending and market interest rates and have a relatively small interest sensitivity. Suppose, for example, that there is a cyclical downturn in total spending. If the central bank withdraws reserves from the system in order to maintain a given level of market interest rates in the face of falling demand for money, the money stock would decrease at a time when additional monetary stimulus is needed. If instead the central bank maintains the original level of reserves in order to keep the money stock at its target level, interest rates must fall. The less interest-sensitive is money demand, the more would interest rates have to decline to offset the depressing effect of reduced

237

spending on the public's desired money holdings. Thus, by maintaining money at the target level, an easing of credit conditions and perhaps a depreciating foreign exchange rate over time would partially offset the original decline in spending, and moderate the cyclical downturn.

However, when the public's willingness to hold monetary aggregates given nominal spending and interest rates is undergoing an abnormal shift, movements in measures of the money stock provide misleading signals of monetary stimulus or restraint. Such shifts in money demand have occurred in response to financial innovations and deposit deregulation as well as varying precautionary motives on the part of the public. As a result, the properties of empirical relationships connecting the money stock to nominal spending and market interest rates have been altered – in some cases permanently. The precise nature of the impact is difficult to assess when the process is underway. For example, in the United States during the 1980s, the disinflation process interacted with sluggishly adjusting offering rates on newly deregulated transaction deposits to raise substantially the responsiveness of the demand for narrow money to changes in market interest rates. The sizeable declines in market interest rates after the early 1980s enhanced the relative attractiveness of returns on interest-bearing fully checkable deposits, which are included in narrow money. Inflows into these accounts were massive, with a significant portion representing savings-type funds.

Faced with unusual money demand behaviour, the central bank would be best advised not to resist departures of money from target but instead to accommodate reserve provision to the shifting demands for money. It could do so by maintaining existing reserve market conditions. Otherwise, the very process of restoring the money stock to target would transmit the disturbance in money demand to spending behaviour and economic activity. The changing conditions in reserve and credit markets associated with returning money to target would be inappropriate for stabilizing spending. Central banks that rely on monetary aggregates as policy guides have interpreted such episodes as demonstrating the need for monitoring overall economic developments and making feedback adjustments to monetary targets in response to evident disturbances of money demand relative to income.

Market interest rates thus would serve as a better policy guide than monetary aggregates if the only disturbances were to the money demand relationship. In a realistic economic context, though, independent disturbances to the relation between nominal spending and market interest rates also are likely to occur. Collection lags for data on economic activity and uncertainties about the structure of behavioural relations in the economy and the permanence of disturbances make the appropriate reaction to unexpected pressures on interest rates and misses of money from target difficult to determine at the time. For example, suppose the central bank sees that an unanticipated rise in interest rates is needed to keep the money stock from overshooting its target. The reason could be an unexpected strengthening of inflation and nominal spending that is boosting money demand, or a surprise upward shift in money demand relative to spending, or some combination of the two. The source of overshoot of money from target could prove self-reversing, or it could be only the beginning of a cumulative departure. Unless uncertainty about the money demand relationship is exceptionally severe, it might be safer for the central bank to permit some upward movement in nominal interest rates than for it simply to keep interest rates stable by fully accommodating reserve provision to the outsized money growth. The latter reaction would provide no counterweight at all to what later could prove to have been an inflationary upturn of nominal spending.

On the other hand, suppose spending had clearly weakened, and the central bank has responded by adding to reserve availability in the face of a very interest-sensitive demand for the targeted monetary aggregate. The resulting fall of interest rates has led to a sizeable overshoot of money from target. In this circumstance, it may turn out better for the economy if the central bank accepts the full overrun of money above target. With a highly interest-sensitive demand for money, only a small reduction in interest rates is implied by keeping money on target when spending turns down. This easing in financial conditions will provide only little offset to the weakness in economic activity, absent an upward adjustment to targeted money growth.

Relying more on interest rates as a policy guide will not necessarily resolve the problem of determining the appropriate central bank reaction to unexpected developments. The relationship between nominal values of spending and market interest rates is qualitatively less predictable and stable over time than the already loose underlying relation between their real values. Determining what level of real interest rates is associated with a given level of nominal interest rates is hampered because the public's inflationary expectations are difficult to measure. Longer-term real interest rates, which are thought to have the most powerful influence on many important components of real spending, are especially difficult to discern since the public's expectations of inflation over the distant future are the most obscure.

Central banks thus face considerable uncertainty about the real interest rate that would be implied initially by the choice of a particular level for the nominal interest rate. Also, unless the resulting level of real interest rates just happened to be consistent with full employment and a stable inflation rate, the implied real interest rate would tend to move over time in a destabilizing direction, as was originally pointed out by Knut Wicksell. Suppose the central bank maintained nominal interest rates over an extended period at a level that from the start yielded an overly stimulative real interest rate. Economic activity would press against the economy's productive and labour capacities, and inflation would tend to accelerate. But as inflation expectations adjusted upward in response to actual inflation, the real interest rate implied by the targeted nominal interest rate would be driven still lower. This fall in the real interest rate would add even more stimulus to nominal spending and inflation. Even so, growth of reserves and money would have to be continually accelerated to maintain the targeted nominal interest rate. An ever faster rise in nominal spending and inflation hence would result from pegging the nominal interest rate at too low a level. Those central banks emphasizing market interest rates as policy guides interpret such possibilities as requiring them to monitor overall monetary and economic developments and to make feedback adjustments over time in setting market interest rates.

Since the potential pitfalls of either monetary aggregates or market interest rates as policy guides have induced central banks to respond to more ultimate gauges of economic performance – such as nominal GNP, prices, and un-employment – in setting intermediate targets, some observers have recommended that central banks should cut through the feedback process by simply targeting one of these ultimate objectives itself. But this approach has disadvantages beyond the fact that the particular objective variable to be selected is of course controversial. Any of these ultimate variables are affected by numerous forces outside the central bank's control, including domestic fiscal policy and foreign fiscal and monetary policies. Data on most of these variables are received with some delay and then subject to sizeable revisions. Finally, an attempt to convert an ultimate objective to a shorter-term policy target would risk unstable macroeconomic outcomes over time in light of the uncertainties and lags in the impact of money policy actions.

For these reasons, central banks have not believed that they can justifiably be held accountable for the near-term performance of the overall economy. Despite the problems of interpreting the various monetary and debt aggregates and interest rates which are more under their near-term control, central banks, as well as many other analysts, view the constellation of these financial variables taken together as offering a surer indication of the longer-term stance of monetary policy itself than current values of ultimate economic variables. While the disadvantages under some circumstances of guiding policy by any single financial measure argue against an overreliance on any one, the advantages of each under different circumstances are viewed as suggesting that, when taken in the context of broader economic developments as well, none can be completely ignored in the conduct, or assessment, of monetary policy.

Nevertheless, the long-run linkage between money growth and inflation together with the traditional concern of central banks for price stability give monetary aggregates a special position among these financial variables. Continuing to focus on average money growth over extended periods, while accounting for the influence of distortions to its demand behaviour, forces central banks to keep longer-term price objectives in mind in the process of adjusting policy actions in response to shorter-term financial and economic developments.

POLICY RULES VERSUS DISCRETION. Some critics of the discretion embodied in such a policy approach place even more weight on the longer-term consideration of providing a nominal anchor to the macroeconomy. They also interpret the difficulty of forecasting both economic developments and the impact of policy actions as implying that central banks should not even attempt to stabilize the economy over shorter periods of time through discretionary policy actions. Given the lags and uncertainties involved, they believe such flexibility in policy is likely to do more harm than good, despite the best of intentions.

These critics have recommended that monetary policy should be based on fixed rules rather than discretion. The most influential has been the proposal of the monetarists to maintain a low, constant money growth rate through thick and thin. These economists, under the intellectual leadership of Milton Friedman, have argued that excessive money growth is the main cause of inflation and that variations in monetary growth historically have been responsible for the large cyclical fluctuations in real output. With constant money growth, self-correcting mechanisms would prevent macroeconomic shocks from having major, sustained impacts on economic activity.

The rational expectations school has added a new wrinkle to the case for policy rules. They believe discretion imparts an inflationary bias to monetary policy because central banks face an irresistible temptation over time to put aside announced long-term plans to maintain price stability in pursuit of short-term production and employment aims. If the public had adjusted price expectations to the central bank's announced intention to maintain price stability, then a temporary increase in money growth would surprise the public and cause a desirable, if short-lived boost to output and employment with little inflationary cost. But with rational expectations, the public would see through this temptation and expect such a policy action. Expectations of inflation would emerge in anticipation of the monetary stimulus, leaving only price increases but no output gains as the policy is implemented. Indeed, if the central bank did not undertake the expected stimulus after all, then output would instead be temporarily depressed. Given this dilemma, central banks would end up providing the monetary stimulus, even though it only validates ongoing inflation and has no output effects.

Following an invariant policy rule would avoid this problem, according to these advocates, by making an anti-inflation policy credible to the public. The public then would expect only policy actions consistent with price stability. This school supports a rule defined in terms of a fixed target for either money growth or the price level.

While monetarist views have affected central bank practice in recent decades, as evidenced by the enhanced reliance on monetary aggregates in actual policy making during the 1970s, central banks have shied away from the adoption of fixed money rules in light of the perceived advantages of policy flexibility. The abstract, even hypothetical, nature of the rational expectations argument has limited its influence. And the substantial disinflation worldwide from the early- to mid-1980s despite continued rapid growth of monetary aggregates appears to have weakened the case of both schools for policy rules.

COORDINATION WITH OTHER DOMESTIC AND FOREIGN POLICIES. The separate influences of domestic fiscal policy and foreign fiscal and monetary policies on macroeconomic outcomes at home raise the issue of coordination with domestic monetary policy. On the domestic side, a more expansionary fiscal policy involving enlarged government spending or reduced taxes, for example, may require that offsetting actions be taken to make monetary policy more restrictive.

241

Even if the policy mix is changed in such a way to keep overall employment, production and prices the same, nominal and real values of market interest rates and foreign exchange rates would be altered, as would the composition of aggregate output in terms of real consumption, investment and net exports.

The traditional view has been that after some point a shift in the policy mix toward more stimulative fiscal policy and more restrictive monetary policy becomes undesirable, since investment and net exports will have to be 'crowded out' by higher real interest rates and exchange rates to make room for larger government purchases or private consumption. A reduced pace of investment would retard capital accumulation and the economy's longer-term growth potential, while lowered net exports would harm export and import-competing industries. The increased government budget deficit would be associated with a larger deficit in the current international payments accounts, implying a faster buildup of both government and external debt. Repayments of both debts over time would become more burdensome for domestic residents by requiring a greater sacrifice of future consumption. If capital inflows were invested effectively, they could provide resources to make future debt-service payments, but if these funds simply helped to finance government budget deficits, they would not support private capital accumulation.

A more recently advanced 'supply side' view is that sizeable reductions in marginal tax rates will encourage private saving, investment, work effort and entrepreneuship. The economy's growth potential will be increased sufficiently that a more restrictive monetary policy need not be adopted, even if government deficits initially are increased. Evidence drawn from the United States following sizeable cuts in marginal tax rates early in the 1980s suggests, however, that the resulting incentive effects on the economy's potential growth rate are relatively minor.

In practice, fiscal policy has not proven to be as flexible a macroeconomic tool as monetary policy, as other social goals beyond countercyclical considerations, as well as legislative delays, have prevented prompt adjustment in spending programmes or tax laws in response to overall economic developments. This situation has placed monetary policy in the forefront in pursuing macroeconomic stabilization objectives. Monetary policy actions become most politically sensitive when fiscal policy is expansionary and private spending and wage and price decisions are causing the economy to overheat. The required turn to a more restrictive monetary policy engenders opposition to higher interest rates, particularly from sectors where employment and production are especially disadvantaged by upward movements in interest and exchange rates. Having monetary policy bear too much of the brunt of countercyclical policy restraint is to be avoided partly because the central bank may not practically be able to bear the political pressures, and partly because economic imbalances across sectors become more pronounced.

Difficulties of achieving the proper mix of monetary and fiscal policy are exacerbated when considered in a multi-country context. International policy coordination is not just an issue of meshing monetary polices, but of coordinating overall macro-policy mixes in general. It also covers a range of possible interactions among countries. A higher degree of policy coordination obviously becomes more necessary in a regime of fixed exchange rates or common trade areas, or to the degree that different countries have accepted common exchange rate objectives. But even without explicit exchange rate objectives, some international policy coordination may still yield benefits given the transmission of effects of policy actions. A general move to restrictive fiscal policy abroad, for example, would reduce foreign spending on domestic exports. Also, the fall in foreign interest rates can heighten the willingness of international investors to hold domestic financial assets; these higher asset demands would act to keep domestic interest rates lower than otherwise but raise the exchange rate, ultimately depressing further the domestic balance of trade. Self-reinforcing cycles can even occur in which more expansive fiscal policies abroad, with a rise in foreign interest rates, produce a depreciation of the exchange value of the domestic currency. The lower value of the currency then leads to higher domestic inflation and inflationary expectations, in turn possibly contributing to a further depreciation of the currency, depending on the domestic monetary policy response.

A process of international policy coordination is in the interest of interrelated nations. Closer coordination could in principle provide for a greater measure of stability in exchange markets, while maintaining some of the features of flexible exchange rates in cushioning international disturbances and in lessening the constraints on policy implied by automatic flows of international reserves under a fixed-rate system. But the interests and circumstances of sovereign nations may well diverge at times. This can occur either because of a somewhat different emphasis on the various ultimate economic objectives or because the countries are experiencing different stages of the business cycle. In such situations, scope for agreement about the appropriate pattern of macroeconomic policies across countries may be limited.

BIBLIOGRAPHY
Axilrod, S.H. 1985. U.S. monetary policy in recent years: an overview. *Federal Reserve Bulletin* 71(1), January, 14–24.
Bank of England, 1984. *The Development and Operation of Monetary Policy, 1960–1983.* London: Oxford University Press.
Friedman, M. 1960. *A Program for Monetary Stability.* New York: Fordham University Press.
Goodhart, C.A.E. 1984. *Monetary Theory and Practice: the UK experience.* London: Macmillan.
Lindsey, D.E. 1986. The monetary regime of the Federal Reserve System. In *Alternative Monetary Regimes*, ed. C.D. Campbell and W.R. Dougen, Baltimore: Johns Hopkins University Press.
McCallum, B.T. 1984. Credibility and monetary policy. In *Price Stability and Public Policy*, Kansas City: Federal Reserve Bank of Kansas City.
Poole, W. 1970. Optimal choice of monetary policy instruments in a simple stochastic macro model. *Quarterly Journal of Economics* 84(2), May, 197–216.
Wallich, H.C. and Keir, P.M. 1979. The role of operating guides in U.S. monetary policy: a historical review. *Federal Reserve Bulletin* 65(9), September, 679–91.

Money Illusion

PETER HOWITT

The term money illusion is commonly used to describe any failure to distinguish monetary from real magnitudes. It seems to have been coined by Irving Fisher, who defined it as 'failure to perceive that the dollar, or any other unit of money, expands or shrinks in value' (1928, p. 4). To Fisher, money illusion was an important factor in business-cycle fluctuations. Rising prices during the upswing would stimulate investment demand and induce business firms to increase their borrowing, thus causing a rise in the nominal rate of interest. Lenders would accommodate them by increasing their savings in response to the rise in the nominal rate, not taking into account that, because of the rise in inflation, the real rate of interest had not risen but had actually fallen (Fisher, 1922, esp. ch. 4).

Beginning with Haberler (1941, p. 460, fn. 1) other writers have used the term money illusion as synonomous with a violation of what Leontief (1936) called the 'homogeneity postulate', the postulate that demand and supply functions be homogeneous of degree zero in all nominal prices; that is, that they depend upon relative prices but not upon the absolute price level. This usage differs from Fisher's in two senses. It refers to people's reactions to a change in the level of prices rather than to a change in the rate of change of prices, and it is cast in operational terms, as a property of potentially observable supply and demand functions rather than as a property of people's perceptions or lack thereof.

Patinkin (1949) objected to the latter use of the term money illusion on the grounds that it failed to take into account the real balance effect. A doubling of all money prices should affect household demand functions even if people are perfectly rational and suffer from no illusions, because it reduces at least one component of the real wealth that constrains their demands – the real value of their initial money holdings. Accordingly he defined the absence of money illusion as the zero-degree homogeneity of net demand functions in all money prices and the money values of initial holdings of assets.

In a fiat money economy in Hicksian temporary equilibrium, under the assumption of static expectations, the absence of money illusion in Patinkin's sense is operationally equivalent to the assumption of rational behaviour, in the following sense. Let each agent's demand functions $\hat{x}_i(p_1,\ldots p_n, W)$ for goods $i = 1,\ldots,n$, together with his demand-for-money function $\hat{M}(p_1,\ldots p_n, W)$ be defined as the maximizers of the utility function $U(x_1,\ldots,x_n; M, p_1,\ldots p_n)$ subject to the budget constraint: $p_1 x_1 + \cdots + p_n x_n + M = W$, where W is initial nominal wealth. The utility function includes M and the money prices p_i because M is assumed to yield unspecified services whose value depends upon the vector of prices expected to prevail next period, and those expected prices are proportional to today's prices.

A rational agent would realize that a proportional change in M and all prices would leave unaffected the purchasing power of M, and thus also the services rendered by M. Accordingly U is said to be illusion-free if it is homogenous of degree zero in $(M, p_1 \ldots, p_n)$. This homogeneity property was first assumed explicitly in the context of demand theory by Samuelson (1947, p. 118) although it was implicit in the earlier analysis of Leser (1943), who used the equivalent formulation: $U(x_1,\ldots,x_n; M/p_1,\ldots,M/P_n)$. It is easily verified that the $\hat{x}$'s are illusion-free in Patinkin's sense if and only if they can be derived from an illusion-free U (see Howitt and Patinkin, 1980).

The assumption of static expectations is crucial to this equivalence. If expected future prices were not proportional to current prices then a proportional change in $p_1,\ldots,p_n$, W would alter intertemporal relative prices and it would not be irrational for the agent to respond by changing his demands. Patinkins's original definition can be generalized to take this possibility into account and to allow for the presence of productive non-money assets by requiring demand functions for real goods to be unaffected by a proportional change in W, all current prices, and all expected future prices, holding constant the rates of return on all non-money assets. If future prices p_i' were uncertain then current demands would depend upon the probability distribution $F(p_1',\ldots,p_n')$, and the proportional change in future expected prices in the above statement would have to be replaced by a change from $F(p_1',\ldots,p_n')$ to $F_\lambda(p_1',\ldots,p_n') \equiv F(p_1'/\lambda,\ldots,p_n'/\lambda)$ where λ is the factor of proportionality.

The absence of money illusion is the main assumption underlying the long-run neutrality proposition of the quantity theory of money. But the presence of money illusion has also frequently been invoked to account for the short-run non-neutrality of money, sometimes by quantity theorists themselves, as in the case of Fisher. On the other hand, many monetary economists have reacted adversely to explanations based on such illusions, partly because illusions contradict the maximizing paradigm of microeconomic theory and partly because invoking money illusion is often too simplistic an explanation of phenomena that do not fit well into the standard equilibrium mould of economics. Behaviour that seems irrational in a general equilibrium framework may actually be a rational response to systemic coordination problems that are assumed away in that framework.

Thus, for example, Leontief (1936) attributed Keynes's denial of the quantity theory to an assumption of money illusion. He interpreted Keynes as saying that the supply of labour depended upon the nominal wage rate whereas the demand depended upon the real wage. A rise in the price level would thus raise the equilibrium quantity of employment. Leijonhufvud (1968, ch. 2) questioned this interpretation and argued that Keynes was dealing with information problems that don't exist in Leontief's general equilibrium analysis. Specifically, Leijonhufvud argued that workers might continue supplying the same amount of labour services in the event of a rise in the general price level, not because they irrationally identified nominal with real wages but because in a world of less than perfect information it would take time for them to learn of the changed value of money.

Likewise, Friedman (1968) objected to the then standard formulation of the Phillips-relation between unemployment and the rate of wage-inflation. Friedman argued that the rate at which firms raised their wage offers and households raised their reservations wages, given any existing amount of unemployment, should depend upon these agents' expectations of the future value of money. To assume otherwise would be to assume money illusion. Friedman's argument implied that an expected-inflation term should be added to the usual specification of the Phillips curve. His analysis of the expectations-augmented Phillips curve was similar to Leijonhufvud's imperfect-information argument.

More recently, Barro (1977) has argued against the assumption of nominal wage stickiness in the work of Fischer (1977) and others, on the grounds that microeconomic theories of wage contracts imply that these contracts should be signed in real, not nominal terms, unless people suffer from money illusion.

Although monetary economists have thus been reluctant to attribute money illusion to private agents they have not hesitated to attribute it to governments. Indeed, as Patinkin (1961) demonstrated, money illusion on the part of the monetary authority is necessary for an economy to possess a determinate equilibrium price level. More recently, several writers have attributed real effects of inflation to money illusion in tax laws (e.g. Feldstein, 1983). Specifically, in many countries interest income and expenses are taxed at the same rate regardless of the rate of inflation, and historical money costs rather than current replacement costs are used for evaluating inventories and calculating depreciation allowances. Because of these efects inflation can distort the after-tax cost of capital.

In short, the attitude of economists to the assumption of money illusion can best be described as equivocal. The assumption is frequently invoked and frequently resisted. The persistence of a concept so alien to economists' pervasive belief in rationality indicates a deeper failure to understand the importance of money and of nominal magnitudes in economic life. This failure is evident, for example, in the lack of any convincing explanation for why people persist in signing non-indexed debt contracts, or why the objective of reducing the rate of inflation, even at the cost of a major recession, should have such wide popular support in times of high inflation.

BIBLIOGRAPHY

Barro, R.J. 1977. Long-term contracting, sticky prices, and monetary policy. *Journal of Monetary Economics* 3(3), July, 305–16.

Feldstein, M. 1983. *Inflation, Tax Rules, and Capital Formation.* Chicago: University of Chicago Press.

Fischer, S. 1977. Long-term contracts, rational expectations, and the optimal money supply rule. *Journal of Political Economy* 85(1), February, 191–205.

Fisher, I. 1922. *The Purchasing Power of Money.* 2nd edn, New York: Macmillan.

Fisher, I. 1928. *The Money Illusion.* New York: Adelphi.

Friedman, M. 1968. The role of monetary policy. *American Economic Review* 58(1), March, 1–17.

Haberler, G. 1941. *Prosperity and Depression* 3rd edn, Geneva: League of Nations.

Howitt, P. and Patinkin, D. 1980. Utility function transformations and money illusion: comment. *American Economic Review* 70(3), September, 819–22.

Leijonhufvud, A. 1968. *On Keynesian Economics and the Economics of Keynes.* New York: Oxford University Press.

Leontief, W. 1936. The fundamental assumptions of Mr. Keynes' monetary theory of unemployment. *Quarterly Journal of Economics* 5, November, 192–7.

Leser, C.E.V. 1943. The consumer's demand for money. *Econometrica* 11(2), April, 123–40.

Patinkin, D. 1949. The indeterminacy of absolute prices in classical economic theory. *Econometrica* 17(1), January, 1–27.

Patinkin, D. 1961. Financial intermediaries and the logical structure of monetary theory. *American Economic Review* 51(1), March, 95–116.

Samuelson, P.A. 1947. *Foundations of Economic Analysis.* Cambridge, Mass.: Harvard University Press.

Money in Economic Activity

D. FOLEY

Money is a social relation. Like the meaning of a word, or the proper form of a ritual, it exists as part of a system of behaviour shared by a group of people. Though it is the joint creation of a whole society, money is external to any particular individual, a reality as unyielding to an individual's will as any natural phenomenon.

To understand the system of social relations of which money is a part, it is necessary to adopt a comparative and historical perspective. Only by seeing the phenomenon of money in contrast with systems of social relations that do not involve money can we get a sense of the characteristic peculiarities of money. Marx's (1867) analysis of commodity production provides such a perspective.

People in every society must produce in order to survive and develop, but their production can be organized through different systems of social relations. An important dimension of these social relations is the degree to which the products are controlled by individual owners acting in their own interests. In a system of commodity production, a product at its creation is the property of one owner, who can exchange it for the products owned by others.

Money appears in systems of commodity production. Because any commodity can be transformed into any other through exchange, commodities appear to be equivalents. It is possible to evaluate any collection of disparate commodities by multiplying the quantity of each one by a price, where the ratio of the prices of any two commodities expresses the ratio in which they exchange, and adding up. Because exchange determines only the ratio of the prices, the units in which value is measured are arbitrary. A similar situation exists in measuring the mass of physical objects. By weighing one mass against another one can establish the proportion of one to another, but to express weight in absolute terms it is necessary to establish a conventional standard (like the kilogram or pound). In a commodity-producing society some system evolves for measuring and transferring value separated from particular commodities, the money form of value. Monetary units such as the dollar, franc, pound, mark, or yen, measure value separated from particular commodities.

Although the money form of value is a universal characteristic of commodity systems of production, different specific forms of money have evolved in different times and places. The earliest form of money is commodity money. One particular product, often a precious metal such as gold, takes on the role of measuring the value of all other commodities. In a commodity-money system the monetary unit, for example the dollar, is defined legally as a certain amount of gold. Since gold exchanges at a particular ratio with every other commodity, this definition establishes a dollar price for every commodity as well.

It is also possible for commodity systems to operate with an abstract unit of value, a monetary unit implicitly defined by prices negotiated by buyers and sellers of commodities. In this situation, the dollar is not defined as a particular quantity of some commodity, but commodity producers, knowing at any moment how much value the dollar represents, continue to establish prices in terms of dollars. Commodity money systems are subject to instability because the exchange ratios of the money commodity against other commodities constantly change. Abstract unit of account systems are subject to instability because the prices producers choose may drift upward or downward over time.

In a commodity money system agents may issue promises to pay a certain amount of money at a particular time in the future, or on demand. These promises to pay, liabilities for the issuer and assets for the holder, if they are credible, can take the place of the money commodity in many situations. For example, if a producer agrees to sell his product for a certain money price, he may accept a credible promise to pay gold instead of gold itself. Likewise, if an individual needs to hold a stock of money to provide for contingencies, she may decide to hold widely acceptable promises to pay rather than gold itself, if that is more convenient. The same thing can happen in an abstract unit of account system. Promises to pay pure value may be acceptable in transactions, and used as stores of value.

In systems where credit is highly developed, what does it mean for one agent to promise to pay money? How can this promise be fulfilled? In a commodity money system, payment ultimately means delivery of a certain quantity of the money commodity. In an abstract unit of account system, payment normally means delivering a third party's promise to pay, where the third party's liability is more acceptable than the debtor's. For example, private producers may pay each other by transferring the liabilities of banks, deposits. Banks in turn may pay each other by transferring the liabilities of the State, bank reserves or currency. In a commodity money system every agent faces an ultimate requirement to pay in the money commodity. In an abstract unit of account system, however, the State does not have to pay its liabilities by transferring something else.

It is surprising how little difference there is in the day-to-day practice of systems with and without a money commodity. For most individual agents there is one type of highly acceptable liability (bank deposits, for instance) in which the agent must settle its accounts. The same thing is true in a money commodity system. The fact that at the top of the pyramid of agents whose liabilities are more and more socially acceptable the State has to pay in gold in a commodity money system, and does not have to pay any particular thing in an abstract unit of account system makes no difference to the individual agents. Even in a commodity money system, the development of a pyramid of agents whose liabilities have different degrees of acceptability insulates most of the agents in the system from the money commodity itself. Only in periods of crisis, when the State faces severe difficulties in maintaining the convertibility of its liabilities into the money commodity, will the money commodity influence the financial decisions of individual agents.

Liabilities of high social acceptability, like currency issued by the State, or bank deposits, may come to be preferred as the means of payment for individual transactions, though in almost all commodity producing societies other liabilities also perform important payment functions. For example, endorsed bills of exchange of private traders have often circulated as widely accepted means of payment among firms in capitalist societies. Furthermore, the issuers of liabilities of high acceptability find that agents are willing to hold them even when they pay a lower rate of return than other assets. If the issuers of these liabilities can exercise some monopoly power, as banks organized under the leadership of a State-sponsored central bank can, they will restrict the interest paid on their liabilities to a minimum. This minimum may in some cases reach zero, so that the most socially accepted liabilities pay a zero interest rate. Agents continue to hold these liabilities as their assets because of their wide acceptability as payment, and because they serve very well as a reserve against the contingency that the agent will not be able to borrow.

From this examination of the nature of money as a social relation, we can draw several important conclusions on which to base a discussion of money and economic activity. First, the money form of value, value separated from a particular commodity, is inherent in the organization of production through exchange. Second, the emergence of money takes place simultaneously with the growth of exchange itself. Third, while the money form of value is a universal characteristic of commodity production, the forms of money are diverse and changing. In particular, the liabilities, or promises to pay, of economic agents can serve in place of a money commodity, and can take the place of the money commodity altogether. Fourth, whether there is or is not a money commodity, there tends to develop a hierarchy of liabilities of different degrees of acceptability. Payment for agents at one level of this pyramid requires their delivery of liabilities of agents at the next level up. The existence of this pyramid creates considerable flexibility in the financing of economic activity.

The relation between money and economic activity is two-sided. Money forms of value are a reflection of the particular organization of economic activity through commodity production. The liabilities that serve to finance economic activity are created in the course of financing economic activity itself. From this perspective it is tempting to argue that money is a reflector of economic activity, and that monetary phenomena are determined by the independent development of economic activity. As we shall see, this is an important theme in the development of monetary theory.

But money also serves as a regulator of economic activity, because it is the link between the individual producer and the social character of production. In order to undertake production, an agent must finance it by getting control of an acceptable monetary asset. If an agent does not already own a sufficient quantity of these assets, it must convert its own liability into a liability of higher acceptability by borrowing. The terms on which agents can make this transformation regulate their initiation of production in two senses. First, financing determines which agents will be able to carry out their plans. Second, financing determines the total volume of economic activity that can be initiated. In its role as regulator of economic activity, money appears, especially from the perspective of the individual economic agent, to be the independent factor to which economic activity has to adapt itself.

Theories of money can be seen first in terms of which of these aspects of the relation between money and economic activity they emphasize as their starting point, and second in terms of the way they account for the final synthesis of the two points of view. Those theories that posit an independent role for money in determining economic activity have some level at which money is itself determined by economic activity, and those theories that emphasize money as a reflector of economic activity also envision circumstances where money regulates and influences the scale of economic activity.

In the 18th and early 19th centuries, the writers who had the most influence on the later development of monetary theory, Hume, Smith, Ricardo, and Marx, all place the main emphasis on money as a reflector of levels of economic activity determined by non-monetary factors.

David Hume (1752) makes two, somewhat contradictory, arguments concerning the reasons why the quantity of money has no lasting effect on the levels of economic activity. The first is that the money prices of commodities are proportional to the quantity of money in a country. As a result, the real quantity of money, correcting the quantity of money for the level of money prices, is endogenous. Since the real quantity of money is relevant for economic decision making, and particularly for decisions regarding the initiation of economic activity, once prices have adjusted, the physical quantity of money commodity in the country makes no difference. But in a second essay Hume argues that in fact the physical quantity of money in a country is also endogenous, here implicitly assuming that the gold prices of commodities are determined by non-monetary factors, essentially by world prices. Here his argument is that a country with a relatively small quantity of money commodity will have low prices relative to the rest of the world, which will create a balance of trade surplus and attract the money commodity to that country. This process will continue until the price level in the country has risen to the level of world gold prices. There are two processes of adjustment in Hume's argument, a middle run in which money prices of commodities are proportioned to the quantity of the money commodity, and a long run in which, because prices of commodities are determined by world prices, the quantity of the money commodity in the country adjusts.

But Hume makes yet a third remark about the relation of money to economic activity, which raises an important theme for later writers. He argues that there is a short run in which increases in the quantity of money in a country do directly increase the level of economic activity because commodity prices have not fully adjusted to the quantity of the money commodity. Later writers attempt to flesh out this argument by specifying the exact mechanism through which changes in the nominal quantity of money can affect the level of economic activity.

Adam Smith (1776) emphasizes quite a different aspect of the relations of money to economic activity. Smith's discussion of credit and banking centres on the idea that the substitution of credit, particularly banknotes, for precious metals as a medium of circulation can free social capital tied up in stocks of the money commodity to set production in motion. In this perspective credit has a significant effect on the level of economic activity. Smith is concerned to enunciate rules of banking that will prevent an overissue of banknotes and maintain convertibility of banknotes into the money commodity, rules which are the origin of the real bills doctrine. Smith recommends that banks lend only to real creditors who are already owed money by real debtors as the result of bona fide commodity transactions. Such loans will be automatically liquidated when the real debtor pays real money (that is, the money commodity) to the creditor and the creditor in turn pays the money into the bank. Essentially Smith argues for a system in which borrowers are forced at frequent, periodic intervals to clear their positions and demonstrate their continued solvency. He claims that a banking system that follows these rules will have no difficulty in maintaining convertibility, so that its banknotes will circulate at par against the money commodity, and can replace a certain proportion of the money commodity as a medium of circulation.

Smith views a properly regulated banking system as providing the appropriate amount of money endogenously through the expansion and contraction of credit. There are two levels to Smith's argument. At the first level, the introduction of banks and credit money have a once and for all effect on economic activity by releasing social capital previously tied up in stocks of the money commodity for production. Once the banking system is in place and functioning to its maximal feasible extent according to the rules of the real bills doctrine, however, the quantity of money and credit, now endogenous to the system, has no independent effect on the level of economic activity (nor, apparently, on prices, which Smith sees as being regulated rapidly by world prices).

Both Smith and Hume are at pains to establish that the quantity of money does not influence the level of interest rates, which they view as being determined by the level of profit rates in a country. In their view there is a conventional relation between the level of profit rates and interest rates. A low interest rate reflects a low profit rate as a result of the healthy development of commodity production in a country and the exploitation of profit opportunities, not an abundance of the money commodity.

David Ricardo's (1811) thinking on monetary matters arose from his study of the problem of the price of gold bullion in terms of pounds during the Napoleonic Wars, when the Bank of England suspended the convertibility of its banknotes into gold. During this period the market price of gold bullion rose to a substantial premium over the official, mint price of gold. This prompted a debate over the reasons for the premium and the appropriate policy to deal with it. A number of people argued that the premium reflected real factors, such as poor harvests, that had created a balance of trade deficit for England, and had driven the pound to a discount against foreign currencies defined in terms of gold. Ricardo insisted, instead, that the premium reflected an overissue of banknotes by the Bank of England. He claimed that this overissue put more notes in the hands of the public than it wanted to hold, and that in attempting to get rid of the excess, the public tried to buy gold bullion and drove up its price. For Ricardo, the policy appropriate to the situation was one of restricting the issue of banknotes as a prelude to resuming conversion of notes into gold. He further argued that any impact of real factors, like bad harvests, on the price of gold bullion must take place by way of monetary changes. In other words, in the absence of an overissue of paper currency, and a consequent rise in the price of bullion, a bad harvest would lead to a rise in other commodity exports to pay for the import of grain, not to a depreciation of the pound in terms of gold.

Ricardo's discussion raises a new question, which has great importance for the later development of monetary systems. This is the question of the effect of the issue of banknotes that, unlike Smith's convertible notes, are not convertible into the money commodity at a guaranteed rate of exchange. The broad thrust of Ricardo's argument is that the issue of such notes has no effects on the economy, because overissue simply leads to a discount of the notes against the money commodity. Once again, the quantity of real money has become endogenous, now not through changes in the prices of commodities in terms of the money commodity, but through changes in the discount of paper banknotes against the money commodity.

Ricardo later goes considerably further than this analysis and explicitly argues for the independence of levels and directions of economic activity from monetary factors. Because he believed that the only rational end of economic activity was consumption, Ricardo argued, following Say, that every commodity offered for sale represented a demand for some other commodity, and thus, that in the aggregate the value of commodities offered on the market equalled the demand. Thus money is purely a medium for the exchange of commodities against each other, and has no independent role in determining economic activity; money is a veil.

Karl Marx (1867) develops his theory of money as a critique and correction of the ideas of these earlier writers. He has three important themes of correction in his approach to money. First, he argues that the prices of commodities in a commodity money system are prior to the quantity of money, so that the quantity of money theory of the price level is mistaken. Second, he rejects Ricardo's espousal of Say's Law on the ground that the movement of money into and out of hoards may create a discrepancy between the aggregate supply of commodities and the aggregate demand. Third, Marx argues for viewing the quantity of money commodity as endogenous to the economic system, and insists that a sharp distinction be made between the effects of exogenous issues of nonconvertible paper money, and the endogenous movements of the money commodity. Still, Marx's overall view emphasizes the primacy of production decisions limited by the accumulation of capital in regulating the level of economic activity, and portrays monetary events as primarily reflecting or communicating forces set in motion at the level of production.

In Marx's theory the money price of a commodity reflects the relation between the cost of production of the commodity and the cost of production of the money commodity. In the simplest case in which costs of production are proportional to labour times expended, this implies that the money price of a commodity is just the ratio of the labour time expended in producing it to the labour time expended in producing a unit of the money commodity. If, for example, it takes one hour of labour time to produce a bushel of wheat, and two hours to produce an ounce of gold, the gold price of a bushel of wheat will be $\frac{1}{2}$ ounce of gold. In Marx's analysis monetary units, like the dollar or pound or franc, are simply conventional names for specific quantities of gold. If an ounce of gold is defined to be equal to 20 dollars, for instance, then the price of a bushel of wheat will be 10 dollars in the example above. In this way, the money commodity takes on the special role of expressing the abstract labour contained in other commodities. But this role depends on the cost of production of the money commodity, not on the quantity of it that happens to be in a certain country at a certain time.

How, then, does the quantity of money adjust to changes in the scale of economic activity? Marx introduces the idea that agents hoard money, so that there are reserves of the money commodity available to be brought into circulation in response to increases in economic activity, and ready to absorb excess quantities of the money commodity if economic activity slackens. Marx's recognition of hoards is a key distinction between his vision of monetary theory and that of Hume and Ricardo. It leads logically to another important difference in Marx's treatment of Say's Law. Because Marx included the possibility of hoarding in his theory, he saw the possibility that the proceeds from sales of commodities might be hoarded rather than spent, thus breaking the close connection between the aggregate supply of commodities and aggregate money demand asserted by Ricardo and Say.

In his discussin of inconvertible paper money issued by the State in a system based on a commodity money, Marx returns to a position very similar to Ricardo's early analysis of the price of gold bullion. Following Smith, Marx argues that the issue of paper can displace gold without a depreciation of the paper, as long as the quantity of paper issued is smaller than the requirements of circulation. Under these circumstances all the paper will be absorbed by circulation, displacing an equal value of gold, and will circulate at par against gold. If, however, the State issues more paper than this, agents trying to dispose of the excess will bid the paper to a discount against gold. The quantity of money theory of prices holds for inconvertible paper money in Marx's view, but only through the mechanism of the premium for gold against the paper money. The quantity of gold itself has no impact on gold prices, because these are determined by costs of production.

In Marx's view the level of economic activity is regulated primarily by the historical accumulation of value as capital. At any moment the technology in use establishes capital requirements for the production of various commodities. The amount of capital value available from past accumulation sets a limit to the scale of economic activity. Money in normal circumstances adapts passively to this level, either through the adjustment of hoards, or through the expansion and contraction of credit. In periods of crisis, however, the stagnation of money in reserve hoards is for Marx, the mechanism by which aggregate demand is reduced. Marx's account of the exact relation of economic activity to money in periods of crisis is incomplete. It is clear that he viewed the existence of money, and the possibility of hoarding as preconditions for crisis, and as important channels in the development of crises. He also strongly suggests that the underlying causes of crises lie in the evolution of production itself, for example, in the tendency of rate of profit to fall with capital accumulation and capitalist development of production.

The classical economists and Marx left a well-developed account of the relation of money to economic activity, an account which shaped later thinking in decisive ways. These theorists assumed unquestioningly that they were dealing with a commodity money system. The only exception to this rule is the analysis of inconvertible paper money issued by the State, and coexisting with a commodity money system. The characteristic theme of classical analysis was the subsidiary importance of money in relation to production. Money was seen as adapting to economic activity, either by automatic adjustments in the quantity of money, or in real quantities of money through changes in the prices of commodities.

The century after 1875 was a period of rapid and thoroughgoing transformation of monetary systems and financial institutions in the industrialized capitalist countries. With the growth of national markets and firms operating on a national and, increasingly, international scale, national markets for credit also developed. Large banks began to play a central role in the mobilization and channelling of national capital funds. Periodic monetary panics, involving external or internal drains of gold from the reserves of banks, began to occur. National banking systems became oligopolized and regulated. Thus the monetary phenomena that Smith, for example, analysed in the context of a largely agrarian and commercial capitalist society came to play a decisive role in the financing and construction of large-scale industrial development.

The important capitalist nations during this period extended their influence over the whole rest of the world in the first wave of capitalist imperialism. The world monetary system came to play a more and more important part in regulating economic activity on a world scale. The rivalries intensified by imperial competition between European powers set off a chain of disastrous social and military crises, beginning with World War I. The world monetary system was fundamentally and irreversibly transformed by these crises. During the war, all

255

the participant nations suspended convertibility of their currencies into gold, and erected elaborate systems of control over movements of capital. As a result the link between gold and national currencies became much weaker. The governments of the European powers discovered that their domestic monetary and credit mechanisms depended very little on convertibility for their day to day functioning. They also discovered the enormous latitude for State policies opened up by their abandonment of the promise to convert currency into gold. Although most political leaders expected the gold standard to return after the war, commitments to convertibility turned out to be fragile and temporary. Since 1914, convertibility of national currencies into a commodity money has been the exception rather than the rule, attainable only for short periods as the result of intensive diplomatic compromise.

The earlier monetary theory we have discussed might lead one to predict that under these circumstances national currencies would gradually lose their monetary role in competition with a spontaneously maintained world commodity money standard, so that all the national currencies would find their own discount or premium against gold, which would still function as a commodity money. While something like this did occur between the First and Second World Wars, after World War II a surprising evolutionary development occurred, in which one national currency, the dollar, despite its tenuous and tentative convertibility into gold, emerged as a world monetary standard. When the United States finally abandoned convertibility of the dollar into gold in 1971, it became clear that gold had lost its central position in the world monetary system. The industrialized world functioned with the dollar, an abstract unit of account, whose value in terms of commodities is determined by the pricing decisions of commodity buyers and sellers, as the standard of value.

These historical and institutional developments called into question much of classical monetary theory, which was based on the assumption of a commodity money system. In particular, those theories that argued that the value of the monetary standard was determined by the cost of production of the money commodity were left with the need to propose an alternative mechanism for determining the value of the monetary unit. The development of monetary theory in this period reflects the attempts of economists to grapple with this fundamental problem.

Irving Fisher (1911), writing in the heyday of US trustification about the turn of the 20th century, returned to the simplest formulation of the quantity of money theory of prices put forward by Hume as the starting point for his account of the relation between money and economic activity. Fisher posits the existence of a given amount of money, exogenously determined in the system. Because he assumes that this total quantity of money must circulate (thereby abstracting from the possibility of hoards) at a single exogenously given rate (the velocity of money), Fisher argues that the total monetary value of the transactions in an economy is determined independently of the level of economic activity. If, for example, there exist $100 billion dollars, exogenously supplied, and the velocity of money is five transactions per year on average, then the total transactions of the economy must total $500 billion per year. How can this be reconciled with the actual level of economic activity? Either the volume of transactions at given prices must change so that the total equals $500 billion, or the prices at which transactions occur must change to achieve the same result. Fisher followed Hume in arguing that, while in the short run a change in the quantity of money or velocity might have some impact on the level of economic activity in the society, in the long run the whole adjustment would be made in the prices of commodities. Fisher believed that the market system would lead to a given level of production of commodities determined by available resources and technological possibilities independently from monetary factors. Thus the only remaining variable free to adjust is the level of commodity prices. Fisher resurrects the classical presupposition that monetary factors do not influence economic activity, at least in the long run, on the basis of this analysis.

The monetary theory of John Maynard Keynes (1936) responds to the drastic changes in monetary systems engendered by World War I and the Great Depression. Keynes envisions a monetary system with a central bank at its centre. The liabilities of this bank may or may not be convertible into a money commodity. The liabilities of the central bank serve as the reserves of a commercial banking system which issues deposits. Keynes explicitly allows for the existence of other competing monetary assets, bonds and equities, in this system. Keynes poses the question of how the financial system absorbs the reserves and deposits created by the banking system. He argues that rates of return on bonds and equities must adjust until wealth holders are content to hold these assets and deposits in the proportions in which they are being supplied to the public. Thus a change in the reserve policy of the central bank forces a change in the rates of return to bonds and equities.

Since the rates of return on bonds and equity establish the cost of capital funds to firms, changes in these rates of return alter the incentives for firms to make long term investments. A fall in the interest rate engendered by an expansion of bank reserves encourages fixed investment, and this increase in spending by firms raises the level of aggregate demand in the whole economy, normally by a multiple of the initial increase, because households tend to spend part of their additional income as demand expands. In this view there is a close relation between the reserve creation of the central bank and the level of economic activity, mediated by the interest rate on bonds, the price of equities, and the fixed investment policies of firms.

Keynes presents this theory analytically as a correction of Fisher's arguments. First, Keynes insists that the velocity of money, the ratio of desired holdings of money to the value of transactions, responds systematically to the level of interest rates. Second, Keynes argues that prices are not the only variable available to adjust the value of transactions, given the quantity of money and the velocity of money. The other variable is the volume of transactions itself, which changes with the level of economic activity called forth by aggregate demand. While Keynes does not rule out the possibility that price adjustments may, under certain circumstances, be involved in reconciling the value of transactions to the quantity of money and velocity, he deemphasizes this case in arguing that typically the level of economic activity and hence the volume of transactions adapts. Furthermore, Keynes suggests that the relation between money demand, interest rates, and the level of economic activity (in Fisher's terms, the velocity of money) is volatile, subject to sharp changes depending on the mood of wealth holders and their expectations and fears about the future.

Keynes couches his theory in quite traditional terms. He shares with Fisher the concept of a demand for money, or velocity, that establishes a relation between the quantity of money the system will absorb and the levels of prices, interest rates, and economic activity. He also shares with Fisher the procedure of eliminating variables one by one as possible equilibrating factors and arguing that the remaining variable must be the one that adapts. Thus his differences with traditional theory turn on which variable he views as predetermined, and on the emphasis Keynes puts on variations in interest rates as mediating the response of the economic system to changes in the quantity of money. Thus Keynes manages to reverse the classical presumptions that money affects prices but cannot alter the level of interest rates or economic activity, without adopting the view that money is largely endogenous to the economic system.

In historical terms Keynes's theory is a step toward constructing a monetary theory that corresponds to the realities of fully developed industrial capitalism. In his deemphasis of convertibility as a limit on the operations of the central bank Keynes creates a theory that does not depend on the existence of a money commodity. In the place of the traditional emphasis on the money commodity and the relation of domestic money to it, Keynes's gives the centre of the stage to the problem of the regulation of aggregate demand and investment. Keynes's vision of the economic system is not that of a self-regulating entity which the economist seeks to understand, but of a complex set of causal linkages that a policymaker seeks to guide.

Keynes's theory of money establishes the framework within which the most influential post-World War II monetary theorists have worked. The basic elements, a demand for money which is a function of income, wealth, and the rates of return on alternative assets, an exogenously given supply of money, and a connection between money and real activity through changes in the rates of return and prices of nonmonetary financial and real assets, serve as the building blocks for both the new quantity of money theory of prices, and extensions of Keynesian theory. But within this framework, different scholars emphasize one or another element to reach quite different policy conclusions.

In the decade after 1945 Keynesian orthodoxy took the position that 'money doesn't matter', in that spending decisions of consumers and firms were largely independent of asset rates of return, and more responsive to expectational variables. This view was supported by the idea that close substitutes for monetary assets could be produced by banks and other financial actors. Thus any attempt to restrict economic activity by limiting the expansion of bank reserves would be circumvented by the substitution of other liabilities. This extreme nonmonetary interpretation of Keynes fell into disfavour as the advanced capitalist countries in the postwar period began to rely more and more heavily on monetary policy as a tool for regulating aggregate demand and the external value of their currencies.

A strong reaction to this deemphasis of monetary factors in the determination of aggregate demand came in Milton Friedman's (1956) resurrection of the quantity of money theory of prices within the Keynesian framework. Friedman argued that as a matter of empirical fact the demand for money is a highly stable function of a small number of relevant variables. He accepted Keynes's idea that the supply of money was exogenously determined by central bank policy, and concluded that changes in the supply of money would have regular and predictable effects on money income and asset rates of return. Friedman also put forward the claim that there are few good substitutes for money (although there has been some uncertainty as to exactly what his theory regards as a monetary asset), so that the demand for money is an inelastic function of the rates of return on competing assets. This implies that changes in the supply of money will be reflected in changes in money income rather than in rates of return. This line of argument leads naturally back to Fisher's conclusion that the level of real economic activity is determined by real factors independent of money, so that the ultimate effect of changes in the supply of money is entirely absorbed by changes in money prices. This series of empirical hypotheses allows Friedman to restore the claims of Fisher's quantity of money theory of prices within Keynes's theoretical framework. Because the new quantity of money theory of prices depends so heavily on empirical claims, it has come under strong questioning as econometricians have attempted to test it with historical data. The demand for money defined in any particular way exhibits more instability than Friedman claimed, and in some definitions a higher elasticity with respect to rates of return on competing assets than is necessary for Friedman's strong conclusions to hold. While it is possible to redefine the monetary aggregate to improve the statistical evidence for the new quantity of money theory of prices, this path opens up potential criticism of ex post theorizing, that is, choosing the definition of the monetary aggregate to save the theory in its confrontation with evidence.

Another pole of Keynesian interpretation is represented by the work of James Tobin (1982). Tobin also adopts Keynes's conception of a demand for money, but supplements it with demand functions for all other financial and real assets. In this vision money is one part of a spectrum of financial assets, all of which must find their place in wealth holders' portfolios through a mutual adjustment of rates of return and assets prices. For Tobin the possible impacts of monetary changes on economic activity are varied and complex, because they depend on the exact response of the whole structure of rates of return on competing assets to the monetary change, and to the possible reactions of these changes in rates of return on decisions to consume and invest. Tobin accepts Friedman's conclusion that the impact of monetary changes will be absorbed in money prices, but only for a very long run. In the more policy-relevant middle run, there are substantial effects monetary policy can have on the level and direction of economic activity. An expansive monetary policy, by lowering rates of return on bonds and raising the prices of equities, will encourage investment, thus raising the whole level of economic activity, and shifting the emphasis of production toward investment and growth. A contractionary monetary policy, even if it is offset by expansive fiscal policy, so that the overall level of economic activity remains unchanged, will tend to choke off investment and deter long term growth.

These Keynesian lines of thought have been enriched and somewhat modified by incorporating them into models of open economies, in which trade and capital flows are important, as in the work of Robert Mundell (1971). In an open economy with a convertible currency, the supply of domestic money cannot be exogenous. If the central bank expands the supply of money, it will find the public exchanging domestic monetary claims for international reserve assets to offset the expansion. In this context the main scope for monetary policy is at the international level, in the concerted efforts of all the central banks to expand or contract liquidity. In an open economy with a floating exchange rate, and capital markets open to the world, the rates of return on domestic assets will be pegged to world rates of return. In this situation a change in the supply of money has its main effects through changes in the exchange rate. A central bank can influence domestic economic activity in the short run by expanding the supply of money, driving the exchange rate down, and thus expanding the demand for exports. These effects will dissipate over time as domestic price levels adjust, so that the long run conclusions of the quantity of money theory of prices still hold in the open economy framework.

The new quantity theory's claim that in the long run monetary policy cannot affect real economic activity has been transferred even to the short run in the theories of Robert Lucas (1981) that apply the concept of 'rational', or self-fulfilling expectations to simple, stylized macroeconomic models. In this view the public is very quick to learn whatever systematic rule the central bank follows in formulating monetary policy. Once they have learned it, the public will tend to offset the central bank's operations with speculative movements of private portfolios, or through instantaneous price adjustments so as to neutralize any real effects of the policy. Unanticipated or unsystematic changes in the supply of money can affect real economic activity precisely because the public cannot distinguish these changes from changes in the underlying parameters of tastes, technology and resources that are thought to determine real decisions. Thus money itself can have short run effects on economic activity, but the rational expectations school argues that these possible effects can never be used for policy ends in a systematic fashion. It is unclear how general these results are, especially in circumstances where there are important differences in information and beliefs in different segments of the public, and where costs of learning the true structure of the economy (if such a structure actually exists) are significant.

The research of Don Patinkin (1965) and Kenneth Arrow and Frank Hahn (1971) on the insertion of money into fully specified general equilibrium theory has yielded some interesting clarifications of old arguments, but has not been able to reach sharp and sweeping conclusions like those of the new quantity of money theory of prices. By treating real balances of monetary assets as another good symmetrical with produced and consumed goods, Patinkin has shown that out of equilibrium the stock of real balances in principle affects the demands and supplies of all other assets. This argument is fatal to Fisher's simple procedure of separating the determination of relative prices and of the level of money prices. Hahn points out the paradox involved in assuming that money (as a thing, now, not a social relation) is valued only for having a positive price. In general in any monetary general equilibrium economy there exist equilibria in which money has a zero price, that is, a nonmonetary equilibrium. Since the non-monetary equilibrium is quite different from the monetary equilibria, and may involve much lower levels of trade and production, this abstract observation leads to a qualitative understanding of the role of money in facilitating economic activity. This general equilibrium modelling generally accepts the framework of the new quantity of money theory of prices in positing the existence of a single, given, monetary asset with no close substitutes, and in abstracting from the questions of how monetary liabilities come to exist, and whether or not they can be produced by private agents.

Hyman Minsky (1982) puts forward, in contrast, a theory of the relation of money to economic activity in which qualitative changes in the private issuance of monetary liabilities plays a central role. In Minsky's view, firms issue liabilities to finance production based on uncertain (and not necessarily self-fulfilling) expectations about future profitability. As an economic expansion develops, these expectations become more buoyant, and more liabilities are issued. This process gradually erodes the quality of the liabilities, because there comes to be a larger and larger profitability that profit realizations will not in fact allow all the commitments to be met. Each firm tends to move towards thinner and thinner margins of equity in its financial position; firms that are reluctant to follow this policy find themselves severely punished competitively in the short run. The deterioration of the quality of liabilities sets the stage for a financial crisis, in which many firms face difficulties in meeting their commitments, and new lending is extended only on much tougher terms. In the absence of State intervention to substitute its liabilities in part for lower quality private liabilities, the resulting collapse of the financial system has strong repercussions on levels of economic activity as firms find it difficult to finance new productive outlays. Minsky's account emphasizes the qualitative, rather than the purely quantitative effects of monetary liabilities on economic activity. It also goes beyond quantity of money theories in seeing the space of monetary liabilities as constantly shifting in its properties, as new liabilities are invented and old ones take on a different function with the development of production. In the place of a single, inelastically supplied, monetary liability with known and unchanging properties, the spectrum of financial assets in Minsky's view is filled up with elastically supplied liabilities of unknown and constantly changing properties.

Channels of influence run both from money to economic activity and from economic activity to money. Whether money takes the form of a commodity produced by the system, or of liabilities issued to finance production, the creation

261

of monetary assets is an incident in the cycle of production. But it is at least partly through the availability and cost of finance that levels of planned production are determined, and confined within the productive capacities of the whole society as Michal Kalecki (1971) has emphasized. Different monetary theories have emphasized one or another side of this mutual interaction, without reaching a fully adequate synthesis.

The relation between money and economic activity must be analyzed in explicitly dynamic terms because monetary and financial institutions constitute an important feedback loop in commodity-producing economies. The properties of the equilibria of a system often fail to reveal its dynamic behaviour. In equilibrium situations the powerful forces running from money to economic activity are balanced by those running the other way, and monetary effects tend to disappear from view. The contemplation of such equilibrium situations is an insufficient guide to understanding the effects of money on economic activity in general.

BIBLIOGRAPHY

Arrow, K.J. and Hahn, F. 1971. *General Competitive Analysis.* San Francisco: Holden-Day.

Fisher, I. 1911. *The Purchasing Power of Money.* New York: Macmillan.

Friedman, M. (ed.) 1956. *Studies in the Quantity Theory of Money.* Chicago: Chicago University Press.

Hume, D. 1752. *Writings on Economics.* Ed. E. Rotwein, Madison: University of Wisconsin Press, 1955.

Kalecki, M. 1971. *Selected Essays on the Dynamics of the Capitalist Economy.* Cambridge: Cambridge University Press.

Keynes, J.M. 1936. *The General Theory of Employment, Interest, and Money.* London: Macmillan; New York: Harcourt, Brace.

Lucas, R.E. 1981. *Studies in Business Cycle Theory.* Cambridge, Mass.: MIT Press.

Marx, K. 1867. *Capital,* Vol. I. Ed. F. Engels, New York: International, 1967.

Minsky, H. 1982. *Can 'It' Happen Again?* Armonk: Sharpe.

Mundell, R. 1971. *Monetary Theory.* Pacific Palisades: Goodyear.

Patinkin, D. 1965. *Money, Interest and Prices.* 2nd edn, New York: Harper & Row.

Ricardo, D. 1811. *The Works and Correspondence of David Ricardo.* Vol. III, *Pamphlets and Papers 1809–1811.* Ed. P. Sraffa, Cambridge: Cambridge University Press, 1951; New York: Cambridge University Press, 1973.

Smith, A. 1776. *An Inquiry into the Nature and Causes of the Wealth of Nations.* Ed. E. Cannan, London: Methuen, 1961; New York: Modern Library, 1937.

Tobin, J. 1982. *Essays on Economics: Theory and Policy.* Cambridge, Mass.: MIT Press.

Money Supply

K. BRUNNER

Money is still best defined in the classical tradition to refer to any object generally accepted and used as a medium of exchange. Financial innovations associated with technological or institutional changes do not modify this definition. They do change however the empirical counterpart of the definition and this requires intermittent changes in the measurement procedures for the nation's money supply. This magnitude can be expressed as the sum-total of money held by the domestic public. This eliminates from the money supply all 'intra-system items', i.e. liabilities of money-issuing institutions which are simultaneously assets of some money-issuing institutions. For some purposes domestic money held by residents of foreign countries may usefully be included in the measure of the nation's money supply.

Information about the money supply and knowledge about its behaviour is hardly important for its own sake. Its importance derives from the role of the money supply in the economy's interaction. Shorter-run variations in monetary growth contribute to the variance in economic activity and long-term monetary growth determines approximately the long-term inflation rate. This position in the economic nexus directs attention to the determination of the money supply and its behaviour.

We usefully approach an understanding of the money supply process with the examination of a simple monetary system. A pure commodity money regime in an open ('small') economy offers some important insights into the nature of the money supply process and of monetary regimes. This primitive regime is fully characterized by a demand for money confronting a money stock and a trade balance controlling the rate of change of the domestic money stock.

This regime provides (a potentially moving) anchor for money stock and price level. For any prevailing foreign price level, exchange rate and underlying real conditions (money demand and 'technology') the regime determines an inherent equilibrium stock of money with a corresponding price level. The evolution of money stock and price level over time follows thus a course shaped by the underlying real conditions.

The simple prototype model yields useful insights. A country cannot arbitrarily and permanently change its money stock in the context of a given foreign price level, exchange rate and underlying real factors. Ultimately the system always settles on the equilibrium stock governed by the relevant determinants. These imply that the injection of fiat money is eventually offset by a loss of internationally acceptable commodity money. The pattern changes with the relative size of the country. A comparatively large country can actually retain a portion of the original increase and thus permanently influence the equilibrium money stock. This follows from the fact that a large country's monetary injection may raise other countries price-levels. But the discipline of a fixed exchange rate system constrains ultimately even a larger country. The institutional arrangements of financial intermediation may of course loosen the relation between money stock and the commodity money reserve. The maintenance of a fixed rate system continues however to impose over time in the context of given underlying conditions a negative association between the fiat and commodity component of the monetary base. It may be noted that the admission of domestic production of the money commodity and a non-monetary use of this commodity complicates but does not invalidate the basic result.

The basic long-run pattern of the commodity money regime continues in more complex monetary regimes with fixed exchange rates and a common international reserve. Under these conditions the international monetary system possesses a stable anchor determined most particularly by the demand for money, the technology controlling the production of international reserves and the ultimate constraints imposed on the domestic money supply by international reserves. The underlying anchoring conditions imply that there exists at any moment of time a stock equilibrium both of money supply and price-level. This stock equilibrium shifts over time with the evolution of the underlying anchoring conditions. The survival of this system depends most particularly on the institutional and political choices shaping the relation between international reserves and domestic money supply.

The institutional choices made in the postwar period failed to maintain, or to develop, a new system which anchors both money supply and price-level. This experience motivates a somewhat deeper attention to the process determining the money supply in an economy with extensive financial intermediation. An exploration of the money supply process contributes moreover to a more rational institutional choice lowering short-run monetary and long-run price-level uncertainty in the context of an 'anchored international system'. This exploration involves a deeper study of the relation linking the monetary base with the money supply.

The nation's money supply emerges from a process characterized by the interaction between the various asset-markets. Three groups of agents need be considered in this context. The public supplies financial claims to the banks, holds money, allocates money between currency and transaction accounts at financial intermediaries, and allocates its accounts at these intermediaries between transaction and non-transaction accounts. Banks absorb the claims offered by the public, set the supply conditions for their liabilities and allocate their assets between earning assets and reserves. Lastly, the monetary authorities set the supply conditions of the monetary base, possibly constrain the banks' supply conditions of their liabilities and control the range of admissible assets to be held by banks. All these allocations and interactions are shaped by market conditions and jointly determine money stock, bank credit and prices on the asset markets.

The process of interacting asset-markets can be projected into an expression $M = m \cdot B$, with M = money stock, m = monetary multiplier and B = monetary base. This expression may be interpreted as a semi-reduced or reduced form depending on policy strategies and institutional arrangements. It offers an economically useful logarithmic additive decomposition of the money stock. The underlying analysis describes the money stock as the resultant of the joint behaviour of public, banks and monetary authorities. This behaviour controls the base to the last dollar. The monetary multiplier linking the base with the money stock reflects on the other hand dominantly the behaviour of banks and public. This behaviour proceeds however in the context of an institutional framework conditioned by the monetary authorities. Changes in institutional arrangements may thus affect the responses of the multiplier to the public's or the bank's behaviour.

The summary expression offers an organized frame for the useful exploration of a wide range of questions. We need to remember in this context that the monetary multiplier depends proximately on the public's and the bank's allocation patterns, i.e. on the currency ratio, the transaction account ratio and the banks' reserve ratio. The multiplier depends therefore ultimately on market and institutional conditions. Some of the issues addressed under the title of a money supply theory are indicated in the final paragraphs.

Many discussions in past and recent years bear on the relative importance of the public's, banks' and monetary authorities' behaviour in the money supply process. Several theories assign a dominant rule to banks and public in explanations of the cyclic pattern of monetary growth. This implies that changes in the multiplier should dominate changes in the base over cyclic units. This is however not confirmed by observation in the USA. The multiplier does dominate the shortest run movements in the money stock. The longer the time horizon under consideration the more prominent is the role of the authorities. We find in particular that substantial or persistent accelerations of the money stock are mostly due to the behaviour of the authorities expressed by the base.

A variety of institutional aspects exemplify the possible explorations. The operation of the Central Bank's discount window, whether as a 'lender of first or last resort', influences the banks' reserve ratio and consequently the multiplier. The role of an interbank-deposit structure and the Federal Reserve membership can be systematically examined in this framework. A detailed investigation reveals that a declining membership hardly affects the Federal Reserve Authorities' control over the money supply. The role of liability constraints on banks and on the banks' asset structure can be similarly assessed, and so can the role of low transaction cost 'money market' (e.g. federal funds, Treasury bills) or the effect of credit cards. Institutional differences in these various aspects influence via the proximate determinants the magnitude and response patterns of the multiplier.

The problem of 'reversed causation' exemplifies the importance of institutional aspects. It emerges that the multiplier offers little opportunity for an interpretation of the income-money correlation based on 'reversed causation'. Such causation requires institutional arrangements producing a positive feedback from economic activity to the base. The occurrence of some reverse causation does not form a necessary and general property of monetary processes. It results from policy decisions structuring the monetary regime.

Our last issue attends to the controllability of the money stock. It is frequently denied with little analysis and evidence that the monetary authorities can effectively control the money stock. The truth of this denial would have serious and far-reaching implications. Controllability refers essentially to the variance of the probability distribution of the forecast error of money stock conditional on some policy variables. We can express this idea in the following terms:

$$\text{degree of control} = \frac{1}{V[M - M^*/, IR]}, \qquad M^* = E[M/\pi, IR]$$

where V is the variance of forecast error $(M - M^*)$ conditional on the choice of policy variables π and of the institutional regime IR. Under some choices of π and IR the variance of M is a sum of variances of m and B plus a covariance term. Under other choices the variance of M is fully determined by the variance of m. The degree of control experienced by the Central Bank is thus not imposed 'by immutable nature'. It is conditioned by the choice of policy variables and the institutional regime IR. An evaluation of the possible degree of control can be executed by choosing within the institutional framework of the USA the monetary base as our policy variable. The base is perfectly controllable (potentially) by the Central Bank with the aid of suitable strategies and tactical procedures. Professors James Johannes and Robert Rasche computed the Central Bank's control opportunity based on statistical forecasting techniques addressed

Table 1

	Mean percentage forecast error	Standard deviation of percentage forecast error
1-month forecasts	0.0405	0.745 (82 observations)
3-month moving average forecasts (overlapping)	0.0300	0.439 (74 observations)
6-month moving average forecasts (overlapping)	0.0335	0.266 (62 observations)
12-month moving average forecasts (overlapping)	0.0453	0.145 (43 observations)

to the multiplier m (Johannes and Rasche, 1987). Table 1 summarizes the crucial results.

Several features should be noted. The mean percentage error declines somewhat as the time horizon of control lengthens. The root mean square error (not listed here) exhibits the same pattern. The decline in the standard deviation of the forecast error as the horizon is extended is however substantially more dramatic and important. Serial correlation between the forecast errors is not significant. The mean percentage error for all three horizons is not significantly different from zero. Further examination also shows that the statistical properties of the forecast error did not change over the sample period from November 1977 to the end of 1985. Deregulation and financial innovation did thus not impair the controllability of the money stock. These results imply that control of monetary growth over one year within plus or minus one percentage point of the target point is feasible. This degree of control is quite sufficient for all practical purposes of monetary management.

The potential controllability is in particular sufficient to establish a monetary anchor which jointly determines the stock equilibrium of money supply and price level. The crucial underlying conditions need to impose a control on the monetary base. A wide range of monetary regimes characterized by different institutional arrangements may be considered in this context. A rational choice would have to examine the level of shorter-run monetary and longer-run price level uncertainty typically associated with each regime. The provisions of an underlying anchoring for money supply and price level are however not sufficient. The arrangements may involve an anchor with substantial drift over time or allow substantial variations or more or less durable divergences from the stock equilibrium. Shorter-run monetary uncertainty emerges in the latter case and longer-term price level uncertainty in the first case.

BIBLIOGRAPHY
Johannes, J. and Rasche, R. *Controlling Growth of Monetary Aggregates*. The Hague: Kluwer-Nijhoff.

Natural Rate and Market Rate

AXEL LEIJONHUFVUD

The main analytical elements of Knut Wicksell's *Interest and Prices* can be found in the works of earlier writers. Wicksell was familiar with Ricardo's distinction between the direct and indirect transmission of monetary impulses. Although unknown to Wicksell in 1898, Henry Thornton had provided a clear account of the cumulative process in 1802, as had Thomas Joplin of the saving-investment analysis somewhat later (cf. Humphrey, 1986).

Yet, Wicksell did not just coin the terms 'natural rate' and 'market rate of interest'. His development (1898 and 1906) of these ideas made the nexus between money creation, intertemporal resource allocation disequilibrium and movements in money income the dominant theme in macroeconomics for three decades until it was submerged in Keynesian economics. His starting point was the Quantity Theory, understood as the proposition that in the long run the price level will tend to be proportional to the money stock. His objective was to explain how both money and prices come to move from one equilibrium level to another. This inter-equilibrium movement became his famous 'cumulative process'. The maladjustment of the interest rate was the key hypothesis in Wicksell's explanation.

The 'market rate' denotes the actual value of the real rate of interest while the 'natural rate' refers to an equilibrium value of the same variable. The latter term by itself divulges Wicksell's engagement in the ancient quest for a 'neutral' monetary system, i.e., a system neutral in the original sense that all relative prices develop as they would in a hypothetical world without paper money. Wicksell asserted three equilibrium conditions that the interest rate should satisfy; the first of these was that the market rate should equal the rate that would prevail if capital goods were lent and borrowed in kind (*in natura*). This criterion was later shown by Myrdal, Sraffa and others not to have an unambiguous meaning outside the single input-single output world of Wicksell's example. The further development of Wicksellian theory, therefore, centred around the two remaining criteria: saving-investment coordination and price level stability.

The interest rate has two jobs to do. It should coordinate household saving decisions with enterpreneurial investment decisions and it should balance the supply and demand for credit. If the supply of credit were always to equal saving and the demand for credit investment the two conditions could always be met simultaneously. But there is no such necessary relationship between saving and investment on the one hand and credit supply and demand on the other. In Wicksell's system the banks make the market for credit; they may, for instance, go beyond the mere intermediation of saving and finance additional investment by creating money; the injection of money drives a wedge between saving and investment; this could only be so if the banks set the market rate below the 'natural' value required for the intertemporal coordination of real activities. The resulting inflation and endogenous growth of the money supply would continue as long as the banking system maintained the market rate below the natural rate. Wicksell analysed the case of a 'pure credit' economy in which the cumulative process could go on indefinitely, but he also pointed out that, in a gold standard world, the banks would eventually be checked by the need to maintain precautionary balances of reserve media in some proportion to their demand obligations.

Wicksell used the model to explain long-term trends in the price-level and was critical of those who, like Gustav Cassel, used it to explain the business cycle. Nonetheless, subsequent developments of his ideas went altogether in the direction of shorter-run macroeconomic theory. In Sweden, Erik Lindahl (1939) and Gunnar Myrdal (1939) refined the conceptual apparatus, in particular by introducing the distinction between *ex ante* plans and *ex post* realizations and thereby clarifying the relationship between Wicksellian theory and national income analysis. The attempts by the Stockholm School to improve on Wicksell's treatment of expectations were less successful, however, producing a brand of generalized process-analysis in which almost 'everything could happen'.

In Austria, Ludwig von Mises and Friedrich von Hayek focused on the allocation consequences of the Wicksellian inflation story. The Austrian over-investment theory of the business cycle became known to English-speaking economists primarily through Hayek's *Prices and Production* (1931). In expanding the money supply, the banks hold market rate below natural rate. At this disequilibrium interest rate, the business sector will plan to accumulate capital at a rate higher than the planned saving of the household sector. If the banks lend only to business, the entrepreneurs are able to realize their investment plans whereas households will be unable to realize their consumption plans ('forced saving'). The too rapid accumulation of capital (which also has the wrong temporal structure) cannot be sustained indefinitely. The eventual collapse of the boom may then be exacerbated by a credit crisis as some entrepreneurs are unable to repay their bank loans.

The Austrian *monetary* theory of the cycle has been overshadowed first by Keynesian 'real' macrotheory and later by Monetarist theory. One problem with it is the firm association of inflation with overinvestment. The US stagflation in the 1970s, for example, will not fit. The reasons lie largely in the changes that the monetary system has undergone. Most obviously, commercial banks now lend to all sectors and not only to business. More importantly, however, inflation in a pure fiat regime does not tend to distort intertemporal values in any particular direction (although it may destroy the system's capacity for coordinating activities over time): it simply blows up the nominal scale of real magnitudes at a more or less steady or predictable rate. In contrast, the Austrian situation that preoccupied Mises and Hayek in the late 1920s was one of credit expansion by a small open economy on the gold standard. Given the inelastic nominal expectations appropriate to this regime, the growth of inside money would be associated with the distortion of relative prices and misallocation effects predicted by the Austrian theory.

In England, Dennis Robertson and J. Maynard Keynes both worked along Wicksellian lines in the 1920s. The novel and complicated technology of Robertson's *Banking Policy and the Price Level* (1926) may have made the work less influential than it deserved. Keynes's *Treatise on Money*, although also remembered as a flawed work, nonetheless remains important as a link in the development of macroeconomics from Wicksell to the *General Theory*.

In the *Treatise*, Keynes, like Wicksell, assumes that the process starts with a real impulse, i.e., a change in investment expectations. Unlike Wicksell, he focuses on deflation rather than inflation. For Keynes with his City experience, *the* interest rate was determined on the Exchange rather than set by the banks. Consequently, a deflationary situation with the market rate exceeding the natural rate can only arise when bearish speculation keeps the rate from declining. When saving exceeds investment, therefore, money leaks out of the circular spending flow into the idle balances of bear-speculators. Thus the analysis stresses declining velocity rather than endogenously declining money stock. At this stage of the development of Keynesian economics, the banks are already edging out of the theoretical field of vision and the original connection of natural rate theorizing with criteria for neutral money is by and large severed.

The model of the *Treatise* still assumes that, when market rate exceeds the natural rate, the resulting excess supply of present goods will cause falling spot prices but not unemployment of present resources. Although the focus is on a disequilibrium process, at a deeper level the theory is still comfortingly classical. As long as the economy remains at full employment, the bear-speculators who are maintaining the disequilibrium are forced, period after period, to sell income-earning securities and accumulate cash at a rate corresponding to the difference between household saving and business sector investment. Automatic market forces, therefore, are seen to put those responsible for the undervaluation of physical capital under inexorably mounting pressure to allow correction of the market rate. And the longer those agents acting on incorrect expectations persist in obstructing the intertemporal coordination of activities, the larger the losses that they will eventually suffer.

In the *General Theory*, Keynes starts the story in the same way: investment expectations take a turn for the worse – 'the marginal efficiency of capital declines'; the speculative demand for money prevents the interest rate from falling sufficiently to equate *ex ante* saving with investment. But at this point the *General*

Theory takes a different tack: the excess supply of present resources, which is the immediate result of the failure of intertemporal price adjustments to bring intertemporal coordination, is eliminated through falling output and employment. Real income falls until saving has been reduced to the new lower investment level.

This change in the lag-structure of Keynes's theory ('quantities reacting before prices') is not necessarily revolutionary by itself. But Keynes combines it with the assumption that the subsequent price adjustments will be governed, in Clower's terminology, not by 'notional' but by 'effective' excess demands. For the economy to reach a new general equilibrium, on a lower growth path, interest rates should fall but money wages stay what they are. Following the real income response, however, saving no longer exceeds investment so there is no accumulating pressure on the interest rate from this quarter; at the same time, unemployment does put effective pressure on wage rates. Interest rates, which should fall, do not: wages, which should not, do. From this point, Keynes went on to argue that nominal wage reductions would not eliminate unemployment unless, in the process, they happened to produce a correction of relative prices (an eventuality that he considered unlikely). This argument was the basis for his 'revolutionary' claim that a failure of saving-investment coordination could end with the economy in 'unemployment equilibrium'.

Prior to the *General Theory*, writers in the Wicksellian tradition had generally treated 'saving exceeds investment' and 'market rate exceeds natural rate' as interchangeable characterizations of the same intertemporal disequilibrium. The basic proposition could be couched equally well in terms of quantities as in terms of prices. In the *General Theory*, Keynes moved away from this language. Constructing a model with output and employment variable in the short run was a novel task and Keynes, as the pioneer, was unsure in his handling of expected, intended and realized magnitudes. Thus his preoccupation with the 'necessary equality' of saving and investment (*ex post*) was to produce endless confusion over interest theory. If saving and investment are always equal, the interest rate cannot be governed by the difference between them; nor can the interest rate mechanism possibly coordinate saving and investment decisions. To Keynes, two things seemed to follow. One was the substitution of the liquidity preference theory of the interest rate for the loanable funds theory; the other was the abandonment of the concept of a 'natural' rate of interest (Leijonhufvud, 1981, pp. 169 ff.).

These were not innocent terminological adjustments. The brand of Keynesian economics that developed on the basis of the IS–LM model had only a shaky grasp at the best of times of the intertemporal coordination problem originally at the heart of Keynes's theory. The Keynesian position shifted already at an early stage back to the pre-Keynesian hypothesis of money wage 'rigidity' as the cause of unemployment. This switched the focus of analytical attention away from the role of intertemporal relative prices (the market rate) in the coordination of saving and investment to the relationship between aggregate money expenditures and money wages. This brand of 'Keynesian' theory which excludes the saving-investment problem (i.e., excludes the market-natural rate problem) can hardly be distinguished from Monetarism in any theoretically significant way – unless, of course, the habitual insistence that money wages are more rigid than monetarists would like to believe be judged a significant Keynesian principle.

BIBLIOGRAPHY

Cassel, G. 1928. The rate of interest, the bank rate, and the stabilization of prices. *Quarterly Journal of Economics* 42, August, 511–29.

Hayek, F.A. 1931. *Prices and Production.* London: Routledge & Kegan Paul; 2nd ed, New York: Augustus M. Kelley, 1967.

Humphrey, T.M. 1986. Cumulative process models from Thornton to Wicksell. *Federal Reserve Bank of Richmond Economic Review,* May–June.

Keynes, J.M. 1930. *A Treatise on Money.* 2 vols, London: Macmillan; New York: St. Martin's Press, 1971.

Keynes, J.M. 1936. *The General Theory of Employment, Interest and Money.* London: Macmillan; New York: Harcourt, Brace.

Leijonhufvud, A. 1981. The Wicksell connection. In A. Leijonhufvud, *Information and Coordination,* New York: Oxford University Press.

Lindahl, E. 1939. *Studies in the Theory of Money and Capital.* New York: Holt, Rinehart & Winston.

Myrdal, G. 1939. *Monetary Equilibrium.* Edinburgh: William Hodge.

Palander, T. 1941. On the concepts and methods of the Stockholm School. *International Economic Papers* No. 3, London: Macmillan, 1953.

Robertson, D.H. 1926. *Banking Policy and the Price Level.* New York: Augustus M. Kelley, 1949.

Wicksell, K. 1898. *Interest and Prices.* New York: Augustus M. Kelley, 1962.

Wicksell, K. 1906. *Lectures on Political Economy,* Vol. II. London: Routledge & Kegan Paul, 1934; New York: A.M. Kelley, 1967.

Neutrality of Money

DON PATINKIN

'Neutrality of money' is a shorthand expression for the basic quantity-theory proposition that it is only the level of prices in an economy, and not the level of its real outputs, that is affected by the quantity of money which circulates in it. Thus the notion – though not the term – goes back to early statements of the quantity theory, such as the classic one by David Hume in his 1752 essays 'Of Money', 'Of Interest' and 'Of the Balance of Trade'. At that time the notion also served as one of the arguments against the mercantilist doctrine that the wealth of a nation was to be measured by the quantity of gold (which in 18th-century England constituted a – if not the – major form of metallic money: Feaveryear, 1963, p. 158) that it possessed. The term itself is much more recent. It was introduced into the English-speaking world by Hayek (1931, pp. 27–8), who attributed it to Wicksell (1898). Actually, however, the term in the above sense came into use only later and is due to German and Dutch economists in the decade following World War I to whom (while continuing to attribute the term to Wicksell) Hayek (1935, pp. 129ff) subsequently referred (for details, see Patinkin and Steiger, 1989).

1. The rigorous demonstration of the neutrality of money is based on the critical assumption that individuals are free of 'money illusion'. An individual is said to suffer from such an illusion if he changes his economic behaviour when a currency conversion takes place: when, for example (as in Israel in 1985), a new monetary unit – the 'new shekel' – is introduced in circulation and declared to be equivalent to 1000 old shekels.

It can be shown (Patinkin, 1965) that an illusion-free individual in an economy with borrowing who maximizes utility subject to his budget constraint will have demand functions which depend on relative prices, the rate of interest, and the real value of his initial wealth – which consists of physical capital, bond holdings, and money balances. That is, the demand of this representative individual for the jth good, d_j, is described by the function

$$d_j = f_j(p_1/p, \ldots, p_{n-2}/p, r, K_0 + B_0/p + M_0/p) \qquad (j = 1, \ldots, n-2),$$

where the p_j are the respective money (or absolute) prices of the $n-2$ goods;

273

p is the average price level as defined by $p = \Sigma_j w_j p_j$, where the w_j are fixed weights; r is the rate of interest; K_0 is physical capital, B_0 is the initial nominal value of bond holdings (which, for a debtor, is negative), and M_0 is the initial quantity of money. Thus when the new shekel is introduced in circulation, the price of each good in terms of this shekel (and hence the general price level), the terms of indebtedness, and the nominal quantity of initial money holdings are respectively reduced to 1/1000th of what they were before; hence relative prices and the real value of initial wealth are unaffected; hence so are the amounts demanded of each good.

Mathematically, the foregoing property of the demand functions is described by the statement that these functions are homogenous of degree zero in the money prices *and* in the initial quantity of financial assets, including money. Accordingly, the absence of money illusion is sometimes referred to as the homogeneity property of the demand functions. (For the necessary and sufficient conditions that must be satisfied by the utility function in order to generate such illusion-free demand functions, see Howitt and Patinkin, 1980.) This homogeneity property is to be sharply distinguished from what the earlier literature denoted as the 'homogeneity postulate', by which it meant the invariance of demand functions with respect to an equiproportionate change in money prices alone, and which invariance it erroneously regarded as the condition for the absence of money illusion and hence for the neutrality of money (Leontief, 1936; p. 192; Modigliani, 1944, pp. 214–15): for even in the case of an individual who is neither debtor nor creditor, such a change affects the real value of his initial money balances, hence is not analogous to a change in the monetary unit, and hence – by virtue of the real-balance effect – will generally lead him to change the amounts he demands of the various goods.

For a closed economy, the aggregate value of B_0 is obviously zero, for to each creditor there corresponds a debtor. For simplicity, we can also consider the amount of physical capital, K_0, to remain constant. Disregarding distribution effects, the demand functions of the economy as a whole for the $n-2$ goods can then be represented by

$$D_j = F_j(p_1/p, \ldots, p_{n-2}/p, r, M_0/p) \qquad (j = 1, \ldots, n-2)$$

and the corresponding supply functions by

$$S_j = G_j(p_1/p, \ldots, p_{n-2}/p, r).$$

The general-equilibrium system of the economy is then

$$F_1(p_1/p, \ldots, p_{n-2}/p, r, M_0/p) = G_1(p_1/p, \ldots, p_{n-2}/p, r)$$

$$\vdots \qquad \vdots \qquad \vdots$$

$$F_{n-2}(p_1/p, \ldots, p_{n-2}/p, r, M_0/p) = G_{n-2}(p_1/p, \ldots, p_{n-2}/p, r)$$

$$F_{n-1}(p_1/p, \ldots, p_{n-2}/p, r, M_0/p) = 0$$

$$F_n(p_1/p, \ldots, p_{n-2}/p, r, M_0/p) = M_0/p.$$

The $(n-1)$st equation is for real bond holdings, whose aggregate net value is (as already noted) zero; and the nth equation is for real money balances. Assume that this system has a unique equilibrium solution with money prices $p_1^0, \ldots, p_{n-2}^0, p^0$ and the rate of interest r^0, and that the economy is initially at this position. Let the quantity of money now be changed to kM_0, where k is some positive constant. From the preceding system of equations we can immediately see that (on the further assumption that the system is stable) the economy will reach a new equilibrium position with money prices $kp_1^0, \ldots, kp_{n-2}^0, kp^0$ and an unchanged rate of interest r^0. (Clearly, this conclusion would continue to hold if the supply functions $G_j(\quad)$ were also dependent on M_0/p.) Thus the increased quantity of money does not affect any of the real variables of the system: namely, relative prices, the rate of interest, the real value of money balances, and hence the respective outputs of the $n-2$ goods. In brief, money is neutral: or in the picturesque phrase which Robertson (1922, p. 1) apparently coined, money is a veil. (For empirical studies, see Lucas, 1980, and Lothian, 1985.)

Furthermore, Archibald and Lipsey (1958) have shown that if the initial equilibrium exists not only with respect to the economy as a whole, but also with respect to each and every individual in it (which, *inter alia*, means that each individual was initially holding his optimum quantity of money), then this neutrality will obtain in the long run even if one does take account of distribution effects. That is, even if one takes account of differences in tastes, endowments, and hence individual demand functions – an increase in the quantity of money, no matter how distributed among individuals, will in the long run cause an equiproportionate increase in prices and leave the rate of interest variant. This conclusion in turn follows from the fact that the sequence of short-run equilibria generated by the increase in the quantity of money will in the long run redistribute this quantity in a way that results in an equiproportionate increase in the money holdings of each individual, relative to his holdings in the initial equilibrium position (see also Patinkin, 1965, pp. 50–59).

It should also be noted that the preceding analysis has implicitly assumed a unitary elasticity of expectations with respect to future prices, so that neutrality is not disturbed by substitution between present and future commodities.

2. The conclusions of the foregoing analysis are clearly those of long-run comparative-statics analysis. It was this fact that led Keynes – even in his quantity-theory period as represented by his *Tract on Monetary Reform* (1923) – to disparage their policy implications with the famous remark that '*in the long run* we are all dead' (1923, p. 80, italics in original). It should therefore be emphasized that at the same time they demonstrated the long-run neutrality of money, quantity theorists (including Keynes of the *Tract*) also emphasized its non-neutrality in the short run (Patinkin, 1972a). Thus Hume emphasized that prices do not immediately rise proportionately to the increased quantity of money and that in the intervening period this stimulates production. In Hume's words:

it is of no manner of consequence, with regard to the domestic happiness of a state, whether money be in a greater or less quantity. The good policy of the magistrate consists only in keeping it, if possible, still increasing; because, by that means, he keeps alive a spirit of industry in the nation ... (1752, pp. 39–40).

Hume's emphasis on the irrelevance of the absolute level of the money supply (and hence of money prices) in contrast with the significance of the rate of change of this level was also made by later quantity-theorists. Some of them stressed the stimulating effects of rising prices on 'business confidence' and hence economic activity. A more frequent explanation of the short-run non-neutrality of money was in terms of the shift in the distribution of real income as between creditors and debtors generated by a changing price level. Of particular importance was the danger that a sharply declining price level would increase the number of bankruptcies among debtors, will all its adverse repercussions on the economy. Another source of non-neutrality was the fact that individual prices do not change at the same rate in response to a monetary change. Thus if after a monetary decrease, wage rigidities cause the decline in wages to lag behind that of product-prices, the resulting increase in the real wage rate would generate unemployment; conversely, the lag of wages in the case of an inflation would increase profits and hence stimulate production. This consideration led some quantity-theorists to deny even the long-run neutrality of money on the grounds that profit-recipients had a higher tendency to save than wage-earners, so that the shift in income in favour of profits would increase savings, and that these 'forced savings' would lead to an increase in the real stock of physical capital in the economy, and hence to a decline in the long-run rate of interest.

For Irving Fisher, the important lag was that of the nominal rate of interest behind the rate of (say) inflation generated by a monetary increase. In particular, because of the lack of perfect foresight on the part of savers (who are the lenders), the nominal rate does not rise sufficiently to offset this inflation; and the resulting decline in the real rate of interest causes entrepreneurs to increase their borrowings, hence investments and economic activity in general. Conversely, when prices decline, corresponding misperceptions cause an increase in the real rate of interest and hence a decline in economic activity. Indeed, Fisher (1913, ch. 4) based his whole theory of the business cycle on this process: the cycle was for him 'the dance of the dollar' (Fisher, 1923).

The greatly increased importance of income and capital-gains taxation since Fisher's time is the background of the present-day view – much stressed by Feldstein (1982, and references there cited) – that inflation would have real effects on the economy even if there were perfect foresight, so that the nominal rate fully adjusted itself to the rate of inflation, leaving the real rate of interest unchanged. This is particularly true for the taxation of income from capital, with the simplest example being the increased tax burden on corporations generated by the calculation of depreciation expenses on the basis of historical (as distinct from replacement) costs in an inflationary economy (see also Birati and Cukierman, 1979). This is a specific instance of the short-run non-neutrality of money generated by the existence of a tax structure formulated in nominal terms (as is the case with, for example, specific taxes and income-tax brackets) which are generally adjusted to the rate of inflation only after a lag.

Short-run non-neutrality is a basic feature of Keynesian monetary theory and stems from the contention that in a situation of unemployment, prices will not rise proportionately to the increased quantity of money, and that the resulting increase in the real quantity of money will cause a decline in the rate of increase and hence an increase in the volume of investment and the level of national income. The short-run non-neutrality of money is, however, also a basic tenet of today's monetarists, who contend that though the long-run effect of a change in the quantity of money is primarily on prices, its short-run effect is primarily on output. In Friedman's words: 'In the short run, which may be as much as five or ten years, monetary changes affect primarily output. Over decades, on the other hand, the rate of monetary growth affects primarily prices' (Friedman, 1970, pp. 23–4).

This non-neutrality has been rationalized by Lucas (1972) in terms of the individual's inability to determine whether a change in the price of a good with which he is particularly concerned (e.g., labour, in the case of a wage-earner) is a change only in the price of that good (in which case it represents a change in its relative price, which calls for a quantity adjustment) or is part of a general change in prices which does not affect relative prices. In accordance with this approach, and under the assumption that markets always clear, it has also been claimed that only an unanticipated change in the quantity of money will have real effects; for an anticipated one will be expected by the individual to affect all prices proportionately (Lucas, 1975; Barro, 1976). A far-reaching corollary of this claim is that if, in accordance with the assumption of rational expectations, the public anticipates the actions that government will carry out within the framework of its proclaimed monetary policy, then this policy too will be neutral: that is, the systematic component of monetary policy will not affect any of the real variables of the system (cf. McCallum, 1980 and references there cited). Thus under these circumstances even the short-run Phillips curve is – from the viewpoint of systematic monetary policy – vertical.

Empirical support for the claim that only unanticipated monetary changes will have real effects was at first provided by Sargent (1976) and Barro (1978). Contrary conclusions were, however, reached in subsequent empirical studies by Fischer (1980), Boschen and Grossman (1982), Gordon (1982), Mishkin (1982, 1983) and Cecchetti (1986). These differing conclusions stem from different views about the respective ways to estimate (1) that part of a monetary change that is anticipated and/or (2) the extent of the time lags that must be taken account of in measuring the effects of a monetary change on output. In any event, the weight of opinion today is than both anticipated and unanticipated changes in the money supply have short-term real effects. To the extent that anticipated changes have such effects, this can be interpreted either as reflecting the influence of nominally formulated elements (e.g., the aforementioned tax structure, or long-term wage contracts (Fischer, 1977)) in an economy functioning in accordance with the hypothesis of rational-expectations *cum* market-clearing; or, alternatively, it can be interpreted as a refutation of this hypothesis in part or in whole. Thus once again we are confronted with *la condition scientifique* of our discipline: its inability in all too many cases to reach definitive conclusions about theoretical questions on the basis of empirical studies, an inability which increases directly with the political significance of the question at issue.

3. Neoclassical quantity-theorists contended that a shift in the demand curve for money would also have a long-run neutral effect on the economy. Thus consider the Cambridge cash-balance equation, $M = KPY$, where Y is the real volume of expenditures and K is that proportion of his planned money expenditures, PY, which the individual wishes to hold in the form of money. Assume that the economy is in equilibrium with a fixed quantity of money M_0 and price level P_0. Let there now take place a positive shift in the demand for money – that is, an increase in K. Because of the budget constraint, this must be accompanied by a negative shift in the demand for goods. Consequently, the price level P will decline until equilibrium is reestablished with the same nominal quantity of money, M_0, but at a lower price level, $P_1 < P_0$. Thus the automatic functioning of the market will in the long run generate the additional quantity of real balances that individuals wish to hold, without affecting the output of goods.

This neutrality can also be demonstrated in terms of the general-equilibrium system presented above. In particular, if we assume that the increased demand for money is accompanied by a symmetric decrease in the demand for all other goods and for bonds, then a new equilibrium will be established with all money prices reduced in the same proportion, and with an unchanged rate of interest; correspondingly, the respective outputs of goods are also unchanged. In Keynesian monetary theory, however, the increased demand for money is assumed to be solely at the expense of bond holdings: this, after all, is an implication of Keynes's theory of liquidity preference. Such a shift in liquidity preference will accordingly not be neutral in its effects; instead, it will cause an increase in the rate of interest with consequent effects on investment and other real variables of the system (Patinkin, 1965, chs VIII:5 and X:4).

In an analogous manner, a change in the proportions between inside and outside money generated by a change in the currency/deposit ratio and/or the bank-reserve/deposit ratio will not be neutral in its effects (Gurley and Shaw, 1960, pp. 231–6). It should, however, be emphasized that if the demand and supply functions of the financial sector are also characterized by absence of money illusion, then an increase in outside money will leave these ratios unchanged and hence be neutral (Patinkin, 1965, ch. XII: 5–6).

So far, our concern has implicitly been an increase in the quantity of money generated by a one-time government deficit, after which the government returns to a balanced budget. This results in an initial net increase in the total of financial assets in the economy and is thus the real-world analytical counterpart of an increase in the quantity of money generated by the proverbial helicopter dropping down money from the skies. If, however, the monetary increase is generated by an open-market purchase of government bonds (so that initially there is no change in total financial assets), and if there is a real-balance effect in the commodity market, then, as Metzler (1951) showed in a classic article, the equilibrium rate of interest will decline, so that money will not be neutral in its effects. If, however, individuals fully anticipate and discount the future stream of tax payments needed to service the government bonds (in which case these bonds are not part of net wealth), neutrality will obtain in this case too (Patinkin, 1965, ch. XII:4).

4. The discussion until this point has dealt almost entirely with the neutrality of a once-and-for-all increase in the quantity of money in a stationary economy. An analogous question arises with reference to the long-run neutrality of a change in the rate of growth of the money supply in a growing economy – in which context the notion is referred to as 'superneutrality'. Thus consider an economy in steady-state equilibrium whose population is growing at the rate n. Assume that the nominal quantity of money is growing at a faster rate, $\mu = \dot{M}/M$, so that (in order to maintain the constant level of per-capita real money balances that is one of the characteristics of such a steady state) prices rise at the constant rate $\pi = \mu - n$. Money is said to be superneutral if (say) an increase in the steady-state rate of its expansion, and hence in the corresponding rate of inflation, will not affect any of the steady-state real variables in the system, with the exception of per-capita real-balances: that is, per capita, k; per-capita output, y; and the real rate of interest, r, equal to the marginal productivity of capital. On the other hand, because of the higher costs of holding real balances – in terms of loss of purchasing power, or, alternatively, in terms of the foregone higher nominal rate of interest, i, generated by the increased rate of inflation – the steady-state per capita real value of these balances, m, should generally be expected to decrease.

As already indicated, for Irving Fisher (1907, ch. 5; 1913, pp. 59–60; 1930, pp. 43–4) it was only the absence of perfect foresight which prevented such superneutrality from obtaining; for were such foresight to exist, the nominal rate of interest would simply increase so as to compensate for the inflation and thus leave the real rate of interest (which, under the assumption of continuous compounding, equals $i - \pi$) unchanged. Fisher, however, did not take account of the possible effects of the way the increased amount of money is injected into the economy and/or the possible effects of the resulting decrease in real balances on other markets. Thus by assuming that the government increases the quantity of money in the economy by distributing it to households and thereby increasing their disposable income, Tobin (1965, 1967) – in a generalization of the Solow (1956) growth model to a money economy – showed that a higher rate of inflation will generally cause individuals to change the composition of their asset-portfolios by shifting out of real money balances and into physical capital, thus increasing the steady-state values of k and y – and hence (by the law of diminishing returns) decreasing that of r – so that superneutrality does not obtain.

Tobin's analysis assumes a constant savings ratio. In a critique of this analysis, Levhari and Patinkin (1968) showed *inter alia* that if instead this ratio is assumed to depend positively on the respective rates of return on capital and on real money balances – that is, on the real rate of interest and on the rate of deflation – then an increase in the rate of inflation might decrease steady-state savings and hence k, thus causing an increase in the real rate of interest. Similarly, if real money balances were explicitly introduced into the production function, an increase in the rate of inflation might so decrease these balances as to decrease steady-state per-capita output and hence savings sufficiently to offset the positive substitution effect on k, thus generating a decrease in the latter.

Patinkin (1972b) analyzed superneutrality by means of an IS-LM model generalized to a full employment economy with a real-balance effect in the commodity market (the following largely reproduces the relevant material in this reference). As in Solow (1956), the economy is assumed to have a linearly homogeneous production function, $Y = F(K, L)$, where Y is output, K capital, and L labour, with the labour force assumed to be growing at the exogenous rate n. The intensive form of this function is then $y = f(k)$ and its derivative, $f'(k)$, is accordingly the marginal productivity of capital, so that the equilibrium real rate of interest is $r = f'(k)$. Following Mundell (1963, 1965), the crucial assumption of this model is that whereas investment and saving (and hence consumption) decisions depend upon the real rate of interest, $r = i - \pi$, the decision with respect to the amount of real money balances to hold depends on the nominal rate of interest, i – for the alternative cost of holding money instead of a bond is precisely this rate. The same is true if we measure this cost in terms of the alternative of holding physical capital: for the total yield on this capital is its marginal product (equal in equilibrium to the real rate of interest) *plus* the capital gain generated by the price change (π): that is, it is $r + \pi = i$. Alternatively, if we measure rates of return in real terms, the rate of return on money balances is $-\pi$ and that on physical capital r; hence the alternative cost of holding money is the difference between these two rates, or $r - (-\pi) = i$.

Consider now the commodity market. Let E represent the aggregate real demand for consumption and investment commodities combined. For simplicity, assume that this demand is a certain proportion, α, of total real income, Y. Assume further that this proportion depends inversely on the real rate of interest and directly on the ratio of real money balances, M/p, to physical capital, K. The second dependence is a type of real-balance effect, reflecting the assumption that the greater the ratio of real money balances to physical capital in the portfolios of individuals, the more they will tend (for any given level of income) to shift out of money and into commodities. The equilibrium condition in the commodity market is then represented by

$$\alpha(i - \pi, (M/p)/K) \cdot Y = Y \tag{1}$$

By assumption, $\alpha_1(\ )$ is negative and $\alpha_2(\ )$ positive, where $\alpha_1(\alpha_2)$ is the partial derivative of $\alpha(\ )$ with respect to its first (second) argument.

Consider now the money market. Following Tobin (1965, p. 679), assume that the demand in this market depends on the volume of physical capital and the nominal rate of interest. More specifically, assume that the demand for money is a certain proportion, λ, of physical capital. Thus the larger K, the greater (other things equal) the total portfolio of the individuals, hence the greater the demand for money: this can be designated as the scale of wealth effect of the portfolio. Assume further that the proportion λ depends inversely on the nominal rate of interest. That is, the higher this rate, the smaller the proportion of money relative to physical capital which individuals wish to hold in their portfolios: this can be designated as the composition or substitution effect. The equilibrium condition in the money market is then

$$\lambda(i)\cdot K = M/p \tag{2}$$

where by assumption the derivative $\lambda'(\quad)$ is negative.

Dividing equations (1) and (2) through by Y and K, respectively – and transforming them into per capita form – we then obtain the equations

$$\alpha(i - \pi, m/k) = 1 \tag{3}$$

$$\lambda(i) = m/k. \tag{4}$$

In the steady state,

$$\mu = \pi + n. \tag{5}$$

Since μ and n are both assumed to be exogenously determined, the same can be said for the steady-state value of π. Thus in steady-states, equations (3) and (4) can be considered as a system of two equations in the two endogenous variables i and m/k, and in the exogenous variable π. Assuming solubility of these equations, the specific value of k (and hence m) can then be determined by making use of the additional equilibrium condition that the marginal productivity of capital equals the real rate of interest, or,

$$f'(k) = i - \pi. \tag{6}$$

In accordance with the usual assumption of diminishing marginal productivity, we also have

$$f''(k) < 0. \tag{7}$$

The solution of system (3)–(4) can be presented diagramatically in terms of Figure 1. The curve CC represents the locus of points of equilibrium in the commodity market for a given value of π. Its positive slope reflects the assumption made above about the respective influences of the real rate of interest $(i - \pi)$ and of the real-balance effect (as represented by m/k) on α. Namely, a (say) increase in i increases the real rate of interest and thus tends to decrease α: hence the ratio m/k must increase in order to generate a compensating increase in α and thus restore equilibrium to the commodity market. On the other hand, LL – the locus of points of equilibriums in the money market – must be negatively sloped: an increase in the supply of money and hence in m/k must be offset by a corresponding increase in the demand for money, which means that i must decline. The intersection of the two curves at W thus determines the steady-state position of the economy.

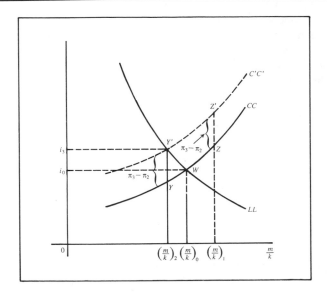

Figure 1

Assume for simplicity that the given value of π for which CC and LL are drawn is $\pi = \pi_2 > 0$, corresponding to the rate of monetary expansion μ_2. Assume now that this rate is exogenously increased to $\mu = \mu_3$, so that (by (5)) the steady-state value of π is increased accordingly to $\pi_3 = \mu_3 - n > \pi_2$. From the fact that π does not appear in (4), it is clear that LL remains invariant under this change. On the other hand, the curve CC must shift upwards in a parallel fashion by the distance $\pi_3 - \pi_2$: for at (say) the point Z' on the curve $C'C'$ so constructed, the money/capital ratio m/k and the real rate of interest $i - \pi$ are the same as they were at point Z on the original curve CC; hence Z' too must be a position of equilibrium in the commodity market.

We can therefore conclude from Figure 1 that the increase in the rate of monetary expansion (and hence rate of inflation) shifts the steady-state position of the economy from W to Y'. From the construction of $C'C'$ it is also clear that the real rate of interest at Y' is $r_3 = i_3 - \pi_3$, which is less than the real rate at W, namely, $r_0 = i_0 - \pi_2$. Thus the policy of increasing the rate of inflation decreases the steady-state value of the real rate of interest, and also the money/capital ratio.

Because of the diminishing marginal productivity of capital, the decline in r implies that k has increased. Thus the fact that m/k has declined does not necessarily imply that m has declined. This indeterminacy reflects the two opposing influences operating on m reflected in equation (2), rewritten here in the *per capita* form as

$$\lambda(i) \cdot k = m. \tag{8}$$

To use the terminology indicated above, the increased inflation increases the steady-state stock of physical capital, and thus exerts a positive wealth effect on

282

the quantity of real-money balances demanded. At the same time, the increased inflation means that the alternative cost of holding money balances (for a given level of k and hence r) has increased, and this exerts a negative substitution effect on the demand for these balances; that is, individuals will tend to shift out of money and into capital. Thus the final effect on m depends on the relative strength of these two forces. As is, however, generally assumed in economic theory, we shall assume that the substitution effect dominates, so that an increase in π decreases m.

We now note that the only exogenous variable which appears in system (3)–(5) is the rate of change of the money supply, as represented by its steady-state surrogate, $\pi = \mu - n$. In contrast, the absolute quantity of money, M, does not appear. It follows that once-and-for-all changes in M (after which the money supply continues to grow at the same rate) will not affect the steady-state values of m, k, and i as determined by the foregoing system for a given value of π. In brief, system (3)–(5) continues to reflect the neutrality of money. On the other hand, because of the Keynesian-like interdependence between the commodity and money markets, the system is not superneutral.

Note that in the absence of this interdependence, the system would also be superneutral. This would be the case either if the demand for commodities depended only on the real rate of interest, and not on m/k (i.e., if there were no real-balance effect); or if the demand for money depended on k, and not on the nominal rate of interest – an unrealistic assumption, particularly in inflationary situations which cause this rate to increase greatly.

The first of these cases is analogous to the dichotimized case of stationary macroeconomic models (cf. Patinkin, 1965, pp. 242, 251 (n.19), and 297–8). It would be represented in Figure 1 by a CC curve which was horizontal to the abscissa. Correspondingly, the upward shift generated by the rate of inflation would cause the new CC curve to intersect the unchanged LL curve at a money rate of interest which was $\pi_3 - \pi_2$ greater than the original one, and hence at a real rate of interest (and hence value of k) which was unchanged; the value of m, however, would unequivocally decline. The second of these cases would be represented by a vertical LL curve. Hence the upward parallel shift in the CC curve generated by inflation would once again shift the intersection point to one which represented an unchanged real rate of interest. In this case (which, as already noted, is an unrealistic one) the value of m also remains unchanged.

5. A common characteristic of the foregoing money-and-growth models is that their respective savings functions are postulated and not derived from utility maximization. An analysis which does derive consumption (and hence savings) behaviour from such maximization was presented by Sidrauski (1967) in an influential article. As before, consider an economy growing at the constant rate n with a linearly homogenous production function having the intensive form $y = f(k)$. Assume now that the representative individual of this economy is infinitely-lived with a utility function which depends on consumption and real balances, and that he maximizes the discounted value of this function over infinite

time, using the constant subjective rate of time preference, q. Under these assumptions, Sidrauski shows that money is superneutral.

As Sidrauski is fully aware, this conclusion follows from the form of his production function together with his assumption of a constant rate of time preference; for this fixes the steady-state real rate of interest at $r = q + n = f'(k)$, which determines the steady-state value of k and hence of r. If, however, the production function depends also on real balances – say, $y = g(k,m)$ – then this superneutrality no longer obtains. For the necessary equality between the marginal productivity of capital and $q + n$ in this case is expressed by the equation $g_k(k,m) = q + n$ (where $g_k(k,m)$ is the partial derivative with respect to k), which no longer fixes the value of k (Levhari and Patinkin, 1968, p. 234). In an analogous argument, Brock (1974) showed that if the individual's utility function depends also on leisure, then an increase in the rate of inflation will affect his demand for leisure, which means that it will affect his supply of labour (i.e. labour *per capita*). Hence even though (in accordance with Sidrauski's argument) the increased rate of inflation will not affect the steady-state values of r, k (i.e. capital per *labour-input*), and y (i.e., output per *labour-input*), it will affect the respective amounts of labour and capital *per capita* and hence output *per capita* – so that it will not be superneutral. Needless to say, Sidrauski's results will also not obtain if the rate of time preference is not constant.

6. The conclusion that can be drawn from this discussion is that whereas there is a firm theoretical basis for attributing long-run neutrality to money (but see Gale, 1982, pp. 7–58, and Grandmont, 1983, pp. 38–45, 91–5), there is no such basis for long-run superneutrality: for changes in the rate of growth of the nominal money supply and hence in the rate of inflation generally cause changes in the long-run equilibrium level of real balances; and if there are enough avenues of substitution between these balances and other real variables in the system (viz., commodities, physical capital, leisure), then the long-run equilibrium levels of these variables will also be affected. An exception to this generalization would obtain if money were to earn a rate of interest which varied one-to-one with the rate of inflation, so that the alternative cost of holding money balances would not be affected by changes in the latter rate; but though it is generally true that interest (though not necessarily at the foregoing rate) will eventually be paid on the inside money (i.e. bank deposits) of economies characterized by significant long-run inflation, this is not the case for the outside money which is a necessary (though in modern times quantitatively relatively small) component of any monetary system.

The discussion to this point has treated the economy's output as a single homogeneous quantity. A more detailed analysis which considers the sectoral composition of this output yields another manifestation of the absence of superneutrality. In particular, it is a commonplace that the higher the rate of inflation, the higher the so-called 'shoe-leather costs' of running to and from the banks and other financial institutions in order to carry out economic activity with smaller real money balances. In the case of households, the resulting loss of leisure is denoted as the 'welfare costs of inflation' as measured by the loss of consumers' surplus: that is, by the reduction in the triangular area under the demand curve for real money balances (cf. Bailey, 1956). In the case of businesses, the costs of inflation take the concrete form of the costs of the additional time and efforts devoted to managing the cash flow. What must now be emphasized is that the obverse side of the additional efforts of both households and businesses are the additional resources that must be diverted to the financial sector of the economy in order to enable it to meet the increased demand for its services. Thus the higher the rate of inflation, the higher (say) the proportion of the labour force of an economy employed in its financial sector as opposed to its 'real' sectors, and hence the smaller its 'real' output. This is a phenomenon that has been observed in economies with two-and especially three-digit inflation (cf. Kleiman, 1984, on the Israeli experience). Viewing the phenomenon in this way implicitly assumes that the services of the financial sector are not final products (which are a component of net national product) but 'intermediate products', whose function it is 'to eliminate friction in the productive system' and which accordingly are 'not net contributions to ultimate consumption' (Kuznets, 1951, p. 162; see also Kuznets, 1941, pp. 34–45).

BIBLIOGRAPHY

Archibald, G.C. and Lipsey, R.G. 1958. Monetary and value theory: a critique of Lange and Patinkin. *Review of Economic Studies* 28, October, 50–56.

Bailey, M.J. 1956. The welfare cost of inflationary finance. *Journal of Political Economy* 64, April, 93–110.

Barro, R.J. 1976. Rational expectations and the role of monetary policy. *Journal of Monetary Economics* 2, January, 1–32.

Barro, R.J. 1978. Unanticipated money, output, and the price level in the United States. *Journal of Political Economy* 86, August, 549–80.

Birati, A. and Cukierman, A. 1979. The redistributive effects of inflation and of the introduction of a real tax system in the US bond market. *Journal of Public Economics* 12, August, 125–39.

Boschen, J.F. and Grossman, H.I. 1982. Tests of equilibrium macroeconomics using contemporaneous monetary data. *Journal of Monetary Economics* 10, November, 309–33.

Brock, W.A. 1974. Money and growth: the case of long run perfect foresight. *International Economic Review* 15, October, 750–77.

Cecchetti, S.G. 1986. Testing short-run neutrality. *Journal of Monetary Economics* 17, May, 409–23.

Feaveryear, A. 1963. *The Pound Sterling: A History of English Money*. 2nd edn, revised by E.V. Morgan, Oxford: Clarendon Press.

Feldstein, M. 1982. Inflation, capital taxation, and monetary policy. In *Inflation: Causes and Effects*, ed. R.E. Hall, Chicago: University of Chicago Press, 153–67.

Fischer, S. 1977. Long-term contracts, rational expectations, and the optimal money supply rule. *Journal of Political Economy* 85, February, 191–205.

Fischer, S. 1980. On activist monetary policy with rational expectations. In *Rational Expectations and Economic Policy*, ed. S. Fischer, Chicago: University of Chicago Press, 211–47.

Fisher, I. 1907. *The Rate of Interest*. New York: Macmillan.

Fisher, I. 1913. *The Purchasing Power of Money: Its Determination and Relation to Credit Interest and Crises*. Rev. edn, New York: Macmillan. Reprinted, New York: Augustus M. Kelley, 1963.

Fisher, I. 1923. The business cycle largely a 'Dance of the Dollar'. *Journal of the American Statistical Association* 18, December, 1024–8.

Fisher, I. 1930. *The Theory of Interest*. New York: Macmillan. Reprinted, New York: Kelley and Millman, 1954.

Friedman, M. 1970. *The Counter-Revolution in Monetary Theory*. London: Institute of Economic Affairs.

Gale, D. 1982. *Money: in Equilibrium*. Cambridge: Cambridge University Press.

Gordon, R.J. 1982. Price inertia and policy ineffectiveness in the United States, 1890–1980. *Journal of Political Economy* 90, December, 1087–117.

Grandmont, J.-M. 1983. *Money and Value: a Reconsideration of Classical and Neoclassical Monetary Theories*. New York: Cambridge University Press.

Gurley, J.G. and Shaw, E.S. 1960. *Money in a Theory of Finance*. Washington, DC: Brookings Institution.

Hayek, F.A. 1931. *Prices and Production*. London: George Routledge.

Howitt, P. and Patinkin, D. 1980. Utility function transformations and money illusion: comments. *American Economic Review* 70, September, 819–22, 826–8.

Hume, D. 1752. 'Of Money', 'Of Interest' and 'Of the Balance of Trade'. As reprinted in D. Hume, *Writings on Economics*, ed. E. Rotwein, Wisconsin: University of Wisconsin Press, 1970, 33–77.

Keynes, J.M. 1923. *A Tract on Monetary Reform*. London: Macmillan. Reprinted, London: Macmillan for the Royal Economic Society, 1971; New York: St. Martin's Press.

Kleiman, E. 1984. Alut ha-inflatzya (The cost of inflation). *Rivon Le-kalkalah* (Economic Quarterly) 30, January, 859–64.

Kuznets, S. 1941. *National Income and its Composition, 1919–1938*. New York: National Bureau of Economic Research.

Kuznets, S. 1951. National income and industrial structure. *Proceedings of the International Statistical Conferences 1947* 5, 205–39. As reprinted in S. Kuznets, *Economic Change*, London: William Heinemann, 1954, 145–91.

Leontief, W. 1936. The fundamental assumption of Mr. Keynes' monetary theory of unemployment. *Quarterly Journal of Economics* 51, November, 192–7.

Levhari, D. and Patinkin, D. 1968. The role of money in a simple growth model. *American Economic Review* 58, September, 713–53. As reprinted in Patinkin (1972c), 205–42.

Liefmann, R. 1917. *Grundsätze der Volkswirtschaftslehre*. Vol. I: *Grundlagen der Wirtschaft*. Stuttgart and Berlin: Deutsche Verlagsanstalt.

Liefmann, R. 1919. *Grundsätze der Volkswirtschaftslehre*. Vol. II: *Grundlagen des Tauschverkehrs*. Stuttgart and Berlin: Deutsche Verlagsanstalt.

Lothian, J.R. 1985. Equilibrium relationships between money and other economic variables. *American Economic Review* 75, September, 828–35.

Lucas, R.E., Jr. 1972. Expectations and the neutrality of money. *Journal of Economic Theory* 4, April, 103–24. As reprinted in Lucas (1981), 66–89.

Lucas, R.E., Jr. 1975. An equilibrium model of the business cycle. *Journal of Political Economy* 83, December, 1113–44. As reprinted in Lucas (1981), 179–214.

Lucas, R.E., Jr. 1980. Two illustrations of the quantity theory of money. *American Economic Review* 70, December, 1005–14.

Lucas, R.E., Jr. 1981. *Studies in Business Cycle Theory*. Cambridge, Mass.: MIT Press.

McCallum, B.T. 1980. Rational expectations and macroeconomic stabilization policy: an overview. *Journal of Money, Credit, and Banking* 12, November, 716–46.

Metzler, L.A. 1951. Wealth, saving and the rate of interest. *Journal of Political Economy* 59, April, 93–116.

Mishkin, F.S. 1982. Does anticipated monetary policy matter? An econometric investigation. *Journal of Political Economy* 90, February, 22–51.

Mishkin, F.S. 1983. *A Rational Expectations Approach to Macroeconometrics*. Chicago: University of Chicago Press.

Modigliani, F. 1944. Liquidity preference and the theory of interest and money. *Econometrica* 12, January, 45–88. As reprinted in American Economic Association, *Readings in Monetary Theory*, Philadelphia: Blakiston for the American Economic Association, 1951, 186–240.

Mundell, R.A. 1963. Inflation and real interest. *Journal of Political Economy* 71, June, 280–83.

Mundell, R.A. 1965. A fallacy in the interpretation of macroeconomic equilibrium. *Journal of Political Economy* 73, February, 61–6.

Patinkin, D. 1965. *Money, Interest, and Prices*. 2nd edn, New York: Harper & Row.

Patinkin, D. 1972a. On the short-run non-neutrality of money in the quantity theory. *Banca Nazionale del Lavoro Quarterly Review* No. 100, March, 3–22.

Patinkin, D. 1972b. Money and growth in a Keynesian full-employment model. In Patinkin (1972c), 195–204.

Patinkin, D. 1972c. *Studies in Monetary Economics*. New York: Harper & Row.

Patinkin, D. and Steiger, O. 1989. In search of the 'veil of money' and the 'neutrality of money': a note on the origin of terms. *Scandinavian Journal of Economics* 91.

Pigou, A.C. 1949. *The Veil of Money*. London: Macmillan; Westport, Conn: Greenwood Press, 1979.

Robertson, D.H. 1922. *Money*. Cambridge: Cambridge University Press.

Sargent, T.J. 1976. A classical macroeconometric model for the United States. *Journal of Political Economy* 84, April, 207–37.

Sidrauski, M. 1967. Rational choice and patterns of growth in a monetary economy. *American Economic Review* 57, May, 534–44.

Solow, R.M. 1956. A contribution to the theory of economic growth. *Quarterly Journal of Economics* 70, February, 65–94.

Tobin, J. 1965. Money and economic growth. *Econometrica* 33, October, 671–84.

Tobin, J. 1967. The neutrality of money in growth models: a comment. *Economica* 34, February, 69–72.

Wicksell, K. 1898. *Interest and Prices: A Study of the Causes Regulating the Value of Money*. Translated from the original German by R.F. Khan. London: Macmillan, 1936.

Open-market Operations

STEPHEN H. AXILROD AND HENRY C. WALLICH

An open-market operation is essentially a transaction undertaken by a central bank in the market for securities (or foreign exchange) that has the effect of supplying reserves to, or draining reserves from, the banking system. Open-market operations are one of the several instruments – including lending or discount-window operations and reserve requirements – available to a central bank to affect the cost and availability of bank reserves and hence the amount of money in the economy and, at the margin, credit flows.

THEORY AND FUNCTION. A distinctive feature of open-market operations is that they take place at the initiative of the monetary authority. They provide a means by which a central bank can directly and actively affect the amount of its liabilities for bank reserves, increasing them by purchases of securities and decreasing them by sales. With reserve provision at the initiative of the central bank, open-market operations facilitate control of the money supply and, from a short-run perspective, the pursuit of a stabilizing economic policy by the central bank and, from a longer-run perspective, of an anti-inflationary policy.

By contrast, in the operation of a central bank's lending function, the provision or liquidation of reserves is at the initiative of private financial institutions. To the extent that this facility is employed too actively or not actively enough and is not offset by the central bank through open-market operations, or by an appropriate discount rate, control of the volume of reserves, and, ultimately, the money supply is weakened.

When open-market operations play the primary role in monetary-policy implementation, such as in the United States, the discount window still serves an important function in the monetary process. Indeed, in the short run, demands at the discount window are not independent of the amount of reserves supplied through the open market. For example, as a central bank restrains reserve growth by holding back on security purchases, some of the unsatisfied reserve demand will at least for a time shift to the discount window. In general, changes in the demand for borrowing will in practice provide some offset to provision of reserves through open-market operations. This may make it more difficult for a central bank to control bank reserves precisely through open market operations. However, precise control is probably not desirable in the short run because demands for, and needs for, money and credit in dynamic, highly active economies are quite variable. In that sense, the discount window provides a safety valve through which reserves can be provided to maintain a suitably elastic currency and to avert disorderly market conditions.

An open-market purchase essentially replaces an interest-earning asset on the books of banks (either a government security or a loan to some entity holding a government security) with a claim on the central bank – that is, with a reserve balance that has been created for the purpose of acquiring the security. This reserve balance is then 'excess' to the banking system. In the process of converting these non-interest-earning excess balances into interest-earning assets, banks will in turn make loans or purchase securities. That will tend to keep interest rates lower than they otherwise would be and lead to an expansion of the money supply through the well-known multiplier process as the original excess reserves turn into required reserves. The associated amount of money will be a multiple of the amount of reserves, with the multiple depending on the required reserve ratio and on the amount of excess reserves banks in the end want to hold at given levels of interest rates.

The power of open-market operations as an instrument of policy does not, however, depend in its essentials on banks being required to hold reserves or being required to hold a high or low fraction of deposits as reserves at the central bank. That might affect to a degree the precision of the relationship between open-market operations and money. But the power of open-market operations to influence the economy derives essentially from the ability of the central bank to create its own product – whether it takes the form of bank reserves, clearing balances, or currency in circulation – without the need to take account of the circumstances that influence ordinary business decisions, such as costs of materials, profit potential, and the capacity to repay debt incurred. Even in the unlikely event that the banks, in the absence of reserve requirements, chose to carry zero reserves and to rely entirely on the discount window, the central bank would have large liabilities outstanding in the form of currency through which it could exert pressure on banks by means of open-market operations. In the United States about three-quarters of the central bank's assets reflect currency liabilities.

In a sense, the product of open-market operations – the non-borrowed portion of the monetary base (roughly the sum of the central bank's deposit or reserve liabilities plus currency in circulation) – can be viewed as being created from outside the economy. It is 'outside' money, exogenous to the economic process, but capable of strongly influencing that process. If the central bank continues to create a product for which there is no need or which the participants in the economy do not wish fully to accept, the economy will devalue that product; excessive money creation will cause the price of money relative to other products to fall. That effectively occurs through a rise in the general price level domestically and devaluation of the currency internationally.

Open-market operations in those countries which have sufficiently broad and active markets so that they can be the central instrument of policy are of course attuned to the nation's ultimate economic objectives and to the intermediate guides for over-all monetary policy used to accomplish these objectives; these guides may encompass money supply, interest rates, or exchange rates. In implementing policy on a day-to-day basis, however, open-market operations require additional guides in those cases where the intermediate objectives of policy are quantities, such as the money supply, that are not directly controllable through the purchase or sale of securities.

In most countries, operations are guided on a day-to-day basis by some view of desirable tautness or ease in the central money market, as judged by an appropriate short-term interest rate, complex of money-market rates, or degree of pressure on the banking system. As money-market and bank reserve pressures change, the banking system, financial markets generally, and the public make adaptations – through changes in interest rates broadly, lending terms and conditions, liquidity and asset preferences – that with some lag lead to attainment of money supply objectives or economic goals more broadly.

It has been argued, chiefly by those who would like policy to focus more or less exclusively on a money supply intermediate target, that open-market operations should be guided not by money-market conditions or the degree of pressure on the banking system but by the total quantity of reserves or monetary base. Because open-market operations are at the initiative of the central bank, they are construed as especially well suited to attainment of such quantitative reserve objectives. Reserves or the monetary base as a guide are thought to bear a more certain relationship to a money-supply intermediate guide than do money-market conditions because the former depend on the multiplier relationship between reserves or the base and money and not on predicting how markets and asset holders will react to a given change in interest rates. However, in practice the multiplier relationship itself is variable (in part because of varying reserve requirements or reserve balance practices behind differing deposits in measures of money) and is not independent of interest rates; for instance, rates affect the demands for both excess and borrowed reserves.

TECHNIQUES. A variety of techniques are available to implement open-market operations. Securities can be purchased or sold outright. The securities may be short- or long-term, although because short-term markets are generally larger and more active most transactions take place in that market.

Open-market transactions may also be undertaken through, in effect, lending or borrowing operations – by purchasing a security with an agreement to sell it back, say, tomorrow or in a few days, or by selling a security with an agreement to buy it back shortly. Whereas outright transactions take place at current market rates on the securities involved, these combined purchase and sale transactions (termed repurchase agreements) yield a return related to the going rate on collateralized short-term loans in the money market. Repurchase agreements have the advantage of greater flexibility. When they run out, after being outstanding overnight or for a few days only, reserves are withdrawn or provided automatically. Outright purchases or sales create or absorb permanent reserves requiring more explicit action to reverse.

Open-market operations are generally conducted in governmental securities, since that is usually the largest and most liquid market in the country. In the United States, domestic operations are confined by law to US government or federal agency securities and all operations must be conducted through the market; purchases cannot be made directly from the government. A large, active market is essential if the central bank is to be able to effect transactions at its own initiative when and in the size required to meet its day-to-day objectives.

The traditional responsibility of central banks for maintaining the liquidity of markets and averting disorderly conditions affects methods of open market operations. In the United States, the bulk of day-to-day open-market operations are undertaken to offset variations in such items as float, the Treasury cash balance, and currency in circulation that affect the reserve base of the banking system. On average per week, such factors absorb or add about 4 per cent (the equivalent of $1\frac{1}{2}$ billion) of the reserve base in the United States. Without offsetting open market operations – sometimes termed 'defensive' operations – typically undertaken through repurchase transactions, money-market conditions and rates would tend to vary sharply from day to day, unduly complicating private decision-making and possibly frustrating the central bank's purposes with respect to controlling the growth of the money supply or the level of interest or exchange rates.

Open-market operations conceptually can be employed to affect the yield curve – for example, to maintain short-term rates while exerting downward pressure on long-term rates. By shifting the composition of its portfolio, the central bank can change the supply of different maturities in the market. An effort to do this in the United States in the early 1960s was not clearly successful. In part, this may be because such an operation requires active cooperation by the Treasury. More fundamentally, most economists have come to believe that expectations so dominate the term structure of interest rates that the central bank, even if aided by a like-minded governmental debt management, would have to engage in massive changes in the maturity structure of securities in the market in order to produce more than a small impact on the shape of the yield curve.

Apart from operations in governmental securities, some central banks undertake open-market operations in foreign exchange. This may be done in an effort to influence the course of exchange rates while at the same time offsetting any effect on bank reserves or other money-market objectives – termed sterilized intervention. However, in certain countries the foreign-exchange market may be the chief avenue available for open-market operations, as is typically the case for small countries in which foreign trade represents a large fraction of their gross national product and exchange-market transactions a large portion of total activity in the open market. In such cases, open-market operations in foreign exchange also

291

tend to affect the bank reserve base either because there is little scope to offset them through domestic markets or because there is little desire to do so if the central bank has a relatively fixed exchange rate objective.

RELATION TO GOVERNMENTAL BUDGETARY DEFICITS. There is no necessary relationship between open-market operations and the financing of budgetary deficits. In a country like the United States open-market purchases are undertaken only as needed to meet money supply and overall economic objectives; they are not increased because a budgetary deficit is enlarged nor decreased when a deficit diminishes. The government must meet its financing needs by attracting investors in the open market paying whatever market interest rate is necessary.

An enlarged deficit would itself lead to increased open-market purchases only if the monetary authority deliberately adjusted its objectives to permit an expansion of bank reserves and money to help finance the government, in which case the deficits would indirectly, through their influence on monetary-policy decisions, lead to inflationary financing. This occurred as a means of war finance during World War II in the United States when the central bank purchased government securities from the market at a fixed ceiling price, thus in effect monetizing the debt; price controls were employed in an effort to suppress the inflation.

But since the early 1950s, debt finance by the US government has had to meet the test of the market unaided by central-bank open-market purchases. Confidence that the central bank will not finance the government deficit is essential to a sound currency. A financial system in which the central bank can refuse to fund the deficit also can provide a powerful incentive to keep deficits from burgeoning.

The typical instances of central-bank monetization of the debt in recent decades have occurred in countries – usually not highly developed ones – with persisting large budgetary deficits who are unable to attract private investors at home or abroad because interest rates offered are artificially low, or the domestic market is undeveloped, or because of a lack of confidence in the security and the currency domestically or on the part of foreign investors. The central bank is then more or less forced to acquire securities directly from the government, automatically creating reserves and money, and leading to inflation and perhaps hyperinflation as the process continues. In those cases, a halt to monetization of the debt through central bank purchases depends essentially on greatly reducing, if not eliminating, budgetary deficits.

It must be recognized, to be sure, that a government deficit may lead to pressures on interest rates that the central bank, usually ill-advisedly, may wish to resist. By encouraging expansion of bank credit and money supply, through open-market operations or otherwise, the central bank may indirectly finance a deficit.

The number of countries in which effective open-market operations can be conducted is surprisingly limited. Required is a securities market sufficiently deep so that the central bank can make purchases and sales sufficient to achieve its reserve objectives without significantly affecting the price of the securities. Otherwise it will be constrained by fear of unintended price effects and would in any event by engaging more in interest-rate manipulation than in control of reserves. Such comparatively price-neutral operations, if possible at all, are feasible usually at the short rather than at the long end. It requires a market for Treasury bills or similar instruments such as exists in, for instance, the United States, the United Kingdom and Canada, but that does not at this time in, for example, Germany and Japan. In the United Kingdom open market operations, in former years, were conducted in Treasury bills; today, commercial bills are primarily employed. Thus, central banks have varying capacities to undertake open market operations; in some cases, where markets for short-term instruments are limited, operations may not be entirely at the initiative of the central bank, nor at a market price in contrast to one set by the central bank (although the price set by the central bank may be based on market conditions).

BIBLIOGRAPHY

Bank of England. 1984. *The Development and Operation of Monetary Policy, 1960–1983.* Oxford: Clarendon Press, especially 156–64.

Board of Governors of the Federal Reserve System. 1984. *The Federal Reserve System: Purposes and Functions.* 7th edn, Washington, DC.

Meek, P. 1982. *US Monetary Policy and Financial Markets.* New York: Federal Reserve Bank of New York. Monetary policy and open market operations in 1984.

Federal Reserve Bank of New York Quarterly Review 10(1), Spring, 1985, 36–56. (Reports for earlier years are available in the same publication.)

Optimum Quantity of Money

PETER HOWITT

The idea of an optimum quantity of money was formulated in the 1950s and 1960s by monetary economists applying standard marginal conditions of social optimality to the particular case of money. The argument runs as follows. Because the function of money can be served by notes whose costs of production are independent of their exchange value, the marginal cost of increasing the real quantity of money is virtually zero. If everyone wanted to hold 5 per cent more, their wishes could be fulfilled by a 5 per cent reduction in all nominal prices. Therefore real money balances should be provided up to the point of satiety; the optimum real quantity of money is that which makes the marginal benefit equal to the zero marginal cost.

This argument implies a failure of Smith's invisible hand in a fiat-money economy, because although society may be able to raise people's real money balances at zero cost by decreasing the price level, no individual can do this. To the individual in a competitive equilibrium the marginal cost of holding money is the nominal rate of interest on the assets that he must sell to acquire more money. As long as the nominal rate of interest is positive he will hold a real quantity of money such that the marginal benefit is still positive.

To give people the incentive to hold the optimum quantity of money, two alternative policies have been proposed. The first is to pay competitive interest on money, so that holding money would entail no private opportunity cost. The second proposal is to maintain a rate of decrease of the price level equal to the real rate of interest, thereby driving the nominal rate of interest, and hence the private cost of holding money, to zero.

The second of these proposals was elaborated upon by Milton Friedman (1969) who coined the phrase 'Optimum Quantity of Money'. However, the proposals and the ideas underlying them had been in the literature on monetary economics for several years prior to Friedman's essay. George Tolley (1957) presented a clear and detailed argument for bringing about the optimum quantity by paying competitive interest on money. The optimum-quantity argument for deflating at the real rate of interest had been made much earlier by Friedman himself (1960, p. 73) and had been elaborated on by such writers as Marty (1961, p. 57).

Although the optimum-quantity argument applies only to fiat money, similar arguments apply to other kinds of money. Thus, for example, as the classical economists explicitly recognized, it is socially wasteful to employ precious metals for monetary purposes when costless notes or tokens could be used instead. Likewise, a direct application of the fiat-money argument implies that the optimum quantity of bank deposits pay competitive interest. Even with competitive deposit-interest the optimum quantity of deposits will not be provided unless banks receive competitive interest on their reserve assets. Otherwise banks would regard the foregone interest on reserves as a component of the marginal cost of issuing deposits, even though there is no corresponding component in the marginal cost to society.

The optimum-quantity argument has had no impact on practical policy discussions, aside from the issues of bank regulation implicit in the preceding paragraph that are tangential to the argument. The logistical problems of paying competitive interest on hand-to-hand currency have been thought to render the idea unworkable. Also, in practice, a central bank that tried to eliminate the opportunity cost of holding money by pegging at a value of zero the nominal rate of interest on some alternative non-money asset would probably produce a Wicksellian cumulative process of the sort that Friedman himself has frequently warned against.

Even the limited proposal that the monetary authority aim at some target of deflation calculated to yield a zero nominal rate of interest in the long run is dubious in a world of limited price-flexibility. For in such a world it is not costless to provide society with more real money balances through deflation. Standard macroeconomic theory predicts that a reduction in the rate of monetary expansion of the sort that would be necessary to achieve long-run deflation starting in a situation of rising or even stable prices would be likely to cause at least a temporary rise in unemployment, the cost of which is not taken into account by the optimum-quantity argument.

Furthermore, the process of deflation itself is likely to impose costs that are ignored by the argument, because of the difficulty of coordinating individual pricing decisions. The argument supposes that in a stationary state all nominal prices can fall continuously at the same rate. In fact, in a world where the overall price-level is falling continuously, individual prices are likely to decrease at discrete points of time. Any good's relative price will drop discontinuously whenever its nominal price is reduced, and will then rise continuously until the next discontinuous reduction. Leijonhufvud (1977) has discussed how the raggedness of the inflationary process can impose costs because of the distortion in resource allocation and the loss of informational content of prices that result from an increased randomness of relative prices. The same is true of the process of deflation.

These practical problems do not necessarily constitute a counterexample to Einstein's dictum that there's nothing more practical than a good theory. It can be argued that the theory underlying the optimum-quantity argument is deficient not because it is simple and ignores practical considerations but because it abstracts from what is important about inflation and money. It involves little more than a transliteration of a welfare theorem that is valid in an idealized non-monetary world of Walrasian general equilibrium to a world with enough frictions to support the institution of monetary exchange. It treats inflation or deflation as nothing more than a tax or subsidy on the holding of money, that can be administered costlessly by a Walrasian auctioneer, rather than a costly process that distorts the transmission of information and the allocation of resources.

Several economists also objected to early formulations of the optimum-quantity argument on the related grounds that these formulations did not make explicit the nature of the gains to society from holding more money. Even the most formal and rigorous versions of the argument modelled the serves of money as one would the services of any other commodity, by including the holding of real balances as an argument of agents' utility and production functions. This left open the question of what the optimum quantity of money would be if account were taken of the special role of money in the process of exchange. In particular, Robert Clower (1970) stressed the fact that because purchases must be paid for with money, the demand to hold money is linked with the demand to purchase goods and with the demand to hold other trade-related inventories, in a way that neoclassical monetary theory does not take into account.

Despite these theoretical objections, and despite the impracticality of the policy recommendations based upon the notion of an optimum quantity of money, the notion has had an important impact upon the development of monetary economics. By posing a provocative result based upon an analogy with non-monetary welfare economics it has stimulated interesting theoretical work aimed at making the role of money and the nature of a monetary economy more explicit than in neoclassical monetary theory.

On the whole, that subsequent theoretical work has tended to confirm the optimum-quantity argument. Inventory-theoretic arguments like that of Clower and Howitt (1978) that take into account the link between holdings of money and other commodity inventories bear out the idea that the interest-opportunity cost of holding money imposes a deadweight loss on society. A similar result has been found by writers like Grandmont and Younès (1973) who have ignored the transactions costs and storage costs essential to the inventory-theoretic approach but have followed Clower's suggestion of making explicit the constraint on individual utility maximization that current purchases must be financed out of prior sales receipts. With such a constraint any cost of holding money acts as a distorting tax on all transactions, because no trades can be made without holding money at least for some minimal period of time.

However, these confirmations of the optimum-quantity argument must be seriously qualified. Both the inventory-theoretic and the cash-in-advance approaches have ignored the price-adjustment problems stressed by Leijonhufvud. Further, these approaches have assumed away externalities that are likely to be important in the use and holding of money. For example, Laidler (1978) has shown how one person's holding of money can confer benefits on other agents in the way that one person's acquisition of a telephone can confer benefits on others. Such externalities are inherent in the process of market exchange in the absence of a costless coordination device like the Walrasian auctioneer; one person's decision to spend resources on transacting will make it easier for his potential trading partners to carry out trades. If Laidler's argument is valid, then even if prices were not costly to adjust, a policy that resulted in a zero private opportunity cost to holding money would not yield the socially optimal quantity of money. It would induce people to hold money up to the point where the marginal private benefit was zero. But at that point the marginal social benefit would still be positive because of the 'spillovers' that the individuals would not take into account when calculating the private benefits.

BIBLIOGRAPHY

Clower, R. 1970. Is there an optimal money supply? *Journal of Finance* 25(2), May, 425–33.
Clower, R. and Howitt, P. 1978. The transactions theory of the demand for money: a reconsideration. *Journal of Political Economy* 86(3), June, 449–66.
Friedman, M. 1960. *A Program for Monetary Stability.* New York: Fordham University Press.
Friedman, M. 1969. *The Optimum Quantity of Money and Other Essays.* Chicago: Aldine.
Grandmont, J.M. and Younès, Y. 1973. On the efficiency of a monetary equilibrium. *Review of Economic Studies* 40(2), April, 149–65.
Laidler, D. 1978. The welfare costs of inflation in neoclassical theory: some unsettled questions. In *Inflation Theory and Anti-Inflation Policy*, ed. E. Lundberg, London: Macmillan.
Leijonhufvud, A. 1977. Costs and consequences of inflation. In *The Microeconomic Foundations of Macroeconomics*, ed. G. Harcourt, London: Macmillan.
Marty, A. 1961. Gurley and Shaw on money in a theory of finance. *Journal of Political Economy* 69, February, 56–62.
Tolley, G. 1957. Providing for growth of the money supply. *Journal of Political Economy* 65, December, 465–85.

Price Level

P. BRIDEL

Until the end of the 19th century, it may be said that the quantity theory was everybody's theory of money and the price level. This does not mean that it was universally accepted: many writers submitted Hume's formulation to some very sharp criticisms. However, short of any viable alternative, all the leading economists adhered to one or another of the marginally different versions of the quantity theory.

The common feature of early-19th-century classical and late-19th-century neo-classical quantity theory is the well-known notion that an expansion or a contraction of the money supply – other things equal – would lead to an equiproportional change in the price level (or alternatively to an equiproportional change in the value of money). That 'other things equal' is reflected in the assumption of a stable demand for money function, or, more specifically, a fixed level of output. The similarities between the Classical and Neo-classical approaches come however to an end here. Whereas in the latter approach the fixed (full employment) output assumption, and hence the causal relationship between money and prices, is the result of a theoretical analysis of the determination of output along marginalist lines, in the former it results from the adoption of Say's Law. In other words, Classical quantity theory is based not on a theory of output but on the lack of such a theory comparable with its theory of value or distribution.

Accordingly, and despite attempts made by some of its leading proponents (like Thornton) to work their way toward a monetary analysis of the economic process as a whole in which price-level issues fall into secondary place, the Classical monetary theory, up until and including J.S. Mill, gave the pride of place to the so-called 'direct mechanism'. This 'transmission mechanism' is older than economic theory itself. Much earlier than Hume's classical version, and well before economics was born as an independent subject, the idea that a change in the money supply would eventually cause prices to rise in the same proportion was part and parcel of most writings on money.

Even if Hume and Cantillon paid great attention to the manner in which a cash injection is disbursed and to the various lags involved in the process, and although they were well aware that an increase of money raises prices equi-proportionately only if everyone's initial money holdings are increased equi-proportionately, their attempts to prove it were thwarted by the very logic of the Classical framework. It is only with the Neoclassical effort to integrate money and value theories that the first serious attempts were made (mainly by Marshall and Wicksell) to escape from this Classical dichotomy and to prove the proportionality theorem by providing a proper stability analysis. However, and at least up until the early 1940s, most economists kept arguing that people spend more money because they receive more cash, not because the value of their real balances has increased beyond the amount determined by the Marshallian k. With his path-breaking analysis of the real-balance effect, Patinkin finally connected people's increased *flow* of expenditures with their feeling that their *stock* of money is too large for their needs. The sweeping endorsement of this theoretical argument by the economics profession allowed an apparently successful counter-attack against Keynes's claim that a fully competitive economy could well get trapped in (unemployment) disequilibria. Despite serious divergences among macroeconomists about the actual workings of the real-balance effect, it was widely held that, if prices and wages are flexible, a Walrasian equilibrium (with a positive value for money) would exist both in the short run and the long run. These investigations also confirmed that money is neutral; that is, excluding all distributional effects, in a neoclassical model coupled with unit-elastic expectations, a once-and-for-all scalar change of all agents' initial cash holdings would change in the same proportion the equilibrium of money prices and nominal money balances at the end of the period, leaving unaltered relative prices and real variables. Price and wage rigidities are thus the only reasons that, in the short run, the excess demands for goods and money might not be homogenous of degree zero and one respectively, with respect to nominal prices and initial balances.

The 'indirect mechanism' has a history that until the interwar period played second fiddle to that of the 'direct mechanism'. It is only with Marshall's, Wicksell's and, later on, Fisher's attempts to give an explicit rôle to the rate of interest in the transmission mechanism connecting money and prices that it rapidly took pride of place in the economist's monetary toolbox. In fact, the argument that monetary equilibrium (and hence the stability of the price-level in an economy) exists only when the money rate in the loan market equals the rate of return on capital (the traditional 'natural' rate) in the capital market is the basic framework within which some of the most famous discussions in the realm of monetary theory took and are still taking place. In all these analyses in terms of saving and investment, cumulative process, Gibson's paradox, forced saving, trade and credit cycles, etc, the price-level plays a crucial rôle as an indicator of the degree of tension within the system. Hence the wealth of introductory chapters on index numbers found in most textbooks and treatises of that period (the most famous being Book II in Keynes's *Treatise on Money* [1930], 1971).

With his cumulative process, Wicksell was indeed the driving force behind the impetus given toward the very end of the 19th century to this 'trailing rate' doctrine. Building on Tooke's 1844 insights, and in contradiction to Ricardo's pronouncements, Wicksell argued that, following a credit expansion, the market rate of interest and the price-level are positively correlated. As a matter of fact, the discrepancy (created by such a credit expansion between the market rate and the expected yield on investment) is a disequilibrium situation in which, period after period, net investment is positive and constantly increasing. Such a cumulative process need neither create inflation if voluntary savings is simultaneously generated via higher market rates (unless a 'pure credit' hypothesis is made) nor be explosive (thanks to the internal drain on banks' reserves). However, in order to preserve price stability, if the economy is operating at full employment and/or if there are signs of inflation, the bank rate would have to be raised in order to ensure that net investment does not exceed voluntary savings. Hence, a stable price level would not only be synonymous with equality between the real (or 'normal') rate of return on investment and the market rate, but also with equality between the market and the bank rates. As Robertson put it later very succinctly:

> It is on the difference between [Savings and Investment] and consequently between 'natural' and market rates that the movement of the price-level... depends (1933, p. 411). Within such a framework there began nearly half a century of intensive theorizing in terms of Wicksell's three criteria. The market rate is in equilibrium if it is equal to the rate of return of capital (or 'natural' rate), at which: (i) the demand for loans is equal to the supply of savings; and (ii) the price level is stable ([1896] 1936, pp. 192–9).

If the market rate trails behind the 'natural' rate, prices will begin to move up; if, furthermore, the bank rate diverges from the market rate, this creates an additional discrepancy between the market rate and the real rate of return on investment: the rate of inflation would of course gather up speed. In macroeconomic terms, the whole of this argument was ultimately incorporated in the loanable-funds theory of interest: the market rate of interest is determined by the demand for (investment demand and demand for cash balances) and the supply of loanable funds (voluntary savings and bank credit). If planned savings are equal to planned investment, net credit creation is equal to the demand for cash, the market rate, the bank rate and the 'natural' rate of interest are one and the same thing and, last but not least, the price level is stable.

Marshall in his stability analysis of the value of money (1923), Fisher in his famous equation (1911), Hawtrey with his purely monetary theory of the cycle (1913), Robertson with his 'four crucial functions' (1928, pp. 105–7 and 182), most members of the Stockholm School (notably Myrdal, 1929), Keynes in his famous 'fundamental equations' (1930) and Hayek (1932) with his forced saving analysis (to name only but a few of the most celebrated contributors to this debate) all tried, by putting a different emphasis on the various components of this indirect mechanism to offer a dynamic analysis of the price level. Having thus added money to a relative-price system in which it has, by definition no part to play, these theorists tried in a certain sense to 'eliminate' it again by defining the monetary policy best suited to make money 'neutral' as concerns the operations of the economic system. By defining the prerequisites for money to be 'neutral', these authors were clearly implicitly (and sometimes explicitly) taking for granted the stability of the system. Rigidities, lags and inelasticities of all types, external shocks and technical progress, and of course monetary impulses could temporarily disrupt the dominant forces at work in an economy; but, ultimately, in the long run, the system would tend towards a full employment equilibrium along Walrasian lines. As Keynes wrote in his *Treatise*: 'Monetary theory, when all is said and done, is little more than a vast elaboration of the truth that "it all comes out in the wash"' (1930, II, p. 366).

Thus by the early Thirties and despite a great deal of activity in the field on monetary theory, the simple and straightforward 'direct' and 'indirect' transmission mechanisms traditionally used to determine the price level were superseded because they proved, as Hayek argued, 'a positive hindrance to further progress' (1931, pp. 3-4). However, the rich harvest of new formulations and the stepping stones laid down by Hayek, a handful of Swedish economists and Hicks in the field of temporary equilibrium sustained no further work after the publication of Keynes's *General Theory of Employment Interest and Money*. With his *magnum opus*, Keynes simply changed the agenda of questions economists were to think about in the next thirty years. In particular, the central part played by the price level as the indicator *par excellence* in the course of the cycle was relegated together with the quantity theory to caricatural classroom teaching.

When Friedman resurrected the quantity theory as a theory of demand for money rather than as a theory of the price level (1950, p. 52), his intentions were originally to develop an alternative to the Keynesian liquidity preference argument. However, by asserting that the demand for money function was *empirically* stable and that it is *autonomously* determined, monetarist economists were able to relate again directly nominal income and price changes to changes in the stock of money. Friedman was thus explicitly in a position to consider his contribution as a theory of the aggregate price level the purpose of which is to provide the missing equation in a Walrasian system (1970, p. 223). The neo-classical synthesis having reached not too dissimilar conclusions, the Monetarist *vs* Keynesian controversy was ultimately seen by both sides as a debate on IS-LM elasticities, speed of adjustment and rigidities. In other words, and to quote Friedman, 'the fundamental differences between [these two streams] are empirical not theoretical' (1976, p. 315). All this suggests of course not only that there is an accepted theory of the economy but also that this theory is capable of yielding both monetarist and other conclusions. In other words, disagreements seem only to arise as far as the speed at which the economy converges to long-run equilibrium is concerned. Besides the fact that it is by no means the case that the IS-LM cross is a generally accepted theory of the economy (the Walrasian story monetarists see behind these two curves would certainly bar them from having income as one of their arguments), the assumptions one finds in the monetarist and New Classical Macroeconomic literature about the neutrality of money are not particularly plausible, let alone theoretically verifiable. In particular, they do not imply the uniqueness of such an equilibrium. Theorists like Hahn (1982) and Grandmont (1983) have shown that there are many, mostly a continuum of rational expectation equilibria over a finite horizon and there may also be many for an infinite horizon. Thus the belief that the long-run equilibrium of a competitive monetary economy is unique and stable and that a scalar change in the quantity of money holdings will generate the same scalar change in all nominal values remains today more than ever at the centre of a formidable theoretical debate. If the neo-classical monetary paradigm has survived, it is more because many economists *think* it yields important insights into the working of decentralized economies than for its theoretical solidity (Lucas, 1984). Hence, and despite the empirical stability of the money demand function reported by many applied economists, and according to the maxim that what is witnessed if not explained is not understood, a proper *theory* of the price level remains yet to be written.

BIBLIOGRAPHY

Bridel, P. 1987. Cambridge Monetary Thought. *The Development of Saving-Investment Analysis from Marshall to Keynes.* London: Macmillan.

Fisher, I. 1911. *The Purchasing Power of Money.* New York: Macmillan, 1922.

Friedman, M. 1950. The quantity theory of money: a restatement. In M. Friedman, *The Optimum Quantity of Money*, London: Macmillan, 1969, 51–67.

Friedman, M. 1970. A theoretical framework for monetary analysis. *Journal of Political Economy* 78, 139–238.

Friedman, M. 1976. Comments on Tobin and Buiter. In *Monetarism*, ed. J. Stein, Amsterdam: North-Holland, 310–17.

Grandmont, J.M. 1983. *Money and Value.* Cambridge: Cambridge University Press.

Lucas, R.F. Review of J.M. Grandmont (1983) *Journal of Economic Literature* 22, 1984, 1651–1653.

Hahn, F.H. 1982. *Money and Inflation.* Oxford: Blackwell.

Hawtrey, R. 1913. *Good and Bad Trade.* London: Constable.

Hayek, F. von. 1931. *Prices and Production.* London: Routledge and Kegan Paul; 2nd edn, New York: A.M. Kelley, 1965.

Hayek, F. von. 1932. A note on the development of the doctrine of 'forced saving'. *Quarterly Journal of Economics* 47, 123–33.

Keynes, J.M. 1930. *A Treatise on Money.* 2 vols, reprinted, London: Macmillan, 1971; New York: St. Martin's Press.

Marshall, A. 1923. *Money, Credit and Commerce.* London: Macmillan.

Myrdal, G. 1929. *Monetary Equilibrium.* London: Hodge, 1939.

Robertson, D. 1928. *Money.* 2nd edn, Cambridge: Nisbet and Cambridge University Press.

Robertson, D. 1933. Saving and hoarding. *Economic Journal* 43, 399–413.

Wicksell, K. 1896. *Interest and Prices.* London: Macmillan, 1936; reprinted, New York: A.M. Kelley, 1965.

Real Balances

DON PATINKIN

By the term 'real balances' is meant the real value of the money balances held by an individual or by the economy as a whole, as the case may be. The emphasis on real, as distinct from nominal, reflects the basic assumption that individuals are free of 'money illusion'. It is a corresponding property of any well-specified demand function for money that its dependent variable is real balances. Indeed, Keynes in his *Treatise on Money* (1930, vol. 1, p. 222) designated the variation on the Cambridge equation that he had presented in his *A Tract on Monetary Reform* (1923, ch. 3: 1) as 'The 'Real-Balances' Quantity Equation'.

Implicit – and sometimes explicit – in the quantity-theory analysis of the effect of (say) an increase in the quantity of money is the assumption that the mechanism by which such an increase ultimately causes a proportionate increase in prices is through its initial effect in increasing the real value of money balances held by individuals and consequently increasing their respective demands for goods: that is, through what is now known as the 'real-balance effect'. This effect, however, was not assigned a role in the general-equilibrium system of equations with which writers of the interwar period attempted to describe the working of a money economy. In particular, these writers mistakenly assumed that in order for their commodity demand functions to be free of money illusion, they had to fulfil the so-called 'homogeneity postulate', which stated that these functions depended only on relative prices, and so were not affected by a change in the absolute price level generated by an equi-proportionate change in all money prices (Leontief, 1936, p. 192). Thus they failed to take account of the effect of such a change on the real value of money balances and hence on commodity demands. This in turn led them to contend that there existed a dichotomy of the pricing process, with equilibrium relative prices being determined in the 'real sector' of the economy (as represented by the excess-demand equations for commodities), while the equilibrium absolute price level was determined in the 'monetary sector' (as represented by the excess-demand equation for money): (Modigliani, 1944, sec. 13). This, however, is an invalid dichotomy, for it leads to contradictory

303

implications about the determinacy or, alternatively, stability of the absolute price level (Patinkin, 1965, ch. 8).

Nor was the real-balance effect taken account of in Keynes's *General Theory* and in the subsequent Hicks (1937)–Modigliani (1944) IS–LM exposition of this theory, which rapidly became the standard one of macroeconomic textbooks. According to this exposition, the only way in which a decline in wages and prices can increase employment is by its effect in increasing the real value of money balances, hence reducing the rate of interest, and hence (through its stimulating effects on investment) increasing the aggregate demand for goods and hence employment. A further and basic tenet of this exposition was that there was a minimum below which the rate of interest could not fall. So if the wage decline were to bring about a lowering of the rate of interest to this minimum before full-employment were reached, any further decline in the wage rate would be to no avail. In brief, the economy would then be caught in the 'liquidity trap'. And even though Keynes had stated in the *General Theory*, 'whilst this limiting case might become practically important in the future, I know of no example of it hitherto' (p. 207), the Keynesian theory of employment was for many years interpreted in terms of this 'trap'.

It was against this background that Pigou (1943, 1947) pointed out that the increase in the real value of money holdings generated by the wage and price decline increased the aggregate demand for goods directly, and not only indirectly through its downward effect on the rate of interest. Pigou's rationale was that individuals saved in order to accumulate a certain amount of wealth relative to their income, and that indeed the savings function depended inversely on the ratio of wealth to income. Correspondingly, as wages and prices declined, the real value of the monetary component of wealth increased and with it the ratio of wealth to income, causing a decrease in savings, which means an increase in the aggregate demand for consumption goods. Pigou's argument (which was formulated for a stationary state) thus had the far-reaching theoretical implication that even if the economy were caught in the 'liquidity trap', there existed a low enough wage rate that would generate a full-employment level of aggregate demand. In this way Pigou (1943, p. 351) reaffirmed the 'essential thesis of the classicals' that 'if wage-earners follow a competitive wage policy, the economic system must move ultimately to a full-employment stationary state'.

In his exposition and elaboration of Pigou's argument (which *inter alia* brought out the significance of the argument for dynamic stability analysis), Patinkin (1948) labelled the direct effect of consumption of an increase in the real value of money balances as the 'Pigou effect'. However, in subsequent recognition of the fact that this effect is actually an integral part of the quantity theory – as well as the fact that Pigou had been anticipated in drawing the implications of this effect for the Keynesian system by Haberler (1941, pp. 242, 389, and 403) and Scitovsky (1941, pp. 71–2) – Patinkin (1956, 1965) relabelled it the 'real-balance effect' and presented it as a component of the wealth effect.

In an immediate comment on Pigou's article, Kalecki (1944) pointed out that the definition of 'money' relevant for the real-balance effect is not the usual one of currency *plus* demand-deposits: for example, in the case of a price decline, the increase in the real value of the demand deposit has an offset in the corresponding increase in the real burden on borrowers of the loans they had received from the banking system. Thus (emphasized Kalecki) the monetary concept relevant for the real-balance effect in a gold-standard economy is only the gold reserve of the monetary system.

More generally, the relevant concept is 'outside-money' (equivalent to the monetary base, sometimes also referred to as 'high-powered money'), which is part of the net wealth of the economy, as distinct from 'inside money', which consists of the demand deposits created by the banking system as a result of its lending operations and which accordingly is not part of net wealth (Gurley and Shaw, 1960). This distinction was subsequently challenged by Pesek and Saving (1967), who contended that banks regard only a small fraction of their deposits as debt, so that these deposits too should be included in net wealth. In criticism of this view, Patinkin (1969, 1972a) showed that if perfect competition prevails in the banking system, the present value of the costs of maintaining its demand deposits equals the value of these deposits, so that the latter cannot be considered as a component of net wealth. This is also the case if imperfect competition with free entry prevails in the system. On the other hand, if – because of restricted entry – the banking sector enjoys abnormal profits, then the present value of these profits should be included in net wealth for the purpose of measuring the real-balance effect.

There remains the question of whether – for the purpose of measuring the real-balance effect – one should include government interest-bearing debt, as contrasted with the non-interest-bearing debt (viz., government fiat money) which is a component of the monetary base. Clearly, in a world of infinitely lived individuals with perfect foresight, the former does not constitute net wealth and hence is not a component of the real-balance effect: for the discounted value of the tax payments which the representative individual must make in order to service and repay the debt obviously equals the discounted value of the payments on account of interest and principal that he will receive. Nor is the assumption of infinitely lived individuals an operationally meaningless one: for as Barro (1974) has elegantly shown, if in making his own consumption plans, the representative individual with perfect foresight is sufficiently concerned with the welfare of the next generation to the extent of leaving a bequest for it, he is acting as if he were infinitely lived.

More specifically, Barro's argument is as follows: assume that an individual of the present generation achieves his optimum position by consuming C_o during his lifetime and leaving a positive bequest of B_o for the next generation. Clearly, such an individual could have increased his consumption to $C_0 + \Delta C_0$ and reduced his bequest to $B_0 - \Delta C_0$, but preferred not to do so. Assume now that the individual also holds government bonds payable by the next generation, and let the real value of these bonds increase as the result of a decline in the price level, expected to be permanent. The revealed preference of the present generation for the consumption-bequest combination C_o, B_o implies that this increase in the real value of its holding of government interest-bearing debt will not cause it to increase its consumption at the expense of the next generation. In brief, government debt in this case is effectively not a component of wealth and hence of the real-balance effect.

Needless to say, the absence of perfect foresight, and the fact that individuals might not leave bequests (as is indeed assumed by the life-cycle theory of consumption) means that government interest-bearing debt should to a certain extent be taken account of in measuring the real-balance effect – or what in this context is more appropriately labelled the 'net-real-financial-asset effect' (Patinkin, 1965, pp. 288–94).

If we assume consumption to be a function of permanent income, and if we assume that the rate of interest which the individual uses to compute the permanent income flowing from his wealth to be 10 per cent and the marginal propensity to consume out of permanent income to be 0.80, then the marginal propensity to consume out of wealth (and out of real balances in particular) is the product of these two figures, or 0.08. However, in the case of consumers' durables (in the very broad sense that includes – besides household appliances – automobiles, housing, and the like), the operation of the acceleration principle implies an additional real-balance effect in the short run. In particular, assume that when the individual decides on the optimum composition of the portfolio of assets in which to hold his real wealth, W, he also considers the proportion, q, of these assets that he wishes to hold in the form of consumers' durables, K_d, so that his demand for the *stock* of consumer-durable goods is $K_d = qW$. Assume now that wealth increases solely as a result of an increase in real balances, M/p. This leaves the representative individual with more money balances in relation to his other assets than he considers optimal. As a result he will attempt to shift out of money and into these other assets until he once again achieves an optimum portfolio. In the case of consumers' durables, this means that in addition to his preceding demand for new consumer-durable goods, he has a demand for

$$C_d = \Delta K_d = q[\Delta(M/p)] = q[(M/p)_t - (M/p)_{t-1}]$$

units, where $(M/p)_t$ represents at time t. In general, the individual will plan to spread this additional demand over a few periods. In any event, once an optimally composed portfolio is again achieved, this additional effect disappears, so that the demand for new consumers' durables (which in the case of a stationary state is solely a replacement demand) will once again depend only on the ordinary real-balance effect as described at the beginning of this paragraph (Patinkin, 1967, pp. 156–62).

It is, of course, true that the process of portfolio adjustment generated by the monetary increase will cause a reduction in the respective rates of return on the other assets in the portfolio, so that the initial wealth effect of the monetary increase will be followed by substitution effects. Now, Keynes limited his analysis in the *General Theory* to portfolios consisting only of money and securities; hence (as indicated above) an increase in the quantity of money could increase the demand for goods only indirectly through the substitution effect created by the downward pressure on the rate of interest. But once one takes account of the broader spectrum of assets held by individuals, one must also take account of the direct real-balance effect on the purchase of these other assets as well.

Various empirical studies have shown that the real-balance effect as here defined (viz., as part of the wealth effect) is statistically significant (Patinkin, 1965, note M; Tanner, 1970). Other studies have demonstrated the statistical significance of yet another definition of this effect: namely, as the effect on the demand for commodities of an excess supply of money, defined as the excess of the existing stock of money over its 'desired' or 'long-run' level (Jonson, 1976; Laidler and Bentley, 1983; cf. also Mishan, 1958). It seems to me, however, that such a demand function is improperly specified: for though (as indicated above) the excess supply of money has a role to play in the consumption function (and particularly in that for consumers' durables), the complete exclusion of the real-balance effect *cum* wealth efffect from the aforementioned demand function implies that in equilibrium there is no real-balance effect – an implication that is contradicted by the form of demand functions as derived from utility maximization subject to the budget constraint (Patinkin, 1965, pp. 433–8, 457–60; Fischer, 1981).

Granted the statistical significance of the real-balance effect, the question remains as to whether it is strong enough to offset the adverse expectations generated by a price decline – including those generated by the wave of bankruptcies that might well be caused by a severe decline. In brief, the question remains as to whether the real-balance effect is strong enough to assure the stability of the system: to assure that automatic market forces will restore the economy to a full-employment equilibrium position after an initial shock of a decrease in aggregate demand (Patinkin, 1948, part II; 1965, ch. 14: 1). On the assumption of adaptive expectations, Tobin (1975) has presented a Keynesian model with the real-balance effect which under certain circumstances is unstable. On the other hand, McCallum (1983) has shown that under the assumption of rational expectations, the model is generally stable.

In any event, no one has ever advocated dealing with the problem of unemployment by waiting for wages and prices to decline and thereby generate a positive real-balance effect that will increase aggregate demand. In particular, Pigou himself concluded his 1947 article with the statement that such a proposal had 'very little chance of ever being posed on the chequer board of actual life'. Thus the significance of the real-balance effect is in the realm of macroeconomic theory and not policy.

Correspondingly, recognition of the real-balance effect in no way controverts the central message of Keynes's *General Theory*. For this message – as expressed in the climax of that book, chapter 19 – is that the only way a general decline in money wages can increase employment is through its effect in increasing the real quantity of money, hence reducing the rate of interest, and hence stimulating investment expenditures; but that even if wages were downwardly flexible in the face of unemployment, this effect would be largely offset by the adverse expectations and bankruptcies generated by declining money wages and prices, so that the level of aggregate expenditures and hence employment would not increase within an acceptable period of time. In Keynes's words: 'the economic system cannot be made self-adjusting along these lines' (ibid., p. 267). And there is no reason to believe that Keynes would have modified this conclusion if he had also taken account of the real-balance effect of a price decline (Patinkin, 1948, part III; 1976, pp. 110–11).

The above discussion has considered only the real-balance effect on the demand for goods. In principle, this effect also operates on the supply of labour: for the greater the real balances and hence wealth of the individual, the greater his demand for leisure as well, which means the smaller his supply of labour. This influence, however, has received relatively little attention in the literature (but see Patinkin, 1965, p. 204; Phelps, 1972; Barro and Grossman, 1976, pp. 14–16).

Another limitation of the discussion is that it deals only with a closed economy. In the analysis of an open economy, the real-balance effect plays an important role in some of the formulations of the monetary approach to the balance of payments.

BIBLIOGRAPHY

American Economic Association. 1951. *Readings in Monetary Theory*. Philadelphia: Blakiston.

Barro, R.J. 1974. Are government bonds net wealth? *Journal of Political Economy* 82, November-December, 1095–117.

Barro, R.J. and Grossman, H.I. 1976. *Money, Employment and Inflation*. Cambridge and New York: Cambridge University Press.

Fischer, S. 1981. Is there a real-balance effect in equilibrium? *Journal of Monetary Economics* 8, July, 25–39.

Gurley, J.G. and Shaw, E.S. 1960. *Money in a Theory of Finance*. Washington, DC: Brookings Institution.

Haberler, G. von. 1941. *Prosperity and Depression: A Theoretical Analysis of Cyclical Movements*. 3rd edn, Geneva: League of Nations; 3rd edn, Lake success, New York: United Nations, 1946.

Hicks, J.R. 1937. Mr Keynes and the 'classics': a suggested interpretation. *Econometrica* 5, April, 147–59. Reprinted in *Readings in the Theory of Income Distribution*. Philadelphia: Blakiston for the American Economic Association, 1946, 461–76.

Jonson, P.D. 1976. Money and economic activity in the open economy: the United Kingdom, 1880–1970. *Journal of Political Economy* 84, October, 979–1012.

Kalecki, M. 1944. Professor Pigou on 'The classical stationary state': a comment. *Economic Journal* 54, April, 131–2.

Keynes, J.M. 1923. *A Tract on Monetary Reform*. London: Macmillan. Repr. as *Collected Works, Vol. IV*. New York: St. Martin's Press, 1971.

Keynes, J.M. 1930. *A Treatise on Money*. Vol. I: *The Pure Theory of Money*. London: Macmillan; New York: St. Martin's Press, 1971.

Keynes, J.M. 1936. *The General Theory of Employment, Interest and Money*. London: Macmillan; New York: Harcourt, Brace.

Laidler, D. and Bentley, B. 1983. A small macro-model of the post-war United States. *Manchester School* 51, December, 317–40.

Leontief, W. 1936. The fundamental assumption of Mr Keynes' monetary theory of unemployment. *Quarterly Journal of Economics* 51, November, 192–7.

McCallum, B.T. 1983. The liquidity trap and the Pigou Effect: a dynamic analysis with rational expectations. *Economica* 50, November, 395–405.

Mishan, E.J. 1958. A fallacy in the interpretation of the cash balance effect. *Economica* 25, May, 106–18.

Modigliani, F. 1944. Liquidity preference and the theory of interest and money. *Econometrica* 12, January, 45–88. Reprinted in American Economic Association (1951), 186–240.

Patinkin, D. 1948. Price flexibility and full employment. *American Economic Review* 38, September, 543–64. Reprinted with revisions and additions in American Economic Association (1951), 252–83.

Patinkin, D. 1956. *Money, Interest, and Prices.* Evanston, Ill.: Row, Peterson.

Patinkin, D. 1965. *Money, Interest, and Prices.* 2nd edn, New York: Harper & Row.

Patinkin, D. 1967. *On the Nature of the Monetary Mechanism.* Stockholm: Almqvist and Wicksell. Reprinted in Patinkin (1972b), 143–67.

Patinkin, D. 1969. Money and wealth: a review article. *Journal of Economic Literature* 7, December, 1140–60.

Patinkin, D. 1972a. Money and wealth. In Patinkin (1972b), 168–94.

Patinkin, D. 1972b. *Studies in Monetary Economics.* New York: Harper & Row.

Patinkin, D. 1976. *Keynes' Monetary Thought: A Study of Its Development.* Durham, North Carolina: Duke University Press.

Pesek, B.P. and Saving, T.R. 1967. *Money, Wealth and Economic Theory.* New York: Macmillan.

Phelps, E.S. 1972. Money, public expenditure and labor supply. *Journal of Economic Theory* 5, August, 69–78.

Pigou, A.C. 1943. The classical stationary state. *Economic Journal* 53, December, 343–51.

Pigou, A.C. 1947. Economic progress in a stable environment. *Economica* 14, August, 180–88. Reprinted in American Economic Association (1951), 241–51.

Scitovsky, T. 1941. Capital accumulation, employment and price rigidity. *Review of Economic Studies* 8, February, 69–88.

Tanner, J.E. 1970. Empirical evidence on the short-run real balance effect in Canada. *Journal of Money, Credit and Banking* 2, November, 473–85.

Tobin, J. 1975. Keynesian models of recession and depression. *American Economic Review* 65, May, 195–202.

Real Bills Doctrine

ROY GREEN

The 'real bills doctrine' has its origin in banking developments of the 17th and 18th centuries. It received its first authoritative exposition in Adam Smith's *Wealth of Nations*, was then repudiated by Thornton and Ricardo in the famous bullionist controversy, and was finally rehabilitated as the 'law of reflux' by Tooke and Fullarton in the currency-banking debate of the mid-19th century. Even now, echoes of the real bills doctrine reverberate in modern monetary theory.

The central proposition is that bank notes which are lent in exchange for 'real bills', i.e. titles to real value or value in the process of creation, cannot be issued in excess; and that, since the requirements of the non-bank public are given and finite, any superfluous notes would return automatically to the issuer, at least in the long run. The grounds for rejecting the real bills doctrine have been many and varied. The main counter-argument is that overissue is not merely possible but inevitable in the absence of any external principle of limitation; in this view, commercial wants are insatiable and excess notes would not return to the issuer but undergo depreciation in the exact proportion to their excess.

By the time the real bills doctrine appeared in the economic literature, fractional reserve banking was already well established, releasing unproductive hoards for trade and investment. This did not satisfy John Law, that 'reckless, and unbalanced but most fascinating genius' (Marshall, 1923, p. 41n.). He outlined a primitive real bills doctrine in the course of his proposal for a land bank, which would issue paper money on 'good security'. He imagined, however, that the need for a metallic reserve was superseded by the abolition of legal convertibility, and that *economic* convertibility would *always* be maintained by conformity with the real bills doctrine (Law, 1805, p. 89).

The problem was that, as a mercantilist, Law identified money with capital; he believed that creating paper money was equivalent to increasing wealth. It was his attempt to 'break through' the metallic barrier that gave him 'the pleasant character mixture of swindler and prophet' (Marx, 1894, p. 441). The spectacular collapse of Law's 'System' set off a negative reaction against financial innovation, which was reflected in Cantillon's 'anti-System' (Rist, 1940, p. 73) and in Hume's opposition to what he called 'counterfeit money' (1752, p. 168). A more positive effect was a shift in the focus of political economy itself to the production process. This shift was led by the Physiocrats and by Adam Smith, whose 'original and profound' (Marx, 1859, p. 168) analysis of money and banking was developed in the context of classical value theory.

A decade before the *Wealth of Nations*, Sir James Steuart had attempted to revive Law's ideas from a 'neo-mercantilist' viewpoint (1767, book IV, pt. 2). For Smith, by contrast, the role of bank credit was to increase not the quantity of capital but its *turnover* (1776, pp. 245–6; also Ricardo, *Works*, III, pp. 286–7). Output was fixed by the level of accumulation, which for for all the classical economists included the speed of its turnover. Credit had the effect both of reducing the magnitude of reserve funds which economic agents needed to hold and of allowing the money material itself – treated as an element of circulating capital and an unproductive portion of the social wealth – to be displaced by paper, thus providing 'a sort of wagon-way through the air'.

Smith followed Law and Steuart, however, in arguing that an overissue of bank notes could not take place if they were advanced upon 'real' bills of exchange, i.e. those 'drawn by a real creditor upon a real debtor', as opposed to 'fictitious' bills, i.e. those 'for which there was properly no real creditor but the bank which discounted it, nor any real debtor but the projector who made use of the money' (1776, p. 239; also p. 231). When a banker discounted fictitious bills, the borrowers were clearly 'trading, not with any capital which he advances to them'. When, on the other hand, real bills were discounted, bank notes were merely substituted for a substantial proportion of the gold and silver which would otherwise have been idle, and therefore available for circulation (p. 231). The quantity of notes was thus equivalent to the maximum value of the monetary metals that would circulate in their absence at a given level of economic activity (p. 227).

This development of the classical law of circulation applied to credit and fiduciary money alike, with the difference that in the latter case overissue in the 'short run' might result in a permanent depreciation of the paper. By contrast, credit-money, i.e. bank-notes, which were exchanged for real bills could never be in long-run excess:

> The coffers of the bank ... resemble a water-pond, from which, though a stream is continually running out, yet another is continually running in, fully equal to that which runs out; so that, without any further care or attention, the pond keeps always equally, or very near equally full (p. 231).

Only what Smith called 'over-trading' would upset this balance, by promoting excessive credit expansion and an accompanying drain of bullion.

Although the real bills doctrine was accepted by the Bank of England Directors as a guide to monetary management, it was challenged in the bullion controversy following the suspension of cash payments in 1797 as 'the source of all the errors of these practical men' (Ricardo, *Works*, III, p. 362; also Thornton, 1802, p. 244 and *passim*). In the view of the 'bullionists',

> The refusal to discount any bills but those for *bona fide* transactions would be as little effectual in limiting the circulation; because, though the Directors should have the means of distinguishing such bills, which can by no means be allowed, a greater proportion of paper currency might be called into circulation, not than the wants of commerce could employ but greater than what could remain in the channel of currency without depreciation (Ricardo, p. 219).

Indeed, there was no other limit to the depreciation, and corresponding rise in the price level, 'than the will of the issuers' (ibid., p. 226).

Nevertheless, the bullionist argument itself was open to challenge, because it confused money with credit. The inconvertible paper of the Bank Restriction was issued not as forced currency but on loan; it was therefore responsible not for increasing the money supply but simply altering its *composition*, by substituting one financial asset for another in the hands of the public. Only when cash payments were restored, however, was any further attempt made to rehabilitate the real bills doctrine, this time as the 'law of reflux': provided notes were lent on sufficient security, 'the reflux and the issue will, in the long run, always balance each other' (Fullarton, 1844, p. 64; Tooke, 1844, p. 60). The 'banking school' called this law 'the great regulating principle of internal currency' (Fullarton, 1844, p. 68). Their opponents, the 'currency school' orthodoxy, 'never achieved better than this average measure of security'; and, after all, the average 'is not to be despised' (Marx, 1973, p. 131). The real bills doctrine made its next appearance in the Federal Reserve Act of 1913. In banking at least, discretion has always been the better part of valour.

BIBLIOGRAPHY

Cantillon, R. 1755. *Essai sur la nature du commerce en général*. Trans. H. Higgs, London: Macmillan, 1931.

Fullarton, J. 1844. *On the Regulation of Currencies*. London: John Murray.

Hume, D. 1752. *Essays, Literary, Moral and Political*. London: Ward, Lock & Co., n.d.

Law, J. 1705. *Money and Trade Considered*. Edinburgh: Anderson.

Marshall, A. 1923. *Money, Credit and Commerce*. London: Macmillan; New York: Augustus Kelley, 1965.

Marx, K. 1859. *A Contribution to the Critique of Political Economy*. Moscow: Progress Publishers, 1970.

Marx, K. 1894. *Capital*, Vol. III. Moscow: Progress Publishers, 1971; New York: International Publishers, 1967.

Marx, K. 1973. *Grundrisse*. Harmondsworth: Penguin.

Ricardo, D. 1951–73. *The Works and Correspondence of David Ricardo*. Ed. P. Sraffa, Cambridge: Cambridge University Press.

Rist, C. 1940. *History of Monetary and Credit Theory from John Law to the Present Day*. London: Allen & Unwin.

Smith, A. 1776. *An Inquiry into the Nature and Causes of the Wealth of Nations.* London: Routledge, 1890; New York: Modern Library, 1937.

Steuart, J. 1767. *An Inquiry into the Principles of Political Oeconomy.* Edinburgh: Oliver & Boyd, 1966.

Thornton, H. 1802. *An Enquiry into the Nature and Effects of the Paper Credit of Great Britain.* London: LSE Reprint Series, 1939.

Tooke, T. 1844. *An Inquiry into the Currency Principle.* London: LSE Reprint Series, 1959.

Seigniorage

S. BLACK

Full-bodied monies such as gold coin contain metal approximately equal in value to the face value of the coin. Under the gold standard, metal could be brought to the mint and freely coined into gold, less a small *seigniorage* charge for the privilege. Subsidiary or token coin and paper money by contrast cost much less to produce than their face value. The excess of the face value over the cost of production of currency is also called *seigniorage*, because it accrued to the *seigneur* or ruler who issued the currency, in early times.

The use of paper money instead of full-bodied coin by modern governments generates a very large social saving in the use of the resources that would otherwise have to be expended in mining and smelting large quantities of metal. The value of this seigniorage can be measured by considering the aggregate demand curve for currency, as a function of the rate of interest. The area under this demand curve represents the aggregate flow of social benefits from holding currency, under certain assumptions. The social cost of holding currency is measured by the opportunity cost of the resources it takes to produce the currency. If gold were used for currrency, its opportunity cost would be measured by the the rate of interest that could be earned on those resources if transferred to some other use. Thus the area under the demand curve between the market rate of interest and the cost of providing paper currency represents the flow of seigniorage or social saving that accrues from the use of paper currency instead of gold.

In the international monetary system, gold remains a very large fraction of total holdings of international reserves (about 45 per cent of total reserves valued at market prices at the end of March 1985). Substitution of fiduciary reserve assets such as Special Drawing Rights created by the International Monetary Fund or United States dollars for gold would generate a substantial social gain in the form of seigniorage equal to the excess of the opportunity cost of capital over the costs of providing the fiduciary asset. If interest is paid to the holders of the reserve asset, the seigniorage is split between the issuer and the holder.

The existence of these large seigniorage gains is what led to the development of the gold exchange standard, under which first British sterling, before World War II, and since then United States dollars and other currencies have substituted for gold in international reserve holdings. As interest rates paid on these reserve assets have risen, more of the seigniorage has accrued to holders of reserve assets.

Further substitution of fiduciary reserve assets for gold in the international monetary system has frequently been suggested, and the Second Amendment to the Charter of the International Monetary Fund adopted in 1978 proposed such a goal. Little progress has been made, however, since the underlying issue is one of trust in the financial probity of the issuer and its continued political stability, as well as its continued willingness to convert reserve assets into usable currencies over long periods of time.

Specie-flow Mechanism

WILLIAM R. ALLEN

The 'specie-flow mechanism' is an analytic version of automatic, or market, adjustment of the balance of international payments. In competitive markets with specie-standard institutions, behaviour will lead to national price levels and income flows consistent with equilibrium in the international accounts, commonly interpreted in this context to mean zero trade balances.

The classic exposition of the mechanism, for the better part of two centuries all but universally accepted, at least as a first approximation, was provided by David Hume in a 1752 essay, 'Of the Balance of Trade'. While it is appropriate to associate the essence of the model with Hume, all the ingredients of Hume's argument had long been available. There were even notable prior attempts to fit the analytic pieces into a self-contained model. Further, even if we give to Hume all the considerable credit due to his systematic, compact statement, his version is not the whole of the specie-flow mechanism; and the specie-flow mechanism is not the whole analysis of balance of payments adjustment.

Hume's presentation is a simple application of the quantity theory of money in a setting of international trade and its financing. With a pure 100 per cent reserve gold standard, and beginning with balance in the international accounts, a decrease in the money stock of country A results in a directly proportionate fall in its price level, which is also a decrease relative to the initially unaffected price levels of other countries; as country A's price level falls, consumer response, in Hume's account, will reduce A's imports and increase its exports; when the exchange rate is bid to the gold point, the export trade balance will be financed by gold inflow, which will raise prices in A and lower prices abroad until the international price differentials and net trade flows are eliminated. The line of causation runs from changes in money to changes in prices to changes in net trade flows to international movements of gold that eliminate the earlier price differentials and thereby correct the trade imbalance and stop the shipment of gold. In equilibrium, the distribution of gold among countries (and regions within

316

countries) yields national (and regional) price levels consistent with zero trade balances.

This theory of trade equilibration links with the Ricardian theory of production specialization. In a comparative advantage model of two countries, two commodities, and labour input, country A has absolute advantages of different degrees in both goods. To have two-way trade, the wage rate of country A must be greater than that abroad, within the wage-ratio range specified by the proportions of A's productive superiority in the two goods. Gold will flow until the international wage ratio yields domestic prices that equate total import and export values.

The conclusion that trade imbalances, and thus gold flows, cannot long obtain was in fundamental contrast to the mercantilistic emphasis on persistent promotion of an export balance and indefinite accumulation of gold. Still, the mercantilists decidedly associated gold inflows with export surpluses of goods and services; a good many writers had posited a direct relation between the money stock and the price level; similarly, it had been indicated that relative national price level changes would affect trade flows. However, while we should bow to such predecessors of Hume as Isaac Gervaise (1720) and Richard Cantillon (1734) and perhaps nod to Gerard de Malynes (1601) for attempts to construct adjustment models, Hume put the elements together with unmatched elegance and awareness of implication – and influence.

Hume's version was specifically a *price*-specie-flow mechanism, with the prices being national price levels (and exchange rates). Even as a price mechanism, the model has problems.

While it is reasonable to presume that price levels will move in the same directions (even if not in the same proportions) as the huge changes in the money stock envisioned by Hume, there remain questions of the impact on import and export expenditures. Vertical demand schedules in country A for imports and in other countries for A's exports would leave the physical amounts of imports and exports unresponsive to price changes. If, following Hume, we upset the initial equilibrium by a large decrease in money and thus in prices in country A, foreign expenditure on A's goods will fall proportionately with the fall in A's prices. The import balance of A will be financed with gold outflow, resulting in a further fall in A's prices and export value and an increase in prices abroad and in A's import expenditure. The gold flow, rather than correcting the trade flow, will increase the import trade balance of A when demand elasticities are zero (or sufficiently small). The import and export demand (and supply) elasticity conditions required for price (including exchange rate) changes to be equilibrating – conditions which are empirically realistic – came much later to be summarized in the 'Marshall-Lerner condition'. Under the most unfavourable circumstances of infinite supply elasticities and initially balanced trade, all that is required for stability is that the arithmetic sum of the elasticities of foreign demand for A's exports and of A's demand for imports be greater than unity.

Aside from the nicety of specifying elasticity conditions for stability, is it appropriate to couch the model in terms of diverging national price levels or of changes in a country's import prices compared to its export prices? Suppose country A has a commodity export balance, resulting perhaps from a shift in international demands reflecting changed preferences in favour of A's goods or imposition of a tariff by A or a foreign crop failure. As gold flows in, A's expenditures expand and prices are expected to rise. Prices of A's *domestic* goods (which do not enter foreign trade) do rise; but prices of *internationally* traded goods are affected little, if at all, for the increase in A's demand for such goods is countered by decrease in demand for them in gold-losing countries. Consumers in A, facing the domestic-international price divergence, shift to now relatively cheapened international goods (imports and A-exportables) from more expensive domestic goods, thus increasing import volume and value and also absorption of exportables. Producers in A shift out of international goods into domestic, thus reducing exports and expanding imports. Corresponding, but opposite, substitutions and shifts are diffused among the other countries. These respective domestic adjustments in consumption and production would continue until the gold flow ceases and the trade imbalance is corrected.

Substantial modern empirical research, however, is more supportive of Hume's changes in the terms of trade or of transitory divergences in relative prices of traded and non-traded goods than of the assumed invariant applicability of the equilibrium 'law of one price' commonly adopted in the modern 'monetary approach' to the balance of payments.

When gold flows into country A, portfolio equilibria of individuals and firms are upset, with cash balances now in excess. People try to spend away redundant balances. Expenditure rises and money income becomes larger. With greater income, demands for goods – including foreign goods – increase: at any given commodity price, quantity demanded has become larger. Import quantities and values rise. Changes in money give rise abroad to opposite portfolio adjustments and changes of income, thereby decreasing A's exports. In all this, there are some changes (upward in A and downward abroad) in prices of domestic goods and production factors, but the adjustment process entails income changes as well as price changes.

Some such role of changes in money income and demand schedules was noted – in different contexts and with different degrees of clarity and emphasis – by many writers in the 19th and early 20th centuries. But single-minded emphasis on income, with little or no explicit role for the money stock and prices, came only with application to balance of payments adjustment of the national income theory of J.M. Keynes. However, such application – with its regalia of marginal propensities and secondary, supplemental repercussions of multipliers – is not contingent on, or uniquely associated with, an international gold standard. Further, neglect of money in the foreign-trade multiplier analysis is a grievous omission. Equilibrium in the income model is characterized by equating of the flows of income leakages (saving, tax payments, imports) and income injections (investment, government expenditure, exports). But such equality of total leakages and injections permits a continuing trade imbalance. And a trade imbalance financed by a gold flow – or accompanied by money change generally – leads to further change in income; that is, income had no reached a genuine equilibrium.

The actual world, even with the classical gold standard in the generation prior to World War I, has not conformed well in institutions and processes with the construct of Hume. A world generally of irredeemable paper money and universally of demand deposits along with fraction-reserve banking and discretionary money policy – a world including the International Monetary Fund arrangement of indefinitely pegged exchange rates – has relied on selected adjustment procedures more than on automatic adjustment mechanisms. So Hume's model in its own terms is inadequate and in important empirical respects is even inappropriate. But it provided analytical coherency and expositional emphasis in an early stage of a discussion which continues to evolve.

BIBLIOGRAPHY

Blaug, M. 1985. *Economic Theory in Retrospect*. Cambridge: Cambridge University Press.
Darby, M. and Lothian, J. 1983. *The International Transmission of Inflation*. Chicago: University of Chicago Press.
Fausten, D. 1979. The Humean origin of the contemporary monetary approach to the balance of payments. *Quarterly Journal of Economics* 93, November, 655–73.
Rotwein, E. (ed.) 1970. *David Hume: Writings on Economics*. Madison: University of Wisconsin Press.
Yeager, L. 1976. *International Monetary Relations: Theory, History, and Policy*. 2nd edn, New York: Harper & Row.

319

Transaction Costs

JÜRG NIEHANS

Transaction costs arise from the transfer of ownership or, more generally, of property rights. They are a concomitant of decentralized ownership rights, private property and exchange. In a collectivist economy with completely centralized decision-making they would be absent; administrative costs would take their place.

In modern economies a substantial, and probably increasing, proportion of resources is allocated to transaction costs. Nevertheless, up to World War II economic theory had virtually nothing to say about them. Over the last few decades a large and diverse literature has developed, but the analytic complexities are such that success still is only partial; important problems remain unsolved.

TRANSACTION TECHNOLOGY. Transaction costs, like production costs, are a catch-all term for a heterogeneous assortment of inputs. The parties to a contract have to find each other, they have to communicate and to exchange information. The goods must be described, inspected, weighed and measured. Contracts are drawn up, lawyers may be consulted, title is transferred and records have to be kept. In some cases, compliance needs to be enforced through legal action and breach of contract may lead to litigation.

Transaction costs face the individual trader in two forms, namely (1) as inputs of his own resources, including time and (2) as margins between the buying and the selling price he finds for the same commodity in the market.

The transaction technology specifies what resources inputs are required to achieve a given transfer. It may be formalized in a 'transaction function' analogous to a production function. In principle, each such function relates to a specific pair (or, more generally, group) of economic agents. In this respect transaction costs are analytically analogous to transportation costs, which relate to a pair of locations. In one way or another, transaction costs are incurred in an effort to reduce uncertainty. For many purposes it may nevertheless be an efficient research strategy to proceed *as if* transaction costs occurred even under full certainty. Transaction costs then become, as Stigler (1967) put it, 'the costs of transportation from ignorance to omniscience'.

While transaction costs are analogous to transportation costs in some respects, they are quite different in others. This is because they relate not to individual commodity flows, but to pairs (or, more generally, to groups) of such flows. There must be a *quid pro quo* in every single transaction. This requirement imposes constraints for which there is no spatial counterpart. While in a Walrasian equilibrium each trader has to observe only his budget constraint, in a transaction cost equilibrium he has to balance his account with every other trader. This gives rise to an additional set of shadow prices, reflecting the burden of the bilateral balance requirement (Niehans, 1969).

Transaction functions may exhibit diminishing, constant, or increasing returns. Scale economics are often pronounced; in many cases, transaction costs are virtually independent of the quantity transferred. The scale effects may relate to the size of the individual transaction, to the size of the participating firm or to the size of the market as a whole.

Only for simple exchange will a transaction function, built in analogy to a production function, provide an adequate description of transaction technology. Many contracts, particularly the more important ones, are far more complicated, often assuming a bewildering (and expansive) complexity. As a consequence, transaction costs become difficult, and perhaps impossible, to quantify. The analysis of more complex contracts, institutions and economic arrangements has thus been forced to rely more on qualitative than on quantitative methods.

THE VOLUME OF TRANSACTIONS. Transaction costs, by and large, reduce the volume of transactions. In general equilibrium without transaction costs, the network of exchanges is indeterminate; there is no constraint on the gross trading volume. With increasingly costly transactions, individuals have an ever stronger incentive to economize transactions.

This can be clearly seen in a single market in which x is exchanged against y. In the budget constraint confronting an individual trader, proportional transaction costs produce a kink. If they amount to θ units of y for every unit of x bought or sold, the constraint will look like the heavy line in Figure 1, where $\bar{x}$ and $\bar{y}$ mark the initial endowment. Depending on the shape of the indifference curves, the individual may wish to buy x (selling y), to buy y (selling x), or not to trade at all. A shift in the market price will let the budget constraint swivel around E. The important point is that, because of the kink, there is a *range* of prices for which trade remains zero.

The reciprocal demand curves for two representative traders will, with transaction costs, have a kink at the origin (Figure 2). This may have the consequence that trade remains at zero (as illustrated) despite considerable changes in tastes and/or endowments. If transaction costs also have a fixed component, the budget constraint assumes the shape of the thin line in Figure 1, and the reciprocal demand curves have an empty space around the origin (not illustrated). The larger transaction costs, both variable and fixed, the more likely

321

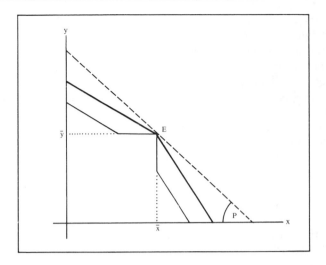

Figure 1

it is that equilibrium is at the no-trade point. In a multimarket framework, therefore, transaction costs can explain why certain potential markets, either for present or future goods, do not exist (Niehans, 1971). There have been numerous studies applying these general considerations to particular markets.

One way of economizing on costly market transactions is the establishment of firms. Coase (1937) regarded the cost of using the price mechanism as the

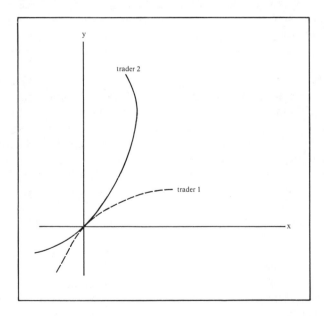

Figure 2

main reason for the existence of firms. For Williamson (1979, 1981) transaction costs are not only the key to an institutional theory of the firm but also to a new type of institutional economics.

THE BUNCHING OF TRANSACTIONS. Fixed transaction costs tend to result in a bunching of transactions. This effect has played a major role in explaining the demand for money. Cash balances are held because for short holding periods the costs of buying and selling an earning asset are too high compared to its yield (Hicks, 1935). Using an elementary inventory model with a sawtooth pattern of total assets, Baumol (1952) and Tobin (1956) derived algebraic demand functions for the demand for money. With fixed transaction costs, the demand for money would rise only with the fixed square root of total assets, but this properly does not hold in more general models. There is a vast literature applying the Baumol/Tobin approach to problems of monetary economics. In the history of economic thought few quantitative models of comparable simplicity have inspired more widespread uses.

EFFICIENCY. Compared to an imaginary state with costless transactions, transaction costs inevitably reduce welfare. In the individual optimization model of above, the set of consumption possibilities shrinks. The welfare loss is reflected partly in the resources allocated to transactions and partly in the suppression of exchanges that would otherwise have been mutually beneficial.

The more interesting question is whether transaction costs make an economy inefficient. A number of contributions to it are surveyed by Ulph and Ulph (1975). The mere fact that the Walrasian auctioneer uses up resources, reflected in a spread between selling and buying prices, does not in itself create efficiency problems. However, increasing returns in transaction technology, particularly in the form of fixed transaction costs, may lead to distortions. It is well known that in the presence of scale economies competition may not lead to an efficient allocation of resources.

Hahn (1971) took the view that transaction costs generally result in an inefficient equilibrium because the multiplicity of budget constraints reduce consumption possibilities. Kurz (1974a, 1974b) made it clear, however, that the alleged inefficiency may just be due to an inappropriate efficiency concept. The real question is whether, with given initial allocation and given transaction technology, the resulting equilibrium could be improved upon by a Pareto-superior reallocation, even though this would again cost resources. In the absence of scale economies, the discussion has produced no reason why, in this sense, transaction costs should generally cause inefficiency.

Efficiency problems also arise in a more general context. Simple exchange is a bilateral transaction. More complicated transactions may range from triangular exchange to multilateral contracts with a large number of parties. With increasing complexity, transaction costs tend to increase very rapidly. Even triangular contracts, therefore, are relatively rare and for more complex transactions the costs may rapidly become prohibitive. This is the basic reason for the emergence of market economies consisting of a network of bilateral exchanges. Politics may be interpreted as the arena in which multilateral transactions are typically made.

In a sense, any deviations from Pareto-optimality can be attributed to transaction costs, because in their absence all opportunities for Pareto-superior contracts would be realized. This is the so-called 'Coase theorem' (Coase, 1960). If, for example, the externalities of water pollution give rise to a social loss, one can imagine a multilateral abatement contract providing for payments from the sufferers to the polluters which is beneficial to all. In a world without transaction costs, therefore, private contracts could take the place of regulation. In the real world, however, as Coase emphasized, multilateral contracts tend to be very costly. Regulation, therefore, may be efficient, not because there is an externality, but because regulation may be cheaper than a multilateral contract. A similar reasoning can be applied to monopoly (Demsetz, 1968).

Buchanan and Tullock (1962) have extended this type of analysis to political decisions, where the individual is assumed to weigh his benefit from collective action against his share of decision-making costs. If the latter are zero for everybody, a unanimity rule would lead to a Pareto optimum, but in the presence of transaction costs the high costs of unanimity are likely to result in other decision rules. In the debate about these propositions it has often been pointed out that the underlying definition of transaction costs may be tautological: whatever produces deviations from Pareto-optimality is implicitly interpreted as a transaction cost.

ARBITRAGE. Transaction costs, like transportation costs, obstruct arbitrage, thus impeding the Law of One Price. Suppose, in an efficient and competitive exchange network, goods, on their way from producers to consumers, pass through the hands of several middlemen. Along each link of the network the increase in price will just pay for the marginal transaction costs. Where transaction costs would exceed the price differential, the transaction does not take place; in the reverse case the shortfall will be eliminated by competition. If between two potential intermediaries no transactions take place, their prices, within the margin of transaction costs are often called 'imperfect'. This should not be regarded as a value judgement. In the presence of transaction costs, efficiency requires a multiplicity of prices.

Transaction costs also limit arbitrage between different assets. In a multicommodity exchange system in which every good can be exchanged against each of the others, perfect markets would result in consistent 'cross rates'. The foreign-exchange market is a good example: in the absence of transaction costs, the sterling rate of the dollar equals the sterling rate of the mark times the mark rate of the dollar. With transaction costs, the equality is replaced by a set of inequalities.

The influence of transaction costs on asset arbitrage was studied for many particular markets, including those for Eurocurrencies (Frenkel and Levich, 1975), bonds of different types (Litzenberger and Rolfo, 1984) and maturities (Malkiel 1966), stocks (Demsetz, 1968, is the forerunner of many studies), take-overs

(Smiley, 1976), stock options (Phillips and Smith, 1980) and commodities (Protopapadakis and Stoll, 1983).

INTERMEDIATION. Imagine an economy in which all exchange consists of bilateral barter. In the absence of transaction costs it would make no difference who trades with whom; on their way from producers to consumers, commodities could pass through any number of hands. The presence of transaction costs makes the exchange network determinate. In such a network, certain traders, in view of their lower transaction costs, probably emerge as middlemen, brokers or intermediaries (Niehans, 1969). A pure intermediary makes his contribution to the social product, abstracting from any associated contribution to production, by helping other traders to economize on transaction costs. Transaction costs, therefore, are the key to an understanding of intermediation and of the structure of markets.

This is especially important in asset markets. For many consumer goods, particularly perishable ones, transaction costs are too high for them to pass through many hands. However, for assets like deposits, securities, foreign exchange, commodity contracts, gold options, insurance contracts, and mortgages, transaction costs are low enough to permit complicated intermediary networks. Benston and Smith (1976) thus argued convincingly that transaction costs are the *raison d'être* of financial intermediaries.

The Eurodollar market offers an instructive example. In the interwar period it became customary to regard banks primarily as producers of money and possibly other liquid assets. From this point of view, the emergence and the functioning of the Eurodollar market appeared as a 'puzzle'. The puzzle was easily solved once it was realized that the market for dollar funds (and other currencies) tended to move wherever transaction costs were lowest (Niehans and Hewson, 1976). The more transaction costs decline under the pressure of financial innovation, the more highly developed will be the division of labour in financial services, the more elaborate the structure of the financial system and the higher the flow of daily transactions compared to the stocks of traded assets. It is tempting, therefore, to interpret the rapid changes in financial markets in recent years largely as a consequence of changing transaction costs.

MEDIA OF EXCHANGE. Transaction costs are also responsible for the use and choice of media of exchange. The lower transaction costs on a given commodity, the more likely that this commodity will serve as money. Thanks to low transaction and holding costs, money helps to save resources that would otherwise have been used up in transactions. More important, it extends the scope of mutually beneficial exchange. In a world with transaction (and holding) costs, money thus has (indirect) utility even though, being a mere token money, it may have no direct utility.

Though this insight is old, its analytical implementation has made progress only in the last two decades. A simple expedient is to express transaction costs as a declining function of cash balances and then treat them like other costs

325

(Saving, 1971, 1972), but this begs the question how exactly such a function is determined.

The services of money for the individual consumer in the presence of transaction costs were analysed by Bernholz (1965, 1967) and, more fully, by Karni (1973). A rigorous analysis would have to be based on a general-equilibrium model of bilateral barter with transaction costs, which is not yet available. Since cash balances are an inventory, this needs to be a multiperiod model in which endowments, tastes and perhaps technology are subject to fluctuations. In order to model such fluctuations in an equilibrium framework, one might visualize those changes in the form of infinite stationary motion in which successive 'days' or 'seasons' are different, but successive 'years' are the same.

Such an economy will generally exhibit a complex pattern of markets in which a given commodity is traded against many (though not all) other commodities. If, from this arbitrary starting point, transaction costs are gradually lowered for one particular good, this good appears as the *quid pro quo* in an increasing number of transactions, while other barter exchanges disappear. There may also be cases with several moneys, each with its comparative advantages (Niehans, 1969). If transaction costs on the medium of exchange (and also its holding costs) are low enough, it will be used as a general medium of exchange. If, in the limit, money can be transferred, produced and held without cost, one arrives at the special case of a Walrasian economy with an integrated budget constraint and neutral money (Niehans, 1971, 1975, 1978), but, in contrast to Walras, with a determinate exchange network.

The rigorous mathematical analysis of the existence, uniqueness and efficiency of monetary equilibria with transaction costs made some progress during the 1970s (see Honkapohja, 1977, 1978a, 1978b and the literature given there). Since then, progress has been slow. The difficult process of adapting the traditional concepts of general-equilibrium analysis to the requirements of an intertemporal transaction-cost economy is still incomplete. This is one area where rigour so far has been at the expense of substance.

BIBLIOGRAPHY

Baumol, W.J. 1952. The transactions demand for cash: an inventory theoretic approach. *Quarterly Journal of Economics* 66(4), 545–56.

Benston, G.J. and Smith, C.W. 1976. A transactions cost approach to the theory of financial intermediation. *Journal of Finance* 31(2), 215–31.

Bernholz, P. 1965. Aufbewahrungs- und Transportkosten als Bestimmungsgründe der Geldnachfrage. *Schweizerische Zeitschrift für Volkswirtschafft und Statistik* 101(1), 1–15.

Bernholz, P. 1967. Erwerbskosten, Laufzeit und Charakter zinstragender Forderungen als Bestimmungsgründe der Geldnachfrage der Haushalte. *Zeitschrift für die gesamte Staatswissenschaft* 123(1), 9–24.

Buchanan, J.M. and Tullock, G. 1962. *The Calculus of Consent: Logical Foundations of Constitutional Democracy*. Ann Arbor: University of Michigan Press.

Coase, R.H. 1937. The nature of the firm. *Economica* 4(16), 386–405.

Coase, R.H. 1960. The problem of social cost. *Journal of Law and Economics* 3, 1–44.

Demsetz, H. 1968. The cost of transacting. *Quarterly Journal of Economics* 82(1), 33–53.

Frenkel, J.A. and Levich, R.M. 1975. Covered interest arbitrage: unexploited profits? *Journal of Political Economy* 83(2), 325–38.

Hahn, F.H. 1971. Equilibrium with transaction costs. *Econometrica* 39(3), 417–39.

Hicks, J.R. 1935. A suggestion for simplifying the theory of money. *Economica* 2(1), 1–19.

Honkapohja, S. 1977. Money and the core in a sequence economy with transaction costs. *European Economic Review* 10(2), 241–51.

Honkapohja, S. 1978a. A reexamination of the store of value in a sequence economy with transaction costs. *Journal of Economic Theory* 18(2), 278–93.

Honkapohja, S. 1978b. On the efficiency of a competitive monetary equilibrium with transaction costs. *Review of Economic Studies* 45(3), 405–15.

Karni, E. 1973. Transaction costs and the demand for media of exchange. *Western Economic Journal* 11(1), 71–80.

Kurz, M. 1974a. Equilibrium in a finite sequence of markets with transactions cost. *Econometrica* 42(1), 1–20.

Kurz, M. 1974b. Arrow-Debreu equilibrium of an exchange economy with transaction cost. *International Economic Review* 15(3), 699–717.

Litzenberger, R.H. and Rolfo, J. 1984. Arbitrage pricing, transaction costs and taxation of capital gains: a study of government bonds with the same maturity date. *Journal of Financial Economics* 13, 337–51.

Malkiel, B.G. 1966. *The Term Structure of Interest Rates: Expectations and Behaviour Patterns*. Princeton: Princeton University Press.

Niehans, J. 1969. Money in a static theory of optimal payment arrangements. *Journal of Money, Credit and Banking* 1(4), 706–26.

Niehans, J. 1971. Money and barter in general equilibrium with transaction costs. *American Economic Review* 61(5), 773–83.

Niehans, J. 1975. Interest and credit in general equilibrium with transactions costs. *American Economic Review* 65(4), 548–66.

Niehans, J. 1978. *The Theory of Money*. Baltimore: Johns Hopkins University Press.

Niehans, J. and Hewson, J. 1976. The eurodollar market and monetary theory. *Journal of Money, Credit and Banking* 7(1), 1–27.

Phillips, S.M. and Smith, C.W. 1980. Trading costs for listed options: the implications for market efficiency. *Journal of Financial Economics* 8, 179–201.

Protopapadakis, A. and Stoll, H.R. 1983. Spot and future prices and the Law of One Price. *Journal of Finance* 38(5), 1431–55.

Saving, T.R. 1971. Transactions costs and the demand for money. *American Economic Review* 61(3), 407–20.

Saving, T.R. 1972. Transactions costs and the firm's demand for money. *Journal of Money, Credit and Banking* 4(2), 245–59.

Smiley, R. 1976. Tender offers, transactions costs and the theory of the firm. *Review of Economics and Statistics* 58(1), 22–32.

Stigler, G.J. 1967. Imperfections in the capital market. *Journal of Political Economy* 75(3), 287–92.

Tobin, J. 1956. The interest-elasticity of transactions demand for cash. *Review of Economics and Statistics* 38(3), 241–7.

Ulph, A.M. and Ulph, D.T. 1975. Transaction costs in general equilibrium theory: a survey. *Economica* 42(168), 355–72.

Williamson, O.E. 1979. Transaction-cost economics: the governance of contractual relations. *Journal of Law and Economics* 22(2), 233–61.

Williamson, O.E. 1981. The modern corporation: origins, evolution, attributes. *Journal of Economic Literature* 19(4), 1537–68.

Velocity of Circulation

J.S. CRAMER

The *velocity of circulation* of money is V in the *identity of exchange*

$$MV \equiv PT \tag{1}$$

which is due to Irving Fisher (1911). On the left-hand side, M is the stock of money capable of ready payment, i.e. currency and demand deposits, or, in modern parlance, M_1; on the right, P is the price level and T stands for the volume of trade. PT is usually identified with total transactions at current value, which must be identically equal to total payments. All these variables are aggregates. The identity defines V as PT/M, that is the ratio of a flow of payments to the stock of money that performs them; its dimension is time^{-1}.

Apart from defining V, the identity (1) also serves for rudimentary quantity theories of money. If V is assumed constant, we have a theory of money demand, with PT determining M. Again, with both V and T constant, changes in M imply changes in P; this is still a popular explanation of inflation, with 'too much money chasing too little goods'. The above quantity theory of money demand has however long been replaced by a more sophisticated argument, whereby money demand is determined along with demand for other assets by yield and liquidity differentials and by net wealth or income Y. This has led, by analogy, to the unfortunate term *income velocity* for the ratio Y/M. It should not be thought that Y here acts as a proxy for PT of the earlier theory: the underlying argument is quite different, and if Y is a proxy at all it represents net wealth. The term velocity is inappropriate in this context. We shall here reserve it for the *transactions velocity* V as defined above, and for its constituent parts.

This V has no place in modern economic analysis; it attracted some interest in the decades before 1940. When we divide M into currency M_c and demand deposits M_d, and acknowledge that there are several different types of transaction, (1) becomes

$$M_c V_c + M_d V_d = \sum_j P_j T_j. \tag{2}$$

328

Among the variables in this expression, M_d and V_d are in principle observable at short notice, and in the absence of production indices and of national income estimates $M_d V_d$ (or $M_d V_d/P$) is a useful indicator of economic activity. It was used as such by authors like Angell (1936), Edie and Weaver (1930), Keynes (1930) and Snyder (1934). As for the data, M_d is demand deposit balances, available from banking returns, and V_d is the ratio of debts to balances, which can also be obtained from banks. The US Federal Reserve Board has long published monthly statistics of this *debits ratio* or *deposit turnover rate*, and still does so; there have been some drastic changes in definition and coverage over the years. The Bank of England provided a similar series from 1930 to 1938. Comparable statistics are available for several other countries.

The main trouble with this approach is that there is more than one type of transaction, and that (bank) payments are not limited to transactions in connection with current production. Some debits even have no economic meaning at all, as when a depositor has several accounts, and shifts funds between them, or when currency is withdrawn. Moreover bank debits can also reflect the sale of capital assets, income transfers, and money market dealings. The latter are by far the largest single category of turnover. These elements hinder the interpretation of V_d, and various attempts have been made to identify and remove them. We refer to Keynes' distinction between *industrial* and *financial* circulation, and to the Federal Reserve's practice of separately recording turnover in major financial centres. Failing a detailed classification of debits by the banks, however, all corrections are limited to approximate adjustments.

The observed value of V_d thus varies considerably with the definition of the relevant payments. For the US we quote the overall annual V_d, inclusive of financial transactions and the money market. This gross V_d rose from just under 30 in 1919 to about 35 in 1929, and then declined until 1945 when it was under 15. After the war it started on a long rise. It was about 50 by 1965, and from then onwards it soared to over 400 in 1984 (Garvy and Blyn, 1970; Federal Reserve Bulletin). In Britain, *net* velocity, exclusive of the money market, was roughly stable at values between 15 and 20 from 1920 to 1940; later it rose from 20 in 1968 to 40 in 1977 (Cramer, 1981). In the Netherlands, similarly defined net debits series show a V_d of between about 40 in 1965 and 45 in 1982 (Boeschoten and Fase, 1984).

It is hard to find a single common interpretation of these movements. The development in the US until the 1960s suggests strong business cycle effects, but the enormous later increase of gross V_d must in large part be due to new techniques like overnight lending and repurchase agreements. These generate a huge amount of debits on the basis of quite small average balances. New banking techniques that go hand in hand with improved cash management explain increases in V_d outside the money market, too. The process is induced by the pressure of rising interest rates. Increased speed and precision of bank transfers permit a reduction of working balances at a given turnover level, and the reduction of demand moreover calls forth additional debits, as when idle funds are shifted to time

329

deposits. Debits may thus increase *because* balances are reduced, and the rise of V_d is accentuated.

As regards currency payments, the currency stock M_c is well documented, but the estimation of velocity V_c or payments $M_c V_c$ presents intractable problems. There are two solutions, but both use major assumptions that defy verification.

The first method is based on the redemption rates of worn-out banknotes of different denominations. Under stationary conditions these rates are the reciprocal of average lifetime, and this turns out to be positively related to face value. While this may well be due to more careful handling of the larger notes, it is usually inferred from this that larger denominations circulate less rapidly and are hoarded more often, and for longer periods, than small notes. Laurent (1970) uses these specific redemption rates to estimate currency payments. He assumes that a banknote is redeemed if and only if it has completed G transfers. Assigning G transfers to notes that are redeemed, and $\frac{1}{2}G$ to notes still in circulation, he builds up cumulative estimates of the transfers performed by each US denomination from 1861 onwards. This yields annual transfers by denomination, and hence total currency payments per year, ignoring coins. All estimates are of course a multiple of the unknown G, which is regarded as a physical constant like the number of times a note can be handled. Laurent assumes implicitly that it equals the number of payments a note can perform in its lifetime. He constructs currency payments series for various G, adds bank debits, and examines the correlation of this sum with GNP over the period 1875 to 1967. The maximum correlation occurs at $G = 129$, and this value is adopted. Since currency in circulation, bank debits, and GNP all share the same real growth and price movements, the constructed payment series will be closely correlated with GNP for *any* G, and the maximum correlation is not a good criterion for determining this constant. It is moreover uncertain that G is constant. Laurent's estimates of currency payments imply that V_c is about 30 from 1875 to 1890; it then rises to a peak of 120 in 1928, and thereafter declines steeply to 32 in 1945, remaining at that level since. We shall argue that this level is too high.

The second method of estimating currency payments is due to Fisher (1909). He observes that most people obtain the currency they spend from banks, and that most recipients return their takings to banks. The currency circulation thus consists of *loops* of payments connecting withdrawals with deposits, and currency payments can be established by multiplying aggregate withdrawals (or deposits) by the average number of intervening payments or the *loop length*. Withdrawals and deposits are of course recorded at the banks, and should be readily available statistics (although in fact they are not); as for the loop length, there is no way of measuring it, and it must be inferred from common sense considerations. In consumer spending the loop consists of a single payment, as households draw cash from the banks and spend it at retail shops that deposit all their takings. This is of course a minimum: some agents do not deposit their currency receipts, but spend them; some agencies, like post offices or stores that cash customers' cheques, act in a double capacity, paying out currency they have received and thus doubling the number of payments it performs before returning to the banks. Such considerations together suggest an average loop length of about two for present-day industrialized countries.

In recent years, V_c has been estimated for two countries for which series or estimates of cash withdrawals could be established. Fisher's method gives a constant V_c of about 18.5 for Britain over the period 1960–78 (Crammer, 1981). For the Netherlands, a combination of Laurent's and Fisher's methods gives a constant value of about 15.3 for the years 1965–82 (Boeschoten and Fase, 1984). These results suggest that currency velocity is a constant, as if it were set by physical limitations to the speed of currency circulation, and that it lies between 15 and 20.

This estimate often arouses strong feelings, as casual observation suggests that currency performs far more than 15 or 20 payments a year. A higher value of V_c does however mean higher currency payments $M_c V_c$, and it is not at all clear where these take place. Even with a velocity of 15 this is a problem, for at this value currency payments in most countries far exceed consumer spending, let alone retail sales. Yet consumer spending is commonly believed to be the major repository of cash. A fair proportion must by our estimate take place elsewhere, and it appears that crime or the informal economy cannot account for this vast amount. Over and again the currency stock is much larger than common sense would suggest. Where are these payments made? Where is all the currency used or hoarded? The plain answer is that no one knows, and that very few people care. Attempts to find the answer by a sample survey have failed (Cramer and Reekers, 1976).

The above results suggest that even for current transactions (excluding the money market) bank velocity is larger than currency velocity, so that the steady and continuing shift from currency to demand deposits must mean a gradual increase in the overall velocity V.

BIBLIOGRAPHY

Angell, J.W. 1936. *The Behaviour of Money.* New York: McGraw-Hill.

Boeschoten, W.J. and Fase, M.M.G. 1984. *The Volume of Payments and the Informal Economy in the Netherlands 1965–1982.* Monetary Mongraphs no. 1, Amsterdam: de Nederlandsche Bank, and Dordrecht: Nijhoff.

Cramer, J.S. 1981. The volume of transactions and of payments in the United Kingdom, 1968–1977. *Oxford Economic Papers* 33(2), July, 234–55.

Cramer, J.S. and Reekers, G.M. 1976. Money demand by sector. *Journal of Monetary Economics* 2(1), January, 99–112.

Edie, L.D. and Weaver, D. 1930. Velocity of bank deposits in England. *Journal of Political Economy* 38, August, 373–403.

Fisher, I. 1909. A practical method for estimating the velocity of circulation of money. *Journal of the Royal Statistical Society* 72, September, 604–11.

Fisher, I. 1911. *The Purchasing Power of Money*, 2nd edn, 1922. Reprinted New York: Kelley, 1963.

Garvy, G. and Blyn, M.R. 1970. *The Velocity of Money.* New York: Federal Reserve Bank, available from Microfilm International, Ann Arbor and London.

Keynes, J.M. 1930. *A Treatise on Money.* London: Macmillan; New York: St. Martin's Press, 1971.

Laurent, R.D. 1970. Currency transfers by denomination. PhD Dissertation, University of Chicago.

Snyder, C. 1934. On the statistical relation of trade, credit, and prices. *Revue de l'Institut International de Statistique* 2, October, 278–91.

Contributors

William R. Allen Professor of Economics, University of California, Los Angeles. Vice President, Institute for Contemporary Studies. President, Western Economic Association; Vice President, Southern Economic Association. 'The International Monetary Fund and balance of payments adjustment', *Oxford Economic Papers* 15 (1962); 'Domestic investment, the foreign trade balance, and the World Bank', *Kyklos* 15 (1962); *University Economics* (with A. Alchian, 1964); 'The position of mercantilism and the early development of international trade theory' in *Events, Ideology and Economic Theory: The Determinants of Progress in the Development of Economic Analysis*, (ed. R. Eagly, 1968); 'Economics, economists, and economic policy: modern American experiences', *History of Political Economy* 9 (Spring 1977); 'Irving Fisher, F.D.R., and the Great Depression', *History of Political Economy* 9 (1977).

Stephen H. Axilrod Vice-Chairman, Nikko Securities Company International; formerly Staff Director for Monetary and Financial Policy, Federal Reserve Board. 'Postwar U.S. monetary policy appraised', (with H. Wallich) in *United States Monetary Policy* (1964); 'Monetary aggregates and money market conditions in open market policy', *Federal Reserve Bulletin* (February 1971); 'Federal Reserve System implementation of monetary policy: analytic foundation of the new approach', (with D. Lindsey) *American Economic Review* (1980); 'Comments', in *Monetary Policy in Our Times* (1985); 'U.S. monetary policy in recent years: an overview', in *Monetary Conditions for Economic Recovery* (1985); 'Overview', in *Debt, Financial Stability, and Public Policy* (1986).

Ernst Baltensperger Professor of Economics, University of Bern. 'The lender–borrower relationship, competitive equilibrium, and the theory of hedonic prices', *American Economic Review* 66 (1976); 'Predictability of reserve demand, information costs, and bank portfolio behaviour', (with H. Milde) *Journal of Finance* 31, (1976); 'Alternative approaches to the theory of the banking firm',

Journal of Monetary Economics 6 (1980); 'Reserve requirements and economic stability', *Journal of Money, Credit, and Banking* 6 (1980); 'Theorie des Bankverhaltens', (with H. Milde) *Studies in Contemporary Economics* (1987); 'Banking deregulation in Europe', (with J. Dermine) *Economic Policy* 4 (1987).

Stanley Black Georges Lurcy Professor of Economics, University of North Carolina. International Affairs Fellow, Council on Foreign Relations, 1975–76; Vice-President, Southern Economic Association, 1983. 'The use of rational expectations in models of speculation', *Review of Economics and Statistics* 54(2), (May 1972); 'International money markets and flexible exchange rates', *Princeton Studies in International Finance* No. 32 (1973); 'Exchange policies for less developed countries in a world of floating rates', *Princeton Essays in International Finance* No. 119, (December 1976); *Floating Exchange Rates and National Economic Policy* 1977; 'The use of monetary policy for internal and external balance in ten industrial countries', in *Exchange Rates and International Macroeconomics* (ed. J. Frenkel, 1983).

Michael D. Bordo Professor of Economics, University of South Carolina; Research Associate, National Bureau of Economic Research. 'The effects of monetary change on relative commodity prices and the role of long term contracts', *Journal of Political Economy* (1980); *A Retrospective on the Classical Gold Standard, 1821–1931* (with Anna J. Schwartz, 1984); 'Explorations in economic history', *Explorations in Economic History* 23 (1986); *The Long-Run Behavior of the Velocity of Circulation: The International Evidence* (with L. Jonung, 1987); 'Why did the Bank of Canada emerge in 1935?', (with A. Redish) *Journal of Economic History* 47(2), (1987); *Money, History and International Finance: Essays in Honor of Anna J. Schwartz* (ed., 1989).

P. Bridel Professor of Economics, University of Lausanne, Switzerland. *Loi des débouches et principe de la demande effective. Contribution à l'histoire de l'analyse économique* 1977; 'On Keynes' quotations from Mill: a note', *Economic Journal* 89 (1979); *Cambridge Monetary Thought: the development of savings-investment analysis from Marshall to Keynes* (1987).

Karl Brunner Professor of Economics, University of Rochester. Founding Editor, *Journal of Monetary Economics*; Founding Editor, *Journal of Money, Credit, and Banking*; Co-editor, Carnegie-Rochester Conference series on Public Policy. *The First World and the Third World* (ed., 1978); *The Great Depression Revisited* (ed., 1981); *Fiscal Policy in Macro-Theory: a survey and evaluation* (1986).

Phillip Cagan Professor of Economics, Columbia University. 'The monetary dynamics of hyperinflations', *Studies in the Quantity Theory of Money*, (ed. M. Friedman, 1956); 'Why do we use money in open market operations?', *Journal of Political Economy* (1958); *Determinants and Effects of Change in the Money Stock 1875–1960* (1965); *The Channels of Monetary Effects on Interest Rates*

(1972); *Persistent Inflation* (1979); 'The uncertain future of monetary policy', *The Sixth Henry Thornton Lecture* (1984).

David Clark Senior Lecturer, School of Economics, University of New South Wales; editorial writer and columnist, *Australian Financial Review. Student Economics Briefs* (1986–89); *Economic Update; the fifty most important graphs that explain the Australian economy* (3rd edn, 1990).

J.S. Cramer Professor of Economics, University of Amsterdam. Member, Netherlands Royal Academy of Arts and Sciences; Fellow of the Econometric Society. 'The volume of transactions and the circulation of money in the United States, 1960–1979', *Journal of Business and Economic Statistics* 4 (1986); *Econometric Applications of Maximum Likelihood Methods* (1986).

A.B. Cramp Life Fellow, Emmanuel College, Cambridge; Research Consultant, Jubilee Centre, Cambridge. Fellow of the Institute for Christian Studies, Toronto. *Opinion on Bank Rate, 1822–60* (1962); *Monetary Management* (1971).

Meghnad Desai Professor of Economics, London School of Economics. 'Growth cycles and inflation in a model of the class struggle', *Journal of Economic Theory* (1973); 'Phillips Curve: a revisionist interpretation', *Economica* (1975); *Applied Econometrics* (1976); *Marxian Economics* (1979); *Testing Monetarism* (1981); 'Men and things', *Economica* (1986).

Duncan Foley Professor of Economics, Barnard College, Columbia University. *Monetary and Fiscal Policy in a Growing Economy* (with M. Sidrauski, 1971); *Money, Accumulation and Crisis* (1986); *Understanding Capital: Marx's economic theory* (1986).

Benjamin M. Friedman Professor of Economics, Harvard University; Director of Financial Markets and Monetary Economics Research, National Bureau of Economic Research. Marshall Scholar, King's College, Cambridge; Junior Fellow of the Society of Fellows, Harvard University. 'Targets, instruments and indicators of monetary policy', *Journal of Monetary Economics* 1 (1975); 'Financial flow variables and the short-run determination of long-term interest rates', *Journal of Political Economy* 85 (1977); 'Crowing out or crowding in? The economic consequences of financing government deficits', *Brookings Papers on Economic Activity* (1978); 'Optimal expectations and the extreme information assumptions of "rational expectations" macromodels', *Journal of Monetary Economics* 5 (1979); 'The roles of money and credit in macroeconomic analysis', in *Macroeconomics, Prices and Quantities: Essays in Memory of Arthur M. Okun* (ed. J. Tobin, 1983); 'Lessons from the 1979–1982 monetary policy experiment', *American Economic Review* 74 (1984).

Milton Friedman Paul Snowden Russell Distinguished Service Professor of Economics, University of Chicago, Emeritus; Senior Research Fellow, Hoover Institution (Stanford University). John Bates Clark Medal (American Economic Association), 1951; Nobel Prize in Economics, 1976; National Medal of Science (USA), 1988; numerous honorary degrees. *Essays in Positive Economics* (1953); *A Theory of the Consumption Function* (1957); *A Monetary History of the United States, 1867–1960* (with A.J. Schwartz, 1963); *Monetary Statistics of the United States* (with A.J. Schwartz, 1970); *Monetary Trends in the United States and the United Kingdom* (with A.J. Schwartz, 1982); *The Essence of Friedman* (1987).

Stephen M. Goldfeld Professor of Economics, Princeton University. Fellow of the Econometric Society. 'Commercial bank behaviour and economic activity: a structural study of monetary policy in the postwar United States', *Economic Analysis Series* N43 (1966); 'Nonlinear methods in econometrics', (with R.E. Quandt) *Economic Analysis Series* 77 (1972); *Studies in Nonlinear Estimation* (ed., with R.E. Quandt, 1976); 'The case of the missing money', *Brookings Papers on Economic Activity* No. 3 (1976); 'Money demand: the effects of inflation and alternative adjustment mechanisms' (with D.E. Sichel) *Review of Economics and Statistics* 69 (1987); 'Budget constraints, bailouts and the firm under central planning', (with R.E. Quandt) *Journal of Comparative Economics* (1988).

Marvin S. Goodfriend Vice President and Economist, Federal Reserve Bank of Richmond; Visiting Professor of Business Economics, Graduate School of Business, University of Chicago. 'Reinterpreting money demand regressions', *Carnegie-Rochester Series on Public Policy* No. 22, (ed. K. Brunner and A. Meltzer, 1985); 'Monetary mystique: secrecy and central banking', *Journal of Monetary Economics* (1986); *Monetary Policy in Practice* (1987).

Charles Goodhart Norman Sosnow Professor of Banking and Finance, London School of Economics; Adviser and Chief Adviser on Monetary Policy at the Bank of England 1968–85. 'The importance of money', (with A. Crockett) *Bank of England Quarterly Bulletin* 10(2), (1970), reprinted in *The Development and Operation of Monetary Policy* (1984); *The Business of Banking, 1891–1914* (1972); *Money, Information and Uncertainty* (1973; 2nd edn 1989); *Monetary Theory and Practice* (1984); *The Evolution of Central Banks* (1985, republished 1988); *The Operation and Regulation of Financial Markets* (ed., with D. Currie and D. Llewellyn, 1987).

Roy Green Economic Advisor, Minister of Industrial Relations, Canberra, Australia. 'Money, output and inflation in classical economics', *Contributions to Political Economy* 1 (1982).

Herschel I. Grossman Merton P. Stoltz Professor in the Social Sciences; Professor of Economics, Department of Economics, Brown University; Research Associate, National Bureau of Economic Research. John Simon Guggenheim Memorial

Foundation Fellow, 1979–80. *Money, Employment, and Inflation* (with R.J. Barro, 1976); 'Tests of equilibrium macroeconomics using contemporaneous monetary data', (with J. Boschen) *Journal of Monetary Economics* (1982); 'The natural-rate hypothesis, the rational expectations hypothesis, and the remarkable survival of non-market-clearing assumptions', *Carnegie-Rochester Conference Series on Public Policy* 19 (1983); 'Seigniorage, inflation, and reputation', (with J. Van Huyck) *Journal of Monetary Economics* (1986); 'The theory of rational bubbles in stock prices', (with B. Diba) *Economic Journal* (1988); 'Sovereign Debt as a contingent claim: excusable default, repudiation, and reputation', (with J. Van Huyck) *American Economic Review* (1988).

Donald D. Hester Professor of Economics, University of Wisconsin, Madison. Guggenheim Fellow; Fellow of the Econometric Society. 'Monetary policy in an evolutionary disequilibrium', in *Financial Innovation and Monetary Policy: Asia and the West* (ed. Yoshio Suzuki and Hiroshi Yomo, 1968), 'Monetary policy in the "checkless" economy', *Journal of Finance* 26(2), (1972); *Bank Management and Portfolio Behavior*, (with J. Pierce) Cowles Foundation Monograph 25 (1975); 'Customer relationships and terms of loans: evidence from a pilot survey', *Journal of Money, Credit, and Banking* 11(3), (1979); 'Innovations and monetary control', *Brookings Papers on Economic Activity* No. 1, (1981); 'On the empirical detection of financial innovation', in *Changing Money: Innovation in Developed Countries*, (ed. Marcello de Cecco, 1987).

Peter Howitt Professor of Economics, University of Western Ontario. 'Stability and the quantity theory', *Journal of Political Economy* 82 (1974); 'Activist monetary policy under rational expectations', *Journal of Political Economy* 89 (1981); 'Transaction costs in the theory of unemployment', *American Economic Review* 75 (1985); 'The Keynesian recovery', *Canadian Journal of Economics* 19 (1986); 'Business cycles with costly search and recruiting', *Quarterly Journal of Economics* 103 (1988).

Susan Howson Professor of Economics, University of Toronto. 'The origins of dear money, 1919–20', *Economic History Review* 28 (1974); *Domestic Monetary Management in Britain 1919–38* (1975); 'The origins of cheaper money, 1945–47', *Economic History Review* 40 (1987).

Dwight M. Jaffee Professor of Economics, Princeton University. Associate Editor, *Journal of Economic Perspectives*. 'A theory and test of credit rationing', (with F. Modigliani) *American Economic Review* 59 (1969); *Credit Rationing and the Commercial Loan Market* (1971); 'Methods of estimation for markets in disequilibrium', (with R. Fair) *Econometrica* 40 (1972); 'On the application of portfolio theory to depository financial intermediaries', (with O. Hart) *Review of Economic Studies* 41(1), (1974); 'Cyclical variations in the risk structure of interest rates', *Journal of Monetary Economics* 1 (1975); 'Imperfect information, uncertainty and credit rationing', (with T. Russell) *Quarterly Journal of Economics* 90(4), (1976).

David Laidler Professor of Economics, University of Western Ontario. Fellow, Royal Society of Canada; President, Canadian Economics Association 1987–88; Baas Lister Lecturer 1972. *Essays on Money and Inflation* (1975); *The Demand for Money – Theories, Evidence and Problems* (1977); 'Adam Smith as a monetarist economist', *Canadian Journal of Economics* 14(2), (May 1981); 'Jevons on money', *The Manchester School* 50(4), (December 1982); *Monetarist Perspectives* (1982); 'The "buffer stock" notion in monetary economics', *Economic Journal* 94 (supplement), (March 1984).

Axel Leijonhufvud Professor of Economics, University of California, Los Angeles. Honorary doctorate, University of Lund. *On Keynesian Economics and the Economics of Keynes* (1968); 'Inflation and economic performance', in *Money in Crisis* (ed. B. Siegal, 1974); *Information and Coordination* (1981); 'Hicks on time and money', *Oxford Economic Papers* (1984); 'Capitalism and the factory system', *Economics as a Process* (ed. R. Langlois, 1986); 'Whatever happened to Keynesian Economics?', *The Legacy of Keynes* (ed. D. Reese, 1987).

David E. Lindsey Member of the Board of Governors of the Federal Reserve System. 'Determining the monetary instrument: a diagrammatic exposition', (with S. Leroy) *American Economic Review* 68(5), (December 1978); 'Recent monetary developments and controversies', *Brookings Papers on Economic Activity* 1 (1982); 'Nonborrowed reserves targeting and monetary control', *Improved Money Stock Control* (ed. L.H. Meyer, 1983); 'Short-run monetary control: evidence under a nonborrowed reserve operating procedure', (with H. Farr, G. Gillum, K. Kopecky and R. Porter) *Journal of Monetary Economics* 13 (January 1984); 'The monetary regime of the Federal Reserve System', *Alternative Monetary Regimes* (ed. C.D. Campbell and W.R. Dougan, 1986).

Bennett T. McCallum H.J. Heinz Professor of Economics, Carnegie-Mellon University; Research Associate, National Bureau of Economic Research; Research Advisor, Federal Reserve Bank of Richmond; Co-Editor, *American Economic Review*; Editorial Board of *Journal of Monetary Economics, Journal of Money, Credit, and Banking, Economics Letters*. 'Rational expectations and the natural rate hypothesis: some consistent estimates', *Econometrica* 44 (January 1976); 'Price level determinacy with an interest rate policy rule and rational expectations', *Journal of Monetary Economics* 8 (November 1981); 'The role of overlapping generations models in monetary economics', *Carnegie-Rochester Conference Series on Public Policy* 18 (Spring 1983); 'Are bond-financed deficits inflationary? A Ricardian analysis', *Journal of Political Economy* 92 (February 1984); 'On "real" and 'sticky-price" theories of the business-cycle', *Journal of Money, Credit, and Banking* 18 (November 1986); *Monetary Economics: Theory and Policy* (1989).

Jürg Niehans Emeritus Professor of Economics, University of Bern. *The Theory of Money* (1978); *International Monetary Economics* (1984); *History of Economic Theory: Classic Contributions 1720–1980* (forthcoming).

Don Patinkin Professor of Economics, Hebrew University of Jerusalem. Rothschild Prize 1959; Israel Prize 1970; President, Econometric Society, 1974; President, Israel Economic Association, 1976; various honorary fellowships and degrees. *Money, Interest, and Prices: An Integration of Monetary and Value Theory* (1956); *The Israel Economy: The First Decade* (1959); *Studies in Monetary Economics* (1972); *Keynes' Monetary Thought: A Study of Its Development* (1976); *Essays On and In the Chicago Tradition* (1981); *Anticipations of the General Theory? And Other Essays on Keynes* (1982).

Anna J. Schwartz Research Associate, National Bureau of Economic Research; Adjunct Professor of Economics, Graduate School of the City University of New York. President, Western Economic Association International, 1987–1988, Doctor of Letters, Honoris Causa, University of Florida, 1987, Honorary Visiting Professor, City University Business School, London, 1984–89. *The Growth and Fluctuation of the British Economy 1790–1850* (with A. Gayer and W. Rostow, 1953; 2nd edn, 1975); *A Monetary History of the United States, 1867–1960* (with M. Friedman, 1963); *The International Transmission of Inflation* (with M. Darby et al., 1983); *Monetary Trends in the United States and the United Kingdom: Their Relation to Income, Prices, and Interest Rates, 1867–1975* (with M. Friedman, 1984); *A Retrospective on the Classical Gold Standard 1821–1931* (ed., with Michael D. Bordo, 1984); *Money in Historical Perspective* (1987).

Otto Steiger Professor of Economics, Universtät Bremen. 'Studien zur Enstehung der Neuen Wirtschaftslehre in Schweden – Eine Anti-Kritik', *Wirtschaftswissenschaftliche Abhandlungen* 28 (1971); *Menschenproduktion: Allgemeine Bevölkerungstheorie der Neuzeit* (with G. Heinsohn and R. Kneiper, 1979); 'Private property, debts and interest or: the origin of money and the rise and fall of monetary economies', (with Gunnar Heinsohn) *Studi Economici*, 38(21), (1983); *Die Vernichtung der weisen Frauen: Beiträge zur Theorie und Geschichte von Bevölkerung und Kindheit* (with G. Heinsohn, 1987); 'The veil of barter: The solution to "the task of obtaining representations of an economy in which money is essential"', (with Gunnar Heinsohn) in *Inflation and Income distribution in Capitalist Crisis: Essays in memory of Sidney Weintraub* (ed. J.A. Kregel, 1988); 'Warum Zins? Keynes und die Grundlagen einer monetären Werttheorie', (with Gunnar Heinsohn) in *Keynes' General Theory nach fünfzig Jahren* (ed., with H. Hageman, 1988).

James Tobin Professor Emeritus of Economics. Nobel Prize in Economics 1981; John Bates Clark Bronze Medal 1955 (American Economic Association); Member, President's Council of Economic Advisors 1961–62; President, American Economic Association 1971; numerous boundary degrees. *Essays in*

Economics Vol 1, Macroeconomics; Essays in Economics Vol. 2, Consumption and Econometrics; Essays in Economics Vol. 3, Theory and Policy; Asset Accumulation and Economic Activity (1980); *Policies for Prosperity* (1987); *Two Revolutions in Economic Policy* (with Murray Weidenbaum, 1988).

S.C. Tsiang President, Chung-hua Institution for Economic Research, Taiwan; Emeritus Professor of Economics, Cornell University. Fellow of the Academia Sinicia; Honorary Fellow, London School of Economics. 'Liquidity preference and loanable funds theories, multiplier and velocity analysis: a synthesis', *American Economic Review* 46(4), (1956); 'The role of money in trade balance stability: synthesis of the elasticity and absorption approaches', *American Economic Review* 51(5), (1961); 'The rationale of the mean standard deviation analysis, skewness preference and the demand for money', *American Economic Review* 52(3), (1972); 'The diffusion of reserves and the money supply multiplier', *Economic Journal* 88 (1978); 'Keynes's "finance" demand for liquidity, Robertson's loanable funds, theory, and Friedman's monetarism', *Quarterly Journal of Economics* 94(2), (1980); *Finance Constraints, Expectations, and Macroeconomics* (ed., with M. Kohn, 1988).

Henry C. Wallich Professor of Economics, Yale University, 1951–74; Member, Board of Governors of the Federal Reserve System, 1974–. Assistant to the Secretary of the Treasury; Member, President's Council of Economic Advisors. 'Debt management as an instrument of economic policy', *American Economic Review* 36 (1946); *Monetary Problems of an Export Economy* (1950); *Mainsprings of the German Revival* (1955); 'Conservative economic policy', *Yale Review* 46(1), (1956); *The Cost of Freedom* (1960); *Monetary Policy and Practice* (1981).

Alan Walters Professor of Economics, Johns Hopkins University. *Money in Boom and Slump* (1968); *An Introduction to Econometrics* (1968); *The Economics of Road User Charges* (1968); *Noises and Prices* (1975); *Microeconomic Theory* (with R. Layard, 1978); *Britain's Economic Renaissance* (1986).

THE NEW
PALGRAVE

MONEY